## Other A to Z Guides from Scarecrow Press

*The A to Z of Buddhism* by Charles S. Prebish, 2001.
*The A to Z of Catholicism* by William J. Collinge, 2001.
*The A to Z of Hinduism* by Bruce M. Sullivan, 2001.

HISTORICAL DICTIONARIES OF RELIGIONS,
PHILOSOPHIES, AND MOVEMENTS
Edited by Jon Woronoff

1. *Buddhism,* by Charles S. Prebish, 1993
2. *Mormonism,* by Davis Bitton, 1994. *Out of print. See No. 32.*
3. *Ecumenical Christianity,* by Ans Joachim van der Bent, 1994
4. *Terrorism,* by Sean Anderson and Stephen Sloan, 1995. *Out of Print. See No. 41.*
5. *Sikhism,* by W. H. McLeod, 1995
6. *Feminism,* by Janet K. Boles and Diane Long Hoeveler, 1995
7. *Olympic Movement,* by Ian Buchanan and Bill Mallon, 1995. *Out of print. See No. 39.*
8. *Methodism,* by Charles Yrigoyen Jr. and Susan E. Warrick, 1996
9. *Orthodox Church,* by Michael Prokurat, Alexander Golitzin, and Michael D. Peterson, 1996
10. *Organized Labor,* by James C. Docherty, 1996
11. *Civil Rights Movement,* by Ralph E. Luker, 1997
12. *Catholicism,* by William J. Collinge, 1997
13. *Hinduism,* by Bruce M. Sullivan, 1997
14. *North American Environmentalism,* by Edward R. Wells and Alan M. Schwartz, 1997
15. *Welfare State,* by Bent Greve, 1998
16. *Socialism,* by James C. Docherty, 1997
17. *Bahá'í Faith,* by Hugh C. Adamson and Philip Hainsworth, 1998
18. *Taoism,* by Julian F. Pas in cooperation with Man Kam Leung, 1998
19. *Judaism,* by Norman Solomon, 1998
20. *Green Movement,* by Elim Papadakis, 1998
21. *Nietzscheanism,* by Carol Diethe, 1999
22. *Gay Liberation Movement,* by Ronald J. Hunt, 1999
23. *Islamic Fundamentalist Movements in the Arab World, Iran, and Turkey,* by Ahmad S. Moussalli, 1999
24. *Reformed Churches,* by Robert Benedetto, Darrell L. Guder, and Donald K. McKim, 1999
25. *Baptists,* by William H. Brackney, 1999
26. *Cooperative Movement,* by Jack Shaffer, 1999
27. *Reformation and Counter-Reformation,* by Hans J. Hillerbrand, 2000
28. *Shakers,* by Holley Gene Duffield, 2000
29. *United States Political Parties,* by Harold F. Bass Jr., 2000
30. *Heidegger's Philosophy,* by Alfred Denker, 2000

# The A to Z of Islam

Ludwig W. Adamec

The Scarecrow Press, Inc.
Lanham, Maryland, and Oxford
2002

# SCARECROW PRESS, INC.

Published in the United States of America
by Scarecrow Press, Inc.
A Member of the Rowman & Littlefield Publishing Group
4720 Boston Way, Lanham, Maryland 20706
www.scarecrowpress.com

PO Box 317
Oxford
OX2 9RU, UK

British Library Cataloguing in Publication Information Available

**Library of Congress Cataloging-in-Publication Data**

Adamec, Ludwig W.
  The A to Z of Islam / Ludwig W. Adamec.
    p. cm.
  Includes bibliographical references.
  ISBN 0-8108-4505-9 (pbk. : alk. paper)
  1. Islam—History—Dictionaries. 2. Muslims—History—Dictionaries. I. Title.
BP50 .A325 2002
297'.03—dc21
                            2002070846

To Rahella

# CONTENTS

vii

# READER'S NOTES

The purpose of this work is to provide for the lay person as well as the serious student a concise dictionary of Islamic history, religion, philosophy, and Islamic political movements. Entries include the biographies and thoughts of medieval thinkers and modern members of the religio-political establishment. Articles describe the major sects, schools of theology and jurisprudence, as well as aspects of Islamic culture to present a brief introduction to the field of Islamic studies.

Muslims believe that the Koran is God's message in Arabic, revealed through the medium of the Prophet Muhammad for the guidance of the Arabs and subsequently for all humanity. Therefore, much of the Islamic terminology is Arabic, a fact which may pose some problems for the beginner.

There is the problem of names: in many parts of the Islamic world individuals have not adopted a family name. Some are known by their personal name (*ism*), such as Ali or Muhammad (as explained in the entry "Names and Name Giving"); others are identified under a group name (*nisba*) indicating a place of origin or residence, such as al-Baghdadi—the one from Baghdad, or al-Siqqilli—the Sicilian. They may be known by their patronymic (*nasab*), as, for example, Ibn Khaldun, the son of Khaldun (listed under "I") or Abu Muslim, the father of Muslim (listed under "A"). The Arabic article "al-" must be ignored in the alphabetical order and only the short name of an individual is given; for example, the full name of Taqi al-Din al-Maqrizi (listed under "M") is Abu 'l-'Abbas Ahmad ibn 'Ali ibn 'Abd al-Qadir al-Husayni Taqi al-Din al-Maqrizi (meaning the Father of Abbas Ahmad, the son of Abd al-Qadir al-Husayni).

"Abd al-," meaning "the servant of," is also spelled Abdul; 'Abd Allah and Abdullah are variant spellings of the same name. The reader may ignore the diacritical mark "ayn" (') which stands for a certain sound in Arabic as do the ligatures "dh," which non-Arabic speakers often pronounce like "z," and "kh" pronounced like "ch" in the German exclamation "ach." The article is transliterated "al" even in "sun letters," for example, al-Shafi'i (not ash-Shafi'i), al-Rashid (not ar-Rashid), al-Dajjal (not ad-Dajjal), al-Salam (not as-Salam), and so forth.

Where possible, headings of entries are given in English and cross listed with the equivalent term in Arabic; for example, the entry on "Almsgiving" also lists the Arabic term "zakat" and refers the reader to the related term "sadaqah." The English word "Judge" is cross listed with "Qadhi," also spelled "cadi" or "kadi" in *Webster's Dictionary*.

A word represented in **bold type** refers the reader to a separate entry. However, names frequently listed, such as God or Allah (the Arabic equivalent), the cities of Mecca and Medina, Sunnis and Shi'ites, the names 'Ali and Muhammad, when they refer to the Prophet and his son-in-law, and Koran are not indicated in bold letters. Some Islamic terms listed in *Webster's Dictionary* are given in the English spelling: Koran, rather than Qur'an; Medina rather than Madina; and Mecca rather than Makka.

Citations from the Koran are from *The Holy Qur'an: English Translation of the Meanings and Commentary*, revised and edited by the Presidency of Islamic researches, IFTA, Call and Guidance, Kingdom of Saudi Arabia. Surahs and verses of the Koran are indicated, listing the Surah first and the verse after a colon; for example, 22:36 indicates Surah 22 and verse 36.

Muslims reckon time from 622, the time Muhammad emigrated from Mecca to Medina; however, all dates in this volume are given as common era (CE). It should be mentioned here that the dates of birth of individuals are often not known and are usually approximations and therefore less reliable than the date of a person's death. Also the records disagree on some dates, which may be reflected in this publication. The Islamic lunar year is shorter than the Western solar year, therefore, lacking an exact equivalent, some sources indicate an event occurring near a break in the solar year, like 911/912; I have listed only the first date.

A chronology provides the dates of important events and a selected bibliography should enable the serious student to pursue more specialized research.

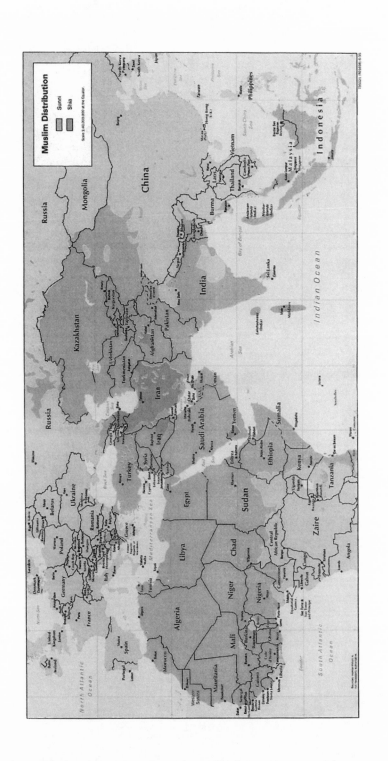

# ABBREVIATIONS AND ACRONYMS

BCE    Before Common Era

CE    Common Era

EI2    *Encyclopaedia Islamica*

EIR    *Encyclopaedica Iranica*

FIC    Front for Islamic Constitution

FIS    Front de Salut Islamique (Islamic Salvation Front)

N. d.    No Date

N. p.    No Publisher

OIC    Organization of the Islamic Conference

PLO    Palestinian Liberation Organization

# CHRONOLOGY

**570**   The traditional date of the birth of the Prophet Muhammad in the "Year of the Elephant." During this year (approximate date) Abraha, Christian king of Yemen, moved against Mecca with an elephant in his advance columns.

**577**   Death of Muhammad's mother Aminah b. Wahb (his father had died soon after Muhammad's birth).

**596**   Muhammad marries Khadija, a wealthy merchant woman.

**602**   Lakhmid dynasty at Hira ended.

**c. 610**   "The Night of Destiny." Muhammad receives his first revelation from Angel Gabriel. Khadija becomes his first convert.

**613**   First group of converts face persecution by the Quraysh, the major tribe of Mecca, which fears to lose its cultural and commercial dominance.

**615**   Exodus of some early converts to Ethiopia because of persecution by Meccans. Ascent of Muhammad to the seventh heaven.

**617**   Conversion of 'Umar ibn al-Khattab.

**619**   Death of Khadija and later Abu Talib, his uncle and protector.

**620** Prophet goes to Ta'if to win converts and find protection; does not succeed. Night journey in which Muhammad is taken from Mecca to Jerusalem and from there to heaven.

**621** First Aqabah covenant with 12 men from the Khazraj and Auz tribes who convert to Islam.

**622** **June:** Muslim converts in Yathrib (later Madinat al-Nabi, "City of the Prophet") promise loyalty and invite Muhammad to Yathrib. **July:** Muhammad flees to Yathrib. First of Muharram begins "Year One" of the Islamic lunar calendar.

**623** Muhammad concludes marriage with 'Aisha, daughter of Abu Bakr. Constitution of Madina establishes coexistence of Muslim and Jewish communities, *umma*. Fatima, daughter of Muhammad, marries 'Ali ibn Abi Talib, cousin of Muhammad.

**624** **March:** Battle of Badr in which Muslims defeat a superior Meccan force. Jewish tribe, Banu Qaynuqa, accused of collaborating with Quraysh, expelled from Medina. The month of Ramadhan proclaimed as the period of fasting. Mecca, rather than Jerusalem, designated as the qiblah, direction of prayer.

**625** **March:** Battle of Uhud in which Muslim forces were defeated by Meccans, who do not follow up on their victory. Jewish tribe, Banu Nadir, accused of collaboration with enemy and expelled from Medina.

**627** Battle of the Ditch, Meccans fail to conquer Medina, which is protected by a ditch (*kandaq*). Jewish tribe, Banu Qurayza, accused of collaborating with the enemy and destroyed.

**628** Muhammad sets out on pilgrimage and is prevented from entering Mecca. Treaty of Hudaybiyyah established a 10-year truce with Meccans to permit Muslim pilgrims to enter Mecca.

**629** Beduin allies of the Quraysh break the Truce of Hudaybiyyah.

**630** Muhammad with about 10,000 men enters Mecca without a fight. Muslims destroy the idols of the Ka'ba, declare the interior sacred, *harram*. "Farewell Pilgrimage" to Mecca by Muhammad.

Muhammad. Shi'ites commemorate the 10th of Muharram (Islamic month) as the martyrdom of Husayn.

**683**     Reign of Caliph Mu'awiyah II (683-684). Medina sacked by 'Umayyads.

**683-692** 'Abd Allah ibn al-Zubayr proclaims himself caliph at Mecca.

**684**     Reign of Caliph Marwan (684-685). Battle of Marj Rahit and defeat of the Qays.

**685**     'Abd al-Malik elected caliph (685-705). Arabizes the administration and issues the first Islamic coins (693). Mukhtar leads 'Alid revolt at Kufa (685-687).

**691**     Dome of the Rock built in Jerusalem. Ibn al-Zubayr killed in battle.

**692**     Hajjaj occupies Mecca.

**694**     Hajjaj becomes governor of Iraq.

**695-698** Consolidation of conquest of the Maghrib.

**705**     Walid I succeeds as caliph (705-715), founds the Umayyad Mosque in Damascus.

**706-715** Qutayba b. Muslim conquers Transoxania.

**711**     Tariq b. Ziyad crosses Strait of Gibraltar (named after him *Jabl al-Tariq*, Mountain of Tariq). Battle of Wadi Baakkah, conquest of Spain.

**713**     Zayd becomes imam of Fiver Shi'ites (Zaydis).

**715**     Sulaymand succeeds as caliph (715-717).

**717**     Umar II, most respected of Umayyad caliphs (717-720). Siege of Constantinople (717-718).

**720**     Yazid II becomes caliph (720-724).

**724**      Reign of Hisham (724-743), noted for his administrative reforms.

**728**      Hasan al-Basri dies.

**731-732** Charles Martel stops Arab advance in the Battle of Tours/ Poitiers.

**743**      Walid II (743-744) killed in a struggle between factions.

**744**      Yazid III succeeds to the caliphate. Ibrahim succeeds to the caliphate. Marwan II succeeds to the caliphate (744-750), last of the 'Umayyads.

**746**      Revolt of Abu Muslim who raised the black banners of the Khorasanian army and assisted in the establishment of the Abbasid Khalifate (749-1258).

**749**      Abu al-'Abbas al-Saffah, proclaimed first 'Abbasid caliph (750-754).

**750**      'Umayyad Caliph Marwan defeated at the Battle of the Greater Zab.

**751**      Battle on the Talas; Arabs defeat Chinese in Central Asia, capture paper makers; begin to manufacture paper.

**754**      Al-Mansur, brother of Abu al-'Abbas, becomes caliph (754-775).

**756**      'Umayyad dynasty of Spain founded (756-1031) by 'Abd al-Rahman I (756-788).

**762**      Baghdad founded as capital of the Abbasid caliphate. 'Alid rebellions. Death of Isma'il; he becomes imam of the Isma'ili (or Sevener) shi'ites.

**767**      Death of Abu Hanifa, founder of Hanifite school.

**775**      Al-Mahdi becomes caliph (775-785).

**778**      Muqanna' leads revolt in Khorasan.

**780**      Revolt of Muqanna' "The Veiled One" crushed.

**785**      Musa al-Hadi begins his short reign (785-786). Great mosque of Cordoba erected. Muqanna commits suicide.

**786**      Harun al-Rashid become caliph (786-809).

**788**      Idrisid dynasty founded.

**793**      Death of Malik ibn-Anas, founder of Malikite school.

**796**      Hakam I in Spain, revolts in Cordoba.

**800**      Rise of the Aghlabid amirs.

**803**      End of Barmakid wazirate.

**809**      Al-Amin becomes caliph (809-813); his brother Ma'mun revolts.

**813**      Al-Amin assassinated and Ma'mun begins his caliphate (813-833), adopts Mu'tazilite school (827), and founds a university in Baghdad, the Bayt al-Hikma (house of wisdom) (830).

**820**      Death of Shafi'i, founder of Shafi'ite school.

**821**      Rise of the Tahirid amirs in Khurasan (822-873).

**831**      Palermo seized by the Arabs.

**833**      Al-Mu'tasim assumes caliphate (833-842). Mu'tazilite "rationalist" school gains ascendancy.

**836**      New 'Abbasid capital built in Samarra.

**837**      Sect of Babak destroyed.

**842**      Wathiq succeeds to caliphate (842-847).

**847**      Mutawakkil becomes caliph (847-861). Mu'tazilite school abandoned.

**855**     Death of Ahmad Ibn Hanbal, founder of Hanbalite school.

**861**     Mutawakkil assassinated. Caliphate of Muntasir begins.

**862**     Caliphate of Musta'in begins (862-866).  Caliph moves from Samarra to Baghdad.

**864**     Zaydi shi'ism established in Daylam, Iran; continues until 1126.

**866**     Caliphate of Mu'tazz begins (866-869).

**867**     Rise of the Saffarid amirs in Eastern Iran.

**868**     Tulunid dynasty founded.

**869**     Zanj Rebellion of black slaves. Muhtadi becomes caliph (869-870). 'Ali ibn Muhammad founds kingdom of black slaves (869-883).

**870**     Mu'tamid becomes caliph (870-892). Conquest of Malta. Al-Bukhari dies.

**871**     Ya'qub al-Saffar rules Persia (871-879).

**873**     Eleventh shi'ite imam dies. Disappearance of the 12th Shia Iman and beginning of "Lesser Occultation" (873-940), followed by the "Greater Occultation" after 940, until the coming of the Mahdi.

**875**     Rise of the Samanid amirs in Transoxania.

**877**     Hamdan Qarmat revolts.

**892**     Caliphate of Mu'tadid begins (892-902).

**894**     Foundation of the Qarmatian state (894-977).

**898**     Foundation of a Zaydi state in Yemen, beginning of Rassi dynasty.

**902**     Al-Muktafi (902-908).

**908**     Al-Muqtadir becomes caliph (908-932), death of rival 'Abdallah ibn al-Mu'tazz.

**909**     'Ubaydullah al Mahdi becomes first Fatimid rulers (909-1171), assumes title of caliph in 911.

**929**     Rise of the Hamdanid amirs in Mesopotamia and Syria.

**930**     Qarmatians take Black Stone from Ka'ba. Abd al-Rahman II (912-961) assumes title of caliph in Spain.

**932**     Qahir becomes caliph (932-934). Buyid Mu'izz al-Dawlah becomes guardian of caliph, founds Buyid Dynast (932-1062).

**934**     Qahir blinded and deposed. Radhi becomes caliph (934-940).

**935**     Ikhshidid dynasty founded.

**940**     Beginning of "Grand Occultation" after fourth representative of the Hidden Imam. Muttaqi becomes caliph (940-944).

**944**     Muttaqi blinded and deposed. Mustakfi becomes caliph (944-946).

**945**     Buyids take Baghdad. Rule Iraq and Iran (932-1062).

**946**     Muti' becomes caliph (946-974).

**951**     The Imam dies. Qarmatians return Black Stone to Mecca.

**953**     Mu'izz becomes Fatimid Caliph (953-975).

**969**     Fatimids conquer Egypt. Foundation of Cairo.

**973**     Fatimids found al-Azhar mosque, the first Muslim university.

**974**     Ta'i' becomes caliph (974-991).

**975**     'Aziz becomes Fatimid caliph (975-996).

**977**     Beginning of Ghaznavid state (977-1186).

**991**    Qadir becomes caliph (991-1031). Recognizes independence of Mahmud of Ghazna and Ghaznawid dynasty (977-1186). Foundation in Baghdad of Shi'ite library, *Dar al'Ilm* (house of knowledge).

**996**    al-Hakim becomes Fatimid ruler at Cairo (996-1021), revered by the Druzes as a deity. Fatimids destroy Church of the Holy Sepulcher in Jerusalem.

**1027**    Hisham III, Last Umayyad in Cordova (1027-1031).

**1031**    Qaim becomes caliph (1031-1075).

**1036**    Mustansir becomes Fatimid caliph (1036-1094).

**1038**    Almoravid (al-Morabitun) Berber Kingdom founded. Beginning of Seljuq sultanate (1038-1194).

**1058**    Al-Mawardi dies.

**1062**    Almoravid Yusuf ib-Tashfin conquers Morocco.

**1071**    Battle of Manzikert. Rum Seljuks established in Anatolia.

**1075**    Al-Muqtadi becomes caliph (1075-1094).

**1090**    Hasan al-Sabbah captures Alamut fortress and begins rule of the Assassins.

**1092**    Nizam al-Mulk assassinated.

**1094**    Al-Mustazhir becomes caliph (1094-1118).

**1099**    Crusaders conquer Jerusalem.

**1107**    Muhammad Ibn-Tumart founds Almohad dynasty.

**1111**    Al-Ghazali dies.

**1118**    Al-Mustarshid becomes caliph (1118-1135).

**1124**    Death of Hasan al-Sabbah.

**1130**     Almohad (al-Muwahhidun) kingdom founded (1130-1269).

**1135**     Al-Rashid becomes caliph (1135-1136).

**1136**     Al-Muqtafi becomes caliph (1136-1160).

**1160**     Al-Mustanjid becomes caliph (1160-1170).

**1170**     Al-Mustadi' becomes caliph (1170-1180).

**1171**     Salah al-Din (Saladin) ends Fatimid regime in Egypt.

**1174**     Saladin captures Damascus and Syria. Ayyubid Dynasty founded.

**1180**     Al-Nasir becomes caliph (1180-1225).

**1187**     Salah al-Din (Saladin) defeats Crusaders at Battle of Hattin, captures Jerusalem.

**1203**     Chingiz Khan (Timuchin) founds Mongol empire.

**1212**     Almohades are defeated at Battle of Las Navas de Tolosa.

**1225**     Al Zahir becomes caliph (1225-1226).

**1226**     Al Mustansir becomes caliph (1226-1242).

**1230**     End of Almohad rule in Spain.

**1242**     Al-Musta'sim becomes last Abbasid caliph (1242-1258).

**1254**     Mamluk rule in Egypt (1254-1517).

**1256**     Mongols captures Assassin fortress of Alamut.

**1258**     Mongols sack Baghdad, end Abbasid caliphate at Baghdad.

**1260**     Mamluks defeat Mongols at 'Ayn Jalut.

**1273**     Jalal al-Din Rumi dies.

1324    Orkhan founds Ottoman empire (1324-1922).

1328    Ibn Taymiyyah dies.

1402    Timur-i Lang (Tamerlain) defeats Bayezid in Battle of Ankara.

1406    Ibn Khaldun dies.

1453    Ottomans capture Constantinople.

1492    Fall of Granada, the last Muslim kingdom in Spain.

1497    Babur captures Samarkand, becomes founder of Mughal dynasty (1526-1858).

1501    Shah Isma'il founds Safavid dynasty, imposes shi'ism in Iran.

1514    Selim defeats Shah Isma'il at Chalidran.

1517    Ottomans conquer Egypt.

1521    Ottomans capture Belgrade.

1529    Ottomans besiege Vienna.

1538    Ottomans annex Hungary, capture Baghdad.

1683    Second siege of Vienna.

1745    Emergence of the Wahhabi (Unitarian) movement.

1798    Napoleon invades Egypt (1798-1801).

1802    Wahhabis capture Mecca and Medina (1802-1804).

1805    Muhammad 'Ali founds Egyptian dynasty (1805-1952).

1812    Ibrahim, son of Muhammad 'Ali, takes Mecca and Medina.

1818    Ibrahim defeats Wahhabis.

1826    Massacre of the Janissaries under Mahmud II.

1828    Parts of Greece gain independence.

1830    French take Algeria.

1850    Execution of the Bab.

1869    Suez Canal openes.

1870    The "Mahdi" Muhammad Ibn ʿAbdallah in Sudan.

1874    Aligarh school (later university) founded by Sir Sayyid Ahmad Khan.

1876    Abdul Hamid becomes sultan/caliph of the Ottoman empire.

1881    French occupy Tunisia. Agha Khan I dies.

1882    The Mahdi drives Egyptians out of Sudan. British invade Egypt, begin colonial rule (1882-1952).

1885    Khartum attacked and Gen. Gordon killed. Mahdi dies.

1898    Sir Sayyid Ahmad Khan dies.

1901    Wahhabi forces take Riyadh. The French invade Morocco.

1907    Anglo-Russian Convention divides Iran, Afghanistan, and Tibet into spheres of influence.

1908    Young Turk revolt.

1914    Ottoman empire enters war against Triple Entente.

1916    **May:** Sykes-Picot Agreement. **June:** Arab Revolt.

1917    **November:** Balfour Declaration promises Jewish "Homeland" in Palestine.

1918    Armistice of Mudros between Ottomans and Allies.

**1920**    Ottoman government signs Treaty of Sèvres.

**1921**    Sons of Husayn, Sharif of Mecca, become kings. 'Abd Allah in Transjordan, Faysal in Iraq.

**1922**    Mustafa Kemal abolishes the sultanate.

**1923**    Turks defeat Greeks, sign Treaty of Lausanne which repeals Treaty of Sèvres.

**1924**    Turks abolish the caliphate.

**1928**    Hasan al-Banna founds Muslim Brotherhood. Assassinated in 1949.

**1938**    Sir Muhammad Iqbal dies.

**1975**    Elijah Muhammad dies.

**1978**    Imam Musa Sadr, leader of Twelver Shi'ites disappears on a trip to Libya.

**1994    November 5:** Emergence of the Taliban, students of religious schools, who capture Kandahar.

**1995    September 5:** Taliban capture Herat.

**1996    September 26:** Taliban take Kabul and two years later control most of Afghanistan.

**1997    October 6:** Taliban issue a decree, prohibiting dolls for children and all photographic images of humans and animals.

**1998    April 22:** A court in Pakistan sentenced a Christian, Ayyub Masih, to death for blaspheming Islam. The sentence was later suspended. **July 28:** The Taliban government decreed that Afghan parents must give their children "Islamic" names. **August 20:** United States launched approximately 75 cruise missiles on a training camp of Osama Bin Laden in Khost province of Afghanistan. **September 11:** Mullah Umar, head of the Taliban movement, issues a decree, prohibiting forced marriages of women. **October:** Taliban require Hindus in Kandahar to wear yellow marks on their clothing. **November 4:**. The United States offered a reward of 5 million dollars for the capture of Osama Bin Laden who enjoys protection in Afghanistan.

**1999** **October 19:** Merve Kawakci was stripped of her citizenship and her seat in parliament when she appeared in an Islamic head scarf. **November 4:** Roman Catholics and Orthodox Christians closed their churches in protest to the Israeli decision to permit building a mosque next to the Church of the Annunciation in Nazareth. **November 14:** The United Nations imposed sanctions on Afghanistan for its refusal to surrender Osama bin Ladin. **November 30:** A bill granting full political rights to women was rejected in Kuwait with a vote of 32 to 30. For approval 33 votes would have been needed.

**2000** **May 20:** Israeli troops withdraw from southern Lebanon as a result of casualties from Hizbullah campaigns. **August 1:** A group of six Iranian religious leaders issued a *fatwa* declaring that women could lead congregational prayers of their own gender. **October 6:** It is reported that the Bahrain government appointed to the consultative assembly four women, one Christian, and one Jewish. **December 19:** The UN Security Council voted to impose sanctions on the Taliban government.

**2001** **January 2:** Mulla Muhammad Umar of Afghanistan issued a decree making conversion from Islam to Christianity a capital crime. **February 26:** Mulla Muhammad Umar called for the destruction of all statues as they were a threat to Islam. **March 6:** Destruction of the giant Buddha statues begins. **May 5:** Taliban government issues a ruling to prohibit foreigners from drinking alcohol, eating pork, listening to loud music, and being in contact with members of the opposite sex. **May 21:** A decree of Mulla Umar demands that Hindus wear a yellow mark on their clothing and homes and prohibits them from wearing a turban. **May 31:** The Taliban government prohibits foreign women to drive cars. **September 11:** Suicide bombers, believed to be members of Osama bin Ladin's al-Qaida organization, crash commercial aircrafts into the World Trade Center and the Pentagon. **September 13:** The United States government mobilizes forces for action against the Taliban. **October 7:** American and British aircraft attack Taliban and al-Qaida bases in Afghanistan. **December 22:** Afghan Interim Government begins its tenure.

# INTRODUCTION

The Arabian Peninsula, heartland of the Arab nation and birthplace of the Muslim Prophet Muhammad, is a vast expanse of deserts with oases on the periphery and covers an area of about 2,750,000 square kilometers. It is a plateau that slopes away from the west to the Persian/Arabian Gulf and Mesopotamia, the present Iraq. Its backbone is a range of mountains running parallel to the Red Sea coast forming the **Hijaz** (barrier), which includes the holy cities of Mecca and Medina. The slope to the east is gradual and long and the fall to the Red Sea is short and steep. Between the Nile and the Indus Rivers there is only one major river system: the Euphrates and Tigris and their tributaries. In the south-center lies the Rub' al-Khali, Empty Quarter, the largest expanse of sand in the world, comprising an area of about 640,000 square kilometers.

Sheltered by impenetrable barriers, nomad Bedouins eked out a precarious existence. Only they knew the location of water holes which made survival possible. They grazed their flocks, moving within confined areas, some tending to limited agriculture in valleys and oases, others depending entirely on their flocks. Dates and the milk and meat from the camel were the major items of nourishment. To possess the "two black ones"—that is water and dates—is the minimum requirement for survival. The camel was the nomad's nourisher, his means of transportation, and his medium of exchange. He drinks its milk, feasts on its flesh, and makes his tent with its hair, which is fashioned into a felt. The dowry of a bride, the price of blood, and the wealth of a chief were counted in terms of camels. The Bedouin has been called the parasite of the camel (Hitti, 21). Without the camel, the desert could not be crossed, and the Arabs could never have conquered an empire. While the camel was the most useful, the horse was the most noble of all animals. In Arabia the horse has been kept pure and free of admixtures; it provided the speed in raids (**ghazwah**), a necessity for survival and to gain booty.

1

**The Message of Islam.** The period of some 200 years prior to the Prophet's message was called the **jahiliyyah**, the "time of ignorance." Arabia was then isolated from the rest of the Near East. Two superpowers ruled in the north, the Eastern Roman, or Byzantine, empire and the Sasanian Persian empire. They employed satellite kingdoms as buffer states to prevent the Arab nomads from raiding the northern territories. The Yemen in the south was contested between the empires of the north. In the **"Year of the Elephant,"** about the early 570s, an Abyssinian army under **Abraha** moved against **Mecca** but was forced to return to Yemen.

Most of the Arabs were pagans, but some were Christian or Jewish. One of the most important cultural centers was the city-state of Mecca, ruled by an oligarchy of merchants from the tribe of **Quraysh.** The Quraysh were subdivided into a number of clans, one of which, the **Banu Hashim**, was the clan of the Prophet. The prosperity of Mecca depended on keeping the caravan routes free from attacks; therefore, they promoted two sacred periods during which raiding and blood feuds were temporarily stopped. Customary tribal law in Mecca was beginning to give way to hegemonic rule by the Quraysh. The Bedouin concept of honor was giving way to the idea of accumulating wealth.

Muhammad was born in the "Year of the Elephant." His mother Amina was of the clan of Zuhra, and his father ʿAbd Allah was of the Hashimite clan of the Quraysh. His father died four months before his birth and his mother died a few years later. As was the custom, he was raised by a Bedouin nurse, Halima, and then stayed with his grandfather **ʿAbd al-Muttalib** and later with his uncle **Abu Talib.** At age 25, Muhammad married **Khadijah**, a wealthy woman of about 40 for whom he had conducted some business. Every year in the month of Rajab, Muhammad would go to Mount Hira and live there and fast. When he was 40, he came home one day, confessing to Khadija that he heard voices. And one day in the month of **Ramadhan**, Muhammad had his first revelation. He heard a voice, commanding him to "Read!" Muhammad answered "I cannot read!" The spirit gripped him again and said:

READ: IN THE NAME OF THY LORD WHO CREATED
CREATED MAN FROM A CLOT
READ: AND IT IS THY LORD THE MOST BOUNTIFUL
WHO TEACHETH BY THE PEN
TEACHETH EACH MAN THAT WHICH HE KNEW NOT.

Then the spirit disappeared and Muhammad went home to Khadijah. His wife covered him with a cloak and Muhammad fell asleep. Suddenly the spirit returned and shouted:

O THOU THAT ARE CLOAKED, ARISE AND WARN!
THY LORD MAGNIFY! THY RAIMENT PURIFY!
AND FROM INIQUITY GET THEE AWAY.

Muhammad woke up and told Khadijah that the spirit had bid him to call men to God. He asked: "Whom shall I call? And who will believe me?" Khadijah was said to have answered: "Call me the first, for I believe in thee." Muhammad began to have additional revelations, and an angel—later identified as **Gabriel**—told Muhammad that he was chosen as the Messenger of God. He gained a small number of converts to his creed: After Khadijah, 'Ali, his cousin and son-in-law, **Abu Bakr,** and the freed slave **Zayd ibn Haritha,** were among the first. The early converts came from three groups: Young men of influential families, who did not themselves wield any power; young men of weaker families and clans; and foreigners and men from outside the clan system, who did not have any powerful protectors. The time was ripe for Muhammad's message: There existed a social malaise as tribal traditional values and the existing social relationships were unable to cope with the problems faced by urban society. A new ideology was needed to replace the bonds of blood with the bonds of religion to provide a new concept of social justice and equality.

Muhammad was soon faced with opposition from the Quraysh, who feared that the new religion would threaten their social and commercial interests. Islam taught worship of one God and condemned the worship of idols. Islam propagated a philosophy of equality, which threatened not only their pagan beliefs but also their wealth and political power. In 619 Muhammad lost his uncle and protector and soon afterward Khadija, his wife. This was serious, because **Abu Lahab,** an old enemy, now became head of the Hashimite clan. Some of his followers, who did not enjoy the protection of a powerful tribe, were forced to migrate to Abyssinia, and Muhammad was forced to flee to **Yathrib,** subsequently called **Madinat al-Nabi,** "City of the Prophet," or simply Medina.

Members of the **Khazraj** and **Aws** tribes at Yathrib converted to Islam and invited Muhammad to come to their city, which was torn by disputes between two Arab and three Jewish tribes. The year 622, marking Muhammad's flight, became the "Year One" of the Islamic era. In Medina, Muhammad was Prophet of the early Arab converts, and statesman and arbiter between them and the Jews. The "**Charter of Medina**" is the first constitution in Islam, regulating the coexistence of a heterogeneous community.

The growth of the Muslim community in Medina considerably alarmed the Quraysh, who feared that the caravan route to the north would be blocked. The first confrontation between the two city-states resulted in the **Battle of Badr** in 624, when a force of some 300 Muslims defeated a superior force of some 1,000 Meccans. This was a severe loss of prestige for Mecca, which lost a number of its most prominent leaders. For the Muslims it was confirmation that Allah was on their side. One of the Jewish tribes, the **Qaynuqa**, was accused of collaboration with the Meccans and expelled from Medina. Another engagement in the **Battle of Uhud** (625) proved a temporary setback, which Muhammad blamed on a lack of steadfastness of the Muslim forces. The second Jewish tribe, the **Banu Nadir**, was now expelled. In 627 the Meccans moved with an army of between 7,500 and 10,000 against Medina, but the Muslim community was saved by digging a trench that the Meccans were unable to cross. This came to be known as the **Battle of the Trench**. The last Jewish tribe, the **Qurayza**, was accused of intriguing with the Meccans and was destroyed. Medina was now a Muslim Arab city, growing in power as converts joined the banners of the new faith.

Realizing the weakness of the Meccans, Muhammad decided to go on a pilgrimage to the **Ka'bah**, a cube-like building in Mecca that had been a shrine since pre-Islamic days. According to legend, the shrine was built by **Adam** and rebuilt by Abraham after the deluge. Angel Gabriel brought the **Black Stone**, which is now in the Ka'bah and instructed the people in the pilgrimage. Muhammad set out in 628 for Mecca with some 1,400 Muslims, but he was not able to enter the city. He concluded with the Meccans the **Treaty of Hudaybiyah**, which was to maintain peace for the subsequent 10 years. Accusing the Meccans of violating the treaty, the Muslim forces took Mecca in 630 at the loss of two Muslim lives.

In the **Year of Deputations**, 630-31, delegations of tribes from all over the Arabian Peninsula came to Medina to offer their allegiance. They agreed to be instructed in the new faith and to pay a poor tax, **zakat**, for the institutional use of the Muslim community. The area of Mecca and Medina was declared **haram**, forbidden to non-Muslims, a prohibition that some believe was later extended to much of the Peninsula. By the time the Prophet Muhammad died in 632, virtually all the Arabs in the Peninsula had offered their allegiance (**bay'ah**) and the Arab nation and the Islamic state were one and the same.

The death of the Prophet caused considerable consternation. It was soon decided that a **khalifa**, successor or **caliph**, was to be elected to lead the Muslim community (**ummah**). Three factions in Medina seemed to vie for power: the Emigrants, **muhajirun,** who came with Muhammad to Medina; the Helpers, **ansar,** Medinans who converted and supported the Prophet; and members of the Quraysh, Meccans who had now become Muslims and felt that their past leadership and blood relationship with the Prophet would especially qualify them for assuming leadership of the state. An assembly of **Companions** of the Prophet seemed unable to agree until 'Umar ibn al-Khattab spontaneously offered bay'ah to Abu Bakr. Others followed suit and he was elected the first caliph.

**The Spread of Islam.** Abu Bakr did not have much time to institutionalize his functions as head of state. Many of the tribes who had nominally become Muslims considered themselves free of any obligation to his successor. Therefore, most of the short reign of Abu Bakr was devoted to reuniting Arabia in the **Wars of Ridda,** defeating the apostates. He was ably assisted by **Khalid ibn al-Walid** and **'Amr ibn al-'As** who eliminated the **Ghazanid** and **Lakhmid** buffer states and moved into Palestine.

Campaigns during the caliphate of 'Umar ibn al-Khattab (634-644) led the Islamic forces into North Africa and Mesopotamia. 'Umar adopted the title **Amir al-Mu'minin,** Commander of the Believers. The Byzantines were defeated in the **Battle of Yarmuk** (636) and the Persian Sassanids at the **Battle of Nihavand** (641). 'Umar was worried about overextending his forces and he cautioned his reckless commander, Amr ibn al-As: "If my letter ordering thee to turn back from Egypt overtakes you before entering any part of it then turn back; but if thou enter the land before the receipt of my letter, then proceed and solicit Allah's aid"(Hitti, 160). Surmising its contents, Amr did not open the letter until he had entered Egypt. At the siege of the fortress of Babylon, Cyrus, in charge of the fortress, tried to bribe the Muslim commander, but his negotiators found that it was impossible to corrupt the enemy. They reported:

> We have witnessed a people to each and every one of whom death is preferable to life, and humility to prominence, and to none of whom this world has the least attraction. They sit not except on the ground, and eat naught but on their knees. Their leader [amir] is like unto one of them: the low cannot be distinguished from the high, nor the master from the slave. And when the time of prayer comes none of them absents himself, all wash their extremities and humbly observe their prayer. (Hitti, 163)

In 643 the Muslim armies reached the borders of India. When 'Umar was assassinated in 644, a council of five Companions elected **'Uthman ibn 'Affan** (644-656), an aristocratic member of the Quraysh, to lead the

Islamic community. 'Uthman was a compromise candidate; he was old and weak and was soon dominated by members of his clan who wanted to take over leading positions in the state. The most important legacy of his rule was believed to be the final collection of the revelations in the **Koran** (Qur'an, constituting the Holy Book of Muslims). Unrest continued in the empire and malcontents from Medina and disaffected groups in Egypt and Iraq turned against 'Uthman and murdered the 80-year-old caliph. **'Ali ibn Abi Talib** was the last of the Rashidun, the **"Rightly Guided Caliphs"** of **Sunni** Islam.

'Ali moved the capital of the Islamic state from Medina to Kufah. One reason may have been that Medina had been tainted by the murder of 'Uthman; another that he felt insecure in the old capital. He was immediately challenged by **Talhah ibn 'Ubaydullah, Zubayr ibn al-Awwam**, and **'A'isha**, Muhammad's widow. They blamed him for permitting 'Uthman's murderers to escape and finally met him in combat in the **Battle of the Camel** (656). Both Talhah and Zubayr were killed and 'A'isha was returned to Medina to resign herself to a life of seclusion. **Mu'awiyah ibn Abu Sufyan**, the governor of Syria and a relative of 'Uthman, was next to challenge 'Ali's authority. He refused to swear allegiance to 'Ali and demanded that he first avenge the murder of 'Uthman, and the two armies met in the **Battle of Siffin** (657). 'Ali's forces were about to gain the upper hand when the Syrians appealed for arbitration and an end to the bloodshed. There was great reluctance among the soldiers to fight fellow Muslims. Both had relatives in the other camp, and 'Ali agreed to submit the dispute to arbitration. This marked the origins of the division of Islam into Sunni, or orthodox Muslims, and **Shi'ites**, the partisans of 'Ali, who felt that he was the rightful successor of the Prophet Muhammad. The **Kharijites**, or seceders, who were followers of 'Ali, turned against him because he had submitted to arbitration. A Kharijite assassinated 'Ali in 661. **Najaf**, 'Ali's burial place in present-day Iraq, is a holy city to Shi'ites.

**The Umayyad Caliphate.** Mu'awiyah had himself proclaimed caliph in 660 when 'Ali was still alive. He was a clever politician and showed himself as a model of an Arabian king. He was quoted as having said: "I apply not my sword where the lash suffices, nor my lash where my tongue is enough." He performed all the functions required of a caliph and said he would resign if all the Muslims could agree on a man more fit to lead them. He based his right to rule on the fact that he alone had sufficient power to maintain and defend the Islamic state. While he was still governor of Syria, Mu'awiyah built the first Islamic navy and in the **Battle of the Masts** (655) he won a naval engagement against the

Byzantine empire. New conquests in the east brought his forces into central Asia, Kabul in 664 and Bukhara in 674. One of his most important governors and military leaders was **Ziyad ibn Abihi** (Ziyad, the Son of His Father whose name was not known). Ziyad crushed the Kharijites again and some of their Bedouin allies. Mu'awiyah assured the continuation of the Umayyad Caliphate (661-750) when he appointed his son **Yazid** (680-683) as his successor. This continued the civil war into the second generation when 'Abdullah, the son of 'Umar; 'Abdullah, the son of Zubayr; and **Husayn**, the son of 'Ali, refused to swear allegiance to Yazid. Husayn, expecting support from the Kufans, moved with a band of some 200 men into Iraq, but he was met by an Umayyad army of some 4,000 men and he and his supporters were killed. His death at **Karbala** in 680 is still mourned by Shi'ites today. They observe the first 10 days of the month of **Muharram** as days of lamentation. This event sealed the schism in Islam.

Yazid was able to defeat **Abdullah Ibn al-Zubayr**, who had proclaimed himself caliph, near Medina in 683. 'Abd al-Malik, the "great Arabizer," succeeded in 685 to mark the high point of Umayyad power. Assisted by his general Ibn Yusuf **al-Hajjaj**, 'Abd al-Malik captured Mecca in 692 and defeated a number of uprisings. He divided the empire into provinces, each of which was in charge of a governor, appointed judges (**Qadhis**) to the major towns, and established a large standing army. The first Muslim coins were struck and the **Arabic** script was improved with the addition of vowel marks. The Umayyads expanded the territories of Islam from Bukhara and Samarkand to Spain; they reached southern France, and they were stopped only at the Battle of Poitiers (or Tours) in 731/2. Accused by the pious opposition as Arab kings, rather than caliphs, resistance to the Umayyads began to grow. **'Umar ibn Abd al-Aziz** II (682-720), known as the "renovator" of Islam, was an exception. With the capture of new lands, Arabs became a minority in the Islamic empire. Their secularism and lack of a clear ideology, ill treatment of newly converted, who were taxed like non-Muslim subjects, and internecine warfare ended in a revolt that established the **'Abbasid Caliphate** (749-1258) with its capital in Baghdad.

The Umayyads got a bad press by 'Abbasid historians, in part, to justify the 'Abbasid revolt, but also with some justification: Of the 14 caliphs only Mu'awiyah, 'Abd al-Malik, and 'Umar were capable rulers; with a weak man in charge, the empire was weakened. The Umayyads, like subsequent Muslim rulers, lacked a clear rule of succession; the Arabs did not follow the law of primogeniture. The practice of polygamy greatly increased the number of eligible successors, and several caliphs were the sons of slave women; if often the oldest male relative was chosen, it was not necessarily the son who succeeded. Cousins, uncles, and others had an equal claim. The result was a measure of internecine conflict that continued throughout the centuries in the Islamic world. The Umayyads failed to engender a sense of loyalty among their most deserving officials. They put to death some of their best generals and deposed their administrative officials to deprive them of their wealth. The Umayyads were Arab kings rather than theocratic rulers, enjoying the pleasures of life, more attuned to the culture of pre-Islamic times. Tribalism and conflicts between Arab tribes continued to divide the Arab-Islamic nation. Non-Arab converts, **mawalis**, were treated as second-class citizens, which encouraged them to join the Shi'ite opposition. But this is to be expected in a period of transition from an Arab-Islamic nation to an Islamic empire.

**The 'Abbasid State.** The Abbasid assumption of power was not just a dynastic change; it was a revolution in the early history of Islam. The short rule of Abu al-'**Abbas al-Saffah**, "The Shedder of Blood" (749-754) was followed by Abu Ja'far **al-Mansur** (754-775), the real founder of a dynasty of 37 caliphs which ended with the Mongol conquest of Baghdad in 1258. He established his capital at Baghdad. Ruthless to real or imagined rivals, he preserved the supremacy of Islamic law and was a good administrator. His thriftiness earned him the title "Father of the Penny" (the penny pincher). On his deathbed he advised his successor "Never allow a thing which has to be done today to remain over for tomorrow. Associate with people from whom you can get good advice. Keep the people and the army contented. Never make your treasury empty. Never go beyond the bounds of moderation . . .," an advice he did not himself often follow. Although the 'Abbasid state was hailed as a return to the theocratic state, it became increasingly patterned after an older, Persian model, with the caliph the august, unapproachable, god-like autocrat. The 'Alids, who supported the revolution, were rudely disappointed when the 'Abbasids restored Sunni orthodoxy. Mansur has been called a treacherous man; he put to death his distinguished general, **Abu Muslim**, and cruelly killed his uncle Abdullah, but he preserved the supremacy of Islamic law and was a good administrator. The empire was organized after the Sassanian model, and ministries of the Army, the Seal, Finances, Post and Intelligence were set up. The only sphere in which Arabic continued to dominate was in the religious sciences. The Abbasids gained valued help in their state building by drawing on the talents of the **Barmakids**, a Persian family of secretaries and **viziers**.

With **Harun al-Rashid** (786-809) the "Arabian Nights" period of the

'Abbassids began. He conducted a brilliant court that attracted the talented and beautiful, including the Barmakids, who were men of great ability and administrative skill and amassed considerable wealth. But it was the end of an era: The Umayyad caliphate continued in Spain and, under Harun's successors, the empire began to lose control of the periphery. Harun hoped to prevent civil war after his death by arranging for an orderly succession; he appointed Muhammad **al-Amin** as his successor in Baghdad and Abu al-Abbas **al-'Ma'mun** as governor of the eastern province of Khurasan and second in line of succession. It was not to be. Ma'mun prevailed in a struggle for power and the unity of the Islamic world was ended both with the establishment of independent sultanates on the periphery and the achievement of hegemony by the Turks, who arrived as slaves and eventually became the masters of large parts of the Islamic world. Ma'mun tried to mend the Sunni-Shi'ite schism; he gave his daughter in marriage to the eighth Shi'ite imam, **'Ali al-Ridha**, and appointed him as his successor. This was not well received by the Sunni **ulama** and only the premature death of al-Ridha caused an end to Ma'mun's efforts. Ma'mun began a short "age of rationalism," and the **Mu'tazilite** dogma became the accepted doctrine. He established the **Houses of Wisdom** where Arabic and foreign sciences were taught. Religion was freely debated among Christians, Jews, and Muslims in Baghdad; and Greek philosophers were translated and later retranslated from Arabic in the West.

Unlike the Umayyad caliphs, the 'Abbasids prided themselves as the heads of a theocratic empire. They patronized the ulama (doctors of Islamic sciences) and made a show of consulting them on matters of state and law. Culturally, first Persian and later Turkish influences dominated; with the loss of its tribal basis, the empire lost its democratic features and the caliphate was transformed into monarchial despotism. The caliphs kept themselves aloof and surrounded themselves with an awe-inspiring court, and the vizier became the alter ego of the invisible caliph. The Muslim historian, al-Fakhri, said about the 'Abbasid caliphate:

> It was a dynasty abounding in good qualities, richly endowed with generous attributes, wherein the wares of science found a ready sale, the merchandise of culture was in great demand, the observances of religion were respected, charitable bequests flowed freely, the world was prosperous, the Holy Shrines were well cared for, and the frontiers were bravely kept.

Under the Umayyads no true orthodoxy prevailed and only with the beginning of 'Abbasid control do we have the creation of a systematic theology. Theological schools emerged in major cities, most importantly in Medina, Damascus, Basrah, and Kufah, which developed such disciplines as law, jurisprudence, grammar, and Koranic exegesis. In each of these towns pious men gathered, usually in **mosques**, to discuss questions of theology. Certain men gained a reputation for their knowledge; others were famous for their asceticism. They argued such questions as free will and predestination, capital sin and the sinner's fate, the divine unity and justice of Allah. The major philosophical trends were espoused by the rationalist Mu'tazilites; the uncommitted **Murji'ites**, who would leave judgment to God; the radical Kharijites, who declared a sinner a **kafir** to be killed; and the fundamentalist **Ash'arites**, whose doctrine became orthodox dogma.

An important dogma in Islam is God's omnipotence with the corollary that nothing happens without God's will. From that it would follow that all is preordained and man could not help committing sins; but al-Ash'ari with his doctrine of **kasb** (acquisition) stated that God produces the act, which is then "acquired" by the individual, giving him a choice, without infringing on God's omnipotence. Al-Ash'ari denied the existence of causality or a natural law, and he demanded the unquestioned acceptance of Divine Law and Revelation. He held that the Koran was the uncreated speech of God and espoused a literalism in which he used logic to expound an extreme **fundamentalism**. The Mu'tazelite school, on the other hand, stood for free will and God's justice, giving man the certainty that choosing the good and avoiding evil will win salvation. They also held that the Koran was created. When Caliph Ma'mun supported the Mu'tazilite doctrine of the createdness of the Koran and forced its acceptance by the ulama, the 'Abbasid caliphs eventually lost their authority to interfere in matters of religion and law.

Muslim historians call the period of the first 10 caliphs the golden age; Mansur (754) was the "Opener," Ma'mun (813) the "Middler," and Mu'tadid (892) the "Closer." The 21 caliphs after al-Mu'tadid were pawns and at times virtual captives of a new type of de facto political rulers, called **sultan**.

Sunni Muslims disagree as to the time the caliphate ended: some would end it after the four Rightly Guided Caliphs (632-661), who were Companions of the Prophet; others end it with the Mongol conquest of Baghdad (1258). The Ottoman conquerors of western Asia and North Africa claimed to have been appointed by a member of the 'Abbasid clan when they captured Egypt in 1517. Thus the Ottoman sultanate/caliphate continued until its defeat in World War I. Shi'ites count the end of the imamat, with the fifth, seventh, or Twelfth **Imam**, respectively.

**Institutional Development.** Political development in the Islamic world was a slow process: In pre-Islamic times and long afterward, the political unit was the biological and sociological unit, the family, the clan, and the tribe. Political unity meant to voluntarily accept arbitration, share resources, and provide for the common defense. An assembly (**majlis**) consisted of the male members of a tribe, which was to make decisions affecting the common interest. A chief (**shaykh**) presided, but he was essentially an arbitrator, a *primus inter pares*. The votes were weighed, not counted; the elders and more prosperous carried the day. There was no priestly class, only a shamanist type of sooth-sayer (**kahin**) who was the custodian of the idols, usually stones that were collected in the Ka'bah. The Kahin did not have any authority over the tribe. In urban areas a kind of city council (*mala'*) existed, but it was not very effective.

Initially, Muhammad's community acted like a clan, but the bonds of Islam began to replace the bonds of blood. The early community consisted of two classes of believers (**mu'minun**): the Companions who followed Muhammad to Medina (muhajirun), and the Helpers (ansar), Medinans of the Aws and Khazraj tribes who converted to Islam. But there were also three Jewish tribes in Medina and together they formed the first Judeo-Muslim community (ummah). Muhammad became the ruler on the basis of a contract, called the **Charter of Medina**, which provided for the common defense and coexistence of the communities. Once Arabia was unified under Islam and new territories were conquered, the ummah included only Muslims, and non-Muslim subjects (**dhimmis**) continued to coexist in autonomous communities, subject to payment of a capitation tax (**jizyah**) and dispensations from military service.

Under the successors of Muhammad's rule, the caliphs served as heads of state, but since Islamic law consisted of God's commands—as collected in the Koran—sovereignty rested with God. The caliph and subsequent rulers could not legislate; they had to enforce the God-given law. Only in matters not conflicting with divine law (**Shari'ah**), the Koran, and Traditions (**Sunnah**) was legislation permitted. With 'Umar I (634-644) a new constitution came into force: No religion other than Islam was to be tolerated in the Arabian Peninsula. The Muslim Arabs were to be a warrior class, racially and political segregated from the conquered in garrison camps (**amsar**). They were not to hold any land outside the Arabian Peninsula, and the dhimmis were to have protection of their life, property, and religion. If they converted to Islam, they no longer had to pay that tax. A land tax, **kharaj**, was first levied only on non-Muslims in the newly conquered territories (as Arabs acquired land, they eventually had to also pay the land tax), and a cadastral survey was conducted for the assessment of taxes. **'Ushr** (a tenth) eventually became a tithe on property owned by

Muslims, and a poor tax (**zakat**) came to be levied. A public register, the **Diwan**, was set up for the distribution of movable booty (**Ghanimah** or **Khums**), of which at first one-fifth went to the ruler for his institutional use while four-fifths was taken by the conquering soldiers. But soon the state took four-fifths and paid pensions to the soldiers, to Muhammad's wives, and to widows and families of martyrs. Pensions were paid on a scale depending on priority of conversion and nearness to the Prophet (wives got 12,000 dirhams), the Companions of the Prophet and those who had participated in the Battle of Badr (5,000 dirhams). 'Umar divided the empire into provinces, each headed by a governor (**Wali**) who also acted as a judge and tax collector ('**Amil**), and judges were eventually appointed for the major towns.

Muslim political philosophers in the 10th and 11th centuries began to define the ideal character of an Islamic state. The caliph was the supreme head of state, ruling with the assistance of a consultative council (**Shurah**). Sunnis believed in the principle of election, which was established with the election of the first four caliphs by a council of companions of the Prophet. Nevertheless, dynastic succession was common and the caliph was essentially an absolute monarch as long as he also held military power. Shi'ites held that the Imam must be a descendant of Ali, nominated by his predecessor. The caliph had to be knowledgeable in Islamic law and the traditions of the Prophet. He had to be of good character and piety, have good judgment in the functions of government and administration, as well as being of sound mind and body. Eventually a doctrine of the caliphate evolved. One Islamic jurist, Abu Hassan **al-Mawardi** (974-1058), defined the functions of the caliph as follows: Protecting Islam from innovation; providing justice; protecting the borders of Islam; executing the penalties of the shari'ah; garrisoning the borders; fighting unbelievers and compelling them to convert or pay the poll tax; levying taxes according to the Koran; regulating the expenditures of the state; appointing the right people to offices; and supervising the administration.

However, when the sultans became de facto rulers, the institution of the sultanate was legitimized as long as sultans performed all the functions the caliph no longer could. For a time, the caliphs had the power to approve the legislation of a sultan, but eventually sultans, like the Shi'ite **Buyids**, ignored or defied the wishes of the caliph.

Already from the begining of the 'Abbasid empire the unity of the Islamic world was lost. In Spain the Umayyad dynasty/caliphate continued from 756-1031 at the capitals of Seville and Cordova, ending the fiction of a united caliphate. The **Idrisids** (788-926) were the first Shi'ite dynasty in Islamic history, founded by Idris ibn 'Abdullah, and established in

Morocco; but they fell prey to the **Fatimids** in the east and the Spanish Umayyads in the west. The **Tulunid dynasty** (868-905) was the first local principality of Egypt and Syria that gained autonomy from Baghdad. The **Ikhshidis** (935-969) established themselves in Egypt, but finally they gave way to the Shi'ite **Fatimids** (909-1171). North Africa was subsequently ruled by the **Ayyubids** who under Salah al-Din (Saladin, 1138-1193) defeated the Crusaders at the battle of **Hittin** (1187) and captured Jerusalem. The **Mamluk** slave dynasties (1250-1517) gave way to the **Ottoman** dynasty (1342-1924), which reunited most of the Islamic world west of the Iranian border.

In the east, territory was lost to the short-lived **Tahirids** (820-873), who were replaced by the Saffarids (867-ca. 1495), who, in turn, were largely replaced by the **Samanids** (874-999). Turks were the founders of the **Ghaznawid dynasty** (977-1186), the **Seljuq dynasty** (1038-1194) (which replaced the Buyids) and the Ottoman dynasty. By the 16th century the Islamic world was divided into the Ottoman empire, controlling the lands west of Iran; the **Safavid dynasty** (1501-1732), which founded modern Shi'ite Iran; and the Moghul (Mughal) empire of India (1526-1858), which existed until defeated by Great Britain in 1858.

**The Development of Islamic Law.** A body of **Islamic law** (Shari'ah) also gradually evolved during the eight and ninth centuries based on the revelations of God's commands collected in the Koran. But it was soon felt that the Koran was not sufficient to cover all aspects of a complex society, and the jurists turned for guidance to the life of the Prophet. Acting on the premise that God would not have chosen Muhammad as prophet if he had not led an exemplary life, the Traditions (Sunnah, actions and sayings of the Prophet), collected in news items (**hadith**), were examined for guidance. A science of hadith criticism evolved in which news items, transmitted by an original witness through a chain of transmitters, were judged according to the reliability of the chain. Six major Sunni collections were compiled with the one of Muhammad Ibn Isma'il **al-Bukhari** being the most authoritative, including some 7,000 traditions with information on such topics as revelation, belief, **prayer** and **ablutions, fasting, pilgrimage, marriage,** and others. The Traditions (Sunnah) thus became a second **pillar** of Islamic law.

Four **Schools of Law** developed in Sunni Islam named after early legal scholars: the **Malikite**—named after **Malik ibn Anas** (d. 795), the Shafi'ite—named after ibn **Idris al-Shafi'i** (d.819), the Hanbalite—named after **Ahmad ibn Hanbal** (d. 855), and the Hanafite—named after **Abu Hanifa** (d.767). These schools recognize each other as orthodox but differ in the application and extent of two additional pillars of Islamic law. The

Hanafite school has the largest number of adherents. It recognizes as a basis of jurisprudence, in addition to the Koran and the Sunnah, **ijma'** (consensus of the Muslim community) and **qiyas** (reasoning by analogy). Legal reasoning is called **ijtihad**, the struggle, or effort, in arriving at a legal decision. By the 10th century Muslim jurists decided by consensus that Islamic law was complete and that independent interpretation (ijtihad), was no longer permissible. Henceforth, Muslims were to follow, or imitate (**taqlid**), God's law and the body of decisions of the four schools. Islamic modernists as well as radical Islamists want to reopen the "Gate of Ijtihad" to permit a reinterpretation of Islamic law to meet new, modern requirements.

Judges (**qadis**) in Shari'ah courts are to apply the law, subject to consultation with legal experts (**muftis**) who issue legal decisions (**fatwas**). A jurist (**faqih**) is trained in an Islamic college (**madrasah**) to serve as a lawyer, teacher, judge, or mufti. Punishments include the penalties for major offenses prescribed in the Koran (**hadd**, pl. hudud), discretionary and variable punishments (**ta'zir**), and retaliation (**qisas**).

Shi'ites find their sources of law in the Koran and the Traditions of the Prophet and the Infallible Imams. In the absence of the **Hidden Imam**, the Imami, or **Twelver Shi'ites** are permitted to legislate on the basis of ijtihad of the qualified scholar (**mujtahid**).

The Shari'ah was unevenly enforced and a dichotomy always existed between God's and the king's law (**qanun** or **'urf**, customary law), and the latter began to infringe on the former. The governor or his deputy presided over the police court or court of tort in cases that did not come under canon law. Muslims are enjoined to command virtue and prevent vice (*al-amr bi'l ma'ruf wa'n nahy 'an al-munkar*) and the governments institutionalized this in a Department of Promotion of Virtue and Suppression of Vice. It was to supervise public morals and command Muslims to attend to the daily prayers. The **muhtasib**, overseer of public morals and market inspector, was appointed to maintain public order, resolve disputes between buyers and sellers, examine weights and measures, and check goods according to quality and quantity. He had to be a jurist to be able to check the preaching of heretical doctrines. He could not act on suspicion, nor could he enter the closed doors of homes. His function was eventually taken over by the urban police in most countries.

With time, especially during the 19th and 20th centuries, the state increasingly restricted the application of Islamic law to personal law, matters of marriage, **divorce**, **inheritance**, and similar matters. Under the influence of colonial rule and modernization, governments adopted Western legal systems to varying degrees.

**Islamic Reform Movements.** In the post-classical age, a number of Islamic reform movements (**Salafiyyah**) emerged, often originating on the periphery of the Islamic world. Some were messianic, like the **Almohades** (1130-1269), **Almoravids** (1061-1147), **Wahhabis**, and the **Mahdi of the Sudan** (1880s-1899). Of these, only the Wahhabis, or Unitarians—as they call themselves—have left a lasting influence. An alliance between the revivalist Muhammad ibn **'Abd al-Wahhab** and the tribal chief Muhammad **ibn Sa'ud** in the late 18th century led to the establishment of the Kingdom of Saudi Arabia as an Islamic state in which the Shari'ah is enforced in all its provisions. Based on the Hanbali school of Sunni Islam, it is the most restrictive of the orthodox schools and, because of the country's relative isolation, it has scarcely been affected by the process of westernization. The rest of the Islamic world has been affected to a varying degree by Western influences, as a result of colonization, integration into the world economy, the rise of nationalism, the cold war, the emergence of Israel, and other factors.

Muslims differ in their interpretation of Islam. Secularists favor the separation of church and state. They tend to be cosmopolitan in outlook, and they favor the organization of the state along Western models and support mass education and scientific investigation. The secularists have achieved their objectives with the establishment of the Republic of Turkey and the victory of the secular policies of **Kemalism**. They can be found among the higher echelons of the military, the bureaucracy, and the urban intelligentsia. **Muslim modernists** want to reinterpret Islam to adapt to the requirements of modern times. They feel that Islam and democracy are compatible and that selective borrowing from the West would benefit their societies and solve their socioeconomic problems. They are often the product of Western education, urban, and professional groups. Important proponents include **Sayyid Jamal a-Din Afghani** (d. 1897) and his disciple **Muhammad Abduh** (d.1905).

Numerically the largest segment of the Muslim population can be classified under the label of traditionalists. They are devout, practicing Muslims, the products of madrasas and Islamic elementary schools, as well as government schools, who accept the leadership of the ulama and, while relatively tolerant, tend to reject alien ideas and practices. They look to the classical and medieval periods of Islam as their model of the Islamic state. They feel that the Koran and the Traditions are sufficient for finding answers to the problems of today and are generally conservative. Most of the traditionalists come from the rural population, circles attached to the mosques and bazaars. They are farmers and craftsmen, but they also include Muslim intellectuals who feel that the Islamic world is in danger.

They favor the establishment of a Muslim, if not an Islamic, state, organized after the example of the classical and medieval models.

A new, radical, **Islamist** movement has emerged in the 20th century that wants to establish an Islamic state and draws its inspiration from the writings of the trinity of **Abu'l A'la al-Maududi** (1903-1979), **Hasan al-Banna** (1906-1949), and **Sayyid Qutb** (1906-1966). To these should be added the Shi'ite **Ayatollah Khomeyni** (1900-1989), who was the first to achieve the objective of establishing a modern theocratic government in the **Islamic Republic of Iran** in 1979.

Islamism is a new term for a radical, fundamentalist movement that is gaining adherents among the youth of the Islamic world. They emerged on university campuses as the opponents of the leftists and they developed a political ideology based on Islam, which advocates restoring power and influence to the Islamic world. They blame the backwardness and decline of the Islamic world on the rulers who did not enforce the injunctions of Islam and permitted the growth of Westernization. They share the basic beliefs of the ulama, but they blame the traditional ulama for having tolerated secular ideologies such as nationalism and socialism. They proclaim holy war against the process of secularization. They maintain that sovereignty belongs to God; the amir is his representative, who rules with the advice of a council (**shurah**) that bases its decisions on the Koran and Traditions. The Islamists preach political sermons and use violence to achieve their objectives, stating that no truly Islamic society existed after the first four Rightly Guided Caliphs. The leaders are intellectuals who see themselves as avant-gardists and the only Islamic party, while their opponents characterize them as fascists. They are organized in centralized, disciplined groups, some in cells, such as the communists and other clandestine parties. They are the product of government education, often members of the lower middle class. Some of them were attracted to Marxism and joined radical Islam after the fall of the communist empire. Many studied Marxism and Western thought, so as to be able to refute them. They want the consensus (ijma) of the community, not of the ulama.

Their program consists of reeducating Muslims to accept their view of a purist Islam and starting a revolution to bring justice and happiness to the people. They accept the principle of private property and profit from lawful efforts, but they want to eliminate social inequalities. They forbid lending money for interest and demand that taxes should be on income and capital, and that the poor must be helped. The Islamists prohibit music, TV, games, compel attendance at prayers, and enforce wearing of traditional dress. Most will give women the right to education, but not coeducation. They build mosques in poor areas and provide social services that the governments failed to provide, such as soup kitchens and aid to families of their **martyrs**. They are missionaries who want to make "true" Muslims out of the believers and want to eliminate all manifestations of Westernization.

There is variety and unity in the Islamic world. Muslims are not a homogeneous, timeless people who can be explained solely by their normative texts, the Koran and the Sunnah. At the present time, the emergence of Islamist revivalism and its political impact is one example of the continuing process of redefinition. Although Muslims believe in the unity of the Islamic community (ummah), there exists no *homo islamicus*, as sometimes represented in Orientalist literature.

# THE DICTIONARY

-A-

**ABADITES.** *See* IBADITES.

**'ABBAS IBN 'ABD AL-MUTTALIB** (573-653). Paternal uncle of the Prophet and head of the Hashimite clan. Abbas fought in the Battle of **Badr** on the side of the Meccans and was taken prisoner by the Muslims. Ransomed, he converted to Islam in 630 and consolidated his link to Muhammad by giving him his sister-in-law, **Maymuna,** in **marriage.** He was a rich merchant and possessed the monopoly of providing water for pilgrims to Mecca. In spite of his former opposition, he was accepted as one of the **Companions** of the Prophet, the "last of the refugees" (**muhajirun**). His great-grandson Abu al-'Abbas al-Saffah was the eponymic founder of the **'Abbasid caliphate.**

**'ABBASID CALIPHATE** (749-1258). The dynasty that succeeded the **Umayyad Caliphate** at the time when the Islamic community (**umma**) evolved from an Arab kingdom into an international Islamic empire. As the number of new converts increased, there was considerable discontent about discriminatory treatment by the Arabs, and a coalition of malcontents, partisans of **'Ali,** and the pious opposition in Medina supported the 'Abbasid revolt. To a certain extent an Iranian revivalism appeared under the guise of international Islam, led by the Khorasanian leader **Abu Muslim** (d. 755). He captured Marv in 747, defeated Marwan II in the battle of the Greater **Zab** in 750, and thus ended Umayyad rule. Abu 'l- 'Abbas al-Saffah (the Shedder of Blood) became the first 'Abbasid **caliph.** His title al-

19

Saffah may have been adopted because of a tradition, according to
which there would be three precursors to the **Mahdi** (Redeemer), one
of them the "Shedder of Blood." The empire enjoyed a period of
greatness, which, however, did not last longer than about 100 years.
Islamic unity was ended when **'Abd al-Rahman** continued the
Umayyad dynasty in Spain (755-1031) and there existed two states
with claims to the **caliphate.**

**Al-Mansur** was the real founder of the dynasty, supported by
the army and bureaucracy; he established his capital at **Baghdad**
(762), which became the intellectual center of the empire. Members
of the **Barmakid** family held the position of first minister (**vizier**) of
the state and were famous as builders and patrons of the arts. The
empire reached its greatness during the reign of **Harun al-Rashid**,
but decline began when two of his sons, **al-Amin** and **al-Ma'mun**,
fought over succession with the latter victorious. Under the influence
of Greek philosophy, al-Ma'mun adopted the **Mutazilite** interpretation on such questions as the createdness of the Koran. This was
followed by an inquisition (*mihna*) during which Islamic scholars
were forced to accept the dogma that the Koran was created, an idea
that was eventually rejected some 25 years later. **Ahmad ibn Hanbal**
(780-855), founder of the **Hanbalite** school of Sunni Islam, refused
to recant.

Under al-Mu'tasim Turkic units, drafted to protect the ruler,
became increasingly powerful and eventually became the real power
behind the 'Abbasid throne. For his own protection and to appease
the citizens of Baghdad who resented the unruliness of the Turkic
troops, al-Mu'tasim had to move the capital to **Samarra** where it
remained from 836 until 892. From the reign of al-Qahir to the time
of al-Qaim, the 'Abbasids suffered the ignominy of being dominated
by the Shi'ite **Buyids.** Trends to Shi'ism were reversed when the
**Seljuq** Turks established their empire at Baghdad, supporting Sunni
orthodoxy and relegating the **caliphs** to an honored, but powerless,
status. Finally, the **Mongol** invasion of the Middle East led to the
destruction of Baghdad in 1258 and the massacre of the members of
the 'Abbasid clan. An uncle of al-Musta'sim continued the 'Abbasid
line in **Cairo** until Egypt was captured by the **Ottomans** in 1517.
The Ottomans later propagated the idea that the last of the Abbasids
appointed Sultan Selim I as his successor.

The 'Abbasids included the following members:

| | |
|---|---|
| 749 Abu al-'Abbas al-Saf-<br>fah | 754 Al-Mansur |
| | 775 Al-Mahdi |

| | | | |
|---|---|---|---|
| 785 | Musa al-Hadi | 940 | Al-Muttaqi |
| 786 | Harun al-Rashid | 944 | Al-Mustakfi |
| 809 | Al-Amin | 946 | Al-Muti' |
| 813 | Al-Ma'mun | 974 | Al-Ta'i |
| 833 | Al-Mu'tasim | 991 | Al-Qadir |
| 842 | Al-Wathiq | 1031 | Al-Qaim |
| 847 | Al-Mutawakkil | 1075 | Al-Muqtadi |
| 861 | Al-Muntasir | 1094 | Al-Mustazhir |
| 862 | Al-Musta'in | 1118 | Al-Mustarshid |
| 866 | Al-Mu'tazz | 1135 | Al-Rashid |
| 869 | Al-Muhtadi | 1136 | Al-Muqtafi |
| 870 | Al-Mu'tamid | 1160 | Al-Mustanjid |
| 892 | Al-Mu'tadid | 1170 | Al-Mustadi' |
| 902 | Al-Muktafi | 1180 | Al-Nasir |
| 908 | Al-Muqtadir | 1225 | Al-Zahir |
| 923 | Al-Qahir | 1226 | Al-Mustansir |
| 934 | Al-Radhi | 1242-58 | Al-Musta'sim |

The 'Abbasid assumption of power was a revolution in the early history of Islam: The **"Rightly Guided" caliphate** was an Islamic theocracy, the **Umayyad caliphate** was a kingdom of the Arabs, and the 'Abbasid caliphate was an Islamic empire. Culturally, first Persian and then Turkish influences prevailed. Only the **Arabic** language and Sunni orthodoxy remained. Politically, the 'Abbasid caliphate was a monarchical despotism; the caliphs kept themselves aloof and surrounded themselves with an awe-inspiring court. Slaves gained influence in the administration and army. As the empire lost territory in the west, the center of power moved to the east. The Golden Age of the empire lasted until the death of the 10th caliph, Mutawakkil in 861 and, thereafter, the decline began. Sectarian conflict prevailed and a military feudalism spread. The **Mongol** invaders destroyed an empire that was already near disintegration.

**'ABD.** Servant, slave. In a compound with one of the names of Allah ('Abd Allah), it designates a believer in the one God, Allah; it is also a common name. *See also* SLAVERY.

**'ABD AL-'AZIZ IBN MUHAMMAD IBN SA'UD** (1721-1803). *See* IBN SA'UD, 'ABD AL-'AZIZ IBN MUHAMMAD.

**'ABD AL-AZIZ IBN SA'UD** (1880-1953). *See* IBN SA'UD ABD AL AZIZ.

**'ABD AL-HAMID II** (r. 1876-1909). **Ottoman sultan/caliph** who fought a losing battle with domestic and foreign enemies. He promulgated the first Ottoman constitution in 1876 and assumed power as a constitutional monarch. But he prorogued parliament for 30 years when it was unable to agree on a budget and tried to limit his own powers. The sultan continued his predecessor's reforms, including the construction of modern government buildings. He greatly expanded the educational system and founded the Dar al-Funun in 1900, which later became **Istanbul** University. Abd al-Hamid built a rail network, including the **Hijaz** railroad that connected Istanbul with Medina and was to facilitate **pilgrimage** as well as serve the strategic purpose of centralizing the powers of the state. To consolidate his power he promoted **pan-Islamism**, Ottomanism, and Turkism to appeal to his varying constituencies, but foreign pressures increased: Great Britain occupied Cyprus (1878) and Egypt (1882), and France took Tunisia in 1881. Austria annexed Bosnia-Herzegovina in 1908. The rise of nationalism among the ethnic minorities and, finally, the Young Turk Revolution, led to the ouster of Abdul Hamid in 1909.

**'ABDALLAH IBN AL-ZUBAYR** (624-692). Born in Medina, the son of Asmah, older sister of **'A'ishah**, the wife of Muhammad, and of **Zubayr ibn al-Awwam, Companion** of the Prophet. **Caliph 'Uthman** ordered Zubayr to make the first recension of the Koran. He was one of the leaders of the pious opposition who fought **'Ali ibn Abi Talib** in the **Battle of the Camel** in 656. He then lived in Mecca and subsequently refused to recognize **Yazid**, son of **Mu'awiyah**, as the new **Umayyad caliph**. Beaten in the battle of **Marj Rahit** in 684, he continued to rule as anti-caliph for 10 years at Mecca. He was defeated by **'Abd al-Malik**'s general **al-Hallaj** in the battle for Mecca and killed in 692.

**'ABD AL-MALIK** (646-705). Fifth **Umayyad caliph** (r. 685-705) and native of Medina who fought secessionist forces, defeating **'Abdallah ibn al-Zubayr** in 692, who had proclaimed himself **caliph** in Mecca. He consolidated the state and centralized power in which he was greatly assisted by his governor of Iraq, **Hajjaj ibn Yusuf**. More of an autocrat than **Mu'awiyah**, he was attuned to the pious opposition in the **Hijaz**. Described as dark, thickset, and with a long beard, he was an astute judge of character, appointing capable people to positions of power. He was known for his eloquence and miserliess,which earned him the nickname "Dew of the Stone." 'Abd al-Malik was the great Arabizer, substituting **Arabic** for Greek and Persian in the administration and issuing the first Islamic coins. During his reign, diacritical markings were added to the Arabic script, permitting greater accuracy in the rendition of Arabic speech. He established a regular postal service,which also served as a system for collecting intelligence. His policy of forcing newly converted Muslims to return to the land and to continue to pay their original taxes caused considerable resentment and contributed to hostility toward the Umayyad regime.

**'ABD AL-QADIR AL-JILANI.** *See* JILANI, 'ABD AL QADIR AL-.

**'ABD AL-RAHMAN, 'UMAR (ABDUL RAHMAN, OMAR** 1938- ).
Egyptian Islamist leader, native of a village in Daqaliyah district in the Nile delta. He went blind in infancy, but he was able to study and obtain a doctorate from **Al-Azhar** University in 1977. Subsequently he taught at a branch of the university at Asyut. He went abroad and took a job as teacher of Islamic studies in Saudi Arabia. Upon his return to Egypt he was arrested for instigating the assassination of President Anwar Sadat but was freed in 1984 for lack of evidence. 'Abd al-Rahman is said to have inspired the **Islamist movements** of **Jama'at al-Islamiya** and **Islamic Jihad** (al-Jihad al-Islami), which deny the legitimacy of any Muslim state that adopts Western government principles and demands the establishment of an Islamic state, governed on the basis of the Koran and Traditions (**Sunnah**). He fled to Sudan and came to the United States in 1990 where he continued his campaign against the Egyptian government. He was arrested and given a life sentence in 1994 for involvement in the bombing of the World Trade Center in New York.

**'ABD AL-RAHMAN** (r. 756-787). Founder of the **Umayyad caliphate** of Spain (756-1031). He escaped the massacre of the Umayyad clan at **Damascus** and made his way to Spain where he was well received. He defeated the **Abbasid** governor at Cordoba in 756 and made the city his capital. Cordoba became a famous center of **Arabic** culture and learning; it took its place as the most cultured city in Europe and with Constantinople and **Baghdad** as one of the three cultural centers of the world.

> With its one hundred and thirteen thousand homes, twenty-one suburbs, seventy libraries and numerous bookshops, mosques and palaces, it acquired international fame and inspired awe and admiration in the hearts of travellers. (Hitti, 526)

Abd al-Rahman III (r. 912-961), the eighth in line of succession, proclaimed himself **caliph** in 929 and his reign marked the height of Umayyad power.

**'ABD AL-WAHHAB, MUHAMMAD IBN** (1703-1792). 'Abd al-Wahhab studied theology with his father and then traveled widely in Arabia, Iran, and Iraq, before going to Medina to study **Islamic law** and **theology**. Influenced by the teachings of **Ibn Hanbal** (780-855) and **Ibn Taymiyyah** (1263-1328), he campaigned for a return to the practices of early Islam. He was shocked by what he considered sinful innovations in the great cities of Islam and allied himself with Muhammad **Ibn Sa'ud** of Dariya in Central Arabia to propagate his reformist ideas. 'Abd al-Wahhab presented his ideas in *The Book of Unity* (kitab al-tawhid), in which he attacked as sinful innovations the doctrines of Sufism, saint cults, and intercession, and demanded the Koran and Traditions (**Sunnah**) as the sole bases of Islamic theology and jurisprudence. He was able to gain a considerable following among the Arab tribes and, although initially defeated, the alliance between the Islamist reformer and the clan of Al Sa'ud led to the conquest of Arabia and the establishment of **Wahhabism** in what came to be the Kingdom of Saudi Arabia.

**'ABDUH, MUHAMMAD** (1849-1905). Journalist, theologian, jurist, reformer, and one of the founders of **Muslim Modernism**. Born in Egypt, he received the traditional education and earned the title of **hafiz** when he had memorized the Koran at the age of 12. He graduated from **Al-Azhar University** in 1874 and immediately started to criticize the traditional **ulama** for its dogmatic and doctrinaire attitude in theology and jurisprudence. He called for a renaissance in the Islamic world and encouraged Muslims to study modern science and technology. He rejected imitation or emulation (**taqlid**) of the law as consolidated in the 10th century, and he advocated the adoption of independent reasoning and judgment (**ijtihad**) in revising **Islamic law**. As a teacher at Al-Azhar, he preached that

**revelation** and reason were inherently harmonious. In his major publication, *The Theology of Unity* (risalat al-tawhid, 1887), he held that what was given in revelation should be rationally possessed.

As a result of the British invasion of Egypt in 1882, Abduh was suspended and joined his mentor, the **pan-Islamist** Sayyid Jamal al-Din **al-Afghani**, in Paris where they published the journal **Al-Urwat Al-Wuthqa** (The Firmest bond). Exiled from France, he returned to Egypt in 1888, where his teachings and moderate views won him many followers. In 1889 Abdu was appointed Grand Mufti of Egypt and in 1894 was elected a member of the Supreme Council of Al-Azhar University. He issued liberal **fatwas** (legal decisions) proclaiming it legal to eat the meat of animals slaughtered by **Christians** and **Jews**; discouraging **polygamy**, as it would require the impossible equal treatment by a man of each wife; and fighting the misuse of **talaq, divorce** of **women** by men. **Rashid Ridha** (1865-1935), his biographer and the most important of his disciples, gradually abandoned his modernist views and moved toward a type of **fundamentalism** akin to the contemporary **Islamism**.

**'ABDUL.** *See* 'ABD AL-.

**ABLUTION.** "Wudhu." Ritual washing prescribed before **prayers**. It is commanded on the authority of the Koran, which says: "O ye who believe! Approach not prayer . . . Until after washing your whole body. If ye are ill, or on a journey, or one of you cometh from the privy, or ye have been in contact with **women**, and ye find no water, then take for yourselves clean sand (or earth), and rub therewith your faces and hands" (4:43). There are three types of ablutions, **ghusl** (greater ablution), which involves washing the entire body; wudhu' (lesser ablution), washing the hands, mouth, nose, face, arms, head, and the feet; and **tayammum**, where, for lack of water, sand or earth is used instead. Shi'ites and **Kharijites** do not permit the use of tayammum. One Islamic scholar proclaimed,

> When a believer washes his face during ablution, every sin he contemplated with his eyes will come forth from his face along with the water; when he washes his hands, every sin they wrought will come forth from his hands with the water; when he washes his feet, every sin toward which his feet have walked will come out with the water, with the result that he will come forth pure from offenses. (Tabrizi, p. 94)

**ABODE OF WAR.** *See* DAR AL-HARB.

**ABORTION.** "Isqat."Abortion is forbidden in Islam except if the life of the pregnant mother is in danger. The practice of infanticide in pre-Islamic Arabia was outlawed in the Koran, which says: "Kill not your children for fear of want: We shall provide sustenance for them as well as for you. Verily the killing of them is a great sin" (S17:31). According to Tradition (**Sunnah**), after 120 days of conception, the fetus receives its soul, therefore abortion is considered homicide. Female infanticide was rationalized by the Bedouins in pre-Islamic Arabia "because **women** have to be adorned in gold and silver only to be married off, thus resulting in a material loss." Women were seen as a liability in battle, as they could not serve as fighters, and they were carried off as part of the booty.

**ABRAHA** (ca. 540-570). Christian viceroy of the Negus in Yemen who invaded the **Hijaz** in about 570 but was not able to capture Mecca. He brought war elephants with his army, animals not known by the desert Arabs; therefore, they named the year of the campaign the "**Year of the Elephant.**" This is traditionally claimed to be the year of the birth of the Prophet Muhammad. Abraha's troops were decimated by smallpox and forced to retreat.

**ABRAHAM (IBRAHIM).** The biblical ancestor of the Arabs and **Jews**. He rebuilt the **Ka'bah**, established the **pilgrimage** to Mecca, and destroyed the idols in the temple (2:125-127, 3:96, 22:26). According to the Koran, Abraham was neither **Christian** nor **Jew**, but a **hanif**, monotheist. He is reckoned to be one of six prophets to whom God delivered special laws. Legend has it that Abraham was buried under a **mosque** in Hebron.

**ABROGATION.** "Naskh." The repeal of a **revelation** by another. The Koran says: "Allah doth blot out or confirm what He pleaseth; with Him is the Mother of the Book"(13:39) and "When We substitute one revelation for another—and Allah knows best what He reveals (in stages)—They say, 'Thou art but a forger' but most of them know not"(16:101). This refers to changes in legal and practical matters, such as the prayer direction (**qibla**), matters of **inheritance**, and penalties for **adultery**.

**ABU.** "Father, or owner of," indicates possession, state, property, or father of the person named; for example, Abu Musa means the father of Musa.

**ABU AL-'ABBAS AL-SAFFAH** (r. 750-754). *See* ABBASID CALIPH-ATE.

**ABU BAKR** (573-634). First of the **"Rightly Guided Caliphs"** and father of **'A'isha**, the favorite wife of Muhammad. He was one of the first three male converts to Islam and the first of a socially prominent position. He was called *al-Siddiq* (the Sincere) and described as a man of fair complexion, thin frame, with a stoop. He spent much of his fortune on buying and manumitting slaves, which was reckoned to be a good deed to be rewarded on the **Day of Judgment**. Elected as khalifa, successor to the Prophet, in 632 by a council in which members of the Helpers (**ansar**) contested the choice of the Immigrants (**muhajirun**). Abu Bakr suggested the selection of **'Umar ibn al-Khattab**, but he, in turn, offered allegiance ( **bay'ah**) to Abu Bakr and the council accepted the choice. Many of the tribes that had allied themselves with Muhammad considered themselves free of any obligation to his successor. Rival prophets appeared, most importantly one **Musaylimah** (Maslamah). Therefore, Abu Bakr's short reign (632-634) was devoted to forcing the tribes to renew their allegiance in what came to be know as the War of **Riddah** (**apostasy**). Abu Bakr's election established the elective principle of leadership in **Sunni** Islam (although, in fact, it was largely dynastic) and the principle of the oath of loyalty by members of the community. The seeds of schism were sown when the partisans of 'Ali, son of **Abu Talib** and cousin of Muhammad, disputed the election. The partisans of 'Ali (*shi'at 'ali*) later evolved into the Shi'ite **sect**. Abu Bakr's major achievements included the consolidation of the young Muslim state. He made the first attempt to collect the scattered **revelations**, which were subsequently collected in the Koran (Qor'an), and he established government by consultation (**shura**). Abu Bakr nominated 'Umar as his successor before he died in 634 in Medina.

**ABU DAWUD.** *See* SIJISTANI, SULAYMAN ABU DAWUD AL-.

**ABU AL-FARAJ.** *See* ISFAHANI, ABU AL-FARAJ AL-.

**ABU HANIFAH, AL-NU'MAN IBN THABIT** (ca. 700-767). Great
Sunni jurist and eponymic founder of the **Hanafi school of law**, the
largest of the four orthodox schools (**madhhab**) and the dominant
school in the **Ottoman empire** (1281-1924). He was born in **Kufah**
and died in prison in **Baghdad** because he refused to serve as a judge
(**qadhi**), or more likely, because he was a supporter of the Zaidi
revolt. He derived his income from trading in silks and did not need
government patronage. Ibn Khallikan described him as tall, of
medium weight, with a somber disposition, "a learned man and a
practiser (of good works), remarkable for self-denial, piety, devotion
and the fear of God; humble in spirit and constant in his acts of
submission to the Almighty." He embarked on the study of law with
**Ja'faral-Sadiq** in Medina as well as with other famed **mujtahids**.

   With Abu Hanifa, the science of Muslim jurisprudence (**fiqh**)
really began. Before him doctrines were formulated in response to
actual problems, whereas he attempted to solve future problems. He
did not declare a sinner to have become an infidel, and accepted
reasoning by analogy (**qiyas**) and permitted the use of personal
opinion (**ra'y**) in the interpretation of law. Because of this he and his
followers were also called *ahl al-ra'y*, the "people of opinion." Abu
Hanifa dictated his teachings to his disciples Abu Yusuf (d.799),
Muhammad ibn al-Hasan, and others who subsequently compiled
them.

**ABU HURAYRAH** (d. 681). "Father of the Kitten," so named because
of his liking for kittens. Before his conversion, his name was Abu
Shams. He was a **Companion** of the Prophet, whom he joined in
Medina in 629 and was appointed governor of Bahrain by Caliph
**'Umar** I. Described as having a reputation for piety and a fondness
for jesting, he was one of the most prolific transmitters of **hadiths**.
There is, however, some doubt that many attributed to him are
genuine. He died in Medina at the age of 78.

**ABU LAHAB.** "Father of the Flame" [Hellfire], a name given by
Muhammad to his uncle whose name was 'Abd al 'Uzza. He was a
mortal enemy of the early Islamic community. After the death of
**Abu-Talib**, head of Muhammad's clan, the Banu **Hashim**, Abu
Lahab withdrew the clan's protection from Muhammad, forcing him
to flee to Medina (**hijrah**). The Koran says: "Perish the hands of the
Father of Flame! Perish he! No profit to him from all his wealth, and
all his gains! Burnt soon he will be in a fire of blazing flame! His

wife shall carry the (crackling) wood as fuel! A twisted rope of palm-leaf fibre round her (own) neck!"(111:1-5). Abu Lahab died shortly after the Battle of **Badr** in 624.

**ABU MUSA AL-ASH'ARI** (614-663). A native of Yemen and **Companion** of the Prophet who converted to Islam after 628. He was a military commander in Yemen, Persia, and Mesopotamia and a transmitter of a number of **hadith**. Governor of **Basra** and **Kufah** under caliphs **'Umar** and **'Uthman**, he was appointed by **'Ali ibn Abi Talib** to represent him at the **Adhruh Arbitration** in 659, which demanded that 'Ali and **Mu'awiyah** resign their claim to the **caliphate**.

**ABU MUSLIM** (d. 755). Son of a Persian slave woman, he was born at Marw (or near Isfahan) and raised in **Kufah**. He conducted pro-**Abbasid** propaganda and headed the Khorasanian forces, which brought the 'Abbasids to power. The rebels, consisting of Persian converts (mawalis), Shi'ites, and Himyarite Arabs, raised the black banners of Muhammad and invaded Iraq. He defeated the **Umayyad Caliph** Marwan II in 750, and 'Abdullah, uncle of the 'Abbasid caliph **al-Mansur**, at Nasibin in 754. He thus secured the **caliphate** for al-Mansur. He was appointed governor of Khorasan, where his tenure contributed to a revival of Persian culture. Becoming apparently too powerful for the caliph, he invited Abu Muslim to the court and had him treacherously assassinated. He was described as "low in stature, of a tawny complexion, with handsome features and engaging manners, his skin was clear, his eyes large, his forehead lofty, and his beard ample and bushy... his legs and thighs short, and his voice soft.... He abstained from intercourse with females, except once in each year. 'Such an act,' said he, 'is a sort of folly, and it is quite enough for a man to be made once a year.'" (Khallikan, II,103)

**ABU NUWAS** (753-813/15). "Father of the Lock of Hair." A native of Khuzistan, Iran, who was educated in **Basra** and **Kufah** in Islamic studies and lived with Bedouins to acquire a command of "pure" **Arabic**. Famed poet and boon companion of Caliphs **Harun al-Rashid** and his son **al-Amin**. He glorified Bedouin life and also wrote hunting and drinking songs (*khamriyyah*), elegies, panegyrics, satires, and religious poems. His drinking and debauchery got him repeatedly imprisoned, but the elegance of his style and command of

Arabic and his accomplishments as a poet, as well as his supposed remorse in old age, saved him from a violent death. From prison he wrote to Fadhl, the **Barmakid vizier**:

> Fadhl, who hast taught and trained me up to goodness
> (And goodness is but habit), thee I praise.
> Now hath vice fled and virtue me revisits,
> And I have turned to chaste and pious ways. (Nicholson, 293)

Ibn Khallikan quotes one contemporary saying:

> I never saw a man of more extensive learning than Abu Nuwas, nor one who, with a memory so richly furnished, possessed so few books; after his decease we searched his house, and could only find one book-cover, containing a quire of paper, in which was a collection of rare expressions and grammatical observations. (I, 392)

**ABU AL-QASIM** (939-1013). Famous surgeon, known as Albucasis in the West, who greatly influenced European surgical practices until the 16th century. He was court physician of the **Umayyad Caliph Abd al-Rahman III** (d.961) at Cordoba, Spain, and there he published his famous treatise *The Method* (al-tashrif liman 'jaz'an al-ta'lif). It was translated into Latin in the 12th century and served as the leading text on surgery.

**ABU SUFYAN** (d. 651). Head of the **Umayyad** clan and leader of a Meccan force which fought Muhammad in the Battle of **Badr** (624) and the Battle of the **Trench** (627), but he submitted to Islam when Muhammad took Mecca in 630. His ties to the Prophet were strengthened when he gave him his daughter **Umm Habibah** in marriage. His son, **Mu'awiyah**, became the founder of the **Umayyad Caliphate**.

**ABU TALIB** (d. 619). Uncle and guardian of the Prophet and father of 'Ali, fourth of the **"Rightly Guided Caliphs."** He was head of the Banu **Hashim**, and he protected Muhammad from persecution by the Meccans, but he never became a Muslim. When he died, **Abu Lahab** succeeded to leadership of the Banu Hashim and Muhammad was forced to flee to Medina.

**ABU 'UBAYDAH.** *See* 'UBAYDAH, IBN AL-JARRAH.

**'ABU AL-WAFA (BUZJANI, 940-997).** *See* WAFA', ABU AL-.

**'ADA.** "Custom." In Islamic jurisprudence, *'ada* is customary law, synonymous with **'urf** or **qanun.** It complements divine law, **Shari'ah,** but must not be contrary to it.

**ADAB.** Polite behavior, good morals, also *belles lettres.* The *Book of Adab* of al-**Bukhari** specifies, for example, how Muslims should greet others: A small group of people should first greet a large one, a riding person should greet the walking person, and the walking person should first greet the sitting one. *See also* EDUCATION.

**ADAM.** The first man and prophet; he had the title "God's Chosen One." God made him of dried clay, and the **angels** were ordered to prostrate before him; only one, **Iblis** (satan), refused, claiming superiority because he was made of fire (15:26-32). Adam was separated from Eve after they were driven from paradise, but he was reunited with her in the valley of **Arafat** near **Mecca.** According to tradition, he built the **Ka'bah** and died in Mecca.

**'ADAWIYYAH, RABI'AH AL-.** *See* RABI'AH AL-'ADAWIYYAH.

**ADHAN (AZAN).** *See* CALL TO PRAYER.

**ADHRUH ARBITRATION (659).** As a result of the Battle of **Siffin** (657) in which **Mu'awiyah** challenged Caliph **'Ali,** demanding vengeance for the murder of Caliph **'Uthman,** 'Ali agreed to arbitration at a time when his forces seemed to gain the upper hand. Following a suggestion by **'Amr ibn al-'As,** the Syrians had fastened copies of the Koran on their lances and called for an appeal to the "Law of the Lord." This appeal resulted in the appointment of two intermediaries, 'Amr for Mu'awiyah and **Abu Musa al-'Ashari** for 'Ali, who were to consult the Holy Book as a basis for arbitration. Instead it became an arbitration by men. Now a large number of 'Ali's forces seceded and the Seceders (**Kharijites**) turned against their **caliph.** The arbiters met at Adhruh in February 658, and 'Amr convinced Abu Musa that both candidates should resign, to which the latter agreed. According to the traditional account Abu Musa was tricked into announcing the demotion of 'Ali, after which 'Amr proclaimed Mu'awiyah caliph. According to the Orientalist Wellhausen, there was no treachery and it was 'Ali who refused to step down. 'Ali was subsequently assassinated by a Kharijite and Mu'awiyah became the first of the **Umayyad** caliphs.

**'ADL, AL-.** "Justice," due to every Muslim. In jurisprudence a person whose testimony is valid. Al-Adl is one of the 99 names of Allah, meaning the Just.

**'ADN.** The Garden of Eden. *See also* HEAVEN.

**ADULTERY.** "Zinah." Adultery is forbidden and punished by stoning, but the penalty requires that there be either four witnesses to the act or else the confession of the culprits. Since four witnesses have not been easily found, this penalty has been rarely exacted. If a husband catches his wife in flagrante delicto, he is authorized to kill her and her partner. The culprits must be free Muslims of maturity and married; the punishment for fornication is one hundred lashes, and only half that number for slaves. False accusation of adultery is punished with 80 lashes. Muslim modernists claim that since witnesses cannot usually be found, this drastic penalty should not be inflicted (24:2-4). In most parts of the Islamic world, zinah is not a capital crime. Islamist radicals, as for example the **Taliban** of Afghanistan, wanted to reintroduce these as well as other Islamic (**hadd**) punishments. Zinah also includes **fornication**. *See also* LI'AN.

**AFGHANI, SAYYID JAMAL AL-DIN** (1838-1897). Father of the **Pan-Islamist** movement, Muslim modernist, and political propagandist who called for the unity of the Islamic world and selective borrowing from the West for the purpose of stemming the tide of Western imperialism. Afghani was the adviser of Muslim rulers in many parts of the Middle East and a political activist in Iran, Afghanistan, India, Egypt, and the **Ottoman empire**. Frequently opposed by the **ulama** and suspected as an intriguer by the temporal powers, he was often on the run. When one of his followers assassinated the Persian ruler Nasr al-Din Shah (r. 1848-1896), Afghani was placed under house arrest by the Ottoman **Sultan Abdul Hamid** (r. 1876-1907). Afghani died in **Istanbul** in 1897. He was not a prolific writer and varied his message to suit a particular audience. He wrote a *Refutation of the Materialists* (al-radd 'ala al-dahriyin) and published the periodical *The Firmest Bond* (al-'urwah al-wuthqa) with his disciple **Muhammad Abduh**. Afghani was the precursor of the **Islamist** movement. Afghans revere his memory and believe him to be a descendant of a family of Sayyids from Asadabad in Kunar province of Afghanistan. Western and Iranian scholars agree on his Iranian origin.

**AFGHANIS.** Radical **Islamists** called Afghanis, mostly of Arab nationality, but also from other Muslim countries, who participated in the war against the Communist regime in Afghanistan. Many of them returned to their countries and continued the **jihad** against their governments with the intention of establishing an "Islamic State." They are said to include some 5,000 Saudis, 3,000 Yemenis, 2,000 Egyptians, 2,800 Algerians, 400 Tunisians, 370 Iraqis, 200 Libyans, some Jordanians, as well as citizens of other Muslim countries. They are a serious threat to the military regime in Algeria, have started terrorist activities in Egypt, and are fighting in regional wars from Bosnia to Kashmir. **Osama bin Ladin** is an "Afghani," accused of instigating the bombings of American embassies in Nairobi and Dar es Salam. He is a wealthy Saudi citizen who had taken refuge with the **Taliban** regime in Afghanistan, as have several thousand others, including one Islamboli, a brother of the assassin of the Egyptian President Anwar al-Sadat.

**AGE OF IGNORANCE.** *See* IGNORANCE, THE AGE OF.

**AGHA KHAN. Imam** of the Nizari branch of the **Isma'ilis**. The Qajar rulers of Iran at times bestowed this title on notables. In 1818 Fath 'Ali Shah gave the title Agha Khan I to Abu al-Hasan 'Ali Shah Mahallati (1800-1881), governor of Kerman province. He fled Iran after an unsuccessful revolt in 1841 and settled in Bombay. He was able to organize Isma'ili communities in India, supported by a court order that gave him control of the **sect**'s property. He was succeeded by 'Ali Shah (1881-1885), who became the official repre-sentative of Iran to the government of India. The third Agha Khan (1877-1957), Sultan Sir Muhammad Shah, was a very active individual. Born in Karachi, he became the head of the Isma'ili community at the age of eight. Although he moved to Europe in 1898, he continued to take charge of the interests of the sect from there. Agha Khan III gave his support to the Allies in the First and Second World Wars. He was president of the All-India Muslim League and involved in raising **Aligarh** College to the status of a university in 1920. In 1937 he was elected president of the League of Nations. The present Agha Khan is Karim IV (b. 1937), who counts himself the 49th successor of the Nisari Isma'ili Imam, attends to the welfare of the Isma'ili community in Africa, Syria, Iran, Tajikistan, India, United States, Pakistan, and Afghanistan. He founded a charitable organization, the Agha Khan Foundation, in 1967 with headquarters in Geneva, which supports developmental assistance in many parts of the world. Muhammad, Karim's grandfather, was on special occasions weighed on a scale and presented with gold and precious stones to an equal amount, a practice that has since been discontinued. The Agha Khan claims descent from Isma'il through the last Grand Master of **Alamut**. *See also* NIZARIS.

'**AHD.** Contract, treaty, pact between **caliph** and community. *See also* COVENANT.

**AHKAM AL-KHAMSAH, AL-.** *See* FIVE PRINCIPAL ACTS OF ISLAMIC LAW.

**AHL.** Originally those living in the same tent, but in combination with other words it denotes persons belonging to the same group. For example, **Ahl al-Kitab**, Peoples of the Book, scriptuaries.

**AHL AL-BAYT.** "People of the House," a term used for the family of the Prophet Muhammad in the Koran (33:33). Shi'ites restrict the term to Muhammad's descendants through 'Ali and **Fatimah** and their sons **Hasan** and **Husayn**, including the Twelve Imams and believe that they embody a special **barakah**, blessing, and authority inherited from their blood relationship to the Prophet. *See also* IMAM.

**AHL AL-DHIMMA.** *See* PEOPLES OF THE BOOK.

**AHL AL-HADITH.** "The People of **Tradition**." A Muslim reformist movement founded in the early 19th century in the Indian subcontinent and now a political movement in Pakistan and Afghanistan. Its founding fathers are **Shah Waliallah** (d. 1762) and Sayyid Ahmad **Barelvi** (d. 1831), who demanded adherence solely to the Koran and Tradition (**Sunnah**), rejected **Sufism** and Shi'ism, and called for the right to **ijtihad**.

**AHL AL-HALL WA 'L-'AQD.** "Men with the power to loosen and bind," that is, representatives of the community with the power to offer the **caliphate** to the most qualified person and to depose a sinful ruler. Once selected, the community offers an oath of allegiance (**bay'ah**). There is disagreement as to the number of persons required, even one was seen as sufficient, which enabled **caliphs** to nominate their sons. The *ahl al-hall* had to be jurists versed in Islamic sciences, capable of exercising **ijtihad** (interpretation of **Islamic law**). Since the demise of the caliphate, the appointment of a ruler has become more of an inauguration ceremony and the *ahl al-hall* have had little success in deposing an autocratic ruler. In modern days, radical **Islamists** claim the right to this function for the entire community.

**AHL AL-HAQQ (AHL-I HAQQ).** "The People of Truth." A syncretist **sect** of a number of groups found predominantly in western Iran and Kurdistan. They recognize the twelve Shi'ite **imams** and count seven successive manifestations of God, believing that humans must pass though a cycle of reincarnations with corresponding rewards. 'Ali, cousin of Muhammad, is one of the manifestations, but the most important is a person called Sultan Sohak (15th century). The sect, also called 'Ali Illahi, is said to combine elements of Shi'ism with **Jewish** and **Christian** practices. Their doctrines are secret, but what is known comes from the *Firqan al-Akhbar*, a publication of a former member.

**AHL AL-KITAB.** *See* PEOPLES OF THE BOOK.

**AHMAD BARELVI, SAYYID.** *See* BARELVI, AHMAD SAYYID.

**AHMAD IBN HANBAL.** *See* IBN HANBAL, AHMAD.

**AHMADIS (AMADIYYAH).** A messianic movement in modern Islam, which originated in British India. It is named after its founder, Mirza Ghulam Ahmad (c. 1839-1908) of Qadian, Punjab, who declared himself the "Renewer of the Faith" in 1882. He eventually laid claim to prophethood. The **sect** divided in 1914, after the death Mirza Ghulam's successor, into the more radical Qadiani, who considered all others infidels, and the Lahori, who held Ahmad to be merely a "renewer" (*mujaddid*) of the faith. The Ahmadis conducted a vigorous missionary activity that brought them into conflict with orthodox Sunni regimes. After the partition of India in 1947 the headquarters of the movement moved to Pakistan. Because of **ulama** opposition in 1974, the government of Prime Minister Zulfiqar Ali Bhutto declared the movement to be non-Muslim. In 1984 the government of President Zia ul-Haq made Ahmadi religious observance a punishable offense, and the head of the Qadianis, Mirza Tahir Ahmad (1982-), was forced to move to London. The Ahmadis present themselves as Muslim modernists and have been successful in winning converts in America, Europe, Asia, and Africa. They are said to number between 500,000 and one million but claim to count from 10 to 20 million. The sect is prohibited in Syria, Uganda, Pakistan, and several other countries.

There are also several **Sufi** orders with this name, most importantly the one of Ahmad al-Badawi (d. 1276).

**AHMAD KHAN, SIR SAYYID** (1817-1898). **Muslim modernist** who demanded reforms and called for the adoption of Western technology and education. After receiving a traditional education, he found work as a writer with the East India Company's court of justice at Delhi in 1841. He advocated coexistence between Muslims and the British, feeling that Muslim interests would be better protected under British rather than Hindu rule. In 1888 he was awarded a Knight Commander of the Star of India. Among his many publications was a commentary on the Bible and the Koran, pointing out the common source of the scriptures. In 1875 Sir Sayyid founded the All-India Muhammadan Anglo-Oriental College at **Aligarh**, which was eventually transformed into the Aligarh Muslim University (which supporters called the Muslim Cambridge). He sought to reconcile faith and reason and favored the adoption of Western concepts, such as science, technology, justice, and freedom. He is credited with being one of the initiators of India's Islamic renaissance and a promoter of the idea of creating a Muslim state, which was finally implemented long after his death with the creation of Pakistan. *See also* ISLAMIC MODERNISM.

**AHSA'I, AHMAD AL-** (1753-1826). A native of Ahsa al-Hasa (now a province of Saudi Arabia) of a Shi'ite family. He was self-taught and, at age 20, went to **Najaf** and **Karbala** for advanced study of Shi'ite jurisprudence (**fiqh**) and theology (**kalam**). Ahsa'i spent about 20 years at Yazd before moving to Kermanshah, where he was excommunicated when he claimed to be inspired in his dreams by the

Prophet and **Imams**. Denounced as an infidel in 1824, he left on a **pilgrimage** to Mecca and died on the way. His followers founded the **Shaykhi** Shi'ite movement, which included Sayyid Ali Muhammad (1820-1850), founder of the Babi, later **Baha'i**, religion. *See also* BAB.

'**A'ISHAH (AYESHA, 613-678).** "Mother of the **Believers**" *(Umm al-Mu'minin)*, the favorite wife of the Prophet Muhammad and daughter of **Abu Bakr**. She was given in **marriage** to Muhammad when she was six years old after his wife **Khadija** died, but the marriage was consummated a number of years later. The Prophet gave some household goods worth 50 (according to *Sirat*, 400) dirham as a dowry for 'A'ishah. A scandal threatened the marriage, when 'A'isha was missing on the return from an expedition. She had left her litter in search of a necklace she had lost and the caravan left without her. Waiting to be rescued, she fell asleep and was found the next morning by a young nomad called Safwan, who brought her back to Medina. Rumors about infidelity finally made Muhammad consult with some of his followers, including '**Ali**, who counseled that he should **divorce** 'A'isha. A **revelation** solved the problem in Surah 24:13, saying, "Why did they not bring four witnesses to prove it? When they have not brought the witnesses, such men in the sight of Allah (stand forth) themselves as liars." This established the requirement in **Islamic law** of witnesses in cases of **adultery**, unless the culprits confess. 'A'isha did not forgive 'Ali for his advice, and she met him with the **Companions Talha** and **al-Zubayr** during the **Battle of the Camel** in 656. The rebels were defeated and 'A'isha was returned to Medina where she lived an honored life until her death in 678. A childless widow at 18, 'A'isha outlived many of the early Companions of the Prophet and became an important transmitter of the sayings and actions (**hadith**) of the Prophet Muhammad.

According to a hadith 'A'ishah declared the following:

> I was preferred over the wives of the Prophet by ten things: "It was asked what are they, Umm al-Mu'minin?" She said: "He did not marry any other virgin but me. He did not marry a woman whose parents were **muhajirun** except me. Allah Almighty revealed my innocence from heaven. **Jibril** brought my picture from heaven in silk and said, 'Marry her. She is your wife.' He and I used to do **ghusl** from the same vessel, and he did not do that with any of his wives except me. He used to pray while I was stretched out in front of him, and he did not do that with any of his

wives except with me. The revelation would come to him while he was with me, and it did not come down when he was with any of his wives except me. Allah took his soul while he was against my chest. He died on the night when it was my turn and he was buried in my room. (Tabaqat, Tr. Aisha Beverley, *Women of Madina*)

**AJAL.** The "appointed time" of death ordained by God.

**AJNADAYN.** Scene of a battle on July 30, 634, about 45 kilometers southwest of **Jerusalem**, in which a united force of Arabs under **Khalid ibn Walid** and **'Amr ibn al 'As** defeated a Byzantine army commanded by the brother of the Greek emperor. This opened the way to the conquest of Palestine.

**AKHBARIS (AKHBARIYYAH).** A traditional school in **Twelver Shi'ite** jurisprudence, which holds that legal opinions should be based on the Traditions (**sunnah**) of Muhammad and the **Imams**, rather than "derived from general principles (**usul**) by analogical reasoning." In other words, religious scholars should not exercise independent judgment (**ijtihad**) in matters of law, as maintained by the **usuli** school. The latter was adopted by the Shi'ite clergy in Iran in the late 17th and early 18th centuries as a justification for its role as the "guardians of the **believers**." The Akhbariyyah school was first established by Muhammad Amin Astarabadi (Akhbari, d. 1624), who rejected the teachings of most jurists after the 10th century. By the 19th century, Agha Muhammad Baqir Bihbihani (1706-1790) was instrumental in contributing to the supremacy of the **usuli** school. *See also* SHI'ISM.

**AKHTAL, GHIYATH AL-TAGHLIBI AL-** (640-710). Christian Arab poet and rival of his contemporaries **al-Jarir ibn 'Atiyah** and Hammam ibn Ghalib **al-Farazdak,** who are considered among the founders of **Arabic** literary criticism. Ostentatiously Christian and not ready to renounce wine, Akhtal refused an offer of a pension of 10,000 dirhams from Caliph **'Abd al-Malik** if he converted to Islam. He was a supporter of the **Umayyad** dynasty, which used him to attack members of the pious opposition. Akhtal was acclaimed as the first among the poets of Islam—and it was said that, if he had lived a single day before the advent of Islam, he would also have been the first of the **Jahiliyyah** poets.

**AKHUND.** A title for religious personalities and scholars. The term was first used in Timurid times (15th century) as an honorific for a great scholar, but it later denoted a simple school teacher with a slightly pejorative connotation. In some areas it also was the designation of theology students. A descendant of an Akhund is called Akhund-zada.

**ALAMUT.** A fortress in the Elburz mountain range about 35 kilometers northeast of Qazvin, captured by **Hasan al-Sabbah** (d. 1124) in 1090. He was the Grand Master of a religious order of **Isma'ilis**, subsequently called the **Assassins**, or *hashishiyun*—hashish smokers. The members of the order were initiated into successive stages of hierarchy, corresponding to their level of advancement, the lowest of which were the **fida'i**, devotees, who were sent on errands of assassination. They were said to have used hashish as part of their rituals and became a threat to the princes and crusader kings in the Middle East. **Nizam al-Mulk**, the **vizier** of the **Seljuq** ruler Alp Arslan, is said to have been one of the more famous statesman who fell under the dagger of a fida'i of the "Old Man of the Mountain." **Hulagu**, founder of the Ilkhanid state in Iran, finally captured Alamut and other Isma'ili fortifications in 1256 and ended the existence of the state, which lasted for 166 years. The word assassin came into Western languages as a corruption of the word *hashishi-yun*. The followers of the Grand Master reckon the **Agha Khan** as their titular head.

**'ALAWIS ('ALAWIYUN).** A term generally applied to all Shi'ites, but more specifically to a religious community of several hundred thousands located in Syria, Lebanon, and southern Turkey. They are also called Nusayris after their eponymic leader ibn Nusayr (d.c. 873), a follower of the 11th Shi'ite **Imam** Hasan al-'Askari (d. 873). Their religious practices are secret but they are known to have a holy book, the *Kitab al-Majmu'* (Book of collection) and are said to combine syncretist elements from Shi'ite **Isma'ili** and even Christian teachings. They observe the Zoroastrian New Year, Easter, and St. Barbara's Day and are said to believe in a holy trinity of 'Ali, Muhammad, and **Salman** al-Farisi. They permit wine drinking, but prohibit drunkenness. They use candles. The 'Alawis practice **taqiyyah** (dissimulation) to protect themselves from persecution. In addition to the Five **Pillars of Islam**, they also accept **jihad** and waliyah, devotion to Imam 'Ali and hatred of his adversaries. During the French occupation of Syria, many 'Alawis joined the armed services, and, after independence, the Arab Socialist (Ba'th) party. Thus they were able to gain control of the country. Hafez al-Asad, an 'Alawi, has been president of Syria since 1971.

Other communities of 'Alawis (Alevi) exist in Kurdish regions of eastern Turkey and in Arabic-speaking areas in the south near the Syrian border. An 'Alawi dynasty established itself in Morocco and continues to lead the country until the present. It was founded by Mawlay Rashid (d.1672), who established his capital in Meknes. It derives its legitimacy from the monarch's claim as a descendant of the House of 'Ali through his son **Hasan**.

**ALCOHOL.** Not expressly forbidden in the Koran, where alcohol is mentioned as *khamr*, wine. The Koran says: "They ask thee concerning wine and **gambling**. Say: 'in them is great sin, and some profit for men; but the sin is greater than the profit'"(2:219). On the other hand, **believers** are promised in heaven "Rivers of wine, a joy to those who drink"(47:15). Jurists decided that it should be forbidden, including all intoxicating spirits. Alcohol was, nevertheless, produced by non-Muslim minorities and accessible even to Muslims in some countries. With independence, governments often established a monopoly in the production and sale of alcoholic beverages, as, for example, Turkey, Egypt, and Algeria, among others. But **Islamist** agitation has now resulted in restricting, or prohibiting, the consumption of alcohol in many parts of the Islamic world.

**ALHAMBRA (AL-HAMRA').** "The Red One" is the name of one of the great architectural monuments of Muslim Spain. It was named thus because of the red stucco used in construction of the palace, built in 1238-1258 under the Nasrite dynasty of Granada. The building covered an area about 740 meters in length and 205 meters at its greatest width. It was surrounded by a strong wall with 13 towers. Partially destroyed as a result of war and an earthquake, the Alhambra was periodically restored to its old glory. In 1492 an army of Ferdinand and Isabella captured Granada, the last Muslim outpost on the Iberian Peninsula.

**'ALIDS.** The descendants of **Hasan** and **Husayn**, the sons of 'Ali and **Fatimah** who claimed the exclusive right to the **caliphate**. Some of them were able to establish dynasties, for example, the **Zaydis**,

**Isma'ilis, Fatimids,** and **Qarmatians.** The term also refers to the partisans of 'Ali. *See also* SHI'ISM.

**'ALI IBN ABI TALIB** (r. 656-661). The fourth of the **"Rightly Guided Caliphs"** and the first **imam** of Shi'ite Islam. He was a cousin of Muhammad and his son-in-law, after his **marriage** to **Fatimah.** One of the early converts to Islam; according to some sources, he was the first male convert after **Khadija,** Muhammad's wife. Division in Islam into the Sunnis and Shi'ites resulted in a dispute over the right of succession to Muhammad after his death in 632. The partisans of 'Ali (*shi'atu 'ali*) maintained that 'Ali had a divine right to succession, to be continued through his sons **Hasan** and **Husain,** and repudiated the first three Sunni Caliphs as usurpers. 'Ali moved his capital to **Kufah** where he had the support of his troops. He was immediately challenged by **Talha ibn 'Ubaydullah** and **Zubayr ibn al-Awwam** in the **Battle of the Camel** (656), named after **'A'isha,** the wife of Muhammad, who surveyed the battle from atop a camel to give moral support to the rebels.

Challenged by **Mu'awiyah,** the **Umayyad** governor of **Damascus,** 'Ali met him in the Battle of **Siffin** (657), which was inconclusive and 'Ali was forced to accept arbitration. This cost him the support of part of his army, and the "Seceders," **Kharijites,** eventually turned against him. He was assassinated by a Kharijite during morning prayer in 661. His tomb in **Najaf,** in present-day Iraq, is one of the most important places of Shi'ite **pilgrimage.** 'Ali was described as a resolute warrior, and revered for his piety, nobility, and learning. He favored the distribution of booty among the Muslim community, and upon his death was said to have only 600 dirhams to his name. Shi'ites attribute to 'Ali and the Imams divine inspiration and infallibility. *See also* ADHRUH ARBITRATION.

**ALIGARH.** A town in India, about 120 kilometers southeast of New Delhi, which is the location of the modernist Aligarh Muslim University. Founded by Sir Sayyid **Ahmad Khan** (1817-1898) as a boys school and college (the All-Indian Muhammadan Anglo-Oriental College at Aligarh) to educate committed Muslims according to Western curricula. It became a university in 1920, the "Muslim Cambridge" as its supporters called it, and **women** were admitted in some faculties in 1938. Many of the graduates achieved positions of prominence in the early 20th century. They led the Muslim League, the Pakistan movement, and the new Republic of

Pakistan. The first vice chancellor of Aligarh after independence was Zakir Husain, who subsequently became president of India.

**'ALIM.** A person who has knowledge (i'lm) of the **Traditions, Islamic law,** and **theology.** In **Arabic** also the term for a secular scholar. The plural, ulama', is taken for the body of scholars, loosely described as clergy. *See also* ULAMA.

**'ALI AL-RIDHA.** *See* RIDHA, 'ALI AL-.

**ALLAH.** "God." The **Arabic** name for the one and only omnipotent, omnipresent, just, and merciful God. To be a Muslim one must testify that "there is no god but Allah and that Muhammad is his prophet." Giving partners to Allah is an unforgivable sin. The Koran says: "Say: He is Allah, the One; Allah, the Eternal, Absolute; He begetteth not, nor is He begotten; and there is none like unto Him"(112). There is no trinity, or son of God; he is the Lord of heaven and earth, the Creator of the universe. He will reward and punish humankind on the **Day of Judgment.** His **revelations** through the medium of Muhammad are the commands of Allah, collected in the Koran. The Koran says: "Certainly they disbelieve who say: 'Allah is Christ the son of **Mary.**' Whoever joins other gods with Allah—Allah will forbid him the Garden [paradise], and the fire will be his abode" (5:72).

**ALLAHU AKBAR.** "God is most great." A formula in Islam, called the *takbir*, occurring in ritual **prayers**, as a **call to prayer**, or as a battle cry during war.

**ALMOHADS (AL-MUWAHHIDUN,** 1130-1269). A Masmuda Berber confederation and Islamic revivalist movement ruling in the Maghreb (northwest Africa) and Spain. The Almohads (Unitarians—those who affirm the unity of God) were inspired by the teachings of **Muhammad ibn Tumart** (1077-1130), who formulated a doctrine of puritanical moral reform but eventually proclaimed himself the **"mahdi,"** the "guided one" who was to appear before the **Day of Judgment**. Ibn Tumart was succeeded by Abd al-Mu'min, who proclaimed himself Ibn Tumart's **caliph** and made his capital at Marrakesh in 1147. The Almohads put an end to the **Almoravids** and founded a dynasty, centered in Seville, which witnessed a short period of great cultural revival before the end of Muslim rule in Spain.

**ALMORAVIDS (AL-MURABITUN,** 1061-1147). A revivalist dynasty of Lamtuna Berber tribes, named after their fortified camps **(ribat)** on the edges of the Saharan desert, who conquered an empire in North Africa and Spain. Yahya ibn Ibrahim, a chief of the "Veiled" Sanhaja branch, returned from **pilgrimage** to Mecca and brought with him the Berber scholar 'Abd Alla ibn Yasin. Yasin provided the ideological impetus for a series of conquests of Morocco and parts of Spain. The state reached its greatness under Yusuf ibn Tashfin (r. 1061-1106), who established his capitals at Marrakesh and Seville in Spain. The Almoravids were eventually replaced by the **Almohads.**

**ALMSGIVING.** "Sadaqah." The Koran says: "Alms are for the poor and the needy, and those employed to administer the (funds); for those whose hearts have been reconciled (converted to truth); for those in bondage and in debt; in the cause of Allah; and for the wayfarer; thus it is ordained by Allah" (9:60). It is one of the obligations subsumed under the code of rituals called the **Five Pillars of Islam** and can be given in cash or in kind. Now largely voluntary, as much as 2.5 to 10 percent was customary. *See also* ZAKAT.

**AL SHAYKH FAMILY.** Name for the descendants of Muhammad Ibn Abd al-**Wahhab** in Saudi Arabia.

**'AMAL.** Action for which one will be rewarded on the **Day of Judgment**.

**AMAL.** "Hope." A populist Shi'ite movement that emerged in Lebanon in 1975 and became a major political factor in Lebanese politics. It superseded the Movement of the Deprived (Harakat al-Mahrumin), headed by Sayyid Musa al-**Sadr** and marked a move to the Left when Nabih **Berri** assumed its leadership in 1980. Amal means hope. It is also the acronym for Afwaj al-Muqawamah al-Lubnaniyah, Lebanese Resistance Detachment. Amal fought Israeli occupiers but also opposed a Palestinian Liberation Organization (PLO) presence in southern Lebanon. It eventually disbanded its military arm and Nabih Berri was elected in 1992 to the position of speaker in the Lebanese parliament. Continued economic distress and Israeli occupation in the south led to the emergence of **Hizbullah**, the Party of Allah, a religio-political party that has since merged with the **Islamic Amal** and eclipsed the popularity of the secular Amal.

'**AMIL.** Until the 10th century a provincial official responsible for the collection of taxes. Later it was the office of the finance minister of a prince.

**AMIN, MUHAMMAD AL-** (787-813). Son of **Harun al-Rashid** and his appointed successor (809-813). He was to be succeeded by his brother **al-Ma'mun,** who served as governor of Khorasan. Educated under the supervision of Fadhl ibn Yahya **al-Barmaki,** Amin decided to appoint his son as his successor rather than accepting Ma'mun as the crown prince. In the succeeding war Amin was defeated and killed, leading to the succession of Ma'mun. According to one account, when Ma'mun's general Tahir ibn al-Husayn besieged **Baghdad,** he asked for permission to take care of Amin as he pleased; in reply Ma'mun sent a shirt with no opening for the head. Thereupon Tahir killed Amin. *See also* TAHIRID DYNASTY.

**AMINAH** (d. ca. 576). Mother of the Prophet Muhammad. She died when the Prophet was about six years old.

**AMIR (EMIR).** From the **Arabic** *amara,* meaning, "to command," it is the title of a military commander, a nobleman, chief, prince, ruler. Amir is also a common name. During the **Umayyad** and early 'Abbasid periods this title was given to heads of ruling families, high Arab officials, and governors. **Islamist** groups call their supreme leader amir.

**AMIR AL-HAJJ.** Leader of the pilgrim caravans, in charge of maintaining order and security while traveling and during the ceremonies. The first Amir al-Hajj was **Abu Bakr,** but the position later became an office entrusted to a notable, and it continued as an honorary position during the **Ottoman empire**. The amir used to receive a part of the property of individuals deceased during **pilgrimage** (hajj). Today, when up to two million pilgrims go on hajj, each country provides its own group leader.

**AMIR AL-MU'MININ.** "Commander of the Faithful," title of the **caliph** or **imam** who also is the commander-in-chief of the Islamic army. Abdullah ibn Jahsh first held the title as a reward for his bravery in battle and subsequently it was adopted by Caliph '**Umar I.** It was later adopted by **sultans,** kings, secular rulers, or military commanders. Mulla **Muhammad 'Umar**, head of the **Taliban** regime of Afghanistan, was given this title by his supporters.

**AMIR AL-UMARA.** "Amir of Amirs," title of the commander-in-chief or governor of a large province in the **Ottoman empire**. The title was first given by the **'Abbasid** Caliph al-Muqtadir (908-932) to the commander of his bodyguard. In the 10th century the title became hereditary under the **Buyids**, but later it lost its importance.

**'AMR IBN AL-'AS** (ca. 575-663). A member of the **Quraysh** and conqueror of Egypt. He was originally an opponent of Muhammad and embraced Islam only shortly before the capture of Mecca, and he became an important general of the Muslim armies. Together with **Khalid ibn Walid** he defeated the Byzantines at the battle of **Ajna-dayn** (634) and at **Yarmuk** (636). The 45-year-old warrior raided Egypt (642) when a messenger of Caliph **'Umar I** brought him a letter advising him to desist from entering Egypt, unless he had already done so. Surmising the contents of the letter, Amr did not open it until he had entered the country. He forced Alexandria to pay tribute, established himself at Babylon in 642, and founded Fustat (later part of **Cairo**). In a letter to 'Umar in Medina, he said: "I have captured a city from the description of which I shall refrain. Suffice it to say that I have seized therein 4,000 villas with 4,000 baths, 40,000 poll-tax-paying **Jews** and four hundred places of entertainment for the royalty." 'Amr became governor of Egypt; he fought against 'Ali at the **Battle of Siffin** in 657 and skillfully represented his clansman, **Mu'awiyah**, in the **Adhruh Arbitration**. He remained governor of Egypt at Fustat under Mu'awiya until his death in 663.

**'AMR IBN AL-KULTHUM** (sixth century). Pre-Islamic poet and chief of the Taghlib tribe who extolled the Bedouin values, and his own nobility and bravery in one of the odes included in the **Mu'allaqat**. An anecdote has him kill 'Amr ibn Hind, the King of Hira, when he arranged to have the poet's mother, Layla, insulted. An Arab proverb says of him: "Bolder in onset then 'Amr ibn al-Kulthum."

**AMSAR.** Garrison towns founded on the borders of deserts by Muslim forces in newly conquered lands. They were populated by Arab warriors and became the nuclei of the first Muslim cities: **Kufah**

(638), **Basra** (635), Fustat (641, now part of **Cairo**), and Qayrawan (670).

**AMULETS.** "Hama'il." Known already in pre-Islamic times, amulets are widely used in the Islamic world. They consist of passages of the Koran, some of the 99 names of God, or **prayers** written on paper or engraved in metal or stone. Small copies of the Koran are often worn around the neck in a silk or leather bag. They are fastened on arms or some other part of the body, but they are also fixed above the doors of houses. They are worn to ward off the **"evil eye,"** to protect individuals from the envy and harm of others.

**ANGELS (MALA'IKA).** Angels are the messengers of God. They are, like men, His servants. They record men's actions and bear witness against them on the **Day of Judgment. Gabriel** (jibril) was God's chief messenger to Muhammad. One angel, **Iblis** (satan), refused to bow before **Adam** and tempted Eve; therefore, he was banished from paradise but given the power to lead astray all those who are not true servants of God. Other angels are **Israfil**, who trumpets in the Last Judgment, and **'Izra'el**, the Angel of Death (*malak al-maut*). **Munkar** and **Nakir** are two guardian angels who interrogate men in the tomb about God and the Prophet. Those who cannot answer will be placed in the "tomb of torment" with snakes and scorpions. Two angels, **Harut** and **Marut**, mentioned in the Koran (2:102), were sent to earth where they sinned and were punished for it. According to a **hadith**, angels are made of light, except for Iblis who is made of fire. **Mikail** provides men with food and knowledge. The Koran (35:1) describes angels: "Messengers with wings, two three, or four (pairs)." *See also* DEVIL.

**ANSAR.** "Helpers," name of the people of Medina who converted to Islam and came to be referred to as the "Helpers of the Prophet" (*Ansar al-Nabi*), a name of honor given to them. The Ansar participated in the **Battle of Badr** against the pagan Meccans, furnishing as many as 238 men of a force of about 300, which defeated the Meccans on March 15, 624. They became members of the "pious" opposition when a member of the **Quraysh** was elected **caliph.** Ansari is a patronymic, meaning descent from a Helper and a common name today. The Koran praises them as "those who before them (the muhajirun), had homes (in Madinah) and had adopted the faith, show their affection to such as came to them for refuge, and entertain no desire in their hearts for things given to the (Quraysh) but give them preference over themselves, even though poverty was their (own lot)" (59:9).

**ANSARI, ABD ALLAH AL-** (1005-1089). Islamic theologian, commentator on the Koran, mystic from Herat, and author of a commentary on **Sufi** theory (*manazil-i sha îrin*) and other works. Brilliant as a youth, he studied at Nishapur under **Shafi'ite** teachers but later adopted the more restrictive **Hanbali** school and opposed **Ash'arite** doctrines. He was born in Herat and spent most of his life in that city, a much celebrated Sufi poet and philosopher, "mystic of love" and "mystic of tawhid" (Unity of God). The **caliph** gave him the title *Shaykh al-Islam*. He wrote both in **Arabic** and Persian; his Arabic collection is said to contain more than 6,000 couplets, and his Persian poetry is said to amount to about 14,000 verses. He went blind toward the end of his life; his tomb is in Gazargah, near Herat, amid ruins from the Timurid period.

**ANTARAH IBN SHADDAT** (d. ca. 615). Pre-Islamic poet and hero. Only one complete qasida of his is extant describing a battle scene and part of the **Mu'allaqat** collection. The son of a black slave woman, Antara was freed by his father when his bravery was needed to fight off Bedouin raiders. He sang: "On one side nobly born and of the best, of Abs am I: my sword makes good the rest" (Nicholson, 115). In modern times, novels, songs, and proverbs celebrate him as a popular hero and a protagonist of Arab union and patriotism.

**APOSTASY.** "Irtidad." Apostasy is forbidden in **Islamic law.** The **kharijites,** an early radical **sect,** proclaimed apostates (murtadd) all Muslims who would not accept their interpretation of Islam. A male apostate could be killed, unless he were a minor, lunatic, or otherwise disabled. If he is married, his Muslim wife is considered **divorced** because he has become an infidel (**kafir**). **Surah** 47:25 reads: "Those who turn back as apostates after guidance was clearly shown to them —Satan has instigated them and buoyed them up with false hopes." *See also* RIDDAH.

**'AQABAH.** A hill near Mecca where in 621 members of the **Aws** and **Khazraj** tribes of Yathrib (Medina) accepted Islam. *See* 'AQABAH, PLEDGE OF.

**'AQABAH, PLEDGE OF.** During the time of **pilgrimage** in 621, a group of men of the **Khazraj** and **Aws** tribes of Yathrib (later Medina) secretly met with Muhammad and adopted Islam. They pledged that: "We will not worship any god but the one God; we will not steal; nor commit adultery; nor kill our children; nor will we slander our neighbor; and we will obey the Prophet of God." This was the first pledge of 'Aqaba, also called the "Pledge of **Women**," because it did not require fighting in the defense of Islam. The men returned to Yathrib and converted others. A year later 73 men and two women came to Mecca and offered their loyalty and invited the Prophet to come to Yathrib. The city was torn by tribal disputes and it was hoped that Muhammad's leadership would restore peace. In the second pledge of 'Aqaba, the new converts agreed to be Helpers (**ansar**) and fight for the Prophet. Muhammad, thereupon, made preparations for his emigration (**hijrah**) to Yathrib, where he founded the first Islamic community.

A **hadith** describes the event as follows:

> 'Ubaydah ibn al-Samit said: I was present at the first 'Aqaba. There were twelve of us and we pledged ourselves to the prophet after the manner of women and that was before war was enjoined, the undertaking being that we should associate nothing with God; we should not steal; we should not commit fornication; nor kill our offspring; we should not slander our neighbors; we should not disobey him in what was right; if we fulfilled this paradise would be ours; if we committed any of those sins it was for God to punish or forgive as He pleased. (Sira, Tr. Guillaume, *The Life of Muhammad*, p. 199)

**AQA KHAN.** *See* AGHA KHAN.

**'AQIDAH.** *See* CREED.

**'AQL.** Intellect, soul, the universal mind, spirit.

**AQSA, AL-.** A **mosque**, built by **Umayyad Caliph Abdul Malik** in the seventh century in **Jerusalem** as part of the sanctuary known as the **"Dome of the Rock."** Partly destroyed in an earthquake, it was rebuilt in about 771 by the **'Abbasid** Caliph **al-Mansur** and restored by **Salah al-Din** (Saladin) in 1187, after his conquest of Jerusalem. It is the third holiest sanctuary (after Mecca and Medina) in Islam and the first Islamic building with a dome. The site is traditionally identified as the starting place of Muhammad's **Nocturnal Journey** to heaven.

**'ARABI.** *See* IBN AL-'ARABI.

**'ARABIC.** The language in which Allah's commands were transmitted through the medium of the Prophet Muhammad. It was the language of the pre-Islamic Bedouin Arabs and is spoken today by some 150 million people, including non-Muslim citizens of the Arab world. It is the language of ritual **prayers** of all Muslims. God's **revelations** were collected in the Koran, which Muslims believe to be inimitable. Because of the sacred character of the language, it has been preserved as a classical language and serves in modified form as the written language even of present-day Arabs, whose spoken dialects vary considerably.

**'ARAFAT.** A valley and a hill, about 27 kilometers southwest of Mecca, and the place where pilgrims (hajji) stay on the ninth day of **pilgrimage**. They rest in tents in the valley and pray and hear the **khutbah**, or sermon, from the place where Muhammad stood during his **Farewell Pilgrimage**. According to tradition, **Adam** and Eve met here on the Mountain of Mercy (jabal al-rahma) again, after being driven from paradise.

**ARKAN.** "Pillars." *See* PILLARS OF ISLAM.

**'ASABIYAH.** Voluntary social solidarity and unconditional loyalty and devotion to one's clan or tribe; tribal "nationalism," also fanaticism. Islam replaced the bonds of blood with the bonds of religion and gave it its own 'asabiyah. **Ibn Khaldun** saw the decline of urban civilization in the loss of asabiyah of its people. With the emergence of nation states in the Middle East, 'asabiyah also stood for Arab nationalism.

**ASCENSION.** *See* NOCTURNAL JOURNEY.

**ASHAB.** *See* COMPANIONS OF THE PROPHET.

**ASH'ARI, ABU 'L-HASAN AL-** (873-935[941?]). A dogmatic theologian, considered the founder of Islamic scholasticism. He was born in **Basra** of Yemeni origin and became a student of al-**Jubba'i**

of the Mu'tazilite school. However, he adopted the teachings of **Ibn Hanbal**. Impressed by the omnipotence of God, he held that God could not be limited. He proclaimed the reality of God's eternal attributes, the Koran as the uncreated word of God, and the absolute sovereignty of God over human actions. He acquired his name from Ashar (the hairy) because he was born with hair on his body. One Friday he was sitting in the great mosque of Basra and shouted: "I am 'Ali ibn Isma'il al-Ashari, and I used to hold that the Koran was created, that the eyes (of men) shall not see God, and that we ourselves are the authors of our deeds; now I have returned to the truth; I renounce these opinions and I take the engagement to refute the **Mu'tazilites** and expose their infamy and turpitude." One scholar commented that "the Mu'tazilites went with their heads up till such time as God produced al-Ashari to the world." He died at **Baghdad**. *See also* ASH'ARITES.

**ASH'ARI, ABU MUSA.** *See* ABU MUSA AL-ASH'ARI.

**ASH'ARITES (ASH'ARIYYAH).** A school of theology founded by Abu 'l-Hasan **al-Ash'ari** (873-935). Al-Ash'ari shaped the intellectual framework for orthodox theology. He studied under the head of the **Mu'tazilites**, al-**Jubba'i**, but he seceded from the "rationalist" school, declaring that **revelation** is superior to reason. He taught that the Koran was the eternal and uncreated word of God, based on the Koranic **Surah** (85:21-22) that says: "Nay, this is a Glorious Qur'an, (inscribed) in a Tablet Preserved!" He accepted anthropomorphisms in the Koran, and, impressed by God's omnipotence, he rejected free will but held that God created in man the power of choice that can be acquired (**kasb**) by man. He rejected all causality as it would limit the power of God and demanded that religious dogma be accepted without questioning? (*bila kayfa*). A famous quote of his states:

> We believe that God created everything by bidding it "Be" [kun].
> . . that nothing on earth, whether a fortune or misfortune, comes to be, save through God's will; that things exist through God's fiat; . . . and that the deeds of the creatures are created by Him and predestined by Him; . . . that the creatures can create nothing but are rather created themselves; We . . . profess faith in God's decree and fore-ordination. (Mir Zohair Husain, *Global Islamic Politics*, p. 91)

Ash'ari's teachings at the **Nizamiyyah** at **Baghdad** became part of orthodox Sunni doctrine. His *Maqalat al-Islamiyyin* (Islamic theological opinions) is a record of the doctrines of a number of sects. Leading Ash'arites included **al-Baqillani** (d.1013), **al-Juwayni** (d. 1086), and **al-Ghazali** (d. 1111).

**ASHRAF.** *See* SHARIF.

'**ASHURA.** "The Tenth." The first ten days of the 10th Muslim month **Muharram** and specifically the 10th day when Shi'ite Muslims commemorate the martyrdom of **Imam Husayn**, son of Ali,  at **Karbala** in 680. Passion plays (ta'ziyah) are publicly performed. Processions wind through the streets with floats reenacting the scenes at Karbala, and mourners flagellate themselves or strike their bodies with their hands, knives, or stones. For Sunnis it is a day of voluntary **fasting**. According to tradition, it is the day on which God began his creation and when **Noah** left the Ark.

**ASMA'I, ABU SA'ID AL-** (741-828). Philologist and representative of the grammarian school of **Basra** whose works have preserved knowledge about early Arab lexicography and poetry. His *Asma 'iyyat* is a collection of some 72 pieces of pre-Islamic and early Islamic poetry. He also wrote about the customs and values of the Bedouins, as well as about animals and plants. **Ibn Khallikan** calls Asma'i "a complete master of the **Arabic** language, and able grammarian, and the most eminent of all those persons who transmitted orally historical narrations, singular anecdotes, amusing stories, and rare expressions of the language" (II, 123). Asma'i was born and died in Marw; he was said to have been quite ugly. Yahya, the **Barmakid vizier** of **Harun al-Rashid**, once asked him whether he was married and since he was not, Yahya gave him a slave girl. Upon seeing Asma'i the girl cried: "How can you give me away to such a man as that? Do you not see how ugly he is." Yahya relented and bought the girl back for 2,000 dinars (Khallikan, IV, 107).

**ASRAFIL.** *See* ISRAFIL.

**ASSASSINS (HASHISHIYUN).** *See* ALAMUT and NIZARIS.

**ASSEMBLY OF CONSTITUTIONAL EXPERTS.** A body of 83 individuals charged by the Revolutionary Council to draft a constitution for the **Islamic Republic of Iran**. The assembly was dominated by Shi'ite clergy and laid the foundation for the theocratic government of Iran, establishing the supremacy of the "Guardianship of the Jurist" (*vilayat-i faqih*). It gave **Ayatollah Khomeyni** and his successors supreme authority as the representative of the **Hidden Imam**. The assembly concluded its work in October 1979, and the draft was ratified by a referendum in December. Secular forces who participated in the overthrow of the Shah of Iran were eventually eliminated, and individuals running for parliamentary elections had to be approved as to their suitability for office by a Council of **Guardians**. Principle 110 of the constitution gave Ayatollah Khomeyni sole power of appointing and dismissing the highest military and government officials, making him a virtual dictator.

**ATABAT.** The Shi'ite shrine cities of Iraq—**Najaf, Karbala**, Kazimayn, and **Samarra**—containing tombs of six of the 12 Shi'ite **imams**. At Kazimayn the Seventh and Ninth Imams are buried, and at Samarra the Tenth and Eleventh Imams. The Twelfth went into **occultation** from Samarra. The Tomb of Caliph 'Ali is located in Najaf and his son **Husayn** was martyred there in 680.

**'ATA', WASIL IBN-.** *See* WASIL IBN 'ATA'.

**ATATÜRK, MUSTAFA KEMAL.** *See* KEMALISM.

**ATHAR.** A relic, trace, tradition—used synonymously with **hadith**, when referring to the saying or action of a **Companion**.

**ATHIR.** *See* IBN AL-ATHIR.

**AVICENNA.** *See* IBN SINA, ABU 'ALI AL-HUSAYN.

**AWLIYAH.** *See* SAINTS.

**AWQAF.** *See* WAQF.

**AWS.** One of two tribes at Yathrib (Medina) who invited the Prophet to take refuge in its town, the other being the **Khazraj**. The Aws were among the early converts to Islam, subsequently called the Helpers (**ansar**). *See also* 'AQABAH, PLEDGE OF.

**AYAHS.** "Signs or miracles," verses in which the 114 chapters (**suras**) of the Koran are divided. There are said to be 6,236 verses. It is also part of the title of a Shi'ite **mujtahid**: **Ayatollah** (Miracle of God).

**A'YAN.** "Notables," prominent persons.

**AYATOLLAH (AYAT ALLAH).** "Sign, or Miracle, of God," title given to the most eminent **Twelver** Shi'ite legal experts. The honorific of Shi'ite **mujtahids** (jurists) in Iran, first used in the 14th century and generally adopted during the Qajar dynasty (1779-1924) (Arab-speaking Shi'ites use the title **Imam**). To qualify for the title one had to demonstrate superior learning and leadership, as well as acclamation by one's peers. The most learned of Ayatollahs were the "Sources of Emulation" (*marja-i taqlid*) who are addressed as Ayatollah al-'Uzma. In his lecture in 1970, Ayatollah Ruhollah **Khomeyni** created the concept of the **vilayat-i faqih**, political and spiritual leadership of the Islamic state, preparing the way for a theocratic regime after the Islamic Revolution of 1979. Khomeyni was proclaimed the highest of Ayatollahs; he was succeeded after his death by Sayyid 'Ali **Khamene'i,** who no longer enjoys the charisma and power of his predecessor. *See also* ISLAMIC REPUBLIC OF IRAN.

**AYN.** "Eye, Well." *See* EVIL EYE.

**AYN JALUT.** "Spring of Goliath." A place in Palestine, near Nazareth, where Baybars, the **Mamluk** general of Egypt, defeated a **Mongol** army under the Christian Turk Kitbuga in 1260. This victory led to the reconquest of Syria and stemmed the tide of Mongol advance into the Near East.

**AYYUBID DYNASTY.** Named after Ayyub ibn Shadhi, but founded in 1174 by **Salah al-Din** (Saladin, 1138-1193) in Egypt. He extended his rule over Syria, Iraq, and South Arabia and destroyed the remnants of the **Fatimid** state, restoring Sunni orthodoxy to Egypt. Salah al-Din defeated the Crusaders in the battle of **Hittin** (1187) and reconquered **Jerusalem.** Before his death he divided the Ayyubid empire as appanages among his relatives, but by the middle of the 13th century the Ayyubid empire fell prey to their slaves, who established the **Mamluk** dynasty with its center in Egypt.

**AZAN (ADHAN).** *See* CALL TO PRAYER.

**AZHAR, AL-.** "The Resplendent," important university in Sunni Islam. It was founded by the **Fatimid** general, Jawahar **al-Siqilli** in 972 in **Cairo** as a Shi'ite college for the propagation of the **Isma'ili sect**. After the **Ayyubids** conquered Egypt, the country reverted to Sunni Islam and Al-Azhar eventually became the dominant orthodox institution and a model also for European universities. The famous historian/sociologist **Ibn-Khaldun** lectured at Al-Azhar in the 14th century, and by the 18th century it dominated the educational scene in the Islamic world. **Shaykhs** of Al-Azhar were members of Napoleon's provincial councils, but six shaykhs were executed after a short revolt in 1798 in Cairo. In the 19th and early 20th centuries shaykhs of Al-Azhar were accused of acquiescing to government edicts. **Muhammad Abduh,** member of the Supreme Council of Al-Azhar, was instrumental in initiating modern reforms in the administration and curriculum. During British colonial rule, members of the faculty and students were often in the forefront of public protests. In the 1950s the government of Gamal 'Abul Nasser strictly regulated the university and its shaykh supported Arab nationalism and socialism. It became a modern university, teaching secular as well as theological subjects and **women** were also admitted. But the majority of the faculty stood for stability rather than revolution and the university even approved of the peace treaty with Israel.

**'AZRA'IL.** *See* 'IZRA'IL.

**AZRAQITES.** An extremist offshoot of the **Kharijite** movement in the late seventh century, named after Nafi ibn Azraq, which declared that all Muslims were unbelievers (**kafirs**) and should be killed with their **women** and children if they did not accept their radical interpretation of Islam. The Azraqites elected the warrior-poet Qatari ibn Fuja'ah as their **caliph** and invaded southern Mesopotamia and Khuzistan, and for a long time they held out against superior government forces. They opposed the **Umayyads** as **apostates**. Being a small movement, their fanaticism caused their eventual destruction. Ironically, while they attacked other Muslims, they did not direct their violence against non-Muslims.

-B-

**BAB.** A title of varied application in Shi'ism, also given to **Sufi shaykhs**. Sayyid 'Ali Muhammad (1820-1850), a native of Shiraz, proclaimed himself the Bab, "The Gateway" to the Truth, and the initiator of a new prophetic age. In the early 1840s he went on **pilgrimage** to **Karbala** and remained there to study with Shi'ite theologians. He became a member of the **Shaykhi** movement, which held among others the view that there always existed a man who was capable of interpreting the will of the **Hidden Imam**. Upon returning to Shiraz in 1844, he announced that the mission of Muhammad was ended and he was to inaugurate a new era. He published the Babi scripture, the *Bayan* (Explanation), which was to replace the Koran. He was arrested, but his teachings found wide acceptance. Eventually, he was sent to Tabriz where he was executed. His followers saw it as a miracle that he was not killed in the first volley—the ropes had been torn or shot through and he might have escaped but was found and shot in the second attempt. The Bab's successors were two half-brothers, Mirza Yahya, the *Sobh-i Azal* (Eternal Dawn) and Mirza Husayn Ali (d. 1892), who headed separate factions; the latter proclaimed himself *Baha Allah*, the "Splendor of God," and his followers came to be known as Baha'is. Baha Allah published his teachings in the *Kitab al-Aqdas* (The most holy book). The Baha'is greatly increased in numbers and founded communities also in Europe and America. After a radical beginning, the Baha'is shed their militancy, abolished **jihad**, and advocated obedience to lawful government, universal peace and brotherhood, and a recognition of all prophets. Babi/Baha'i doctrines suggest a predominance of commercial outlook and progressive spirit. They permitted the taking of interest—which is forbidden in Islam—and favored the emancipation of **women**. 'Abd al-Baha, eldest son of Baha Allah, visited Europe and subsequently introduced new concepts, including the equality of sexes, the harmony of religion and science, the commonality of all religions, and progressive **revelation** (Judeo-Christian-Islamic-Babi, Baha'i), and less emphasis on questions of reincarnation, astrology, faith healing, and spiritualism. Numerology was important, the number 19 having special mystical meaning. In 1923 Haifa in Palestine became the administrative center (the Universal House of Justice) of the Baha'is. The tomb of the Bab is in Haifa and Baha Allah is buried in Acre (Akka), Israel. There are between 500,000 and one million Baha'is in Iran and thousands in England

and America. Since the religion is an offshoot of Islam, the Baha'is in Iran have often been persecuted as heretics, and they are outlawed in Morocco, Egypt, Syria, Iraq, and other countries. *See also* BABI.

**BABAK.** *See* BABIK.

**BABAWAYHI.** *See* IBN BABAWAYHI.

**BABI.** Followers of the "Bab" Sayyid ʿAli Muhammad, who split into two major branches, the *Azali* of Mirza Yahya, who were more radical and are reduced in number to a few thousand mostly in Iran, and the Baha'i of Baha Allah, who evolved into a world religion. *See also* BAB.

**BAB-I AʿLA.** The Sublime Porte—name of the executive offices of the grand **vizier** in the **Ottoman empire**.

**BABIK (BABAK,** r. 816-837). A rebel who established himself in 816/17 in Azerbaijan and for some 20 years defied the power of Caliph **al-Maʾmun's** armies. He founded a **sect,** called Khurramiyyah, which wanted to restore the religion of Mazdak and believed in various mystical doctrines, including the transmigration of souls. Babik was finally defeated by Caliph al-Muʿtasim's general Afshin and put to a torturous death. Babik was of humble origin, the son of an oil seller, and what we know about him and his activities comes mainly from hostile sources.

**BABUYAH.** *See* IBN BABAWAYHI.

**BADR, BATTLE OF.** First military victory of the Muslim community of Medina against a superior force of Meccans. In March 624 a heavily armed Meccan caravan was attacked by a small band of some 300 Muslim raiders who faced an army of about 950 men with 700 camels and 100 horses. In spite of the heavy odds against them, the Prophet persisted in the attack and the Meccans were defeated. A sand storm blowing in the direction of the **Quraysh** impeded their visibility, which was seen as a sign of Allah's support. The battle began with a "war of words" as each hurled insults at the other. Next followed single combat in which the Muslims prevailed, and finally the forces engaged. The unity and greater morale of the Muslim forces eventually led to a rout of the Meccans. They left behind 70

(50?) men dead, including many of their Quraysh leaders; only 14 Muslims were killed. About 50 prisoners were held for ransom. For the Muslim community this was a sign that God was on their side and permitted the consolidation of the early Muslim community. The Koran says: "Allah had helped you at Badr, when ye were helpless: then fear Allah: thus may ye show your gratitude" (3:123).

**BAGHAWI, HUSAYN AL-** (d. 1130 or 1136). A **Shafi'ite** traditionist and commentator on the Koran, he is the author of a collection of **hadith**, titled *Masabih al-Sunnah*, which has been translated into English by James Robson and published in four volumes. Unlike **al-Bukhari**'s and **Muslim ibn al-Hajjaj**'s works, it covers a greater variety of topics and lists only the first transmitter and the text of the hadith, and is therefore more practical for use. The work was later revised and expanded under the title *Mishkat al-masabih* (Niche for light) by Shaykh Wali al-Din Mahmud (d. 1342) and others. Baghawi was born near Herat, present-day Afghanistan. He led an ascetic life, living on bread and olive oil, and refused to accept a portion of the **inheritance** after the death of his wife. Ibn Khallikan says about Baghawi: "A wife of this doctor died, and he refused to accept any portion of the inheritance left by her: he used also to live on dry bread, but having been blamed for this (as an affectation of abstinence), he ate his bread with olive oil."

**BAGHDAD.** The "City of Peace" (*madinat al-salam*) was founded in 762 by the Caliph **al-Mansur** as the capital of the **'Abbasid** dynasty. It was a circular-shaped city, located where the Euphrates and Tigris Rivers came closest, at the crossroads of trade where there was an abundance of water and fertile soil. It took four years to build the town and cost 4,883,000 dirhams. The caliphal palace and the great **mosque** were in the center from which roads connected to the four gates. Baghdad rapidly grew and soon surpassed the older cities in splendor. Although named "City of Peace," Baghdad, the Persian name of a nearby village, was eventually adopted. The city reached its cultural greatness under Caliph **Harun al-Rashid** (786-809) and the succeeding five decades. **Al-Ma'mun** (813-833) founded the **"House of Wisdom"** (*bayt al-hikma*) which became the center for translation of Greek science and philosophy. He sponsored the **Mu'tazilite** rationalists, which culminated in the controversy about the createdness, or eternal existence, of the Koran. Turkish influence grew as **caliphs** surrounded themselves with body guards who became so unruly that the caliphs moved the capital to **Samarra** in 838 for about 45 years. In the middle of the 10th century, the Shi'ite **Buyids** captured the city and limited the helpless caliphs to an undignified existence, until the **Seljuqs** liberated the city in the 11th century. They restored Sunni orthodoxy and gave the 'Abbasid caliphs their dignity, but little real power. The 'Abbasid dynasty was brought to an end when **Hulagu** captured the city in 1258. The **Ottomans** captured the city in 1638 after which it lost its importance to **Istanbul**. Baghdad is an important place of **pilgrimage** for Shi'ites who visit the tombs of the seventh and ninth **imams** and for members of the **Qadiriyyah** Sufi fraternity whose founder 'Abd al-Qadir **al-Jilani** is buried there.

**BAGHDADI, 'ABD AL LATIF AL-** (1162-1231). Encyclopedic scholar and author of numerous books, including a history of Egypt in that, among others, stated that Caliph **'Umar** ordered his general **'Amr ibn al-'As** to burn the library of Alexandria. This fact has not been corroborated by any other source. Born in **Baghdad**, he traveled widely in Syria, Egypt, and Iraq and spent a number of years at the court of **Salah al-Din** (1138-1193).

**BAGHDADI, ABU MANSUR AL-** (d. 1037). **Ash'arite** dogmatic theologian and legist who studied and taught at Nishapur. He published a systematized dogmatic in his *Roots of Religion* and a study of Islamic **sects**, called *Al-Farq bayn al-Firaq*. He died and is buried in Isfarayn in present-day Iran. Ibn Khallikan quotes from the *History of Naisapur*, saying: "He possessed great riches, which he spent on the learned (in the law) and on the Traditionists: he never made of his information a source of profit.... He composed treatises on different sciences and surpassed his contemporaries in every branch of learning ... he gave lessons there (at the mosque of Akil), which were assiduously attended by doctors of the greatest eminence" (Khallikan II, 150).

**BAHA'I.** Follower of Baha Allah, leader of the main branch of the Babi sect. *See also* BAB.

**BAHIRAH.** According to tradition, Bahira, a Nestorian Christian monk who lived near Busra on the caravan route from the **Hijaz** to Syria, recognized the sign of prophethood when he saw the 12-year-old Muhammad. Muhammad was traveling with his uncle **Abu Talib** to

Syria when they came upon the monk. Bahira asked Muhammad several questions and then told Abu Talib that in Muhammad's eyes are the marks of a great prophet. A similar event is said to have happened 12 years later when Muhammad traveled on business for his wife **Khadija** and another monk called Nestor made the same prediction.

**BALADHURI, AHMAD** (d. 892). One of the great historians of the ninth century, a native of **Baghdad** but probably of Persian origin. Two of his historical works still extant are *Futuh al-buldan* (The history of Muslim conquests), an abbreviated version of which has been published in English by P. K. Hitti and F. C Murgotten under the title *The Origin of the Islamic State*. The other is the *Ansab al-ashraf* (Genealogy of nobles), which is also important for the history of the **Kharijites**. Toward the end of his life, he became deranged, purportedly as a result of drinking the juice of the anacardia (balad-hur), and he was chained to his bed in a hospital where he died.

**BANNA, HASAN AL-** (1906-1949). Founder of the **Muslim Brotherhood** (Ikhwan al-Muslimin) of Egypt in 1928 and one of the founding fathers of radical Islam. He was born in Mahmudiyya, a town about 135 kilometers from **Cairo**, and educated in his home town and subsequently in Cairo at the Dar Al-Ulum, an Islamic teacher training college. He taught **Arabic** at an elementary school in Isma'iliya. There he founded the Society of Muslim Brethren, a religio-political organization that eventually spread to other parts of the Islamic world. Al-Banna, an ascetic and charismatic teacher, became the "Supreme Guide" (*murshid al-'amm*) who advocated social and economic reforms, expulsion of the British from Egypt, and the establishment of an Islamic state. He blamed Egypt's social malaise of ignorance, hunger, and disease on the fact that Muslims had strayed from orthodox Islam. He called for the creation of a state that was based on the Koran and the Traditions (**Sunnah**) of the classical period of Islam and demanded the abrogation of secular laws and the enforcement of Islamic canonic law. As a political party, the Ikhwan was never very successful, but it was able to mobilize the masses of lower urban and rural classes. In response to government suppression, the Ikhwan resorted to violence and al-Banna himself became the target of assassination in 1949 (reputedly by government agents). Hasan al-Banna's teachings were carried to all corners of the Islamic world and spawned other, more radical, offshoots that agitated for the overthrow of established governments. A Muslim Egyptian who met Hasan al-Banna' said of him:

> He talked chiefly of religious topics, but not in the accustomed manner of the preacher, with sonorous phrases and learned references. He went staight to the nub of the question, and he spoke with directness and ease. It seemed strange to me, but here was a theologian with a sense of reality, a man of religion who recognized the existence of facts. (Quoted by Wendell, 1975)

**BANU.** Tribe. *See* under tribal name, for example HASHIM, BANU; and UMAYYA, BANU.

**BAQI, JANNAT AL-.** "Tree Garden." Cemetery east of Medina where thousands of **Companions** of the Prophet are buried, including **Hasan** and **Husayn**, the sons of Caliph 'Ali, the Shi'ite **imams Muhammad al-Baqir** and **Ja'far al-Sadiq**, as well as the Caliph **Uthman** and **Malik ibn Anas.** When the **Wahhabis** conquered Medina in 1818 and again in 1925, they razed the graves and tombs, except the one of the Prophet.

**BAQILLANI, ABU BAKR MUHAMMAD AL-** (BAKILANI, d. 1013). **Malikite** jurist and theologian who systematized **Ash'ari** teachings, especially the dogma of atomism, according to which everything is newly created every instant by God. He rejected causality and miracles, except the miracle of the Koran. Baqillani gave a concise statement defining the functions of the **caliph**, saying,

> [the caliph] need not be impeccable . . . having knowledge of the unseen, nor even every aspect of the faith . . . the Imam is [only] appointed to uphold the precepts and the limitations and the commands which the **Messenger** promulgated. For the knowledge of the Community has precedence therein, and in everything he undertakes [the caliph] is the trustee and deputy of the Community, and the Community stand behind him guiding him and setting him right and reminding him and demanding the right from him as it is incumbent upon him, even removing and replacing him if he has committed a crime requiring his deposition. (Binder, 1961, 167)

Al-Baqillani has been called the real founder of the **Ash'arite** school. He was the first to devote an entire book, the *Kitab I jaz al-Qur 'an* to the dogma of the inimitability of the Koran. He resided in **Baghdad** and died there.

**BARAKAH.** "Grace," or blessing, a vital force inherent in a person, place, or thing. Founders and heads of **Sufi** fraternities are thought to possess barakah, a spiritual power that can be transmitted from a saintly person to a disciple or devotee. A saint's barakah provides spiritual blessings, which pilgrims can obtain from shrines of venerated **pirs**. The **Hanbali** school of Sunni Islam rejects the veneration of saints as sinful innovation (**bid'ah**). Shi'ites feel that their **imams** enjoy the special illumination or barakah and are, in fact, infallible; therefore, they are entitled to leadership of the Muslim community.

**BARELVI, SAYYID AHMAD** (1786-1831). Native of Rae Bareli and founder of "The Way of the Prophet Muhammad" (Tariqah-i Muhammadiyah), a revolutionary Islamist movement. He called himself Commander of the **Believers** (*amir al-mu'minin*) and proclaimed a **jihad** against the Sikhs in the Punjab, India. He was defeated and killed, and this ended the dream of establishing an Islamic state in Peshawar, now Pakistan. The Barelvis upheld the doctrine of the unity of God (**tawhid**) and called themselves Unitarians or **Ahl al-Hadith**, while others called them **Wahhabis**. They rejected innovation (**bid'ah**) but accepted **Sufism** and believed in **intercession**, that the spirits of dead saints can be invoked for help. They used **amulets** and accepted most features of popular Islam.

**BARMAKIDS.** The Barmakids of Balkh (now Afghanistan) were a family of secretaries and **viziers** in the service of **'Abbasid caliphs**. Al-Saffah (749-754) put the first Barmakid, Khalid ibn-Barmak, in charge of the divans of the army and the land tax and made him his personal adviser. Caliph **al-Mansur** (754-775) appointed him governor of Fars and Tabaristan provinces and his grandson, Fadhl ibn Yahya, was adopted as foster brother of **Harun al-Rashid** (786-809). Yahya, the son of Khalid, was secretary and tutor to Harun and governor of Azarbaijan, and his 17-year rule (786-803) was called the "reign of the Barmakids." His two sons, Fadhl and Ja'far, became governors and served as military commanders.

The Barmakids amassed fabulous wealth and built beautiful palaces in **Baghdad**; they rivaled in splendor the **'Abbasid** court, which was no doubt one factor in their eventual destruction. After Harun returned from **pilgrimage** in 802, he had all of the Barmakids executed. The Barmakids were good administrators; they sponsored the arts and contributed to a revival of Iranian culture. They had become too rich, powerful, and popular to be seen as a threat to Harun. The name *barmak*, meaning chief priest, was derived from a Buddhist monastery in Balkh. A poet said in praise of the Barmakids: "The sons of Yahya are four in number, like the elements; when put to the test, they are found to be the elements of (which) beneficence (is formed)!" (Khallikan, IV,105).

A memorial presented by an unknown person to Harun al-Rashid was said to have been instrumental in the destruction of the Barmakids. It stated:

> Behold, the son of Yahya has become sovereign like yourself; there is no difference between you! Your orders must yield to his, and his orders dare not be resisted. He has built a palace, of which the like was never erected by the Persian or the Indian (king). Pearls and rubies for its pavement, and the floor is of amber and aloes wood. We fear that he will inherit the empire, when you are hidden in the tomb. It is only the insolent slave who rivals his master in splendor.

Another reason given was that Harun married Ja'far to his sister al-'Abbasa on condition that the **marriage** not be consummated. Al-'Abbasa intrigued to bear Ja'far a child, which greatly infuriated the caliph.

**BASMALAH (BISMILLAH).** A phrase that is invoked at the beginning of an action, translated "in the name of God, the Merciful and Compassionate" *(bism' llah' ar-rahman' ar-rahim)*. It is used at the beginning of a meal, when putting on new clothes, and starting any new work. It occurs at the beginning of every **Surah** in the Koran except the ninth.

**BASRA.** An important Islamic city, founded as a garrison town *(misr*, pl. *amsar)* in 638. It was a center of learning where renowned theologians, poets, grammarians, and historians flourished. **Hasan al-Basri** (642-728), **Abu Bishr al-Sibawayh** (d.796), Abdullah Ibn al-**Muqaffa'** (720-757), and **Abu Nuwas** (753-813), resided in Basra.

With the beginning of **Buyid** rule in the 10th century and the **Ottoman** conquest in the 16th century, the city lost much of its importance.

**BASRI, HASAN AL- (HASAN-I BASRA, 642-728).** Celebrated preacher, ascetic, scholar, and important traditionist, he was born in Medina, the son of a slave, raised and educated in **Basra.** He personally met many of the **Companions** of the Prophet and was known for his uncompromising piety. He is said to have known all the branches of science and was noted for his self-mortification, fear of God, and devotion. He presided over a circle of students who discussed the question of free will and **sin.** Some, later called the **Murji'ites** (those who defer), felt that man had no right to judge sinners, that only God will make his merciful decision; their opponents held that a great sinner had become an unbeliever (**kafir**) and would be punished in hell. One **Wasil ibn 'Ata'** stated that a grave sinner is neither an unbeliever nor a believer but occupies an intermediary position. Then he left and formed his own circle. Hasan al-Basri said Wasil withdrew (*i'tazila*), which became the name of the adherents of the **Mu'tazilite** school. Hasan was claimed later as one of theirs by the **Sufis,** orthodox Sunnis, and the Mu'tazilites. Hasan was quoted to say: "I never saw a certainty of which there is no doubt, bear greater resemblance to a doubtful thing of which there is no certainty, than does death" (Khallikan, I, 370). He was described as the handsomest person in Basra until an accident that disfigured his nose by a fall from a horse. Hasan died in Basra and, according to a contemporary report, "All the people followed the funeral and were so taken up with it, that no afternoon prayer was said that day in the **mosque,** for none remained in it to pray; this, I believe, was till then unexampled in Islamism" (Khallikan, I, 372).

**BAST.** "Sanctuary." Persecuted individuals in Iran could escape arrest by taking refuge (*bast*) in a shrine or major **mosque,** or the residence of a **Mujtahid.** During the Iranian Revolution of 1905-1906, some 12,000 protesters took bast in the British embassy in Tehran, forcing Shah Muzaffar al-Din to grant the drafting of a constitution and the establishment of a parliament. However, on occasions, a ruler violated the sanctity of bast and had a refugee arrested.

**BATINITES (BATINIYYAH).** A generic term for groups and **sects,** mostly Shi'ites, who distinguish the inner (*batin*) esoteric interpretation of the Koran and **Islamic law** from the outer (**zahir**) exoteric form. The esoteric doctrine consists of two main parts: the allegorical interpretation (**ta'wil**) of the Koran and the Traditions (**Sunnah**); and the truths (haqa'iq), a system of philosophy and science coordinated with religion. **Isma'ilis** and **Qarmatians** favored this interpretation and devised levels of initiation according to the comprehension of the believer. Among Sunnis, some **Sufi** orders also accept allegorical interpretation.

**BATTLE OF THE MASTS.** *See* MASTS, BATTLE OF.

**BATUTAH.** *See* IBN BATUTAH, MUHAMMAD IBN 'ABD ALLAH.

**BAY'AH.** An oath of loyalty taken from the chiefs of tribes and notables in pre-Islamic times. It was adopted in Islam upon the election of **Abu Bakr** (632-634) and was subsequently taken upon the election of his successors. Once elected, Muslims owe obedience to the **caliph**, unless he commits a grave **sin** or becomes an **apostate**. The principle of leadership by election became accepted in Sunni Islam, although, in fact, dynastic succession was common. There exists no indication as to the number of electors needed and bay'ah came to be primarily a symbolic act.

**BAYHAQI, ABU'L-FAZL** (995-1077). Secretary to the Ghaznawid court and historian of the dynasty. Of his monumental work, the 30-volume *Mujalladat*, the extant portion covers the period of Mas'ud (1030-1041), called the *History of Mas'ud* or the *History of Bayhaqi*. Bayhaqi was born in 995 in Bayhaq, the present-day Sabzawar in Afghanistan. He studied in Nishapur and was one of the most gifted and graceful writers of Persian prose. He was imprisoned briefly for failure to repay a dowry to a former wife. For about 19 years he worked in the Ghaznawid secretariate.

**BAYT AL-HIKMAH.** *See* HOUSE OF WISDOM.

**BAZ, ABDUL AZIZ IBN ABDULLAH AL-** (1911- ). Grand Mufti of Saudi Arabia and president of the Supreme Religious Council. A native of Riyadh, he went blind as a youth but continued his studies and served as a judge (1938-1952) until he became a professor of jurisprudence at the University of Riyadh (1953-1960). He advanced to the position of vice president of the University of Medina in 1961 and president in 1969. He was quoted as having said that the earth was flat and eventually opposed the stationing of non-Muslim troops in Saudi Arabia during the Gulf War. He issued a **fatwa**, forbidding **women** to drive and supported a petition that demanded, among other things, that Saudi Arabia end its close ties with the West. He became Grand Mufti in 1993.

**BEARDS.** According to a **Tradition** the Prophet said: "Do the opposite of the polytheists, let your beards grow long and clip your mustache." The neotraditionalist **Taliban** of Afghanistan therefore enforced the growing of beards after they achieved power.

**BEKTASHI.** A syncretic, heterodox **Sufi** order (*tariqa*) founded in Anatolia by Haji Bektash in 1337. According to **Ottoman** legend, Haji Bektash initiated the first contingent of the **Janissary** corps and the order became closely associated with the Janissaries, the **pirs** serving as chaplains of its battalions. In the late 16th century the grand master of the order became part of the force with the rank of Chorbaji (Soup Ladler), the equivalent to company commander. Although it eventually represented itself as an orthodox Sunni order, it was eclectic, assimilating **Christian** and Shi'ite elements. Its esoteric doctrines were described thus

> Each human soul is a portion of divinity which exists only in man. The eternal soul, saved by perishable mediums, constantly changes its dwelling without quitting the earth. Morality consists in enjoying the good things of earth without injury to any one, whatever causes no ill to a person is lawful. The wise man is he who regulates his pleasures, for joy is a science which has degrees, made known little by little to the initiated. Contemplation is the best of all joys, for it belongs to the celestial vision. (Canon Sell, *The Religious Orders of Islam*)

It was said that members confess their sins to their spiritual chiefs, and **women** participate unveiled in their religious rites. Celibacy was preferred by the higher ranks. In 1826 the Ottoman **Sultan** Mahmud II destroyed the Janissary corps and abolished the Bektashi order. It revived in the latter part of the 19th century to be again abolished by Mustafa Kemal Atatürk in 1925, but it has continued to exist to the present in Turkey, the Balkans, and especially in Albania, where it was widespread in spite of the communist regime.

**BELIEVERS (MU'MINUN).** Believers in Islam. A **surah** in the Koran states: "Successful indeed are the believers, those who humble themselves in their prayers; who avoid vain talk; who are active in giving **zakat**; who guard their modesty, except with those joined to them in **marriage** bond" (23:1-6). *See also* FAITH.

**BERRI, NABIH** (1938- ). Speaker of the Lebanese parliament since 1992 and leader of Shi'ite **Amal** party since 1980. Born in Freetown, Sierra Leone, of Lebanese parents, Berri came to Lebanon and studied law at the Lebanese University and at the Sorbonne in Paris. In 1975 he joined the paramilitary organization of Amal, headed by Sayyid Musa **al-Sadr**. After the disappearance of Sadr in 1978, Berri advanced in the movement and in 1980 he became chairman of Amal and the leading politician of Lebanese Shi'ites. He participated in the siege of the Palestinian refugee camps and fought **Hisbullah** in 1989, while at the same time conducting military operations into the Israeli-declared "Security Zone."

**BID'AH.** "Innovation," or deviation, from Islamic tradition. Anything that is new and contradicts the Koran and **Traditions** is sinful innovation. There are five categories of bid'ah. A good innovation is accepted if it is in conformity with Islamic teachings.

**BILA KAYFAH.** "Without Questioning." The doctrine of literalism propagated by Abu 'l-Hasan al-**Ash'ari** according to which religious dogma that has been generally approved by the leading Sunni schools should be accepted without further argument. This includes even seemingly anthropomorphist references to God in the Koran.

**BILAL.** A black slave who converted to Islam and was appointed by Muhammad to be the first **mu'ezzin**, or caller to prayer. He was an Abyssinian slave, tortured by his master to recant his conversion but was ransomed by **Abu Bakr.** He accompanied the Prophet on all his campaigns and died in the 640s. Bilal was described as tall, dark, and gaunt, with Negroid features and bushy hair. His grave in **Damascus** has become a place of **pilgrimage**.

**BIRUNI, ABU RAYHAN AL-** (973-1048). Chronicler, astrologer, astronomer, mathematician, and historian at the court of Mahmud of Ghazni. He accompanied the **Ghaznavid** ruler on his campaigns to India and studied Sanskrit and Indian philosophy there. He was one of the most profound and original scholars of medieval Islam. Born near Khiva, he was first at the court of the Khwarizm Shahs in Transcaspia and later was called to the court of Mahmud of Ghazni. He was a prolific scholar, said to have 103 finished and 10 unfinished works to his name and, as tradition has it, his writings have exceeded a "camel-load." Translated into English are his *kitab al-athar al-baqiyah* (Chronology of ancient nations), and *tarikh al-hind* (Description of India).

**BISMILLAH.** *See* BASMALLAH.

**BLACK MUSLIMS.** *See* NATION OF ISLAM.

**BLACK STONE.** The Black Stone (*al-hajar al-aswad*) is a stone, possibly a meteorite, positioned in the eastern corner of the **Ka'ba**, a cube-like building that is the holiest shrine in Islam. According to tradition, the Stone was first placed in the Ka'bah by **Adam** and later again by the Angel **Gabriel**. It is the object of veneration, touched by pilgrims during their circumambulations of the Ka'ba. The **Qarmatians**, a Shi'ite religio-political movement named after Hamdan Qarmat, invaded the **Hijaz** in 930 and carried off the Stone to their camp at al-Ahsa. It was not returned to the Ka'ba until 951. The Stone was broken into seven pieces and is now held together by a silver ring.

**BLOOD MONEY.** *See* DIYAH and RETALIATION.

**BOHRAS.** Originally Hindus who converted to the **Isma'ili** branch of Shi'ism in the 11th century. They broke with the supporters of the **Agha Khan** and accepted the leadership of their "Absolute Preacher." The Bohra community of about one million is located in the Bombay area. There are also small Sunni Bohra communities in India and Pakistan. Another group of Bohras exists in Yemen.

**BOOTY.** *See* GHANIMA.

**BROTHERHOOD, MUSLIM.** *See* MUSLIM BROTHERHOOD.

**BUKHARI, MUHAMMAD IBN ISMA'IL AL-** (810-870). **Imam** Bukhari was one of the great traditionists who compiled one of the six books of **hadith**, titled *Sahih al-Bukhari*, which has been called the most authoritative book after the Koran. A native of Bukhara, hence his name, he traveled to Mecca at age 16, spent six years in the **Hijaz**, and then visited the great cities in Syria and Iraq. He was said to have collected 600,000 hadith, but approved only 7,275. They were divided into such topics as **prayer**, **pilgrimage**, manners, commerce, medicine, and holy war (**jihad**). He was buried in Khartank, a village near Samarkand. Bukhari was describes as "a lean-bodied man and of middle size;" he was quoted as having said: "I never inserted a **Tradition** in my *Sahih* till after I had made an **ablution**, and offered up a prayer of two rakas" (Khallikan, II, 596).

**BURAQ.** The animal on which the Prophet is believed to have performed the **Nocturnal Journey**, called **mi'raj**, or ascent, from Mecca to **Jerusalem** and from there to **heaven**. The Archangel **Gabriel** brought Muhammad the white animal, the size of a mule, with a woman's head, and a peacock's tail and two wings.

**BURDAH.** A cloak, especially the mantle of the Prophet, which, according to **Ottoman** claims, came into their possession and is now exhibited in the Topkapi Serayi.

**BURIALS.** *See* DEATH.

**BURQA'.** A veil and covering that encloses the entire body, worn by **women** in public.

**BUYID (BUWAYHID) DYNASTY** (932-1062). A Persian dynasty from Dailam on the southwestern shores of the Caspian Sea that ruled over Iran and Iraq from 932-1062. The Shi'ite Buyids entered **Baghdad** in 945 and dominated the **'Abbasid caliphs** for 110 years, but they did not depose them. The Caliph al-Mustakfi (944-946) gave Ahmad ibn-Buwayh the title Mu'izz al-Dawlah and made him his commander (*amir a-umara '*), but Ahmad insisted on having his name mentioned in the Friday sermon (**khutbah**) and coins minted with his name as an act of his sovereignty. Under 'Adud al-Dawla (949-983) the dynasty reached its greatest power, but it was eventually eliminated by the **Ghaznavids** and **Seljuqs** who restored orthodoxy and the dignity, if not the power, of the caliphs. Muizz al-Dawla is said to have started the Shi'ite custom of commemorating the 10th of **Muharram** by holding a procession in Baghdad in 952. They promoted the feast of **Ghadir al-Khumm**, the appointment of 'Ali as Muhammad's successor, rebuilt Shi'ite shrines, and supported **Twelver Shi'ism** as equal to Sunnism. The Buyids also introduced the system of military feudalism, giving officers districts to tax in lieu of a salary. The Buyids were great patrons of the arts and sciences and contributed to a revival of Persian culture and **Mu'tazi-lite** doctrines. Buyid supremacy marked the low point in the 'Abbasid caliphate and contributed to a clear division in Sunnite and Shi'ite theology.

## -C-

**CADI (KAZI).** *See* JUDGE.

**CAIRO (AL-QAHIRA).** Cairo is the capital of Egypt (Misr) with a population of about 15 million people. It is the largest city in Africa, located on the Nile River, about 170 kilometers south of the Mediterranean coast. Its general location was the site of such ancient cities as Memphis, about 5,000 years ago, and Babylon dating back some 2,000 years. The nucleus of the modern city was Fustat, a garrison town (**amsar**) founded by 'Amr ibn al-'As in 641. Cairo was founded slightly to the north by the Fatimid commander Jawhar in 969, and as the city grew it eventually incorporated the area of Fustat. The city became successively the capital of the **Fatimid** (909-1171) and **Mamluk** (1250-1717) dynasties, after which Egypt became part of the **Ottoman empire**. The Napoleonic invasion of Egypt in 1798 brought Western influence into the area, which continued to grow under the dynasty of **Muhammad 'Ali** (1805-1848) and during the British occupation of Egypt (1882-1954). A military coup abolished the monarchy and established a government under military control, which continues to this day.

Cairo became one of the major intellectual centers of the Islamic world. The city is rich in architectural treasures, cathedral mosques, great fortresses, and **Al-Azhar**, the oldest existing university in the world. **Ibn Khaldun**, the famous Arab philosopher of history taught there, as did **Muhammad Abduh**, the famous Muslim modernist. Under the regime of Gamal Abdul Nasser (1954-1970), Cairo became the center of Arab nationalism and, as a result of the founding of the **Muslim Brotherhood** by **Hasan al-Banna**, it became a center of the **Islamist** movement, which spread from there throughout the Islamic world.

**CALENDAR.** The Islamic calendar year begins with the **Hijrah**, the emigration of Muhammad from Mecca to Yathrib/Medina on July 16, 622. It is divided into "lunar" years of about 354 days and is shorter than the Western "solar year;" and, therefore, the months do not coincide with the seasons. The first month, **Muharram**, is dedicated by Shi'ites to the commemoration of the martyrdom of **Imam Husayn**, the son of 'Ali. It begins with the sighting of the new moon. Rabi' al-Awwal is the month of the Prophet's birthday. **Ramadhan** is the month of daylight **fasting** and **Dhu 'l-Hijja** the month of **pilgrimage**. The Muslim months have 29 or 30 days and are named as follows:

1. Muharram—the sacred month
2. Safar—the month that is void
3. Rabi' al-Awwal—the first of spring
4. Rabi' al-thani—the last of spring
5. Jamad al-Ula—the first dry month
6. Jama al-akhira— the last dry month
7. Rajab—the revered month
8. Sha'ban—the month of division
9. Ramadhan—the hot month
10. Shawwal—the month of hunting
11. Dhu 'l-Qa'da—the month of rest
12. Dhu 'l-Hijja— the month of pilgrimage

The days of the week in **Arabic** are counted from Sunday, First Day, to Thursday, Fifth Day; then comes **Friday**, the Day of Congregation (Jum'a) and Saturday, the Day of Sabbath (*Sabt*). In most Muslim countries dates show both the Islamic lunar year (qamari) and the Gregorian solar year (shamsi); for example, 1999 is equivalent to 1420/21. *See also* FESTIVALS.

**CALIPH (KHALIFAH).** In Sunni Islam, the caliph was the successor of Muhammad in leadership of the Islamic community. (The Shi'ites use the term **imam**, but count only Ali as the legitimate successor of the Prophet and then count his descendants down to the Twelfth Imam.) The Sunnites accept the first four caliphs, the Rightly

**Guided Caliphs** (*Rashidun*), as the legitimate successors of the Prophet. To qualify for the position, a caliph must be an adult Muslim man, sane, of sound mind and body, free, and a just person. He receives his power by nomination and election, but there is no indication as to the number of electors and their qualifications. **Abu Bakr** was elected by a council of **Companions** of the Prophet, **'Umar** was nominated by the dying **Abu Bakr**, and **'Uthman** was appointed as a compromise candidate. In the beginning of the **Umayyad caliphate**, election was usually symbolic and, in fact, the dynastic principle predominated. Some scholars, like **Ibn Taymiyyah**, claimed that

> with the orthodox caliphs ended the era of prophetic succession. After the prophetic caliphate there is mulk [kingship]—no longer the ideal form of government—but sovereignty belongs to the shari'ah. That is cooperation of the **ulama** and the umara (amirs). (Qamaruddin Khan, *The Political Thought of Ibn Taymiyyah*. Islamabad, Research Institute, 1973)

But most Sunni schools accept the legitimacy of the **'Abbasid Caliphate**, which ended with the **Mongol** conquest of **Baghdad**. The **Umayyad** caliphate continued in Spain during the early 'Abbasid period, and some accept the continuation of the 'Abbasid caliphate in Egypt until the capture of Egypt by the **Ottomans** in 1517. Ottoman rulers in the 19th century claimed that the last Abbasid caliph in **Cairo** had appointed Sultan Selim as his successor and, therefore, the caliphate continued until the defeat of the **Ottoman empire** in the First World War. It was abolished by the government of Kemal Atatürk in 1924.

Although usually respected and revered, the caliph held no power to make pronouncements on dogma. When this was done in the middle of the ninth century, the jurists, **ulama**, reacted by proclaiming **Islamic law** complete and prohibited any legislation as sinful innovation (**bid'ah**). The caliphate was often weak, and during the **Buyid** occupation of Baghdad in the ninth and 10th centuries, it suffered the humiliation of being dominated by Shi'ite rulers. Eventually, the caliphs accepted the political realities and recognized secular rulers, the **sultans**, giving them the authority to legislate provided they did not infringe on the Islamic law (shar'iah). Some present-day **Islamist** and fundamentalist groups want to restore the caliphate and establish an Islamic state in which the shari'a is the sole law.

**CALIPHATE, CLASSICAL CONCEPT OF.** Political philosophers have agreed that the caliphate is necessary and prescribed by the **Shari'ah** and that the **caliph** (or **imam**) has to possess the necessary qualifications as well as the requisite military power. He is elected by those with the "power of loosening and binding" (**ahl al-hall wa 'l-aqd**), but there is no agreement as to the number of electors required. After accepting homage (**bay'ah**), the caliph assumes a contractual obligation to perform a number of functions and Muslims are bound to obey him. According to **al-Ghazali**, even if he is a tyrant he should be obeyed to prevent civil war. As to the qualifications of the caliph, al-**Mawardi** gave the following: justice (*adalah*); knowledge ( *ilm*) of Islamic law and theology; sound sight, hearing, and speech; sound limbs; administrative competence (**kifayah**); courage and energy in war; and descent from Muhammad's tribe, the **Quraysh**. The functions of the caliph include: upholding religious orthodoxy, enforcing judicial verdicts, maintaining security, applying the Koranic penalties for offenses, garrisoning the frontiers, waging holy war against infidels, collecting legally authorized tributes (*fay'*) and alms taxes (**zakat**), paying salaries and expenses, appointing trust-worthy officials, and personally supervising governmental and religious business (*Nazihat al-Muluk*, by Ghazali, tr. by F.R.C. Bagley). Al-Ghazali gives six physical and four moral qualifications: The former are: adulthood, sanity, liberty, male sex, Qurayshite descent, and sound sight and hearing. The latter are: military prowess, administrative competence, piety, and knowledge (Ibid. liii). *See also* AL-BAQILLANI, ABU BAKR MUHAMMAD; IBN TAYMIYYAH, AHMAD.

When the **'Abbasid** caliphs lost most of their power to the **sultans,** the concept of legitimate leadership was extended to include the "pious sultan," who was to have the same qualifications and functions. **Islamists,** who want to establish an Islamic state, envision the **Amir** as conforming to this model.

**Twelver Shi'ites** consider the imams to be the only legitimate leaders of the community but accept the leadership of the highest clergy as the representatives of the **Hidden Imam**. Under Ayatollah **Khomeyni** the concept of the guardianship of the highest Islamic jurist (vilayat-i faqih) was promulgated, establishing a theocratic state in Iran. See also 'ABBASID CALIPHATE; FATIMIDS; ISLAMIC REPUBLIC OF IRAN; UMAYYAD CALIPHATE.

**CALL.** *See* DA'WAH.

**CALL TO PRAYER.** "Adhan." The call to the five daily ritual **prayers** by the **muezzin** (*mu 'adhdhin*) from the door of a **mosque** or from the top of a minaret of a large mosque. The muezzin chants the following formula with some repetitions: "Allah is most great. There is no god but Allah. I testify that Muhammad is the apostle of Allah. Come to prayer. Come to salvation. Allah is most great. There is no god but Allah." At the morning prayer the words "prayer is better than sleep" are added. The Shi'ites add the words "come to the best work!" And also "I testify that Ali is the wali (protected friend) of Allah." **Bilal**, a black slave, was the first mu'ezzin.

**CAMEL, BATTLE OF.** Named after the camel on which 'A'ishah sat, during a battle in 656 between 'Ali, the fourth **caliph**, and a force led by 'A'isha, daughter of Muhammad, al-**Zubayr** ibn al-'Awwam, a cousin of the Prophet, and **Talhah** ibn 'Ubaydullah. The coalition was defeated and Zubayr and Talhah were killed; 'A'ishah was captured and returned to Medinah and restricted to honorable confinement.

**CANON LAW.** *See* ISLAMIC LAW.

**CARRION.** It is unlawful to eat "dead" meat. *See* FOOD.

**CHADOR.** "Tent," or portable dwelling. Also the traditional garment covering a woman from head to toe, which in some Muslim countries is obligatory. Wearing of the chador, also called chatri or burqa, was prohibited in Turkey in the 1920s and in Iran in 1936, and it was discouraged in other Islamic countries, but agitation by radical elements has contributed to forcing a partial or complete reintroduction, as for example in Afghanistan. *See also* VEIL.

**CHILDREN.** According to tradition, infants who die have a natural inclination to Islam and are therefore saved from hellfire. At the birth of a child a **mulla** recites the **adhan** into the right ear of the child. The child is given a name on the seventh day of birth; and when it is able to talk, it is taught the **basmala**. Children are exempt from **fasting** during **Ramadhan**; they are not to be killed in battle.

**CHISHTIS (CHISHTIYYAH).** A **Sufi** order, named after Khwajah Mu'in al-Din Chishti. He was born in 1142 in Chisht, a village in Herat province of present-day Afghanistan and died in Ajmir, India, in 1236. The Chishtiyyah Order has most of its followers in India, where the tomb of the saint in Ajmir is an important place of **pilgrimage**. Originally the Chishtiyyah were a puritanical and pacific order, emphasizing the oneness of God (*wahdat al-wujud*) and invoking the names of God in their **dhikrs**. There were also other **pirs** with the name Chishti.

**CHRISTIANS.** Islam recognizes Christianity as a revealed religion and Christ as a prophet, but not the son of God, and objects to what it considers accretions, such as the trinity, and the refusal of Christians to accept Islam. The Koran (5:14) says: "From those too who call themselves Christians, We did take a covenant, but they forgot a good part of the Message that was sent them: so we stirred up enmity and hatred between the one and the other, to the **Day of Judgment**. And soon will Allah show them what it is they have done." The Koran accepts the immaculate conception of Christ by **Mary** (Maryam). **Christians** (as well as **Jews**, and other monotheists) are "**Peoples of the Book**" (*ahl al-kitab*), with a revealed scripture, and they are not to be forcefully converted to Islam. A Muslim man can marry a Christian woman. In Islamic states they are protected in their lives and religion, but pay a special tax (**jizyah**) and were usually exempt from military service. In the **Ottoman empire dhimmis**, as they were called, were organized in autonomous communities (**millets**), and led by their patriarchs, bishops, or rabbis.

**CIRCUMCISION.** "Khitan." Practiced traditionally by the Arabs even before Islam, male and female circumcision is not mentioned in the Koran. The times for circumcision vary from the seventh or 40th day after birth to between seven or 12 years of age. The **Malikite** school considers khitan meritorious, but not obligatory, whereas the **Shafi'ites** requires it for both males and females. Circumcision was also considered a remedy for various diseases prevalent in the desert environment of Arabia. In parts of Africa, Southeast Asia, and the Arabian Peninsula female circumcision is still practiced.

**CIVIL LAW.** *See* QANUN.

**COFFEE.** A beverage that was introduced into Yemen from Abyssinia and came to be widely accepted in the **Ottoman empire**. It was first the beverage of **Sufi** fraternities who drank it as part of their ceremonies and eventually coffee houses (*buyut al-qahwah*) were established in major towns and even in **Istanbul**, in spite of **ulama** opposition. When the Ottoman army had to withdraw from Vienna after an unsuccessful siege in 1529, they left some sacks of coffee beans behind. The Viennese experimented for a while and eventually they brewed a decent cup, which could be relished in the proliferating cafés of the city. Today, to offer coffee is part of Middle Eastern hospitality, but from Iran eastward, tea is the most common beverage.

**COMMANDER OF THE FAITHFUL.** *See* AMIR AL-MU'MININ.

**COMMENTARIES ON THE KORAN.** *See* EXEGESIS.

**COMPANIONS.** "Ashab" or "Sahaba." The Companions of the Prophet were close associates of the Prophet, most importantly the first four **caliphs**, the contemporaries, and those who had seen him. Eventually anyone who had seen the Prophet or came in contact with him came to be called a Companion; according to some biographers there were as many as 144,000. They are the transmitters of **hadith** who recorded the actions and saying of the Prophet, constituting together with the Koran the core of **Islamic law**. Works listing the names and biographies of Companions were compiled to serve the task of evaluating the quality of a hadith. Shi'ites (except for **Zaydis**) do not recognize the legitimacy of the first three caliphs and accept only hadith from the Prophet and the **imams**.

**CONCEALMENT.** In Shi'ite Islam, discretion or concealment (*taqiyya*, or *kitman*) is permitted under compulsion, threat, or fear of injury. The Koran allows denial of faith as long as one keeps believing in one's heart. **Surah** 16:106 says: "Any one who, after accepting faith in Allah, utters unbelief, except under compulsion, his heart remaining firm in faith—but such as open their breasts to unbelief on them is wrath from Allah, and theirs will be a threatful chastisment." Therefore, it is permissible also for Sunnis. *See also* GHAYBAH.

**CONCUBINAGE.** As a result of war, **slavery** existed and **women** were part of the spoils. Concubinage was inferred as permissible on the basis of Surah 23:5-6 "(The **Believers**) who guard their modesty, except with those joined to them in the **marriage** bond, or (the captives) whom their right hands possess, they are free from blame."

Modernists maintain that it is forbidden because of the injunction that all males and females must be married. *See also* ʿABD.

**CONVERSION.** One converts to Islam by testifying before two witnesses that one believes there is only one God and that Muhammad is the Prophet of God. Orthodox consensus requires that there are six conditions before reciting the word "**kalima**:" It must be repeated aloud, it must be perfectly understood, it must be believed in the heart, it must be professed until death, it must be recited correctly, and it must be professed and declared without hesitation. The convert is then committed to the obligations of performing the five daily **prayers**, paying the poor tax (**zakat**), **fasting** during **Ramadhan**, and performing **pilgrimage** to Mecca if he can afford it during his lifetime. The convert no longer pays the poll tax (**jizyah**); he usually adopts a Muslim name and enjoys all the privileges granted to Muslims.

A **hadith**, narrated by Abu Saʿid, says:

> If any person embraces Islam sincerely, then Allah shall forgive all his past sins, and after that starts the settlement of accounts: the reward of his good deeds will be ten times to seven hundred times for each good deed and a bad deed will be recorded as it is. (Bukhari, II, 32)

**COVENANT.** "Mithaq." The dominant opinion of commentators accept that there is an implied covenant (*mithaq*), taken from the posterity of **Adam**, that is, humanity, which creates a spiritual obligation of obedience to God's commands. It is based on a Koranic passage (7:172) that says, "When the Lord drew forth from the children of Adam—from their loins—their descendants, and made them testify concerning themselves (saying) 'Am I not your Lord (who cherishes and sustains you)?' They said 'Yeah! We do testify! (This) lest ye should say on the **Day of Judgment**: Of this we were never mindful.'" According to tradition the souls of Muhammad, **Noah**, **Abraham**, **Moses**, and **Jesus** were present at the Covenant.

A document called the "Covenant of ʿUmar," in fact, an abstract of many letters, gives a description of the situation at about 800 CE of the "**Peoples of the Book**." They are monotheists with a scripture and prophets recognized in Islam, like Moses and Jesus, and are in possession of a protective treaty, **dhimma**, which guards their personal safety, property, and religion. They were relegated to second-class status and under obligation to pay a poll tax (**jizyah**).

Dhimmis were not to be ostentatious in performing their religious performances, not to be armed. In most parts of the Islamic world, non-Muslims now have equal citizen rights.

**CREATEDNESS OF THE KORAN.** Controversy on this issue led to acceptance in Sunni Islam that the Koran is uncreated and existed with God. *See also* ASH'ARITES; IBN HANBAL; MU'TAZILITES.

**CREATION.** Muslims believe that God created **heaven** and earth and all that is between them. According to **Traditions,** God created the earth on Saturday, the hills on Sunday, the trees on Monday, all unpleasant things on Tuesday, the light on Wednesday, the beasts on Thursday, and **Adam**, the last of Creation, after the afternoon prayer on Friday. Surah 41:9 reads: "Say: is it that ye deny Him who created the earth in two days? And do ye join equals with Him? He is the Lord of (all) the worlds. He set on the (earth), mountains standing firm, high above it, and bestowed blessings on the earth, and measured therein its sustenance in four days, alike for (all) who ask. Then He turned to the sky, and it had been (as) smoke: He said to it and to the earth: come ye together, willing or unwillingly. So, He completed them as seven firmaments in two days, and He assigned to each heaven its duty and commands."

**CREED.** "Aqida," pl. "Aqa'id." Belief in God, **angels, prophets, scripture,** and the **Day of Judgment**. Muslims believe in one God, Allah, who is the Creator, Supreme Power, Judge, and Avenger but is also the Compassionate and Merciful One. **Angels** are Allah's messengers and, like humans, his creatures and servants. Surah 4:136 says: "O ye who believe! Believe in Allah and His **Messenger,** and the scripture which He hath sent to His Messenger and the scripture which He sent those before (him). Any who denieth Allah, His Angels, His Books, His Messengers, and the Day of Judgment, hath gone far, far astray."

**CRUCIFIXION.** The Koran denies the crucifixion of **Jesus:** "That they said (in boast), 'We killed Christ Jesus the son of **Mary,** the **Messenger** of Allah;' But they killed him not, nor crucified him. Only a likeness of that was shown to them" (4:157).

## -D-

**DAHNA.** The ten days of **Muharram**, during which Shi'ites mourn the assassination of **Husayn.**

**DAHRI.** "Atheists;" or materialists, characterized in the Koran as saying: "What is there but our life in this world? We shall die and we live, and nothing but time (*dahr*) can destroy us" (14:24).

**DA'I.** Literally, "he who summons." The term was applied to Shi'ite missionaries or propagandists during the latter part of the **Umayyad** and **Fatimid** periods. The **Druzes** are named after Darazi, one of their da'is.

**DAJJAL, AL-.** "False." A false messiah or Antichrist who will come before the appearance of Christ to lead people into disbelief. Sunnis believe that **Jesus** will destroy the Dajjal and the **Day of Judgment** will follow. Shi'ites link his appearance as a precursor to the **Mahdi**. The Dajjal was described as a plump, one-eyed man with a ruddy face and curly hair and the letters k-f-r (kufr—unbelief) on his forehead.

**DAMASCUS (DIMASHQ).** Said to be the oldest inhabited settlement in the world and at present the capital of Syria. It was the seat of the **Umayyad caliphate** from 661 to 750. The city surrendered in 635 to Muslim forces under **Khalid ibn al-Walid** after a six-months' siege. Khalid promised the residents protection (**dhimma**) and security for their lives, property, churches, and the walls of the city upon payment of a poll tax (**jizyah**). According to some sources, the Great Mosque of Damascus was for a time shared with the **Christians**. **Mu'awiyah** was appointed governor of the city and in 661 he became the first Umayyad ruler at Damascus. With the establishment of the **'Abbasid caliphate**, **Baghdad** became the capital of the Islamic empire. Some Sunnis rank the city as the fourth holiest after Mecca, Medina, and **Jerusalem**.

**DANCING.** Dancing in Islam is a reprehensible act, *makruh*, but not expressly forbidden, *harram*, in the Koran or Traditions (**Sunnah**). In many countries dancers are a caste, usually young men, who are often not native to the area in which they perform. Tribal and folk dances are performed in public on special occasions, such as weddings, when the participating men dance to the accompaniment of drums and various instruments. Female belly dancers perform in metropolitan areas in many parts of the Arab world. Only among the most Westernized do men and **women** dance together. Mystical orders perform ecstatic dances as part of their rituals. Radical **Islamists** or neo-fundamentalists, such as the **Taliban** rulers of Afghanistan, forbid dancing and music. This prohibition is deduced from a passage in the Koran that says: "Nor walk on the earth with insolence" (17:37). *See also* MEVLEVIS.

**DAR AL-HARB.** The "abode of war" is that part of the world in which Islam does not prevail. It can also be applied to a Muslim state that is under non-Muslim control, if the edicts of Islam are suppressed. After the First World War, a movement in India proclaimed the state *dar al-harb* and some 50,000 Muslims made the **"hijra"** (emigration) to Afghanistan, which was an independent Muslim state. **Muslim modernists** do not accept this classification by the jurists, saying it has no basis in the Koran or **Traditions**. *See also* DAR AL-ISLAM and DAR AL-SULH.

**DAR AL-HIKMAH.** "House of Wisdom." A foundation established by the **Fatimid** ruler of **Cairo**, al-**Hakim**, in 1005 for the purpose of teaching and propagating Shi'ite doctrine. The "*dar al-hikmah*," also called "*dar al- Ilm*," House of Wisdom and Science, included a library with some 6,500 volumes, lecture rooms, and rooms for translation of manuscripts. It was connected to the palace. In addition to the Islamic sciences, its curriculum included astronomy and medicine. The library was headed by the Fatimid chief missionary (*da i al-du at*). The institution survived until the conquest of Egypt by the **Ayyubids** under **Salah al-Din** (Saladin, 1169-1193).

**DAR AL-ISLAM.** The "abode of Islam" defines that part of the world ruled by a Muslim and where the edicts of Islam have been fully promulgated. Non-Muslim monotheists were protected subjects (**dhimmis**), but not full citizens. They were protected in life and property and permitted to worship God according to their own customs. Certain restrictions applied to them, as for example the paying of a poll tax (**jizyah**). The Dar al-Islam is territorial, whereas the community of **believers** (**ummah**) is universal; it includes individual Muslims wherever they may be.

**DAR AL-SULH.** The "abode of truce" is that part of the world that is in a treaty or tributary relationship with the Islamic world (**dar al-islam**). It originally applied to areas whose inhabitants had voluntarily surrendered to Muslim conquerors on the condition that they be allowed to retain their lands and practice their religion and customs. This category is not accepted by some schools, but **Muslim modernists** would apply this term to the entire non-Muslim world, implying an end to the obligation of perpetual warfare against the "abode of war" (**dar al-harb**).

**DARAZI, MUHAMMAD IBN ISMA'IL AL-** (d. 1019). **Isma'ili** missionary whose followers came to be known as the **Druzes**. Darazi (d. 1019) was a Persian who entered the service of the **Fatimid Caliph al-Hakim** in 1017. He started preaching that the divine spirit, transmitted through 'Ali and the **imams,** had become incarnated in al-Hakim. This caused a public riot and Darazi had to flee from **Cairo** to Syria where he was killed in battle (or was assassinated at the instigation of a rival). His teachings found acceptance in the mountains of Lebanon, leading to the creation of the Druze community.

**DARWISH (DERVISH).** A **Sufi,** religious mendicant, the Persian equivalent of **faqir.**

**DAUGHTERS OF THE PROPHET.** *See* FATIMAH; RUQAYYAH; UMM KULTHUM; ZAYNAB B. KHADIJAH.

**DA'WAH.** "Call." Appeal to conversion by missionary activity rather than by **jihad.** In modern times, **Islamists** call Muslims to accept their **fundamentalist** beliefs based on the Koran and early **Traditions.**

**DA'WAH, HIZB AL-.** "Islamic Call" Party founded in Iraq in 1969 in response to government suppression of Shi'ite political activity. A religious procession in 1974 resulted in political demonstrations, which were severely suppressed and five of its leaders were executed. Da'wah militants tried to assassinate Tariq Aziz, the deputy premier, and, with the start of the Iran-Iraq War in September 1980, they began a campaign of sabotage and armed attacks. Eventually Saddam Husayn's government was able to destroy them as a fighting force.

**DAY OF JUDGMENT.** Muslims believe in the resurrection of the body and the Day of Judgment when God will reward or punish men according to their deeds. Surah 18:49 states: "And the book (of deeds) will be placed (before you); and thou wilt see the sinful in great terror because of what is (recorded) therein; they will say, 'Ah! woe to us! What a book is this! It leaves out nothing small or great, but takes account thereof!' They will find all that they did, placed before them: and not one will thy Lord treat with injustice." There will be a number of signs preceding the **Last Day**: The appearance of the Antichrist (**Dajjal**), the decline of faith on earth, tumults and sedition, commotion in heaven and earth, the sun and moon will be darkened, and Christ will appear to fight the Dajjal.

**DEATH.** Burial ceremonies include the ritual washing of the corpse, which is then enveloped in a shroud (Shi'ites permit a coffin); a ritual prayer is said for the dead, and the funeral service is performed. The corpse is buried with the head in the direction of Mecca. The Koran says: "Every soul shall have a taste of death: and only on the **Day of Judgment** shall you be paid your recompense. Only he who is saved far from the fire and admitted to the garden will have succeeded: For the life of this world is but goods and chattels of deception" (3:185). The Koran is silent on funerals, but according to **Tradition**, the dead are to be handled with respect, buried swiftly, and mourners are to refrain from excessive lamentation. According to a **hadith** transmitted by **Abu Bakr**, Muhammad said that "No prophet was ever buried except in the place where he died." Therefore, a grave was dug at the spot where Muhammad died (*Muwatta*, 16.10.27 ).

**DELUGE.** "Tufan." The story of the deluge is given in the Koran: "We, when the water (of **Noah**'s Flood) overflowed beyond its limits, carried you (mankind) in the floating (Ark), that We might make it a reminder unto you, and that ears (that should hear the tale and) retain its memory should bear its (lesson) in remembrance" (69:11-12).

**DEOBAND.** An Islamic college (*dar al-ulum*, later **madrasah**), founded in 1866 in Deoband, a town near Delhi, India, by the **Hanafi** mystic Muhammad 'Abid. The Deobandis are strictly orthodox but accept the dogma of **intercession** and permit **prayer** at the tombs of prophets and saints to appeal for God's assistance. They are traditionists and insist on following the law (**taqlid**) and reject independent reasoning (**ijtihad**) of the jurists to interpret **Islamic law**. The Deobandis were hostile to the modernism of **Aligarh** and, because many graduates supported the Shah **Waliallah** reformist movement, they were called **Wahhabis** by their critics. They founded a political party, the Jami'at-i 'Ulama-i Islami, in Pakistan which established hundreds of madrasahs in the tribal belt of the Afghan frontier. The students of these schools, many of them orphans, were provided free education, food, shelter, and military training during the war against the communist government of Afghanistan in the 1980s. These students later became the core of the **Taliban** forces that conquered most of Afghanistan. The Jami'at-i 'Ulama-i Islami and their Taliban brothers have now won followers in neighboring countries who are spreading their **Islamist** ideology.

**DEPUTATIONS, YEAR OF** (630-631). After the fall of Mecca and the conversion of the **Quraysh**, tribal deputations from all over Arabia came to Medina to submit to the new predominant power and accept Islam.

**DEVIL.** The devil, *Iblis*, or *Shaytan*, in Islam is a fallen **angel** who refused to bow before **Adam** when commanded by God. For this he was expelled from **heaven** until the **Day of Judgment**, to be the "Adversary," tempting human beings to sin. *See also* IBLIS.

**DEVOTEES OF THE PEOPLE.** *See* FIDA'IYAN-KHALQ.

**DHIKR (ZIKR).** "Remembrance." In **Sufism**, dhikr, is the remembrance of God, his commands, death, and the **Day of Judgment.** It is a recitation of a litany consisting of the glorification of the names of God, selections from the Koran, and special **prayers**. Dhikr may be performed in private meetings or mosques and involve rhythmical body movements and breathing techniques, while uttering the various formulas and names. Dhikr Allah, the Remembrance of Allah, is a striving for union with God, performed under the supervision of a master; it also includes dancing in which the practitioners reach a state of ecstasy. Dhikr can be performed in a loud voice, or silently, when a person shuts his eyes, closes his lips, and fixes his attention on inhalations and exhalations, thinking *la ilaha* "there is no god" at exhalation and *illa Allah* "except God" at inhalation.

**DHIMMI (ZIMMI).** *See* PEOPLES OF THE BOOK.

**DIN.** "Religion." Muslim theologians distinguish between religious belief (**iman**) and acts of worship and religious duties (**'ibadat**), all of which are included in the term *din*, religion.

**DINAR.** From *denarius* (Greek/Latin). The gold coin of the early Islamic period, weighing until the 10th century 4.25 grams. It was divided into 10 **dirhams** and later into 12. First copied by the **Umayyads**, the dinar was struck as an Islamic coin during the reign of Caliph 'Abd al-Malik (d. 705). The dinar is still the name of some Middle Eastern currencies.

**DIRHAM.** Monetary unit named from *drachme*, the currency still in use in Greece. It is a silver coin, originally of 2.97 grams (or 50 grains of barley with cut ends), later of varying value. Ten or 12 dirhams equalled the value of one gold **dinar**.

**DITCH, BATTLE OF THE.** *See* TRENCH, BATTLE OF THE.

**DIVORCE.** "Talaq." According to tradition, "with Allah the most detestable of all things is divorce" (Bukhari, VIII, 63). The various orthodox schools and **sects** disagree on the details, but generally a man can divorce his wife by repudiation, repeating three times "I divorce thee," and a woman has the right to divorce under certain conditions that require dissolution by a court. If a husband is missing for four years, a woman can sue for divorce according to the **Malikite** and **Shafi'ite** schools of jurisprudence; Shi'ites agree with this period, but the **Hanbali** school favors a waiting period of 100 years, making divorce in that case impossible. Divorce by mutual consent is immediately effective, and courts accept such grounds against the husband as impotence, **apostasy**, madness, dangerous illness, among others. After repudiation, the man must wait for three menstrual periods to be certain that there is no pregnancy before the divorce is legal. During this waiting period, *idda*, the man can relent his decision and his **marriage** remains legal. If a man divorces his wife three times, she has to be married to another man, before he can marry her again: "So, if a husband divorces his wife (irrevocably) he cannot, after that, remarry her until after she has married another husband and he has divorced her" (2:230). Part, or all, of the **dowry** must be given the woman upon divorce, and **women** get custody of the children, in some cases until the age of seven and in others until puberty. In a number of countries in the Islamic world divorce is possible only in a court of law, Turkey and Albania, for example; but in most countries personal law is still under the jurisdiction of **Islamic law**, modified more or less to give women protection from certain abuses. Divorce is relatively rare, because marriage is often  concluded within a clan; cousin marriages are frequent, and alliances are formed through marriage. Therefore, a certain stigma attaches to divorce. *See also* LI'AN.

**DIWAN.** A word adopted from Persian for an anthology, financial register, or government department. The French word *douane*, customs, is derived from it. Under **'Umar** I (634-644), it was a register for the distribution of state income in the form of pensions paid to members of the early community according to closeness to the Prophet and early conversion to Islam. The allocations were as follows:

| | | |
|---|---|---:|
| Those who fought at Badr | (Dirhams) | 5,000 |
| Those who were Muslims before al-Hudaybiyah | | 4,000 |
| Muslims in the reign of Abu Bakr | | 3,000 |
| Fighters at Qadisiyyah and in Syria | | 2,000 |
| Muslims after Qadisiyyah and the Yarmuk | | 1,000 |
| Various minor groups | | 500, 300, 250, 200 |
| Muhammad's widows | | 10,000 |
| Wives of men at Badr | | 500 |
| Wives of next three classes | | 400, 300, 200 |
| Wives of others and children | | 100 |
| (Watt, 1974, 49) | | |

Under the **'Abbasids**, the term diwan was used for government departments, and, under the **Ottomans**, it designated a council of court and eventually an administrative department of government. In literature it means a collection of poetry of an individual.

**DIYAH.** "Blood Money." In pre-Islamic Arabia, blood money was to be paid in retaliation for injury or death. The principle became part of **Islamic law** as **retaliation** (*qisas*). The Koran says: "Life for life, eye for eye, nose for nose, ear for ear, tooth for tooth, and wounds equal for equal." But if any one remits the retaliation by way of charity, it is an act of atonement for himself (5:45). This amounted to a recommendation for mercy, which did not exist in pre-Islamic times. Blood money is still demanded, especially in tribal areas of some parts of the Middle East. During their occupation of India, the British Indian government codified tribal law, including the blood money to be paid for injury or death. Examples include: The compensation for murder of a man was 3,000 rupees, half that amount for a woman; accidental death of a man was 1,550 and half for a woman. Cutting off a hand or a foot demanded a compensation of 1,000 rupees; breaking a hand or a foot or rendering an eye blind cost 500 rupees. Facial wounds demanded greater compensation than wounds covered by clothing. In a tribal war, peace was possible when the casualties were equal; otherwise, the party with a blood debt had to pay the difference. Retaliation for murder could be forgiven if the next of kin agreed to accept blood money. This was often seen as dishonorable; therefore, blood money had to be paid secretly, and, if refused, the next of kin was permitted to kill the culprit. The amount of blood money also varied with the importance or wealth of a person, tribe, or community. In Afghanistan, the state had extended its jurisdiction into criminal law, but the present **Taliban** regime has enforced qisas, as a public event.

Some Shi'ite schools counted six types of compensation: either 100 camels, 200 cows, 1,000 sheep, 100 two-piece garments, 100 **dinars** in gold coinage, or 10,000 in silver. The diyah for a **dhimmi** or **slave** was less.

**DOME OF THE ROCK.** A shrine that stands on the rock of the Temple Mount in **Jerusalem** from which the Prophet ascended to heaven in the **Nocturnal Journey** (*mi'raj*). The sanctuary was built during the period of the **Umayyad Caliph 'Abd al-Malik** in the late seventh century and is part of the **Al-Aqsa** Mosque complex.

**DÖNME.** The followers of Shabbetai Tsevi (1626-1676), who proclaimed himself the messiah of Muslims and **Jews**. He went to **Istanbul** in 1666 to overthrow the **Ottoman sultan** and inaugurate his kingdom. Forced to convert, he adopted the name Mehmet 'Aziz Effendi, and many of his followers also adopted Islam, but they seemed to have secretly continued practicing Judaic rites. Their descendants were largely concentrated in Salonika, which had the largest Jewish community in the **Ottoman empire**. There is no evidence that they maintained their beliefs and practices. Many of the Young Turk leadership who fought **'Abd al-Hamid**'s absolutism were Dönmes, but they had assimilated with the Muslim Turks and rejected a return to Judaism.

**DOWRY.** *See* MARRIAGE and MAHR.

**DRUZES.** A religious community with a worldwide population of about one million, found primarily in Lebanon, Syria, and in smaller numbers in the Israeli-occupied Golan Heights. The Druzes are named after one of their early missionaries, **Muhammad al-Darazi** (d. 1019), who converted the early communities on Mount Lebanon where most of them are still settled. They call themselves Unitarians (*muwahhidun*). The religion recognizes the **Fatimid** caliph **al-Hakim ibn Amr Allah** (r. 996-1021) at **Cairo** as a manifestation of God. Other missionaries included **Hamza ibn 'Ali** who announced that al-Hakim had temporarily withdrawn from the world when he mysteriously disappeared. Baha al-Din al-Samuki (al-Muqtana?) succeeded after the disappearance of Hamza; he codified the new religious teachings in the six books known as *al-hikma al-sharifa* or *rasa'il al-hikma* (The noble knowledge). The Druze faith is exclusive and secret; therefore, accounts of their rites are unclear. They do not accept two of the **Five Pillars of Islam**: **fasting** during **Ramadhan** and **pilgrimage** to Mecca. In 1043 the "door of conversion" was shut and no new converts were admitted. Although monotheistic like their Islamic origins, Druzes believe in the transmigration of souls, prohibit **polygamy**, temporary **marriage** (*mut'ah*), practice dissimulation (**taqiyya**), and are known for their strict morality. They are divided into the "sages, *'uqqal*," who are initiated into the faith and are the leaders of the community, and the "ignorant, *juhhal*". Although at times considered heretics, they are accepted as **Peoples of the Book** by Muslims. In Syria and Lebanon they have supported Arab nationalism, Palestinian rights, and profess themselves to be Muslims. Druzes in Israel have served in the Israeli military. During their invasion of Lebanon, Israel missed a chance to win the support of the Druzes and Shi'ites in Lebanon.

**DU'A.** "Call." The individual, informal **prayer** that is offered on special occasions, as for example, at the birth of a child or visit to a grave. The Prophet described du'a as "the kernel of worship." According to a **hadith** transmitted by **'A'isha**, the Prophet abstained from performing the du'a because of fear that the people would do the same and it would become obligatory (**fardh**). (Muwatta, 9.8.32.)

-E-

**EDEN.** "'Adn." Paradise. *See* HEAVEN.

**EDUCATION.** Classical Islamic education consisted of two levels: elementary (kuttab or maktab) and secondary (**madrasah,** "a place to study"). Education was informal, conducted at home, in a **mosque,** or in a building attached to a mosque. Elementary schools taught reading and writing skills; the textbook was usually the Koran but writing was practiced from secular works, so as not "to dishonor the sacred book." Teaching included the **prayers** and rituals and simple arithmetic. Some students memorized the Koran and thus earned the title **hafiz.** In non-Arab areas, some Turkish and Persian poetry was usually memorized. Secondary education included the study of the Islamic sciences, the Koran, **hadith,** jurisprudence (**fiqh**), and ancillary fields, such as **Arabic** grammar, philology, etc. Philosophy or the rational sciences were not included, and medical studies were by apprenticeship. Students attended the lectures of a teacher who would certify that a certain course had been completed, and he could then teach the subjects he had mastered. He would have a license (*ijaza*) to answer juridical questions. It would read like the following:

> The most eminent, unique, learned lawyer . . . read with me the whole of *al-muhadh'dhab* in law with all proofs from the Koran and Sunna and, where there are no proofs, the meaning, correct reading, and implications of the text, the agreement, the adductions and extension of it so that he is worthy that advantage may be taken of him and may be handed on by his teaching. (Szylowicz, 61 )

Graduates would travel to various cities to collect hadith and to study with noted Islamic scholars. Higher education produced the **ulama,** Islamic functionaries, the judges, **muftis,** etc. A distinction was usually made between the Islamic and foreign sciences. The former consisted of Koranic exegesis ( *ilm al-tafsir*), the science of hadith ( *ilm al-hadith*), jurisprudence (*fiqh*), scholastic theology (*ilm al-kalam*), grammar (*nahw*), lexicography (*lugha*), rhetoric (*bayan*), and literature (*adab*). Foreign sciences included philosophy (*falsafa*), geometry (*handasa*), astronomy (*ilm al-nujum*), music (*musiqi*), medicine (*tibb*), and magic and alchemy (*al-sihr wa 'l-kimiya*).

Special buildings for education, madrasahs, were first erected in the 10th century; they included living quarters for students.

Education was free and informal. The first Islamic universities were the Fatimid Al-**Azhar** at **Cairo** (972) and the 11th century Sunni **Nizamiyyah** at **Baghdad**, which became models for educational institutions elsewhere. During the **Ottoman** period the classical system continued and reached its height by the 17th century. The medieval secretary (*katib*) needed, in addition to a natural gift for expression and a general knowledge of everything (*adab*), eight kinds of tools: "1) a thorough knowledge of Arabic, accidence and syntax, and 2) of lexicography and the distinctions between eloquent, obsolete, unusual, etc., expression; 3) an acquaintance with proverbs and *ayyam* (war) tales of the Arabs and with other incidents current among the people; 4) a wide reading in prose and poetry of early authors and a memorization of a great deal of their work; 5) a solid knowledge of political theory and the science of administration; 6) knowledge by heart of the Koran and 7) of the traditions issuing from the Prophet; and 8) command of prosody and poetics" (Von Grunebaum, 1956, 253-254).

Modern reforms in the Islamic world began as a reaction to Western imperialism. Muhammad Ali of Egypt and Ottoman **sultans** felt a need to modernize their armies and began to introduce reforms along European lines. In the early 19th century foreign teachers were imported and native students were first sent abroad to study in Europe. Military academies and medical and administrative colleges were established, resulting in the beginning of a dual educational system: the traditional and the modified modern system, which trained different elites competing for government positions. This educational dualism exists in most parts of the Islamic world to the present.

In the 18th and 19th centuries missionary schools were established in the Middle East that provided education in Arabic and local languages. Some of their textbooks and curricula were gradually adopted by local schools. American missionaries founded the Syrian Protestant College in 1866, which eventually became the American University of Beirut, and French Jesuits founded the St. Joseph University in Beirut in 1875. Other European powers established schools. Local authorities established schools and teachers colleges (*dar al-ulum*), but by 1939 there were fewer than a dozen colleges in the Middle East. Only after the Second World War did higher education, patterned after Western models, greatly expand. By the 1980s there existed about 100 colleges and universities in the Middle East.

**ELIJAH MUHAMMAD** (1897-1975). Leader of the **Nation of Islam,** which transformed itself into one of the most powerful Afro-American organizations. Born Paul Robert Poole in 1897 in Georgia, Elijah Muhammad moved to Detroit in the 1920s where he came under the influence of Fard Muhammad and succeeded him in the leadership of the early Muslim community. He successfully reformed thousands of Afro-Americans in the ghettos and won notable converts in the persons of Malcolm X and Muhammad Ali. Wallace (Warith) Deen Muhammad, son of Elijah, assumed leadership of the movement and made the transition to orthodox Islam, calling the movement "The American Muslim Mission."

**EMIGRANTS.** See MUHAJIRUN.

**EMIGRATION.** "Hijrah." The flight of Muhammad from Mecca to Yathrib (Medina) on July 16, 622. It marks the date from which Muslims count the Islamic **calendar.**

**EMIR.** See AMIR.

**ENJOINING THE GOOD AND FORBIDDING EVIL.** One of the obligations of every Muslim, based on the Koran (22:41, *al-amr bi 'l-ma 'rufwa an'n-nahy 'an al-munkar*), which became institutionalized in offices like the **Muhtasib.** In some Arab Gulf countries this institution is still practiced and in the newly established "Islamic states," such as Iran and Afghanistan, a ministry employs guardians who ensure that **women** are properly attired, people attend ritual prayers, and public morality is enforced. *See also* ISLAMIC REPUBLIC OF IRAN.

**ERBAKAN, NECMETTIN (ARBAKAN NAJM AL-DIN,** 1926- ). Turkish **Islamist** and prime minister (1996-1997), who led his Refa party to victory in municipal elections in 1994-1995 and won the position of prime minister in parliamentary elections in 1996. Because of his policy of re-Islamization, which went counter to **Kemalist** principles, he was forced to resign.

**EVIL EYE.** It is the common belief that certain individuals have the power of looking at people, animals, and inanimate objects to cause harm. It has existed since pre-Islamic times and the Koran warns to seek refuge "from the mischief of the envious one as he practices envy" (113:5). Talismans and images with an eye are used to ward off the evil eye. An **amulet** may read as follows: "O God, tear forth his eye who would curse therewith, snatch the evil thought from his forehead and the word from his tongue. Let his mischief fall upon his own head, upon his goods and on those most dear to him" (Canon Sell, 64). According to a **hadith** the Prophet permitted the use of talismans to ward off the evil eye (Muwatta, 50.2.3).

**EXCOMMUNICATION.** "Takfir." Modern radical revivalist movements that urge excommunication of Muslims who have been lax in the performance of the ritual obligations of Islam and have accepted a measure of secularism. They oppose Muslim rulers as **apostates** because they have permitted Islamic lands to fall into a condition of **jahiliyyah** (ignorance of the true mission of Islam). The movement calls for the establishment of an Islamic state in which all manifestations of Westernization are abolished and the **Islamic law (Shari'ah)** is the only law of the state. It tries to mobilize the masses to accept its purist concept of Islam and proclaims holy war (**jihad**) against its enemies. Some **Islamist** movements like **Takfir wa al-Hijrah** demand that the **believers** make the migration to an Islamic community or state. In their radicalism and **fundamentalist** beliefs they resemble the **Kharijites,** who proclaimed that all Muslims who did not make the migration (**hijrah**) to their camp were infidels.

**EXEGESIS OF THE KORAN.** "Tafsir." Abdallah ibn al-'Abbas (d. 686) is said to have been the first to write a commentary on the Koran, but Muhammad already provided verbal explanations. As time passed, difficulties had to be explained and eventually commentaries examined philological, historical, and juridical questions. In addition to literal interpretation, some Shi'ites (and **Sufis**) focused on an allegorical interpretation. An extensive Sunni tafsir literature exists, produced by such scholars as Al-**Tabari** (d. 923), Fakhr al-Din Radhi (**Razi,** d. 1209), Ibn Kathir (d. 1373), Al-**Suyuti** (d. 1505), and the Shi'ite al-Tabarsi (d. 1153). Modern authors who published exegetic works are Muhammad **Abduh** (d. 1905), Rashid **Ridha** (d. 1935), and the Islamist Sayyid **Qutb** (d. 1966). Recent authors have tried to show that even the most recent technical innovations were predicted in the Koran.

# -F-

**FADLALLAH, MUHAMMAD HUSAYN (FAZL ALLAH,** 1935- ).
Shi'ite religious scholar and spiritual leader of the Lebanese **Hizbullah** (Party of God). Born of a Lebanese family in **Najaf,** Iraq, he was educated at the Shi'ite university at Najaf. He came to Lebanon in 1966 and established cultural youth clubs, free clinics, and community centers to attract the youth to religion. He was inspired by the Islamic revolution in Iran and in 1982 became Hizbullah's spiritual leader. He participated in a council that drafted the Lebanese Islamic Constitution, but he had reservations about giving autocratic power to an individual. Nor did he want to reestablish the **caliphate.** While not participating in any violent actions, he did not rule out the possibility of violent revolution and was suspected of supporting military activities.

**FAITH, ARTICLES OF.** "Iman." The doctrine in Islam that includes: the belief in God (Allah), **angels, prophets, scripture,** the last day, and the Divine Decree. A passage in the Koran says: "O ye who believe! Believe in Allah and his **Messenger,** and the scripture which He hath sent to his messenger and the **scripture** which he sent to those before (him). Any who denieth Allah, His angels, His books, His messengers, and the **Day of Judgment,** hath gone far, far astray"(4:136).

Belief in Allah is expressed in the shahada, or profession of faith: "There is no god, but Allah" (*la ilaha illah llah*). Allah has 99 "beautiful names," most important of which are *al-rahman al-rahim*, "The Compassionate, The Merciful." All **Surahs** of the Koran, except the ninth begin with the **basmalah,** "In the name of Allah, Most Compassionate, Most Merciful." Allah has neither beginning nor end, he has knowledge of all things, he is almighty, he has hearing, sight , and speech. Most important is the oneness of God; it is a great offense to give partners to God. God is eternal and everything from the seven heavens downward is created by him. God reveals himself in the Koran and to understand Him, one must ponder the Koran in its entirety. He is utterly transcendent and yet nearer to man "than his jugular vein."

Angels have specific activities: They praise Allah, and are His messengers, guardians of the Koran in **heaven,** guardians of man, recorders of man's deeds, receivers and punishers of sinners, and guardians of **hell.** They are made of fire. The **jinn** are like man, good and evil, and will be judged like man. They differ from man in that they are created of fire rather than clay. The rebellious jinn are **devils** (*shaytan*), and the fallen angel (**Iblis**) is their chief.

Great Prophets include: **Adam**, God's chosen one; **Noah**, God's preacher; **Abraham**, God's friend; **Moses**, speaker with God; **Jesus**, God's spirit; and Muhammad, God's messenger and last prophet. Muhammad is merely a man and has no superhuman powers. The Shi'ites believe that he had a special **barakah**, and that his descendants, the **imams**, were infallible.

Scripture (*kitab*) comes to man through his messengers. The Koran is the word of Allah to Muhammad; Moses received the Torah (*tawrat*), David the Psalms (*zabur*), and Jesus the Gospel (*injil*).

Resurrection and the Last Day are preceded by a number of signs: The appearance of the **Dajjal**, Antichrist; the decline of faith on earth; tumults and sedition; commotion in heaven and earth; the sun and moon will be darkened, leading to the second advent of Christ. The archangel **Israfil** will sound the trumpet, and Allah will appear. Then follows the weighing of the deeds at which the archangels **Gabriel** and Michael will preside, and everyone crosses a narrow bridge from which the infidels will fall into hell. The only sure way of going to paradise is to be a **martyr** for the faith. Others must repent and believe and be righteous in their actions.

The fifth article of belief is the "divine decree and predestination" (*al-qadha wa 'l-qadar*), which recognizes the absolute power of God but does not exclude a measure of free will. Al-'**Ashari** has tried to resolve this question with the mechanism of "acquisition" (**kasb**), according to which God creates the actions of his creatures, but they are then acquired by the individual. *See also* PILLARS OF FAITH.

**FAKIR.** *See* FAQIR.

**FANA'.** "Extinction," when everything will perish on the **Last Day**. In Islamic mysticism it is the last stage of the journey, the passing away from the self, the union with God. *See also* SUFISM.

**FAQIH.** A jurist (pl. *fuqaha*), interpreter of Islamic jurisprudence (**fiqh**). The *fuqaha* function as **judges**, jurisconsults, and **muftis**, giving legal opinions (**fatwas**). The institution of the faqih became important in the 10th century, but it lost its importance in parts of the Islamic world where the traditional system was supplanted by European codes and courts. In the **Islamic Republic of Iran** the principle of the guardianship of the jurisprudent (**vilayat-i faqih**) over all spiritual and temporal authority of the state was proclaimed by Ayatollah **Khomeyni.**

**FAQIR.** "Poor." In **Arabic** it is the designation of a religious menticant, also called **darwish.** In the West the term has been applied to a public performer or magician.

**FARABI, ABU NASR MUHAMMAD AL-** (ca. 870-950). One of the greatest Muslim philosophers who published in the fields of logic, politics, ethics, natural science, psychology, mathematics, music theory, and other subjects. He was of Turkic origin, born in Farab, Turkestan, and studied in **Baghdad** and other cities of the Islamic world and finally settled in Aleppo, Syria. He tried to create a synthesis of Platonic and Aristotelian philosophy and **Sufism** and aimed at the reconciliation of philosophy and religion. Called the "Second Master" (next to Aristotle) his major works include the *risalat fusus al-hikam* (Epistles on the gems of wisdom), *risalat fi ara ahl al-madinah al-fadhila* (Opinions of the people of the model state), *al-siyasah al-madaniyah* (Political economy), among others. **Ibn Khallikan** writes of him that

> he excelled all the people of Islamism and surpassed them by his real acquirements in that science; he explained its obscurities, revealed its mysteries, facilitated its comprehension and furnished every requisite for its intelligence, in works remarkable for precision and style and subtlety of elucidation. (III, 308)

**FARAJ, ABU AL-.** *See* ISFAHANI, ABU AL-FARAJ AL-.

**FARAZDAK, HAMMAM IBN GHALIB AL-** (640-728). A native of **Basra** and one of the great poets of the **Umayyad** period. A contemporary of **al-Jarir** and **al-Akhtal**, he was a bitter rival of Jarir and tended to be supported by Akhtal. He was described as "reckless, dissolute, and thoroughly unprincipled" and apart from his gift of vituperation "there was nothing in him to admire" (Nicholson, 243). His panegyrics of the 'Alids and lampoons of important individuals resulted in his banishment and flight. Farazdak tricked Nawar, his cousin, into **marriage** only to **divorce** her soon afterward, a step he bitterly regretted, and "the repentance of Farazdak" became a proverbial expression.

**FARDH (FARZ).** A religious duty (pl. *fara'idh*) enjoined in the Koran, the performance of which is incumbent on all Muslims. Fulfillment of such a duty is rewarded and neglect is punished. In the **Hanafi** school a distinction is made between fardh as a "duty on the basis of cogent arguments" and **wajib**, necessity, on the grounds of probability. *Fardh al- ʿayn* is an individual duty, binding on all adult Muslims, such as **prayer** and **fasting**. *Fardh al-kifaya* is a communal duty, binding on the Muslims as a group, which is fulfilled if a sufficient number performs it, for example, **pilgrimage**, visiting the sick, and returning a greeting.

**FAREWELL PILGRIMAGE.** *See* PILGRIMAGRE, FAREWELL.

**FASTING.** Daylight fasting (*sawm*) is obligatory during the 30 days of the month of **Ramadhan**. The Koran enjoins: "[Fasting] for a fixed number of days; but if any of you is ill, or on a journey, the prescribed number (should be made up) from days later"(S.2:184). Voluntary fasting is recommended on various occasions, especially on the 10th of the month of **Muharram**, the month of Shaʿban, on alternate days, etc. According to a **Tradition**, the Prophet said: "Every good act that a man does shall receive from ten to seven hundred rewards, but the rewards for fasting are beyond bounds, for fasting is for God alone, and He will give the rewards." Fasting includes refraining from drink or sexual intercourse, the inhaling of tobacco smoke, and swallowing of spittle that could have been ejected. It begins at daybreak when one can distinguish a white from a black thread. The end of fasting is generally announced by the firing of a cannon.

**FATALISM.** Impressed by the omnipotence of God, al-**Ashʿari** rejected free will and all causality as limiting the powers of God, hence contributing to a tendency of fatalism in Islam. He quotes the Koranic saying: "Nothing will happen to us except what Allah has decreed for us"(9:51). But another **Surah** says: "Whatever good (O man!) happens to thee is from Allah; but whatever evil happens to thee, is from thyself" (4:79). Al-Ashʿari reconciled this with the doctrine of acquisition (**kasb**). *See also* KISMET and PREDESTINATION.

**FATIHA.** The "Opener," or first **Surah** in the Koran, is part of the Muslim **prayer**. It can be translated as follows: "In the name of Allah, Most Gracious, Most Merciful, Praise be to Allah the Cherisher and Sustainer of Worlds: Most Gracious Most Merciful; Master of the **Day of Judgment**. Thee do we worship, and Thine aid we seek. Show us the straight way, the way of those on whom Thou hast bestowed Thy Grace, those whose (portion) is not wrath. And who go not astray" (1:1-7).

**FATIMAH.** Daughter of the Prophet and **Khadijah** who married Muhammad's cousin **'Ali ibn Abi Talib** at Medinah in 624. Since he was poor, Ali gave his coat of mail (or a sheepskin) as a dower; it was worth four **dirhams**. They had two daughters and three sons, **Hasan, Husayn,** and Muhsin; the latter died in infancy. Their descendants through Husayn are revered by **Twelver Shi'ites** as infallible **imams,** whereas Sunnites count 'Ali as the fourth of the **Rightly Guided Caliphs.** For Muslims, Fatimah is the example of the virtuous woman; she died in about 633 at age 29. The founders of the **Fatimid** caliphate claimed descent from 'Ali and Fatimah.

**FATIMIDS** (909-1171). An **Isma'ili** Shi'ite dynasty, claiming 'Alid descent through **Fatimah,** which ruled Egypt and parts of North Africa, as well as Syria, the Holy Places of Mecca and Medina, and for a short time even extended their power to **Baghdad** and Sicily. Sunni opponents deny their link to Fatimah and call them 'Ubaydi-yun, the descendants of 'Ubaydallah al-Mahdi (909-34), the first of the Fatimid rulers. They established their capital at **Cairo** in 969 and founded **Al-Azhar** University as an Isma'ili research center. Under the rule of **al-Hakim** (996-1021), the Fatimids sent their missionaries to distant lands. One of them, Muhammad **al-Darazi,** converted the **Druze** community in Lebanon that still carries his name. A Persian Isma'ili, **Hasan al-Sabbah,** visited Cairo and then established a base in **Alamut,** founding the Order of the Assassins. The Fatimids were finally replaced by the Sunni **Ayyubid** dynasty of **Salah al-Din** (Saladin).

The Fatimid dynasty included the following members:

| 909 | Ubaydullah al-Mahdi | 975 | Al-'Aziz |
| 934 | Al-Qaim | 996 | Al-Hakim |
| 946 | Al-Mansur | 1021 | Al-Zahir |
| 953 | Al-Muizz | 1036 | Al-Mustansir |

| 1094  Al-Must'ali | 1149  Al-Zafir |
|---|---|
| 1101  Al-Amir | 1154  Al-Fa'iz |
| 1130  Al-Hafiz | 1160-71  Al-Adid |

**FATWA (FETVA).** A formal legal opinion by a **mufti**, or canon lawyer, in answer to a question of a judge, *kadhi*, or private individual. Fatwas cover legal theory, theology, philosophy, and creeds, which are not included in **fiqh** books. Fatwas are informational and advisory and generally not enforced by the state. Until the 19th century, the **Ottoman empire** maintained a hierarchy of muftis, headed by the grand mufti of **Istanbul** who held the title of **Shaykh al-Islam**. He had the function of certifying the legality of secular laws, *qanun*, issued by the government and appointed muftis to the major towns in the empire. **Muhammad Abduh**, grand mufti of Egypt issued a number of liberal fatwas, and the grand mufti of **Jerusalem**, **Amin al-Husayni** (b. 1890s) issued fatwas opposing the British mandatory power over Egypt and the Zionist movement. In most Muslim countries, fatwas were relegated to personal law, such as **marriage** and **divorce**, when the state extended its jurisdiction in criminal and civil law. Famous fatwas from Shi'ite Iran were the prohibition of smoking, which led to the "Tobacco Revolt" of 1891, and the fatwa issued by Ayatollah **Khomeyni** in 1989, calling for the execution of Salman Rushdie for blasphemy as a result of publication of the book *The Satanic Verses.*

**FAY'.** *See* GHANIMA.

**FESTIVALS.** Islamic festivals include Shi'ite and Sunni observances of **'Ashura'**, the 10th of the month of **Muharram**, the Prophet's Birthday ('id al-milad al-nabi), the Breaking of the Fast (**'id al fitr**) in the month of **Ramadhan**, Muhammad's Ascension (laylat al-mi'raj), Fasting (**sawm**) during the month of Ramadhan, and the Feast of Sacrifice (**'id al-adha**). Muslims exchange presents and give gifts to their servants and the poor.

**FIDA'I (pl. FIDA'IYAN).** One who sacrifices his life, a guerrilla soldier. Various religio-political movements adopted this designation, as for example the devotees of the grand master of the **Assassins**, the **Fida'iyan-i Islam**, and the **Fida'iyan-i khalq** of Iran. In the 1950s the term designated guerrilla fighters against the British forces in

Egypt and later Palestinian guerilla fighters who conducted raids against Israel.

**FIDA'IYAN-I ISLAM (FIDA'IYYUN).** A Shi'ite religio-political movement founded in 1945 in Tehran by Sayyid Mujtaba Navvab Safavi (1923-1956). The Fida'iyan (Devotees) were a radical, movement that wanted to establish a government guided by **Islamic law**. Navvab had the support of Ayatollah Abu al-Qasim Kashani in his fight against the Iranian monarchy. The Feda'iyan assassinated high government officials, including the court minister, Abd al-Husayn Hazhir, and the prime minister, Husayn 'Ali Razmara, both in 1949. During the National Front government of Muhammad Musaddiq (1951-1953), Navvab broke with Kashani and many of the Feda'iyan were arrested. In 1955 Navvab and three of his comrades were sentenced to death and executed. The movement supported the Palestinian Arabs and opposed Iranian membership in the **Baghdad** Pact. It favored an increased role for the **ulama** in the state, Islamic **education**, and the introduction of Koranic punishments, including mutilation for theft and stoning for **adultery**. The movement considered the **Baha'is** heretics. Its violence led to increased suppression by the state, but many of its demands were realized after the Islamic Revolution of 1979. *See also* ISLAMIC REPUBLIC OF IRAN.

**FIDA'IYAN-I KHALQ.** "Devotees of the People." A movement of university students and intellectuals founded in 1970 by the merger of two leftist groups, which started guerrilla activities against the regime of the shah of Iran. They attacked official buildings, especially police stations and banks, trying to rouse the Iranian people to revolt. After the Iranian revolution of 1979, they cooperated with the **Khomeyni** regime, but they were eventually destroyed by the revolutionary government and disbanded in 1987. *See also* ISLAMIC REPUBLIC OF IRAN.

**FINES.** *See* DIYAH.

**FIQH.** "Understanding; jurisprudence." The science of knowledge and interpretation of law, both civil and religious; it encompasses all branches of Islamic studies. It is the core of Islamic **education**. The books of fiqh provide details about the obligations of the individual in **Islamic law (Shari'a)**. The faqih (pl. *fuqaha*), canonic lawyer, must be a learned and pious scholar. He interprets the law on the basis of the **Koran** and the Traditions (**Sunnah**), and depending on the school, on consensus of the scholars (**ijma**) and analogical reasoning (**qiyas**). The *kitab al-fiqh al-akbar* (Book of great fiqh) by **Abu Hanifa**, founder of the **Hanafite school of law**, is a treatise on theology rather than on fiqh. Sunnis recognize four schools, or rites of fiqh, and Shi'ites adhere to the Ja'farite school, named after the sixth **imam**, Ja'far al-Sadiq (d.765). Shi'ites also permit **ijtihad**, independent reasoning and judgment by learned theologians (**mujtahids**).

**FITNAH.** "Trial, revolt." In Islamic history, a period of dissension or civil war.

**FIVE PILLARS OF ISLAM (ARKAN AL-DIN).** The belief and actions required of a Muslim can be summarized as follows: profession of faith, performance of ritual **prayers**, **almsgiving**, **fasting**, and **pilgrimage**. The profession of faith (**shahada**) consists in testifying that "there is no god but Allah and that Muhammad is the **Messenger** of Allah." To become a Muslim six conditions must be fulfilled: The shahda must be repeated aloud, it must be perfectly understood, it must be believed in the heart, it must be professed until death, it must be recited correctly, and it must be declared without any hesitation.

The ritual prayer (salat) is performed five times during a day: at dawn before sunrise, after the sun passes the zenith, in the late afternoon, immediately after sunset, and between sunset and midnight. Prayers can be performed anywhere, but on **Fridays** preferably in a **mosque**. The person turns in the direction of Mecca (**qiblah**), and performs the bowings (ruku') on a mat or carpet. **Women** pray at home or in a separate area of a mosque.

Fasting (sawm) during the day is obligatory in the month of **Ramadhan**. It begins on the eve of Ramadhan, that is, on the 29th of the month of Sha'ban and ends at sunset on the last day of Ramadhan. **Believers** are to avoid all sins, abstain from eating, drinking, or having sexual intercourse.

Almsgiving (**zakat**) is enjoined to help the poor, destitute, those in debt, travelers, those who are fighting in the cause of Islam, **slaves** to buy their freedom, and for those who perform a public service. It is a tax on savings, not on income. In many countries it has become a voluntary tax.

Pilgrimage (**hajj**) is an obligation only for those who can afford the expense. It can also be performed for a person by a substitute.

Some consider holy war (**jihad**), as a sixth pillar of Islam, which is satisfied if a "sufficient number" of Muslims perform it, but most schools now justify it only as a war of defense against aggression.

**FIVE PRINCIPAL ACTS IN ISLAMIC LAW.** Human acts are divided into five categories (*al-ahkam al-khamsa*) as follows: (1) Obligatory (**fardh** or **wajib**) duties whose performance is rewarded and whose omission is punished. This includes such acts as **prayer**, **almsgiving**, **fasting**, etc. (2) Recommended (sunnah, masnun, **mandub**, and mustahabb) whose performance is rewarded but whose omission is not punished, for example, supererogatory prayers. (3) Indifferent (**mubah** or ja'iz), actions whose performance or omission is neither rewarded nor punished. (4) Reprehensible (**makruh**), actions that are not forbidden and will not be punished, as for example certain dietary rules. (5) Forbidden (**haram**), actions that are forbidden and punishable, for example, **adultery**.

**FIVERS.** Shi'ite followers of the Fifth **Imam** Zayd ibn 'Ali (ca. 698-740). *See* ZAYDIS.

**FOOD.** Food must be lawful (**halal**) and earned lawfully. No animal, except fish and locust, is lawful unless it is ritually slaughtered by cutting the throat. Meat of all quadrupeds that seize their prey with their teeth and all birds that seize it with their talons is forbidden. The Koran enjoins **believers**: "O ye who believe! Eat of the good things that We have provided for you. And be grateful to Allah, if it is Him ye worship. He hath only forbidden you dead meat, and blood, and the flesh of swine, and that on which any other name hath been invoked besides that of Allah. But if one is forced by necessity, without willful disobedience, nor transgressing due limits—then is he guiltless" (2:172-173). The prohibition of wine also includes all intoxicating beverages as well as opium and similar drugs. Muslims are permitted to eat in the company of **Peoples of the Book** (ahl al-kitab), which includes **Christians** and **Jews**; the golden rule is to eat in moderation. *See also* ALCOHOL.

**FORGIVENESS.** God is Merciful, He forgave **Adam** and Eve the sin of eating from the forbidden tree and he wants men to also be forgiving. He never forgives **shirk**, idolatry, and those who disbelieve or commit repeated acts of unbelief. The Koran says: "Those who disbelieve and hinder (men) from the path of Allah, then die disbelieving—Allah will not forgive them" (47:34). According to one **hadith** "anyone who does **wudhu'**, and makes sure he does it correctly, and then does the **prayer**, will be forgiven everything that he does between then and the time when he prays the next prayer" (Muwatta, 2.6.30).

**FORNICATION.** "Zina." Fornication is prohibited in Islam. Like **adultery**, it must be established by proof provided by four witnesses or by confession. The confession can be retracted. The punishment for fornication is one hundred lashes, which should be given with moderation and not aimed at the same location. The law is based on the passage in the Koran that says: "The woman and the man guilty of fornication—flog each of them with a hundred stripes: let not compassion move you in their case, in a matter prescribed by Allah, if ye believe in Allah and the **Last Day**: and let a party of the **believers** witness their punishment"(24:2). Any person who wrongfully accuses a chaste woman of fornication must be punished with 80 lashes. *See also* ADULTERY.

**FREE WILL.** *See* ASH'ARITES; FATALISM; KISMET; PREDESTINATION.

**FRIDAY.** "Jum'ah." Friday, rather than Sunday, is the Islamic holiday. It is the Day of the Assembly when Muslims are enjoined to attend midday **prayer** at a congregational **mosque**. A preacher **(khatib)** delivers a sermon **(khutbah)** in which the name of the legitimate ruler is invoked. Therefore, the khutbah had also political importance as, at the outbreak of a rebellion, the name of the ruler is omitted, or a challenger has his name proclaimed. In some countries, as for example in Saudi Arabia and Afghanistan, attendance at the Friday prayer is obligatory, and no one may loiter in the streets or conduct business at prayer times. According to tradition, Friday is the day on which the **creation** was finished, or when **Adam** entered paradise and was again expelled, Muhammad came to Medina on a Friday, and Friday will also be the **Day of Judgment**.

**FUNDAMENTALISM.** Fundamentalism is a term that was originally applied to conservative Protestant movements in the United States. It has subsequently been applied to any major religion with tendencies like authoritarianism, messianic spirit, subordination of secular politics to religious beliefs, belief in the infallibility of holy scripture, charismatic leadership, and enforced moralism. The designation "fundamentalist" has been applied to puritanical Islamic revivalist movements such as those promoted by Muhammad ibn Abd al-**Wahhab** (1703-1792), **Hassan al-Banna** (1906-1949), Sayyid Abu'l A'la **Maududi** (1903-1979), Ayatollah Ruhollah **Khomayni** (1900-1989), and Mulla Muhammad **'Umar** (b. ca. 1960) of Afghanistan. Supporters of Muslim "fundamentalism" have come to be called **Islamists**.

**FUNERALS.** *See* DEATH.

**FURQAN.** "Criterion." A name for the Koran, because it divides or makes a distinction between good and evil. Surah 25, named al-Furqan, states that God's highest gift to humanity is the criterion for judgment between right and wrong, and those who do not heed it will be "full of woe on the **Day of Judgment**."

**FUSTAT.** *See* CAIRO.

## -G-

**GABRIEL (JIBRIL).** The Archangel Gabriel is believed to be the **angel** of **revelation**. He led **Adam** from paradise to Mount **Arafat** where he found Eve, and he accompanied the Prophet on Muhammad's **Nocturnal Ascension** (*lailat al-mi'raj*) from **Jerusalem** to **heaven**. He (and the angel Michael) will supervise the weighing of good and bad deeds. The Koran is believed to have been communicated to Muhammad by means of the angel Gabriel.

**GAMA'AT AL-ISLAMIYYAH (JAMA'AT).** An **Islamist** movement founded with the support of the Egyptian government of President Anwar Sadat in 1971 as a check on the Marxist movements in schools and universities. The Islamists grew in numbers and in 1978 gained 60 percent representation in the university student union election. As a result of the Egypt-Israeli peace treaty of 1979, they turned against the government. They applauded the assassination of Sadat in 1981 and continued their activities against the regime of

Husni Mubarak. Under the guidance of **Shaykh Muhammad Abu Nasr**, they set up a network of private **mosques** that provided, among other things, health, welfare, and educational facilities. Aug-mented by Egyptians, who had been fighting the communist government in Afghanistan, the movement eventually tried to desta-bilize the country by attacking foreign tourists and the economic benefits derived from tourism. The government responded with mass arrests, but it has not succeeded in crushing them.

**GAMBLING.** Gambling is forbidden in Islam. **Surah** (2:219) says: "They ask thee concerning wine and gambling. Say: 'In them is great sin, and some profit for men; But the sin is greater than the profit.'" Or another (5:90) that says: "O ye who believe! Intoxicants and gambling, sacrificing to stones, and (divination by) arrows, are an abomination - of Satan's handiwork: eschew such (abomination) that ye may prosper." According to tradition, the evidence of a gambler is not admissible in a court of law. However, in most Muslim countries various types of gambling have been tolerated. The **Taliban** regime in Afghanistan, which desires to establish an Islamic state in which the **Shari'iah** is enforced, has forbidden all games of chance and betting on pigeons and quails, among others.

**GARRISON TOWNS.** *See* AMSAR.

**GENGHIS (CHINGIZ) KHAN.** *See* MONGOL INVASION.

**GENIE.** In **Arabic** "jinn;" they are said to be spirits who enjoy a certain amount of free will and will therefore be called to account on the **Day of Judgment**. They are created of fire, unlike man who is created of clay, as stated in the Koran: "We created man from sounding clay, from mud molded into shape; and the jinn race, We had created before, from the fire of a scorching wind" (15:26-27).

**GHADIR AL-KHUMM.** A small lake near Mecca where, according to Shi'ite belief, Muhammad had promised 'Ali "as much power as he held." This was taken as 'Ali's appointment to succeed the Prophet after his death. Shi'ites celebrate this event each year in the Islamic month of Dhu 'l-Hijjah.

**GHANIMA.** "Booty" in the early wars of conquest, which consisted of movable property. The soldiers traditionally received four-fifths and one-fifth went to Muhammad, the **caliphs**, or, later, the heads of state to defray the costs of government. When an area, or city, surrendered peacefully (*sulhan*), no plunder was permitted and the new subjects paid only their taxes but, if an enemy resisted until defeat (*anwatan*), leaving the decision to God, even the population could become *ghanima*. The spoils of war acquired without fighting, called *fay'*, are divided into five equal shares: for God (missionary activity), for the Prophet's institutional use, for kinsmen in need, and for orphans, the needy, and wayfarers. The Koran says: "And know that out of all the booty that ye may acquire (in war), a fifth share is assigned to Allah and to the **Messenger**, and to near relatives, orphans, the needy, and the wayfarer" (8:41). Subsequently, the state took four-fifths of the booty and provided pensions to the soldiers.

**GHASSANIDS.** An Arab kingdom of Monophysite **Christians** in the Syrian desert, which served as an auxiliary force of the Byzantine empire. It acted as a buffer state to protect the Byzantines from Bedouin raids. The state came to an end when Persia captured **Jerusalem** and **Damascus** in 613/14. The Ghassanids fought on the side of the Byzantines at the battle of **Yarmuk** (636). **Labid**, one of the seven poets of the **Mu'allaqat**, flourished in the Ghassanid state.

**GHAYBAH.** "Occultation." Meaning also absence or concealment. The **Twelver Shi'ites** believe that the twelfth **imam**, Muhammad al-**Muntazar** (878), did not die but went into concealment to guide the community and to reappear as the messianic **mahdi**. He then will restore justice and equity after a long reign of injustice and oppression. There are two periods of ghaybah, the lesser and the greater concealment. The lesser occultation lasted for 60 years during which the Imam guided the community through four intermediaries. After the death of the fourth intermediary in 940, the greater occultation began, which has lasted until the present. In the absence of the imam, the **ulama** is collectively responsible for the interpretation of shi'ite doctrine.

**GHAZALI, ABU HAMID MUHAMMAD AL-** (1058-1111). Jurist of the **Shafi'ite** school, philosopher, theologian, mystic, and one of the most influential thinkers. He was born at Tus, near the present city of **Mashhad** in eastern Iran and educated in Nishapur. Still a child, he memorized the Koran and subsequently studied the **Traditions** and **Islamic law** under the famous theologian **Imam** al-Haramayn al-

**Juwayni**. In his works *al-munqidh min al-dalal* (Deliverance from error) and *tahafut al-falasifa* (The incoherence of the philosophers), al-Ghazali attacked the philosophers and **batinites** who advocated an esoteric, inner *(batin)*, interpretation of the Koran. He served as chief teacher at the **Nizamiyyah** in **Baghdad** from 1091-1095, when he suffered a spiritual crisis and dedicated himself to **Sufism**. Ghazali said about his conversion: "This did not come about by systematic demonstration or marshaled argument, but by a light which God Most High cast into my breast" *(Deliverance from Error*, from Denny, p. 193). He traveled widely and eventually settled down to compile his encyclopedic work, *ihya ulum al-din* (The revival of the religious sciences). He was instrumental in reconciling Sufism with orthodox Islam.

**GHAZI**. Originally "one who conducts a raid" *(ghazw)*; also a veteran, or hero, in a religious war. Ghazi became a title for a victorious leader in war, but it was also adopted as a family name. It is synonymous with **mujahid,** a fighter in a holy war **(jihad)**.

**GHAZNAVID DYNASTY** (977-1186). A dynasty of Turkic origin founded by Nasir al-Dawla Sebuktegin (r. 977-997) with its administrative capital in the city of Ghazni. During the reign of Sultan Mahmud of Ghazni (r. 998-1030) the Ghaznavid empire extended from the Tigris River to the Ganges River and from the Indian Ocean to the Amu Darya. **Ibn Khallikan** puts it thus: "he [Mahmud] continued to pursue his conquests in India, and he carried his arms into regions which the banner of Islamism had never yet reached, and where no surat nor verse of the Koran had ever been chanted before" (III,332). Ghazni experienced a period of enormous wealth, most of it amassed by Mahmud during some 17 campaigns into the Indian subcontinent. He attracted some 400 scholars and poets to his capital, including Abu al-Qasim Firdawsi and Abu Rayhan al-**Biruni**. Although the dynasty counted 19 rulers over a period of two centuries, the empire began to disintegrate soon after Mahmud's death.

**GHAZWAH (GHAZW)**. "Raiding." Originally a Bedouin raid for booty in which camels were used to cross the desert and horses for a lightning attack on the object of prey. After Islam it designated forays into hostile territory, the no-man's land between the **dar al-Islam** and the **dar al-harb**. The word razzia in some Western languages is derived from ghazwah, meaning a police raid. One **Umayyad** poet says about ghazwah: "Our business is to make raids on the enemy, on our neighbour and on our own brother, in case we find none to raid but a brother" (Hitti, 25).

**GHUSL.** Ritual washing, which is obligatory before **prayer** after a major impurity caused by orgasm, menstruation, childbirth, etc. It is also obligatory on Fridays, and during the two festivals, the 'Id al-Fitr and the 'Id al-Adha. A pilgrim to Mecca will perform ghusl before entering the sanctuary. It requires that the entire body be washed, beginning with the head, the body, starting from the right side, and finally cleaning the interstices of the body. The water must moisten every part of the body. If there is no water, a symbolic washing (**tayammum**) can be made by wiping with sand the face and arms. *See also* ABLUTION.

**GOD.** *See* ALLAH.

**GUARDIANS COUNCIL.** As a result of the Iranian revolution in 1979, a council of 12 guardians was set up to pass on the legitimacy of all laws and regulations of government. Six of the members were jurists, appointed by Ayatollah **Khomeyni** and, subsequently, by a Leadership Council, and six were nominated by the head of the judiciary and approved by parliament for a six-year term. Together they certified that all parliamentary legislation was in conformance with the Iranian constitution and **Islamic law**. In the parliamentary elections of 1992 and 1999, large numbers of reformist candidates were disqualified. *See also* ISLAMIC REPUBLIC OF IRAN.

**-H-**

**HABIBAH.** Wife of Muhammad. *See* UMM HABIBAH.

**HADD (HUDUD).** Mandatory punishments imposed in classical **Islamic law** in cases of **adultery, fornication,** and false accusation of adultery, as well as for theft, highway robbery, **apostasy,** and drunkenness. For these offenses, punishments are fixed and details as to their execution specified in the **Traditions** or the Koran. For example, the punishment for adultery is stoning or one hundred lashes for fornication, but strict rules of evidence require either a confession from the culprits or the testimony of four male witnesses. The amputation of a hand for theft requires either a confession or two witnesses. Furthermore, the stolen property has to exceed a certain value and the theft must not be between relations. The punishment for wine drinking, not mentioned in the Koran, is 80 lashes according to the Traditions. Because of the severity of hadd punishments, they have not been imposed in most parts of the Islamic world. Only in Saudi Arabia and in the self-described "Islamic States"of Pakistan and Sudan, and most recently in Afghanistan, have **hadd** punishments been exacted.

**HADITH.** It has been defined as "the story of a particular occurrence, and Sunnah as the rule of law deduced from it. It is the practice of the Prophet, his model behavior" (Fyzee, 19). Next to the Koran, the **Sunnah**, Tradition, is the second source of the doctrine and ritual of Islam, political theory, and **Islamic law**. During the life of the Prophet Muhammad, stories as to his actions and sayings were collected by eyewitnesses and then told to others. These stories were transmitted by word of mouth. A chain (**isnad**) of credible transmitters was produced that preceded the text (**matn**), which went somewhat like this: "Muhammad bin Abdullah said to us that Abu Khalid said that Abu Malik said that Sa'd bin 'Ubaydah said that the son of 'Umar said that the Prophet said 'Islam is founded on five things . . .'" The hadith were eventually recorded in writing and a science of hadith criticism classified hadiths as: Sound (*sahih*), if there was no weak link in the chain of transmitters and corroboration existed from others; Good (*hasan*), if there was a weak link or the character of the transmitter was doubtful; and Weak (*dha'if*), if there were several weak links or the narrator was unreliable. This resulted in the production of biographical works that described the qualifications and character of transmitters.

Six major collections of hadith were eventually compiled, which were accepted by all Sunni Muslims. They included those of al-**Bukhari** (d. 870), **Muslim ibn al-Hajjaj** (d. 875), **Ibn Maja** al-Qazvini (d. 886), Abu Dawud al-**Sijistani** (d. 888), Abu 'Isa al-**Tirmidhi** (d. 892), and Abu Abd al-Rahman al-**Nasa'i** (d. 915). The collections of al-Bukhari and al-Muslim are considered the most reliable. **Malik ibn Anas** (d.795) and **Ahmad ibn Hanbal** (d.855), the founders of two orthodox schools, also produced collections. One collection by Husayn al-**Baghawi**, titled *Mishkat al-Masabih*

(Niche for lights), has been translated into English by James Robson and published in four volumes. In addition to the hadith of the Prophet, Shi'ites also use those of their **imams**. Authoritative collections of the Shi'ites were compiled by Muhammad ibn Yaqub al-**Kulayni** (d. 939), **Ibn Babawayhi** (Babuya, d. 991), and Muhammad al-**Tusi** (d. 1067).

The hadith provide a wealth of information regarding the personality, family, and activities of the Prophet and serve as examples of emulation, providing guidance in matters of jurisprudence not stipulated in the Koran. A Western, revisionist, school supports the Goldzieher-Schacht thesis that the majority of hadith were "back-projected as the sayings of the Prophet only at a much later date." Another view holds that the Sunnah is actually the local practice of the people of Medina; but this interpretation is not likely to find acceptance in the Islamic world.

**HAFIZ.** One who has memorized (*hafaza*) the Koran. As part of Islamic **education**, many scholars memorized the Koran in early youth, before progressing to higher education. One who has memorized the Koran carries the title "Hafiz." Encouragement for this task is found in the Koran, which says: "And we have indeed made the Qur'an easy to understand and remember" (S.54:17). Hafiz and Hafiza are also male and female names.

**HAFSAH.** Daughter of Caliph 'Umar ibn al-Khattab and one of the wives of Muhammad. Hafsah was the widow of a man killed in the battle of **Badr**. Her father offered her to **Uthman** and **Abu Bakr** in **marriage** and when they did not accept her, the Prophet married her, giving her a **dowry** of 400 **dirhams**. According to tradition, Hafsah was the custodian of the first official copy of the Koran, compiled during the **caliphate** of Abu Bakr (632-634) or 'Umar. The version accepted as definitive by Muslims was, however, compiled during the period of Caliph 'Uthman (644-656). Hafsah enjoyed considerable influence and recorded a number of **Traditions** of the Prophet. She died at age 60 in 667.

**HAGAR (HAJAR).** Concubine of **Abraham** and mother of his son Isma'il. When Abraham built the foundation of the **Ka'bah**, he abandoned Hagar and Isma'il in the desert, and their search for water led them to discover the **Zamzam** well. According to tradition, Hagar's descendants were the Arabs and Sarah's the **Jews**.

**HAJJ.** *See* PILGRIMAGE.

**HAJJAJ, IBN YUSUF AL-** (661-714). A schoolmaster of Ta'ef in **Hijaz** who became an important general in the service of the **Umayyad caliphs** '**Abdul Malik** (685-705) and **al-Walid** (705-715). He besieged Mecca for seven months and defeated and killed the anti-caliph 'Abd Allah ibn **Zubayr** in 692. He pacified Arabia and Iraq, where he served as governor for about 20 years until his death. He arrived at **Kufah** with an escort of only 12 cameleers and proclaimed from the city **mosque:** "O people of al-Kufah! Certain am I that I see heads ripe for cutting, and verily I am the man to do it. Methinks I see blood between the turbans and the beards . . ." (Hitti, 207). He is said to have sacrificed some 120,000 lives before he was able to establish his tyrannic control over Persia and Iraq. Under his direction, vowel markings were introduced into the **Arabic** script to make the pronunciation of the Koran more precise. Hajjaj was buried in Wasit (middle), the city he founded between **Kufah** and **Basra.**

**HAKIM, ABU'L 'ALI AL-MANSUR AL-** (r. 996-1021). The sixth **Fatimid caliph** at **Cairo,** described as a whimsical tyrant who promoted **Isma'ili** propaganda in a predominantly Sunni country. He enforced discriminatory restrictions on **Christians** and **Jews** who had attained high positions at court during the reign of his father, and he instituted puritanical reforms, prohibiting **women** to appear in the streets. At one time he ordered all the dogs in the city to be killed, then he forbade the sale of grapes and ordered all the jars of honey broken and the contents poured into the Nile. He founded "A House of Wisdom" (**dar al-hikmah**) in 1004 for the training of Isma'ili missionaries. Two of his missionaries (**da'is**), **Hamza** al-Zuzani and **Darazi,** urged him to proclaim his divinity, which led to civil war and the flight of Darazi, who founded the **Druze** community in Lebanon. Al-Hakim disappeared during one of his nocturnal wanderings about the city; the Druzes expect him to return at the end of time as the **Mahdi. Ibn Khallikan** says of him: "He was prodigal of wealth and fond of shedding blood: a great number of persons holding eminent stations in the administration of the state were put to death by him in an arbitrary manner" (III, 449).

**HALAL.** "Permissible." That which is lawful and allowed as compared to that which is forbidden (**haram**). It includes proper behavior in law as well as the consumption of **food.** Halal food includes meat of animals that have been ritually slaughtered, game over which the name of Allah has been pronounced, and various types of seafood. *See* FIVE PRINCIPAL ACTS IN ISLAMIC LAW.

**HALIMAH.** A Bedouin woman who acted as wet nurse of Muhammad during his early childhood. It was the custom of city nobility temporarily to leave their infants with Bedouins in the desert, away from the unhealthy conditions of urban life.

**HALLAJ, HUSAYN IBN MANSUR AL-** (857-922). A Persian **Sufi** poet who was born in Tus (or Bayza in Fars?) and executed as a heretic. A cotton carder by trade, he traveled as far as Turkestan and northern India and was able to win many disciples, who ascribed to him supernatural powers. He stressed a spiritual relationship between human beings and God, denied the necessity of **pilgrimage**, and suggested that saved funds ought to be spent on the support of orphans. An **'Abbasid** inquisition had him flogged and tortured, then decapitated and burned, because of his ecstatic utterance: "I am the Truth"(*ana al-haqq*), that is, God. One of his verses states: "I am He whom I love, and He whom I love is I, We are two souls dwelling in one body. When thou seest me, thou seest Him: And when thou seest Him, thou seest us both" (Hitti,436). **Ibn Khallikan** said of Hallaj "some (are) extolling him to the utmost, whilst others treat him as an infidel" (I, 423). Members of the **ulama** said he merited death and he was handed over to the police guards with the instructions to administer a flogging of 1,000 strokes and "if al-Hallaj does not expire under the bastonnade, cut off one of his hands, then one of his feet, then the other hand, then the other foot; then strike off his head and burn his body" (I, 425).

**HAMAS.** Acronym, for a Palestinian Islamist revivalist movement, the Movement of Islamic Resistance (Harakat al-Muqawamah al-Islamiyah). It was established in December 1987, at the beginning of the *intifadah*, the Palestinian uprising against Israeli occupation on the West Bank and Gaza Strip. It rose out of the **Muslim Brotherhood** and combined a network of social welfare activities with political and military action. Its military wing, the Qassim Brigade (Kata'eb 'Izz al-Din al-Qassam), conducted armed attacks against Israeli targets. Unlike the nationalist Palestinian Liberation Organization (PLO), Hamas wants to "re-Islamize" society with the objective of creating an **Islamic state**. Hamas has been able to win the support of 30 to 40 percent of the Palestinian population because of frustration with the lagging peace process.

Israel originally welcomed the emergence of Hamas "in order to help create a force that would stand against the leftist forces which support the PLO" (Gen. Yitzhak Segev, quoted in *What Kind of Nation?* by Graham Usher). But it embarked on armed actions against Israeli targets in retaliation for the al-**Aqsa** mosque massacre in **Jerusalem** in 1990 in which 18 Palestinians were killed. In the ensuing conflict Israel sentenced Shaykh Ahmad Yasin, the "spiritual guide" of Hamas, to life imprisonment, assassinated 'Imad 'Aql, leader of the Brigade, and attempted to assassinate Khalid Mash'al, head of the Hamas' political bureau in Amman, Jordan (King Husayn demanded the freeing of Shaykh Yasin after the Mossad assassination attempt). In recent times, Hamas agreed to a "truce" if Israel withdrew to its 1967 borders. Some attribute the movement's activities to a conservative turn in Israel and the election of Binyamin Netanyahu as the prime minister in 1996.

**HAMDAN QARMAT.** *See* QARMATIANS.

**HAMZA IBN ALI IBN AHMAD.** An **Isma'ili** missionary (**da'i**) of the **Fatimid Caliph al-Hakim**. He promoted the idea that Hakim was a manifestation of God, a doctrine eventually accepted by the **Druzes**. He disappeared or was assassinated in 1021.

**HANAFI.** *See* ABU HANIFAH and SCHOOLS OF LAW.

**HANAFIYYAH, MUHAMMAD IBN AL-** (637-701). Son of Caliph 'Ali by a woman of the Hanifa tribe and therefore not a descendant of the Prophet. He was not politically active and reluctantly carried the banner of his father 'Ali at the **Battle of the Camel**. As 'Ali's only surviving son, he was recognized by the **Kaysaniyyah** as their **imam**. **Al-Mukhtar** revolted in **Kufah** in 685-87, in the name of al-Hanafiyyah, proclaiming him the expected **mahdi** in **occultation** on Mount Radwa. Hanafiyyah eventually declared his allegiance to Caliph **Mu'awiyah** and retired to Medina.

**HANBAL, AHMAD IBN.** *See* IBN HANBAL, AHMAD.

**HANBALI.** *See* IBN HANBAL and SCHOOLS OF LAW.

**HAND.** Muslims traditionally use the right hand for "honorable purposes" and the left hand for necessary, but unclean actions. When eating with one's fingers, as is customary in many parts of the world, one is supposed to eat with the right hand.

**HANIF.** "One who is inclined to Islam," the term for a monotheist in pre-Islamic Arabia. **Abraham**, the Biblical ancestor of Muslims and **Jews**, is a hanif. The Koran says: "They say: 'Become Jews or **Christians** if ye would be guided (to salvation).' Say thou: 'Nay! (I would rather) the religion of Abraham the True, and he joined not gods with Allah" (S.2:135). A Hanif rejects idolatry and worships God with complete devotion and undivided loyalty. It was the religion of Abraham (*Hanifiya*), who was neither Jew nor Christian.

**HANIFA, ABU.** *See* ABU HANIFAH.

**HANIFITES.** *See* SCHOOLS OF LAW.

**HARAM.** "Sanctuary." The areas of Mecca and Medina, the *Haramayn*, which are sacred and forbidden to non-Muslims. Haram is that which is forbidden and sinful and will be punished on the **Day of Judgment**. In jurisprudence it is an unlawful act, subject to punishment by an Islamic **judge** (kadhi). *See also* FIVE PRINCIPAL ACTS IN ISLAMIC LAW.

**HARIM (HAREM).** The **women**'s quarters of an apartment that any unrelated men were forbidden to enter. Muslim rulers maintained special quarters in which their wives and female servants were kept. The custom is based on the injunction of the Koran, which says: "There is no blame (on those ladies if they appear) before their fathers or their sons, their brothers, or their brothers' sons, or their sisters' sons, or their women, or the **(slaves)** whom their right hand possess" (33:55). As an institution, the harim was taken from Byzantine practices and continued by **caliphs** and secular rulers down to the **Ottoman empire**, when it included several hundred women. Only a few were the actual wives of the **sultan**; the majority were servants and slaves. The mother of the reigning sultan was the queen of the harim, which was organized in a highly hierarchical system. The harim system ended in 1909 with the Young Turk revolution and the removal of Sultan Abdul Hamid.

**HARUN AL-RASHID** (r. 786-809). The fifth 'Abbasid caliph whose reign was the high point of 'Abbasid rule in **Baghdad**. A contemporary of Charlemagne in the West, Harun exceeded the European rulers in power and territorial possessions. He was served by the Persian **Barmakid** family of **viziers**, but he eventually he eliminated them when they began to rival his power and wealth. Harun repeatedly fought **Kharijite** revolts and could not prevent the emergence of the **Idrisids** (789-926) and Aghlabids (800-909) in North Africa as independent states. As a youth, Harun led an army against the Byzantines, forcing Constantine VI to pay a tribute of some 70,000 **dinars**. In the West he came to be known from the tales of *Thousand-and-one-Night*.

**HARUT AND MARUT.** Two **angels** who deplored sinful humanity and were sent by God to earth and became sinful themselves. They taught magic to people without warning them of its evil uses; therefore, they were punished. "They learned from them (the angels) the means to sow discord between man and wife" (2:102).

**HASAN AL-BANNA.** *See* BANNA, HASAN AL-.

**HASAN AL-BASRI.** *See* BASRI, HASAN AL.

**HASAN IBN 'ALI** (625-670). Son of 'Ali and **Fatima** and grandson of the Prophet Muhammad. Hasan was politically inactive and surrendered his rights to the **caliphate** to the first **Umayyad caliph, Mu'awiyah**. The Shi'ites count him as the second **imam**.

**HASAN AL-SABBAH (HASAN-I SABBAH**,1055-1124). A propagandist (**da'i**) of the **Isma'ili sect** who established his base in the fortress of **Alamut**, and as grand master sent his devotees (**feda'i**) on errands of assassination. The members of the **sect** are said to have used hashish in their ceremonies and, therefore, came to be known as the *hashashiyun*, from which the word assassin derives.

**HASHIM, BANU.** *See* HASHIMITE CLAN.

**HASHIMITE CLAN.** The noble, but small, clan of the Prophet, named after its eponymic ancestor, Hashim Ibn al-Manaf (d. 540). The Hashimites were part of the **Quraysh** tribe and were able to protect Muhammad from Meccan persecution. It was only when his grandfather, 'Abd al Muttalib, and his uncle, **Abu Talib**, died, that Muhammad was forced to flee to Medina. The rulers of Jordan (1922-present) claim Hashimite descent and designate their state the Hashimite Kingdom of Jordan.

**HASHISHIYUN.** *See* ALAMUT and NIZARIS.

**HATIM AL-TA'I** (d. ca. 605). A man who personifies the Bedouin ideal of generosity and hospitality. He was in charge of his father's camels when he encountered three travelers and slaughtered three camels for them when they asked only for some milk. *See also* HOSPITALITY.

**HAYTHAM, IBN AL-** (ALHAZEN, 965-1039). Arab mathematician, astronomer, and physicist from **Basra**. In his *Kitab al-Manazir* (in Latin Opticae thesaurus) he rejected theories of Euclid and Ptolemy that visual rays travel from the eye to the object. In what came to be known in the West as "Alhazen's problem," he solved an equation of the fourth degree. Al-Haytham was invited to **Cairo** by the **Fatimid caliph al-Hakim** to study the feasibility of controlling the flooding of the Nile.

**HEAVEN.** "Jannah." Heaven is the abode of the virtuous in the next life. The **Arabic** word, *jannah,* means garden; another term, *firdaws* (probably of Persian origin), means paradise. Heaven is described as a garden with flowing streams, a place of bliss and perpetual happiness (2:25). Surah 3:15 reads: "Say: Shall I give you glad tidings of things far better than those (wealth)? For the righteous are gardens in nearness to their Lord with rivers flowing beneath; therein is their eternal home; with spouses purified and the good pleasure of Allah." Also: "And he will be in a life of bliss, in a garden on high, the fruits whereof (will hang in bunches) low and near. 'Eat ye and drink ye, with full satisfaction; Because of the (good) that ye sent before you, in the days that are gone!'" (69:21-24). There are several types of heaven, including the Seventh Heaven. "But for such as fear the time when they will stand before (the Judgment Seat of) their Lord, there will be two gardens . . . abounding in branches . . . in them (each) will be two springs flowing (free) . . . in them will be fruits of every kind two and two . . . . They will recline on carpets, whose inner linings will be of rich brocade: the fruit of the garden will be near (and easy to reach) . . . in them will be (maidens), chaste, restraining their glances, whom no man or **jinn** before them has touched (55:46-56). While some Muslims tend to take the descriptions of the joys of paradise literally, others see them as metaphors.

**HELL.** Hell (*jahannam*), the abode of polytheists and sinners. There is disagreement as to who will be condemned to eternal hell fire. Some theologians believe that Muslims who sinned, but repented, will be only temporarily in hell, while others would assign Muslims who committed a great **sin** forever to hell. According to tradition, there are seven gates of hell: one a purgatory for Muslims, and individual sections for **idolaters**, **hypocrites**, **Christians**, **Jews**, and others (15:44). The sinners will neither live nor die and will be tormented forever. Their food will consist of thorny bushes and the fruit of the *zaqqum* tree: "In front of such a one (sinner) is hell, and he is given, for drink, boiled fetid water. In gulps will he sip it, but never will he be near swallowing it down his throat; death will come to him from every quarter, yet will he not die; and in front of him will be a chastisement unrelenting" (14:16-17).

**HELPERS.** *See* ANSAR.

**HENNAH (HINNAH).** The leaves of a bush widely grown in the Middle East that are ground and mixed with various ingredients to make a paste used as a cosmetic for **women**. They dye their palms, soles of the feet, finger tips, nails, or face in a bright red color. With certain admixtures it is used to dye men's hair and beards. Originally Hennah was believed to have magical powers, for example, protection from the "**evil eye**."

**HEREAFTER, THE.** The concept of life after death, *akhirah*, resurrection, judgment, and reward or punishment on the **Day of Judgment.** God has created humankind and will recreate man a second time: "Say, He will give them life Who created them for the first time! For He fully knows all creation." **Abraham** was shown how God will revive the dead in the hereafter: "He (Abraham) said: 'Oh! How shall Allah bring it (ever) to life, after this (its) death?' But Allah caused him to die for a hundred years, then raised him up (again). He said: 'How long didst thou tarry (thus)?' He said: '(Perhaps) a day or part of a day.' He said: 'Nay, thou hast tarried thus a hundred years: But look at thy food and thy drink; they show no signs of age: and look at thy donkey: and that we may make of thee a sign unto the people. Look further at the bones, how We bring them together and cloth them with flesh.' When this was shown clearly to him, he said: 'I know that Allah hath power over all things'" (2:259). Belief in the hereafter is one of the basic tenets of Islam. *See also* HEAVEN and HELL.

**HIDDEN IMAM.** The twelfth **Shi'ite imam**, Muhammad **al-Muntazar** who disappeared in 878 and is believed to be in **occultation** and expected to return at the end of time. During the first stage, the Lesser Occultation (878-940), the Hidden Imam was represented by four intermediaries who had the authority to speak on his behalf. After this, the Greater Occultation began and the **ulama** is believed to act as his representatives.

**HIJAB.** "Cover, Veil." One of a number of terms for the **veil** and the seclusion of **women**. In the Koran, the term is taken for seclusion: "O ye who believe! Enter not the Prophet's houses—until leave is given you . . . and when ye ask (his ladies) for anything ye want ask them before a screen: that makes for greater purity for your hearts and for theirs" (33-53). The veil existed in the Hellenistic-Byzantine and the Sassanian empires and was worn by aristocratic ladies in urban environments. Adopted in Islam, the veil became obligatory for women, but the type of veil varied in different parts of the Islamic world. Nomad and peasant women would wear a kerchief that did not limit them from work. In cities, women would wear the burqah **chador** or chatri that covers the head and the entire body. As a result of Westernization, women began to appear on the streets without a veil, and modernizing reformers tried with varying success to abolish the veil. The Islamic revival, beginning in the 1970s led to the adoption of the "Islamic" dress as a political statement in many parts of the Islamic world and even among Muslims in the West.

**HIJAZ.** A province in west-central Saudi Arabia in which the holy cities of Mecca and Medina are located. Pilgrims from all over the world visit the two cities, which are off limits to non-Muslims. Hijaz means "barrier," named after a range of high mountains, which rises parallel to the Red Sea coast and in the east gradually declines to form the Arabian plateau.

**HIJRAH (HEJIRA).** "Emigration." The beginning of the Islamic **calendar** was determined to be July 16, 622, when Muhammad and a small group of his followers fled from Mecca to Yathrib (Medina).

It was during the month of **Muharram**, the first month of the Islamic lunar year. **Muhammad's** teachings had aroused the hostility of the powerful **Quraysh**, who feared the new Islamic community as a threat to their social and economic interests. When **Abu Lahab** became head of the **Hashimite clan**, Muhammad lost the protection of his clan, and his enemies conspired to kill him. Once established in Medina, the Muslim community grew to the extent that it recaptured Mecca and unified Arabia under Islam.

**HILA** (pl. **HIYAL**). "Evasion," or subterfuge, used to circumvent the dictates of law, as for example, to permit the taking of interest. The transaction is represented as the sale of an item, repurchased for a smaller amount, or to make the transaction a partnership. Such stratagems came into use during the **'Abbasid** period, mainly in the **Hanafi school of law**, but they were also adopted by others.

**HILAL.** "Crescent." A symbol carried in Muslim banners. The Red Crescent (*al-hilal al-ahmar*) is the Muslim equivalent of the Western Red Cross. The appearance of the crescent marks the beginning of the Muslim month and the beginning of the sacred seasons.

**HILLI, 'ALLAMAH IBN AL-MUTAHHAR AL-** (1250-1325). An Islamic scholar and jurist of the **Twelver Shi'ite** school, known as the "wise man of Hilli." Born in Hilla, Iraq, and educated in **Baghdad,** he became famous for his works on grammar, logic, **hadith, tafsir** (commentary on the Koran), and biography. He was a supporter of the **usuli** movement, which favored the use of independent judgment (**ijtihad**) in matters of law. His treatise on the *al-bab al-hadi 'ashar* (Principles of Shi'ite theology) is still used by Shi'ites today. Hilli is buried in **Mashhad**.

**HIRAH AL-.** Capital of the **Lakhmid** buffer state between the nomads of Arabia and Sassanian Persia that flourished under its king, Imru' al-Qays (d. 328). Three of the seven authors of the **Mu'allaqat** enjoyed the patronage of the al-Hirah courts, which were famous for sponsoring prize-winning competitions. The population was largely Christian, spoke **Arabic**, but used Syriac in writing. The Muslim general, **Khalid ibn al-Walid**, conquered al-Hirah in 633.

**HISBAH.** The state institution that promotes virtue and forbids vice: *al-amr bi al-ma'ruf wa-al-nahy 'an al-munkar*. Although every Muslim has the obligation to admonish fellow Muslims to good conduct, the hisbah has a function in public law. The **muhtasib**, the person responsible for the hisbah, has been a combination of market inspector and overseer of public morals, who could investigate and judge an offender and administer punishment, usually a number of lashes. In most Islamic countries the urban police have taken over this function, and in some, such as Afghanistan, the hisbah institution has been reintroduced.

**HISHAM, ABD AL-MALIK IBN.** *See* IBN HISHAM, ABU MUHAMMAD ʿABD AL-MALIK.

**HITTIN (HATTIN).** A place in Palestine where **Salah al-Din** (Saladin) defeated the Crusader army in 1187. The battle prepared the way for the conquest of **Jerusalem** three months later.

**HIZB.** A part, division, such as a part of the Koran; also political party.

**HIZB AL-DAʿWAH.** *See* DAʿWAH, HIZB AL-.

**HIZB-I ISLAMI.** "Islamic Party." Two **Islamist** parties with this name in Afghanistan, headed by Gulbuddin Hekmatyar and Yunus Khalis, fought against the Marxist government in the 1980s with considerable assistance from the United States, Pakistan, and governments from the Gulf states. As radical Islamists, they were ideologically trusted to be implacable enemies of the communists. Many Arab **mujahidin** favored these parties and fought on their side; the skills they acquired in weaponry and guerrilla warfare were later employed in fighting the governments in their countries of origin. Some stayed in Afghanistan, such as **Osama bin Laden**, and supported the **Taliban** regime, which for four years controlled most of the country. *See also* AFGHANIS.

**HIZBULLAH (HIZB ALLAH).** The Party of God (Allah), a term which was adopted by Shiʿite **Islamist** parties in Iran and Lebanon. In Iran, Hizbullah rose as a revolutionary movement in the late 1970s when it contributed to the downfall of Muhammad Reza Shah and became a vanguard of the Islamic Republican Party. It contributed to the consolidation of the new regime, but it did not emerge as a separate party. The movement established links with the Lebanese forces and contributed to their training and financial support.

In Lebanon the Hizbullah emerged in the late 1970s among Shi'ites with support from Iran. Its spiritual leader was Sayyid Muhammad Husayn **Fadlallah**, and Shaykh 'Abbas Mussavi was secretary general until his assassination by Israeli agents in 1992. Supported with volunteers from Iran, the party opposed the Maronite regime of President Amin Gemayel and cooperated with like-minded Islamist parties. It proclaimed its objective to fight American and French influence in Lebanon, eliminate Israeli occupation of Lebanese territory, and establish an Islamic system of government. It staged assassinations and suicide attacks on the American and French embassies and peacekeeping forces, including the attack in 1983 on the U.S. marine barracks that resulted in the death of 241 American soldiers.

Hizbullah became a major force in the struggle against Israeli occupation in southern Lebanon, exacting a continuing toll in lives that the Israeli government could not stop. In 1992 and 1996, Hizbullah participated in Lebanese elections and obtained a minority of 27 parliamentary seats allotted to the Shi'ite community. The successes of the Lebanese Hizbullah against the South Lebanon Army and its Israeli supporters resulted in increasing appeals for unilateral withdrawal of Israeli forces from its self-declared security zone, which was completed in 2000. Hizbullah's secretary-general, Shaykh Hasan Nasrallah was elected in 1992, after the Israelis assassinated his predecessor Shaykh Abbas Musawi. A number of splinter groups, the **Islamic Amal**, **Islamic Jihad**, and Islamic Resistance were either part of Hizbullah or merged with the movement. The Party of God prevailed when Prime Minister Ehud Barak pulled out all Israeli troops in June 2000.

**HOLIDAYS.** *See* CALENDERS and FESTIVALS.

**HOLY WARRIOR.** *See* MUJAHID.

**HOSPITALITY.** "Diyafah." A virtue obligatory by **Tradition** and enjoined in the Koran: "And do good to parents and kinfolk, orphans, those in need, neighbors who are of kin, neighbors who are strangers, the companion by your side, the way-farer (ye meet), . . ."(4:36). Pre-Islamic poetry extolls the virtue of **Hatim al-Ta'i**, who slaughtered three camels to entertain three travelers who only wanted a little milk. Hospitality is one of the obligations of the code of manly virtue, **muruwwa**, which demands courage, loyalty, and generosity.

Originally the code of the Bedouin Arabs and an act that permitted survival in a hostile environment, hospitality is an obligation observed throughout the Islamic world.

**HOUSE OF WISDOM.** An academy with a library and translation bureau founded in **Baghdad** in 830 by Caliph **al-Ma'mun** (r. 813-833), which became the most important educational institution in the **'Abbasid** period (749-1258). Scholars translated Greek works in medicine by Galen (d. ca. 200), mathematics by Euclid and Ptolemy, and philosophy by Plato and Aristotle at a time when Europeans were almost totally ignorant of Greek thought and science.

**HUDAYBIYAH.** A valley on the road from Jeddah to Mecca where Muhammad concluded a treaty with the **Quraysh** in February 628. Muhammad moved from Medina to Mecca, accompanied by a force of 1,400 of his followers. He halted at Hudaybiyah and stated that he wanted to perform the **pilgrimage** to the **Ka'bah**. After some negotiations, Muhammad agreed to postpone his entry to Mecca for a year, and to conclude a truce for 10 years. He also agreed to return subjects of the Quraysh who had accepted Islam, although Muslims who defected were not to be extradited. In the following year, the Muslims performed their pilgrimage and, in 630, they took Mecca, claiming a violation of the treaty by the Quraysh.

**HUDUD.** *See* HADD.

**HUJJATIYAH SOCIETY.** A Shi'ite religio-political school founded in the early 1950s by Shaykh Mahmud Halabi in **Mashhad**, Iran. Hujjat, meaning proof, refers to a person who is an intermediary to the **Hidden Imam**. The Society organized campaigns of intimidation of **Baha'is** as heretics, and after the Iranian Revolution it was suspected of rejecting the concept of the **vilayat-i faqih**, the rule of the jurisconsult Ayatollah Ruhollah **Khomeyni.** Therefore, it was eventually forced to suspend its activities.

**HULAGU** (1217-1265). Grandson of the **Mongol** conqueror Genghiz Khan and founder of the Ilkhanid dynasty of Iran. He invaded Iran and captured the fortress of **Alamut** of the Assassins in 1256 and took **Baghdad** in 1258. He ordered the execution of the **'Abassid** caliph Al-Musta'sim and members of his family and thus ended the classical **caliphate**. One member of the 'Abassid family managed to escape and established himself as caliph under **Mamluk** protection in **Cairo**. Hulagu invaded Syria and took Aleppo and Hama, but he could not capture **Damascus**. The Mongols were finally stopped by the Mamluks under Baybars at **'Ayn Jalut** in 1260. Although largely shamanist by religion, the Ilkhanids eventually adopted Islam and assimilated with the local population.

**HUNAYN, BATTLE OF.** A valley on the road from Mecca to Tayef, where Muhammad fought the tribes of Hawazin and Thaqif which planned to recapture Mecca in 630. The tribes attacked Muhammad's forces and after some success were decisively defeated. According to the Prophet's biographers, some 6,000 **women** and children and large herds of camels were taken as **booty**. Many of the survivors embraced Islam and the prestige of the Muslim community was greatly enhanced. The Koran related that an unseen army of **angels** supported the Muslims: "Assuredly Allah did help you in many battle fields and on the day of Hunayn: Behold! Your great numbers elated you, but they availed you nought; the land for all that it is wide did not constrain you, and ye turned back in retreat. But Allah did pour His calm on the **Messenger** and on the **believers**, and sent down forces which ye saw not: He punished the unbelievers: thus doth he reward those without faith"(9:25-26).

**HUR.** The **women** of **paradise**, described in the Koran: "We shall wed them to maidens with beautiful, big, and lustrous eyes" (44-54). Commentaries explain the word Hur as connoting the idea of purity, beauty, and truth.

**HURAYRAH, ABU.** *See* ABU HURAYRAH.

**HUSAYN IBN 'ALI** (626-680). Second son of **'Ali ibn Abi Talib** and **Fatimah** and grandson of the Prophet Muhammad. Muhammad had no male heirs, therefore Husayn and his brother, **Hasan**, were considered by the partisans of 'Ali as rightful successors to the leadership of the Islamic community. When 'Ali was assassinated in 661, Iraq opted for Hasan, but he abdicated in a deal with **Mu'awiyah**, which gained him a considerable pension and retirement in Medina. Husayn refused to acknowledge Mu'awiyah and, following a call by the people of Iraq, he set out for **Kufah**. Deserted by most of his followers, he was confronted at **Karbala'** by an army of some 4,000 troops, headed by **Sa'd ibn-Abi Waqqas**, and he was killed with his family and companions. The 10th of **Muharram** (680) has since been mourned by Shi'ites with passion plays, reenacting the scenes at Karbala (*see* ASHURA'). Shi'ites consider him the second infallible **imam**, and Sunnis respect him as the grandson of the Prophet.

**HUSAYNI, AMIN AL-** (1895-1974). Grand **Mufti** of **Jerusalem** (1926-1937) and head of the Arabic High Command in Palestine (1936). Educated at **Al-Azhar** University in **Cairo** and the School of Administration in **Istanbul**, he became a major force against the British mandatory power of Palestine and was eventually forced to flee in 1937. He spent the years during the Second World War in Italy and Germany from where he conducted anti-Allied propaganda. He was a leading member of the Palestinian Nationalist Movement.

**HUSAYNIYYAH.** A special site for ritual commemoration of the martyrdom of **Imam Husayn**. Husayniyyahs exist in every Shi'ite community in Iraq, Iran, and Lebanon and, with different names, also in Bahrain, Oman, and India. First introduced in **Baghdad** by the **Buyyids** (932-1055) and eventually institutionalized under the **Safavid** dynasty (1501-1722), the practice of commemoration spread throughout the Shi'ite world and has become a common feature in every community.

**HYPOCRITES, THE.** "Munafiqun." Medinans and members of tribes who adopted Islam but deserted Muhammad before the battle of **Uhud** in 625. They wanted to ally themselves with the growing strength of Islam but were ready to desert or intrigue against the early Islamic community. By extension, the term hypocrites has come to be referred to opportunists who did not become Muslims by conviction. The Koran says: "When the hypocrites come to thee, they say, 'We bear witness that thou art indeed the **Messenger** of Allah. Yea, Allah knoweth that thou art indeed His Messenger. And Allah beareth witness that the hypocrites are indeed liars. They have made their oaths a screen (for their misdeeds): Thus they obstruct (men) from the path of Allah: Truly evil are their deeds" (63:1-2).

- I -

'IBADAT. God's commands concerning worship and ritual. They include ritual **prayer** (salat), **fasting** (sawm), **almsgiving** (zakat), **pilgrimage** (hajj), and they constitute part of the **Five Pillars of Islam**, the first of which is the **profession of faith** (shahada). *See* FAITH, ARTICLES OF and FIVE PILLARS OF ISLAM.

IBADITES (ABADITES). Followers of the Ibadiyya, a **Kharijite** offshoot named after its eponymic ancestor, Abdallah Ibn Ibad (d. 680), who lived in **Basra** in the second half of the seventh century. They rejected the intolerance of other Kharijites and did not consider Muslims of other **sects** to be unbelievers (**kafirs**). They opposed political assassinations and believed in the election of their **imam**. Unlike the orthodox schools, they believe that the Koran is created. They live in parts of northwest Africa as well as in Oman and the United Arab Emirates. The head of the Ibadites established his center at Nazwa in the Sultanate of Oman.

IBLIS. A **devil** (*shaytan*) and a fallen **angel** (or rebellious **jinn**) who refused to bow before **Adam** and tempted Eve to eat from the tree of immorality; therefore, he was expelled from paradise and given the power to lead astray all those who are not true servants of God. He is made of fire, whereas man is made of clay, and he will exist until the **Day of Judgment** when he will be destroyed. The Koran says: "And behold, We said to the angels: 'Bow down to Adam:' and they bowed down: Not so Iblis: he refused and was haughty: he was of those who reject faith" (2:34). Also "(Allah) said: 'What prevented thee from prostrating when I commanded thee?' He said: 'I am better than he: Thou didst create me from fire, and him from clay;'" and "(Allah) said : 'get thee down from it: it is not for thee to be arrogant. Here: get out for thou art of the meanest (of creatures)'"(7:12-13).

IBN AL-'ABBAS, 'ABDALLAH (619-687). Son of 'Abbas ibn 'Abd al Muttalib, the uncle of the Prophet. He was a **Companion** of the Prophet and Islamic scholar, the first to produce a commentary of the Koran. Originally a partisan of 'Ali, who appointed him governor of **Basra**, he made peace with the **Umayyads**. He participated in many campaigns, acted as an adviser to **caliphs**, and retired to Tayef, where he died.

IBN ABIHI. *See* ZIYAD, IBN ABIHI.

**IBN AMAJ, AL-QAZVINI** (d.886). Author of one of the six "sound" collections of **hadith**.

**IBN AL-ARABI MUHYI AL-DIN** (1165-1240). Islamic mystic and philosopher of the Ta'i tribe, educated in Seville, Spain, where he lived for 30 years. He traveled widely in the Middle East and settled in Malatya, near **Damascus**, where his tomb is a much-visited shrine. Some 150 of his numerous works are still extant, most famous of which are his *futuhat al-makkiyah* (Meccan revelations) and *fusus al-hikam* (Gems of wisdom). In these works he expounded his ideas as a fusion of literal belief and belief submerging into spiritual illumination and divine inspiration. His concept of the "Perfect Man" (*al-insan al-kamil*) shows man as the image of God whose mission is to reveal the perfection of God. One of his students said: "I followed his lessons upwards of ten years, and I never saw him with a book in his hand; and yet he dictated to his pupils camel-loads of (philological) information." Condemned as a pantheist by **Ibn-Taymiayyah** and **Ibn Khaldun**, he was defended by Firuzabadi (d. 1414), **al-Suyuti** (1445-1505), and **al-Sha'rani**.

**IBN AL-ATHIR, 'IZZ AL-DIN** (1160-1234). Arab historian and biographer, born in southeastern Turkey and educated at Mosul, **Baghdad**, and **Jerusalem**. He was with **Salah al-Din**'s (Saladin) army in Syria and served as minister at various princely courts. He published the *kitab al-kamil fi 'l-tarikh* (Complete history of the world), starting with **Adam**, and a work on **Traditions**, *usd al-ghaba* (Lion of the jungle), which contains biographies of some 7,500 **Companions** of the Prophet. **Ibn Khallikan** placed him in the first rank of traditionists, historians, and genealogists. Considered arrogant and conceited by some, he was appreciated by others for his independent and original mind.

**IBN BABAWAYHI (BABUYAH**, 923-991). Famed Shi'ite scholar, jurist, and collector of **hadith**. Educated by his father, he continued his studies at Rayy with noted scholars and traveled widely in the Islamic world. Author of one of the Shi'ite *Four Books* of hadith (*kutub al-arba 'a*), he was the last prominent member of the Shi'ite traditionist school of **Qom**. His *risalat al-i 'tiqadat* (Shi'ite creed) shows the doctrinal development of Shi'ism. Most of his 200 publications are lost.

**IBN BAJJAH, IBN AL-SA'IGH (AVEMBACE,** ca 1095-1138). Spanish-Arab philosopher, natural historian, music theorist, composer, and musician. He spent some 20 years as **vizier** of the governor of Murcia and Zaragoza until the region was captured by King Alphon-so. He wrote, among others, commentaries on the writings of Aristotle. He tended to a pantheistic-materialistic philosophy, which exposed him to the accusation of heresy. Khakan, a Muslim contemporary, called him an infidel and atheist, saying: "Faith disappeared from his heart and left no trace behind; his tongue forgot (the praises of) the Merciful, neither did (the holy) name cross his lips" (Ibn Khallikan, III,131).

**IBN BATUTAH, MUHAMMAD IBN 'ABD ALLAH** (1304-1368[1377?]). A native of Tangiers who started out on a **pilgrimage** to Mecca in 1325/26 and continued to visit most countries in the Islamic world. He had a traditional education and later studied with noted Islamic scholars and wrote about his travels to the **Ottoman empire**, the steppes of the Golden Horde, India, East Asia—including China—and East and West Africa. After his return to Tangiers 24 years later, he set out for Spain and then crossed the Sahara into Black Africa. It is doubtful whether the "Arab Marco Polo" actually visited the Volga regions, but he included descriptions of all these areas in his travel accounts, entitled *Tuhfat al-Nuzzar fi Ghar'ib al-Amsar wa- 'Aja'ib al-Asfar.* It has been translated in French, and parts appeared in English under the title *The Travels of Ibn Batouta.* His rule was "never travel the same road a second time" and he seems to have adhered to it.

**IBN HANBAL, AHMAD** (780-855). Islamic scholar and eponymous founder of the Hanbali **school of law**. He was a student of **al-Shafi'i**, founder of the Shafi'ite school of law. His is the most conservative, but smallest, of the four Sunni schools. It limits the jurists only to the Koran and the **Sunnah** for a decision of law. Ibn Hanbal was born in **Baghdad** and traveled widely in the Arab world in search of **Traditions** of the Prophet. His *Musnad* is a collection of some 28,000 Traditions. Ibn Hanbal resided in Baghdad, where he was an opponent of the **Mu'tazilite** school, which held that the Koran was created. During the inquisition, *mihna,* he refused to recant and was imprisoned during the reigns of the caliphs **al-Ma'mun** and al-Mu'tasim. Vindicated under the rule of Caliph al-Mutawakkil, Ibn Hanbal saw Sunni Islam accept the dogma of the uncreatedness of the

Koran. Historians relate that his funeral was attended by 800,000 men and 60,000 **women** and that 20,000 **Christians** and **Jews** converted to Islam on the day. The **Wahhabis** (Unitarians) of Saudi Arabia are followers of the Hanbali school. *See also* CREATEDNESS OF THE KORAN.

**IBN HAZM, ABU MUHAMMAD 'ALI** (994-1064). He is said to have been the "greatest scholar and most original genius of Muslim Spain." He was a literalist (**zahirite**) and so virulently critical of other scholars that it was said, "The tongue of Ibn Hazm and the sword of al-**Hajjaj** ibn Yusuf were brothers." Born in Cordoba of a family of Christian converts, he held high offices at princely courts but retired to devote himself to the writing of poetry, biographies, and history. He was said to have produced some 400 works; the best known in the West is *tawq al-hamamah fi al-ulfa wa al-ullaf* (The dove's neck ring: on love and lovers). Because of his unorthodox beliefs he was several times imprisoned and most of his works were burned. **Ibn Khallikan** called him a man of "profound humility equal to the greatness of his talents," and quotes one ibn Bashkuwal as saying: "Of all the natives of Spain, Ibn Hazm was the most eminent by the universality and depth of his learning in the sciences cultivated by the Muslims; add to this his profound acquaintance with the (**Arabic**) tongue, and his vast abilities as an elegant writer, a poet, a biographer, and a historian" (II, 268).

**IBN HISHAM, ABU MUHAMMAD 'ABD AL-MALIK** (767-833/34). Arab Islamic scholar of south Arabian origin and a native of **Basra**, who lived in Egypt where he edited **Ibn Ishaq**'s *sirat rasul Allah* (*Biography of the Prophet*). Only Ibn Hisham's recension is extant. It has been translated into German by G. Weil with the title *Das Leben Mohammeds* (Stuttgart, 1894) and into English by A. Guillaume with the title *The Life of Muhammad*.

**IBN ISHAQ, MUHAMMAD** (704-767). Author of the first biography of Muhammad (*sirat rasul Allah*), which is extant only in the recension of **Ibn Hisham**. Ishaq was born in Medina and died in **Baghdad**. He studied with his father and with Medinan scholars and moved to Hira and **Kufah** to teach and write before spending the rest of his life in Baghdad. The traditionist Ibn Shihab al-Zuhri said of him: "Medina would never lack *ílm* (knowledge) as long as Ibn Ishaq is there."

**IBN KHALDUN, 'ABD AL RAHMAN IBN MUHAMMAD** (1332-1406). Arab philosopher of history and "Father of Sociology," born in Tunis where he worked as a secretary. In Fez he was secretary and chief judge. In Oran he wrote the famous *Muqaddima* (*Prolegomena*), the introduction to his book on the origins of the Arabs, Berbers, and Persians. He held that history is subject to universal laws and presented a theory of cyclical change of humanity from barbarism to rural and urban culture. He coined the term 'asabiyah as the binding element of society, which is strong among the nomad conquerors who founded kingdoms. Gradually it weakens, leading to decay within a few generations, and falls prey to new nomad conquerors. At that time the cycle of evolution begins anew. Ibn Khaldun served a number of princes, in Tunis, Fez, and Egypt. He was imprisoned and forced to escape to **Cairo**, where he became chief judge in **Mamluk** Egypt in 1384. He taught at **Al-Azhar** University and had an encounter with **Timur-i Lang** (Tamerlane) at **Damascus**. The nomad conqueror permitted him to return to Cairo in 1401, where he died in 1406.

**IBN KHALLIKAN, SHAMS AL-DIN** (1211-1282). Born at Arbela in Iraq of a family descended from the **Barmakids.** He was educated at Aleppo and **Damascus**, where he achieved the position of chief judge in 1261 and, after a short assignment in Egypt, again in 1278. Ibn Khallikan was described as "a pious man, virtuous, and learned; amiable in temper, in conversation serious and instructive. His exterior was highly prepossessing, his countenance handsome and his manners engaging." Ibn Khallikan was the first Muslim writer to compile a biographical dictionary in alphabetical order of some 800 great men; it is entitled *wafayat al- 'ayan* (Deaths of eminent men). The British scholar Reynold A. Nicholson called it the "best general biography ever written" (Nicholson 452). It was translated by M. de Slane, (1842-74) with the title *Ibn Khallikan's Biographical Dictionary* (De Slane, IV, xv).

**IBN MAJAH, ABU ABDULLAH MUHAMMAD** (824-886). A Persian from the town of Qazwin. He was a famous traditionist and compiler of the *Kitab al-Sunnan* (Book of **Traditions**), one of the six canonical collections of Sunni **hadith**. Ibn Majah traveled widely in the Islamic world, collecting traditions from outstanding scholars. He is also known for his commentary on the Koran.

**IBN AL-MUQAFFA'.** *See* MUQAFFA', IBN AL-.

**IBN QUTAYBAH.** *See* QUTAYBAH, MUHAMMAD IBN MUSLIM AL-DINAWARI AL-.

**IBN RUSHD, ABU AL-WALID MUHAMMAD (AVERROËS,** 1126-1198). Arab philosopher, theologian, jurist, physician, and great authority on Aristotle's philosophy. He was born in Cordoba, Spain, and later served as chief judge in his hometown until he was banned as a heretic in 1195. He died in Marrakesh. Ibn Rushd wrote a refutation of Abu Muhammad **al-Ghazali**'s *tahafut al-falasifa* (Refutation of the philosophers) and he was accused of denying the immortality of the human soul and the resurrection of the body after death. He held that only spirits, not bodies, would be resurrected and felt that God knows only universals, not particulars. Ibn Rushd separated religion from philosophy and favored an allegorical interpretation of the Koran. In the West he became famous as Averroës for his *Commentaries on Aristotle.*

**IBN SA'D, ABU ABDULLAH MUHAMMAD** (764/5-845). One of the great Islamic biographers. His *kitab al-tabaqat al-kabir* (Great book of classes) is one of the earliest collections and an important source for the Prophet's biography and for early Islamic history. He was born in **Basra** and educated at **Baghdad**. He was secretary of Umar al-**Waqidi**, the Arab historian. Volume 8 of the *Tabaqat* was translated into English by Aisha Bewley under the title *The Women of Medina.*

**IBN SA'UD, 'ABD AL-AZIZ IBN 'ABD AL-RAHMAN IBN FAISAL AL-** (1880-1953). Great-grandson of Muhammad ibn Saud (r. 1747-1765), the founder of the Saudi dynasty and of modern Saudi Arabia. Driven from his native Najd in 1891, he lived in exile in Kuwait. With a band of only 40 men, Ibn Saud was able to recapture the castle of the Rashidi governor in Riyadh in 1902. Supporters flocked to his banners and he took Hasa on the Gulf in 1913. Neutral during the First World War, he had conquered the **Hijaz** by 1925 and, in the Treaty of Jidda, Great Britain recognized the independence of the new state. It was renamed the Kingdom of Saudi Arabia in 1932. In 1933 Saudi Arabia signed the first agreement with the American Oil Company, which struck oil in 1938 and by 1953 the kingdom obtained £5,000 ($2.5 million) a week in royalties.

Ibn Saud founded the tribal Brotherhood (**Ikhwan**), which was formed into an effective army. He wanted his followers to become sedentary and settle in camp communities. Disagreements about raiding into neighboring countries led Ibn Saud to destroy the Ikhwanis in the Battle of Sibilla. He restored the puritanical **Wahhabi** (Unitarian) creed to much of his realm, which accepts only the Koran and early Traditions (**Sunnah**) and rejects later developments of the classical period as innovations (**bid'ah**) and sinful. It forbids **intercession** and the veneration of tombs. Saudi kings draw their legitimacy as the "pious **sultans**" who perform all the functions formerly performed by the **Rightly Guided Caliphs**. Ibn Sa'ud had several wives and over 40 sons and an equal number of daughters. The dynasty continued under Sa'ud (1953-1964), Faisal (1964-1975), Khalid (1975-1982), and Fahd (1982- ).

**IBN SA'UD, 'ABD AL-'AZIZ IBN MUHAMMAD** (1721-1803). Son of Muhammad Ibn Sa'ud (r. 1747-1765). He was the amir of the **Wahhabis** who captured Riyadh in 1773 and in 1786 founded the first Sa'udi state in the Najd. After the death of **'Abd al-Wahhab** in 1792, he held both spiritual and temporal power. His army sacked **Karbala** in 1801 and captured **Mecca** and **Medina** in 1803, but his grandson, Abdullah ibn Sa'ud (1814-1818) was defeated by the army of **Muhammad 'Ali** of Egypt. The House of Sa'ud was able to recover from the disaster and **Ibn Sa'ud** (1880-1953) was able to conquer most of the Arabian Peninsula.

**IBN SINA, ABU 'ALI AL-HUSAYN IBN 'ABD ALLAH (AVI-CENNA)** (980-1037). Born near Bukhara of Persian parents, Ibn Sina traveled to study with famous doctors. "At the age of ten years, he was a perfect master of the Koran and general literature, and had attained a certain degree of information in dogmatic theology, the Indian calculus (arithmetic), and algebra . . . . In the sixteenth year of his age, physicians of the highest eminence came to read, under his tuition the works which treat of the different branches of medicine and learn from him those modes of treatment which he had discovered by his practice" (**Ibn Khallikan**, I, 440). Known in the West as Avicenna, he was a philosopher, physician and author of the *al-qanun fi tibb* (Canon of medicine) which made him famous in Europe. He also wrote the *kitab al-shifa* (Book of healing), a philosophical encyclopedia that earned him the title "Prince of Physicians." Translated into Latin, it served as a major medical text in medieval Europe and is still studied in the East today. He combined Islamic mysticism with Platonic idealism and asserted man's free will. Because he denied predestination Ibn Sina was declared an unbeliever (**kafir**), and Caliph Mustanjid ordered his books to be burned. Ibn Sina died in Hamadan.

**IBN TAYMIYYAH, AHMAD** (1263-1328). Born in Harran in northern Syria and educated in **Damascus** he became a jurist of the **Hanbali school of law**, teaching at Damascus and **Cairo**. His father and grandfather were famous authorities of the Hanbali school. A strict traditionist and opponent of **Sufism**, Shi'ism, saint cults, shrines, and philosophy, Ibn Taymiyyah was a "literalist" accepting anthropomorphic references in the Koran. He held that the Koran must be interpreted according to the letter, not understood through reason; **revelation** is the only source of knowledge, and the Koran and **Sunnah** are the only authentic guides in all matters. Ibn Taymiyyah denied the legitimacy of theology and the obligation to follow the decisions of the early schools of jurisprudence. He condemned many practices of popular Islam as sinful innovations (**bid'ah**), was repeatedly imprisoned, and died in jail. One of his major works is *kitab al-radd 'ala al-mantiqiyyin* (Book of the refutation of the logicians). His teachings have inspired revivalist movements, including 19th-century **Wahhabism** and present-day **Islamists**. A chief of **Shafi'ite** school in Syria said of Ibn Tyamiyyah:

> If he were asked a question in any of the sciences, it would appear as though he knew that science masterfully, to the exclusion of other sciences; and it would be judged that no one knows it as well as he. The jurists of all schools would benefit from his knowledge in their own schools, and would learn about them what they would not have known before. . . . It is not known that any scholar could win a debate against him. . . . He was master at interpretation, expression, organization, categorization and clarification. . . . (Victor E. Makari, *Ibn Taymiyyah's Ethics: The Social Factor*, pp. 26-27)

**IBN TUMART, ABU 'ABD ALLAH MUHAMMAD** (1077-1130). A Berber native of Morocco and ideologue of the **Almohad** dynasty who eventually proclaimed himself as the **Mahdi**. A member of the Masmuda tribe, he was educated at Alexandria and **Baghdad** and subsequently organized the Masmuda in a campaign against the **Almoravids** (1061-1147). He emphasized the unity of God and demanded puritanical moral reform based on the Koran and **Traditions**. Ibn Tumart's creed has been described as a mixture of messianic Shi'ism, **Ash'arite** dogmatics, **Zahirite** legal theory, some **Mu'tazilite** ideas, and **Kharijism**. His writings on theology, philosophy, and law were translated from Berber into Latin. Ibn Tumart was described as

> pious and devout, he lived in squalid poverty, subsisting on the coarsest fare and attired in rags; he generally went with downcast eyes; smiling whenever he looked a person in the face, and ever manifesting his propensity of devotion. He carried with him no other worldly goods than a staff and a skin for holding water; his courage was great; he spoke correctly the **Arabic** and the Maghrib (Berber) languages; he blamed with extreme severity the conduct of those who transgressed the divine law, and not content with obeying God's commandments, he labored to enforce their strict observance. (Ibn Khallikan, III, 206)

**IBRAHIM.** Arabic for Abraham. *See* ABRAHAM.

**'ID.** "Festival." *See* FESTIVALS.

**'ID AL-ADHA.** The Feast of Sacrifice on the 10th of the month of Dhu al-Hijja of the Islamic **calendar**. It is an Islamic holiday in Muslim countries, also called the Greater Bairam in Turkey (or 'Id al-Kabir or Bakr-i 'Id), which marks the end of the month of **pilgrimage**. Pilgrims and Muslims throughout the world slaughter a sheep, or camel, or purchase meat from a butcher as a sacrifice and distribute most of it to the poor. Large quantities of meat are shipped every year from Saudi Arabia to Afghanistan and other countries for distribution to the poor. Major purification, **ghusl**, is obligatory before prayer at a **Friday mosque**. It goes back to the tradition of **Abraham** attempting to sacrifice his son at the command of God.

**'ID AL-FITR.** The Feast of Breaking the Fast, celebrated on the first of the month of Shawwal, the day following the fast month of **Ramadhan**. The celebration begins with the appearance of the new moon, and the following day people pay their poor tax, *zakat al-fitr*, before attending prayer at a **Friday mosque**. It is a joyful celebration as it marks the end of the hardships of **fasting** for an entire month. New clothing is traditionally purchased on this occasion for family and servants, making it an occasion of gift-giving. The holiday is also called *'Id al-Saghir* (or Lesser Bayram) the Minor Feast, or *'Id al-Sadaqah*, the Feast of Alms.

**'IDDA.** "Number." The number of days a **divorced** or widowed **woman** must wait before she can remarry. *See* WAITING PERIOD.

**IDOLATRY.** Islam demands a strict monotheism; giving "partners to God" is idolatry **(shirk)** and an unforgivable sin. The **Hanbali** school, unlike the other orthodox Sunni **schools of law**, prohibits any intermediaries between God and mankind, forbidding the cult of **saints**, soothsayers, the healing properties of **amulets**, and the worship of holy shrines. All Sunni schools prohibit representational art—whether statues or images of living things (although this is no longer enforced in many parts of the Islamic world). Therefore, floral motifs and the **Arabic** script are used for ornamentation. The Koran says: "They disbelieve who say: 'Allah is one of three (in a Trinity) for there is no god except One God . . .'"(5:73). And "Say, to Allah belongs exclusively (the right to grant intercession . . ." (39:44). The **Twelver Shi'ites**, on the other hand, permit even portraits of **Imam** 'Ali.

**IDRISI, AL-SHARIF AL-** (1100-1165). Arab geographer who traveled widely in Europe, Africa, and Asia, and at the court of the Norman king Roger II in Sicily, he produced a geographic work that summed up all the previously known features of the world and made original contributions in his work, entitled *Nuzhad al-Mushtaq fi Ikhtiraq al-Afaq* (The recreation of him who yearns to traverse the lands).

**IDRISID DYNASTY** (788-985). First Shi'ite dynasty in Islamic history, founded by Idris ibn Abdullah (d. 793), a grandson of **Hasan** the son of Ali. He escaped to northern Morocco after an unsuccessful uprising in Medina, and the Berbers recognized him as their **imam**. He was poisoned at the instigation of **Harun al-Rashid** (786-809), the **'Abbasid caliph** at **Baghdad**. His son Idris II founded his capital in Fez, Morocco, but the state disintegrated soon thereafter as a result of attacks from the **Fatimids** in the east and the Spanish **Umayyads** in the west. Their major contributions included converting the Berbers and helping to maintain Sunni predominance by fighting their **Kharijite** neighbors. The Idrisids founded the Sharifian dynasty in Morroco, which rules the country to the present.

**IFTAR.** "Breaking." The breaking of fast at sunset during the month of **Ramadhan**. Cannon shots usually announce the time when it is permissible to eat, and people in the streets, bazaars, and homes begin their evening meal. Shortly before dawn, people eat once more to last them during the daylight **fasting**, which can be quite long during the hot summer months.

**IGNORANCE, THE AGE OF.** Muslims call the pre-Islamic period the "Age of Ignorance" (*jahiliya*). It was the age of tribalism and is reckoned to cover the period of about a century before the advent of Islam. It is also the heroic age of the great Bedouin poets, who extolled the virtues of Bedouin life: courage, loyalty, and generosity. The Seven Odes (**Mu'allaqat**) and similar collections of this period are considered superior to any poetry composed thereafter.

**IHRAM.** "Prohibiting." The state of ritual purity before **prayer**; also during **pilgrimage** (hajj) before entering the perimeter of the city of Mecca (**haram**). The pilgrim (hajji) performs the **ablution** (ghusl) and puts on a dress, consisting of two unsewn sheets or, in the case of **women**, a long robe. Women do not veil their faces during ihram. In the state of consecration all Muslims are manifestly equal before God.

**IJMA'.** "Collecting." The consensus of the community but subsequently only of the competent jurists on a point of theology or law, expressed in words, or deeds, as well as in silent agreement. In the early **Umayyad** period, the Caliph **'Umar II** instructed his governors in the provinces that cases should be decided by consensus of the jurists in each region. Together with the **Koran**, Traditions (**Sunnah**), and reasoning by analogy (**qiyas**), ijma' is one of the four pillars of Sunni **Islamic law** (Shari'ah). Ijma' is based on a saying of the Prophet that states: "My people will never agree in an error." The number required to validate a practice or belief varied with the four orthodox schools of jurisprudence, ranging from the entire community (**ummah**) to local groups or the **Companions** of the Prophet. Limited at first to the Companions of the Prophet, ijma' came to designate the agreement of the learned and had to be determined by retrospection.

Ijma' permitted the acceptance of **Sufism,** and other **innovations,** that were at first thought to be sinful.

**IJTIHAD.** "Exertion." The exercise of personal reasoning and private judgment or "informed opinion" (**ra'y**) and reasoning by analogy (**qiyas**) in questions of **Islamic law** not expressly provided for in the Koran and the Traditions (**Sunnah**). An example of this is the prohibition of all intoxicants, not just wine, mentioned in the Koran. Eventually, it came to be accepted by the four Sunni **schools of law** but exercised by those qualified to make a decision, the **mujtahids,** whose agreement became law on the basis of consensus (**ijma'**). Eventually, the four orthodox schools declared the "gate of ijtihad" closed and demanded imitation or emulation (**taqlid**) and condemned any further employment of ijtihad as sinful innovation (**bid'a**). **Muslim modernists** and their radical opponents, the **Islamists,** favor the reopening of the "gate of ijtihad" for different reasons. The modernists feel that it is necessary to reinterpret the bases of Islamic religion and law in light of modern developments; whereas, many Islamist reject much of what was produced during the period of classical Islam as innovation and want to establish an Islamic state on the model of Muhammad's community. Shi'ites have always accepted the ijtihad of the qualified doctors (mujtahid). *See also* MU'ADH, IBN JABAL.

**IKHSHIDID DYNASTY** (935-969). A dynasty founded by Muhammad ibn-Tughj (d. 496) in Egypt. He was a Turk from Ferghana who was made governor of Egypt by the **'Abbasid caliph** al-Radhi (r. 934-940). He made himself independent and annexed Syria and Palestine and, eventually, also the holy cities of Mecca and Medina to his domains. After his death, al-Misk **Kafur** (Musky Camphor), an Abyssinia eunuch, became the de facto ruler (946-968). The dynasty ended in 969 as a result of **Fatimid** attacks.

**IKHWAN.** "Brethren." **Wahhabi** Bedouin followers of Abd al-Aziz **Ibn Sa'ud** who formed armed militias and settled in village camps in 1912. They were an important factor in establishing their **imam** as king of Saudi Arabia, but they proved to be hostile to reforms promoting modernization and at times resisted attempts at limiting their political influence.

**IKHWAN AL-MUSLIMIN, AL-.** *See* ISLAMIST MOVEMENT and MUSLIM BROTHERHOOD.

**'ILM ('ELM).** The word *ilm* means knowledge, especially that of the Islamic sciences. An *alim* is a doctor of Islamic sciences, and the plural of the word **ulama** is applied to the body of Islamic jurisconsults and theologians.

**'ILM AL-FIQH.** *See* FIQH.

**'ILM AL-HADITH.** *See* HADITH.

**'ILM AL-TAFSIR.** *See* EXEGESIS.

**IMAM.** A leader who stands in front (*amama*) of the congregation at **prayer**. The term is also the title of the first four Sunni **caliphs** and the founders of the four orthodox schools of jurisprudence. Shi'ites use the term for the descendants of Ali and **Fatimah** whom they consider the rightful successor to the Prophet Muhammad in leadership of the Islamic community. Shi'ites are divided between those who accept, respectively, **Zayd**, the son of Ali (d. 740), the Fifth Imam; **Isma'il** (d. 760), the Seventh Imam; and Muhammad al-**Muntazar** (disappeared 878), the Twelfth Imam. They are the descendants of the Prophet and considered free of sin, infallible, and intermediaries with Allah. The **Twelver Shi'ite** (or Imamis) believe that Muhammad al-Muntazar, who disappeared as an infant, went into occultation and will return as the Messiah (**mahdi**) on the **Day of Judgment**. In the meantime, the Twelver Shi'ite jurist/theologians rule on the imam's behalf. The Shi'ite imams include the following:

'Ali ibn Abu Talib (d. 661)
al-Hasan (d. 669)
al-Husayn (d. 680)
'Ali Zayn al-'Abidin (d. 712)
Zayd ibn 'Ali (d. 740) Muhammad al-Baqir (d. 731)
Ja'far al-Sadiq (d. 765)

Isma'il (d. 760)
Musa al-Kazim (d. 799)
'Ali al-Radhi (d. 818)
Muhammad al-Jawad (d. 835)
Ali al-Hadi (d. 868)
al-Hasan al-Askari (d. 874)
Muhammad al-Muntazar (878).

See also HIDDEN IMAM; 'ISMA'ILIS; KHOMEYNI; VILAYAT AL FAQIH; ZAYDIS.

**IMAMIS.** Referring to **Twelver Shi'ites**. *See* SHI'ISM.

**IMAN.** "Faith." The six articles of Islamic faith include belief in God, the **angels** of God, the book of God (**Koran**), the **prophets** of God, the **Day of Judgment**, and the Divine Decree. Shi'ites must also believe in the infallible **Imams**. 'Amal, actions, are summarized under the term the **Five Pillars of Islam** as follows: (l) Profession of faith, shahada. (2) **Prayer**, salat. (3) **Fasting**, sawm. (4) **Almsgiving**, zakat. (5) **Pilgrimage**, hajj. To become a Muslim one has to testify that there is no god but Allah and that Muhammad is the **Messenger** of Allah (*La ilaha illa' llah wa Muhammad Rasul Allah*). *See also* CREED and FAITH, ARTICLES OF.

**IMITATION.** *See* TAQLID.

**IMMORALITY.** Immorality is forbidden by God and encouraged by **Iblis** (Satan). It is immoral to commit **adultery** (4:19, 25; 17:32), engage in homosexuality (7:80, 27:54, 29:28, 33:30 and 65:1), marry the wife of one's father (4:22), and commit slander (24:16, 17). A sinner must ask God's forgiveness and resolve not to commit such an act again.

**IMRU 'L-QAYS** (ca. 500-540). Grandson of the last king of Kindah, who was rejected by his father because of his dissolute life. He was to avenge the murder of his father and sought the support of the Emperor Justinian at Constantinople, but he died, reputedly of poisoning by the emperor. Known as the "Vagabond Prince," wandering from tribe to tribe, he is recognized as the greatest of pre-Islamic poets. Nicholson says of him: "Muhammad described him as 'their [poet's] leader in Hell-fire,' while the Caliphs **'Umar** and 'Ali, . . . notwithstanding, extolled his genius and originality" (105). Hailing a starved wolf as a comrade, he says: "Each of us what thing he finds devours: Lean is the wretch whose living is like ours"(ibid.). His prized poems are part of the **Mu'allaqat**.

**INHERITANCE, LAW OF.** The purpose of the law of inheritance is to prevent the possibility of concentration of wealth. In the tribal society of pre-Islamic Arabia **women** possessed no right of inheritance; in fact, they were often part of the objects to be inherited. The Koran said: "From what is left by parents and those nearest related there is a share for men and a share for women, whether the property be small or large—a determinate share" (4:7). Also: "O ye who believe! Ye are forbidden to inherit women against their will. Nor should ye treat them with harshness, that ye may take away part of the dower . . . "(4:19). The law of inheritance is complex; generally a female inherits a half of the share of a man. The property is to be distributed among ascending as well as descending relatives. No more than a third of the estate can be willed to a designated heir after all outstanding debts have been paid. In certain tribal societies, as for example the Afghan frontier, **women** do not receive their inheritance and a brother, or nearest male relative, marries the wife of the deceased.

**INQUISITION.** *See* MIHNA.

**INSHALLAH (IN SHA'A ALLAH).** A phrase, meaning "if God wills," which is used when talking about the future. It recognizes the supreme power of Allah, who alone decides the events of the future. Westerners who expect a firm commitment wrongly interpret the saying as evasive and tantamount to meaning "perhaps." It is based on the injunction in the Koran, which says: "Nor say of anything 'I shall do so and so tomorrow'—except if Allah so wills" (18:23-24).

**INTERCESSION.** "Tawassul." According to several verses in the Koran, the concept of intercession on the **Last Day** to save a sinner from punishment is not accepted. There are, however, some verses that hint at the possibility of intercession (43:86), which some have interpreted to mean that it is possible if good and bad deeds are evenly matched. According to one tradition, the Prophet Muhammad would intercede on the **Day of Judgment** "until all his community had gone to paradise before him." Shi'ism accepts the intercession of the **imam. Sufism** and popular Islam accept the cult of **saints** and intercession, but it is forbidden by the **Hanbali school of law.**

**INTEREST.** "Riba'" Taking of interest is forbidden in Islam (2:275). The prohibition has been evaded by legal subterfuge (**hila,** pl. hiyal), as for example when the money lender buys something and later sells it back for a lower amount. Islamic banks do not pay interest but charge fees or make a person who opens an account a partner who shares in the profit (and theoretically in the loss) of the bank.

**IQBAL, SIR MUHAMMAD** (1877-1938). Poet in Persian and Urdu, philosopher, and a founding father of the State of Pakistan. He was the product of a traditional and Western education, with a doctorate from Munich, Germany, and he taught **Arabic**, history, and economics at the Oriental College at Lahore. Iqbal was a **Muslim modernist** who favored the reinterpretation of Islam on the basis of **ijtihad** to reflect the interests of society. He held that

> Islam properly understood and rationally interpreted is not only capable of moving along with the progressive and evolutionary forces of life, but also of directing them into new and healthy channels in every epoch. (Mir Zohair Husain, 105)

He favored the partition of India to protect the culture of Muslims in what would have been a predominantly Hindu state. In Urdu and, primarily Persian, he called for reforms and the creation of a sound and prosperous Muslim nation.

**IRAN.** *See* ISLAMIC REPUBLIC OF IRAN.

**IRTIDAD.** *See* APOSTASY.

**ISFAHANI, ABU AL-FARAJ AL-** (897-ca.967). Arab literary historian and critic who won fame for his *kitab al-aghani* (Book of songs), which contained about 2,000 favorite songs of his time, annotated with anecdotes, biographical information, and excerpts from poetry. He was born in Isfahan, a direct descendant of the **Umayyad caliphs**, and educated at **Kufah** and **Baghdad**. One of his teachers was **Tabari**, the grammarian and **hadith** scholar. Criticized for his dirty appearance, drunkenness, and Shi'ite tendencies (he is said to have been a **Zaydi** Shi'ite), he was nevertheless one of the most widely quoted authorities on **Arabic** culture. It was at the Hamdanid court of Prince Sayf al-Dawlah at Aleppo where he wrote the *Book of Songs*. **Ibn Khaldun** says of the work:

> [It] is the Register of the Arabs. It comprises all that they had achieved in the past of excellence in every kind of poetry, history, music, etcetera. So far as I am aware, no other book can be put on a level with it in this respect. It is the final resource of the student

of belles-lettres, and leaves him nothing further to desire. (Nicholson, 32)

**ISFAHANI, ABU NU'IM AL-** (948-1038). **Shafi'ite** jurist and mystic of Isfahan, who published *hilyat al-awliyah* (The Jewel of the saints), a biographical dictionary of **Sufism**.

**ISHAQ, MUHAMMAD IBN** (704-767). *See* IBN ISHAQ, MUHAMMAD.

**ISLAM.** "Submission." A monotheistic religion that continues the prophetic Judeo-Christian tradition and recognizes Muhammad as the last of the **prophets**. It is the religion of about 800 million people, living predominantly in Asia, and with minorities all over the world. There are more than 2 million Muslims in the United States. The word Islam is **Arabic** and means submission, the obligation to "submit" to the commands of Allah, the Omniscient and Omnipotent God. Theologians distinguish between religious belief, or faith (**iman**), acts of worship and religious duty ('**ibadat**), and right-doing (ihsan)—all of which are part of the terms **din**, religion.

Muslims believe in one God, Allah, who is the Creator, Supreme Power, Judge, and Avenger but who is also the Compassionate and Merciful One. **Angels** are Allah's messengers and, like humans, His creatures and servants. They record men's actions and bear witness against them on the **Day of Judgment**. The Angel **Gabriel** is God's chief **messenger**. There are also **jinn**, spirits, who are good or evil like men. The fallen, or evil, jinn are called shaytans, **devils**, whose leader is **Iblis** (Satan). He is given "authority over those who should be seduced by him." God sends His prophets to bring His message. The major messengers include **Adam**, **Noah**, **Abraham**, **Moses**, and **Jesus**, but Muhammad is the last of the prophets and the Koran is the last message, superseding the Torah (Tawrah) of Moses, the Psalms (**Zabur**) of David, and the Gospel (Injil) of Jesus. Muslims believe in a Day of Judgment, when the good will enter paradise and the evil will be condemned to eternal hellfire. Personal responsibility before God is important in Islam, and there is no belief in atonement.

Religious duties ('Ibadat) can be summarized under a code of rituals called the "**Five Pillars of Islam**," as follows:

The profession of faith (**shahadah**). A Muslim says: "I testify that there is no god but Allah and I testify that Muhammad is the

**Messenger** of Allah." Anyone who sincerely testifies to that is a Muslim.

Prayer (salat) which is to be performed five times a day, facing the prayer direction (**qibla**), the location of the **Ka'ba**, a cube-like building in Mecca (built by Abraham, according to the Koran). Prayers include recitation of the Arabic text accompanied by rhythmical bowings (rak'ah) and can be performed in public or private. A ritual washing (**wudhu**) is required before prayer. If there is a congregation, one person is the leader (**imam**), and the rest perform their prayers in unison. ʿ he muezzin (mu'adhdhin) sounds the call to prayer (**adhan**), often from the top of a minaret. The Friday sermon (**khutbah**) also has political significance because the name of the ruler is invoked, indicating the political loyalty of the congregation.

Almsgiving (**Zakat**) is the requirement to give either a percentage of one's wealth or of one's yearly income to the poor. This obligation is not uniformly enforced in the Islamic world.

Fasting (Sawm) is enjoined during the Muslim month of Ramadhan, "the month during which the Koran was sent down." From sunrise to sundown the believer is to abstain from food or drink, which poses considerable hardship when the fast occurs during the long, hot, summer months. Children, the ill, pregnant **women**, travelers, and soldiers in war are exempt, but those prevented must make up this obligation at a later time.

Pilgrimage (Hajj) is a legal obligation of every adult Muslim of either sex to travel at least once in a lifetime to Mecca, provided the person is economically able to do so, and one who has performed pilgrimage carries the honorific title of "hajji."

"Striving in the Way of God," (**Jihad**) is considered by some one of the Pillars of Islam. It is now interpreted as a war in defense of Islam, or any effort in a good cause. The fallen **martyr** is assured of immediate salvation and **heaven**.

Duties to one's fellow men (mu'amalat)and right-doing (ihsan) demand private and public morality, the avoidance of actions, that are forbidden, **haram**, or reprehensible, **makruh**. Minor differences exist in the performance of these obligations within the four orthodox Sunni schools. Sunni Islam does not recognize a central church with power to make decisions on dogma, nor are its practitioners a clergy that stands between mankind and God. They are members of the **ulama**, a body of scholars of the Islamic sciences who constitute the teachers, judges, **muftis**, and jurists of the Islamic world. They find the law on the basis of the four **Schools of Law** but do not legislate. The Shi'ite school of jurisprudence is based on the **Ja'farite** school, named after the Sixth Shi'ite **Imam, Ja'far al-Sadiq** (699-765).

**ISLAMIC AMAL.** A movement established in 1982 by Husain Musawi who left **Amal** and allied himself with the Iranian Revolutionary Guards in the Baalbek Valley of Lebanon. The movement merged with **Islamic Jihad** and **Hizbullah** to fight Israeli occupation forces but eventually lost its influence to Hizbullah.

**ISLAMIC CALENDAR.** *See* CALENDAR.

**ISLAMIC CONFERENCE ORGANIZATION.** *See* ORGANIZATION OF ISLAMIC CONFERENCE.

**ISLAMIC DRESS.** A dress for **women,** which covers most of the body and head, but leaves the face free. It is worn in areas where the **veil** is not obligatory by **Islamist** women as a political statement and as a sign of orthodoxy. The Koran says: "And say to the believing women that they should lower their gaze and guard their modesty; that they should not display their beauty and ornaments except what (ordinarily) appear thereof; that they should draw their veils over their bosoms and not display their beauty except to their husbands, their fathers, their husband's father, their sons, their husband's sons, their brothers and their brothers' sons" (24:31). *See also* CHADOR.

**ISLAMIC JIHAD.** A pro-Iranian Shi'ite group, founded in Lebanon in 1982, which declared war on the American and Western presence in Lebanon. It is held responsible for the 1983 bombing of the United States Embassy in West Beirut and the attack on the U.S. Marine headquarters which cost the lives of 241 soldiers. In 1982 the group took the vice president of the American University of Beirut hostage in retaliation for the kidnaping of four Iranian diplomats by Maronite militias. It facilitated a hostages-for-arms deal between the United States and Iran, and eventually an exchange of Israeli, Lebanese, Palestinian, and Western detainees and hostages. It appears to have ceased its activities and some of its members merged with **Hizbullah**.

**ISLAMIC JIHAD.** An offshoot of the **Muslim Brotherhood** of Egypt, which claimed to have been a major force in the *intifada,* the resistance to Israeli occupation of Palestine. It opposed the accord of

September 1993 between Israel and the Palestinian Liberation Organization (PLO) and continued armed attacks on Israeli targets. It has considerable support in the Gaza Strip where Jihad publishes a weekly newspaper.

**ISLAMIC LAW.** Islamic law (*shari'ah*, from *shar'*, the path leading to the water hole) is God-given and a prescription for the right life in this world and for salvation in the world to come. During his lifetime, the Prophet Muhammad transmitted Allah's commands. These were eventually collected in the book of readings, or recitations, the Koran. The Koran is the basis of law for all Muslims, although various **sects** and schools have differed in its interpretation. When no conclusive guidance was found in the Koran, the Traditions (**Sunnah**), or practice of the Prophet were consulted. There are six "correct" books of Sunni Traditions, compiled by **al-Bukhari, Muslim ibn al-Hajjaj, Abu Daud al-Sijistani, Muhammad ibn Isa al-Tirmidhi, Abu 'Abd Allah Ibn Maja,** and **Ahmad al-Nasa'i.**

Four **Schools of Law** eventually developed in Sunni Islam named after early legal scholars, the **Malikite,** named after **Malik ibn Anas** (d. 795); the **Shafi'ite,** named after ibn Idris al-**Shafi'i** (d.819); the **Hanbalite,** named after **Ahmad ibn Hanbal** (d. 855); and the Hanafite, named after **Abu Hanifah** (d.767). The Hanafite school has the largest number of adherents. It recognizes as a basis of jurisprudence, in addition to the Koran and the *Sunnah*, consensus of the scholars (**ijma'** ), and reasoning by analogy (**qiyas**). Legal reasoning is called **ijtihad,** the struggle, or effort, in arriving at a legal decision. By the 10th century Muslim jurists decided by consensus that Islamic law was complete and that independent interpretation, *ijtihad,* was no longer permissible. Henceforth, Sunni Muslims were to follow, or imitate (**taqlid**), the existing body of law. **Muslim modernists** as well as radical **Islamists** want to reopen the "Gate of Ijtihad" to permit a reinterpretation of Islamic law in order to meet new, modern requirements.

Judges (qadis) in **Shari'ah** courts are to apply the law, subject to consultation with legal experts (**muftis**), who issue legal decisions (**fatwas**). A jurist (**faqih**) is trained in an Islamic college (**madrasah**) to serve as lawyer, teacher, judge, and mufti. Punishments include the penalties for major offenses prescribed in the Koran or **Traditions** (**hadd,** pl. hudud), discretionary and variable punishments (**ta'zir**), and **retaliation** (qisas). Religious injunctions (*al-ahkam al-khamsa*) are five: (1) obligatory (**fardh** or wajib), duties whose performance is rewarded and whose omission is punished, and (2) forbidden (**haram**), actions which are forbidden and punishable; (3) meritorious (**mandub**, also called sunnah, masnun, and mustahabb), actions whose performance is rewarded but whose omission is not punished; (4) reprehensible (**makruh**), things the believer is advised to refrain from; and (5) indifferent (**mubah** or ja'iz), actions whose performance or omission is neither rewarded nor punished. *See* FIVE PRINCIPAL ACTS IN ISLAMIC LAW.

Shi'ites of the **Twelver Usuli** school of jurisprudence find their sources of law in the Koran and the Traditions (*Sunnah*), the statements, deeds, and tacit consent of the Prophet and the **imams**, as well as the consensus (ijma') of the Shi'ite jurists, and the application of reason (*'aql*). It follows from the principle that "whatever is ordered by reason is also ordered by religion (*kull ma hakam bih al-'aql, hakam bih al-shar'*). The most important sources for Shi'ite law are the *al-kutub al-arba'a* (Four books). In the absence of the **Hidden Imam**, the qualified scholars (**mujtahid**) of the Twelver Shi'ites are permitted to legislate on the basis of ijtihad.

Islamic law is an ideal law as it includes man's obligation to God (*'ibadat*), ritual worship, as well as matters of hygiene and etiquette and his obligations to his fellow men (*mu 'amalat*). There has always existed a dichotomy of "God's law" and the "King's law" and customary practices continued, provided they did not conflict with Islamic law. Rulers and governments enacted statutes according to the needs of the day. Police courts existed and judges based their decisions on local custom. Toward the end of the 19th century, Islamic law was increasingly relegated to matters of personal status. Great Britain introduced "Anglo-Muhammadan" law and the French employed their civil, criminal, and commercial codes. After the demise of the **Ottoman empire** as a result of the First World War, independent Muslim states continued this process. But no Muslim country went as far as Turkey which abolished all aspects of Islamic law and established a secular republic in the 1920s. Saudi Arabia, Oman, Sudan, Yemen, and Afghanistan are the only countries that rely predominantly on the Shari'ah.

**ISLAMIC MODERNISM.** *See* MUSLIM MODERNISM.

**ISLAMIC REFORM MOVEMENTS.** *See* SALAF and SALAF-IYYAH.

**ISLAMIC REPUBLIC OF IRAN.** The Islamic Republic of Iran was established in 1979 when a national revolt resulted in the overthrow of the Pahlavi monarchy. Soon the Shi'ite clergy under the leadership of Ayatollah Ruhullah **Khomeyni** was able to prevail, gradually eliminating all secular parties. Khomeyni proceeded to realize his concept of the Islamic state, which was to be governed under the principles of **Islamic law**. Although permitting such modern institutions as a representative government and parliament, he claimed for himself the governance of the supreme jurist (**vilayat-i faqih**). He was to rule in the absence of the **Hidden Imam**. Khomeyni was assisted by a 12-member **Guardians Council**, which had veto power over all legislation and political appointments. The Revolutionary Guards were established as the military arm of the new regime.

It took some time for the regime to consolidate its power, confronted by armed resistance by political groups, primarily the **Fida'iyan-i Khalq,** a leftist **Islamist** party. Relations with the United States, characterized as the "Great Satan," deteriorated in November 1979 when young supporters of Khomeyni occupied the U.S. embassy and took its staff hostage for 444 days. In late 1980, Iraq invaded Iran in an indecisive, but very bloody war, which lasted until August 1988. When Khomeyni died in June 1989, he was succeeded as the supreme jurist by Ayatollah 'Ali **Khamenei** who had similar powers but no longer enjoyed the charisma of his predecessor. When Sayyid Muhammad **Khatami** was elected president in a landslide election on May 23, 1997, there was hope that a liberalization in policies was imminent. But the conservatives continue to control all levers of power and have prevented any political or social reforms.

**ISLAMIC SALVATION FRONT (FRONT DE SALUT ISLAM-IQUE, FIS).** A radical Algerian Islamist movement that resorted to terrorism when it was denied victory in the general elections of December 1991. In the first free election in Algeria, the FIS called for the establishment of an Islamic state in which **Islamic law** would replace secular law. The FIS won 55 percent of the vote in regional elections in 1989 and 49 percent in the first round of general elections on December 26, 1991. To prevent an FIS victory, the military took control of the government in mid-January 1992, prohibited all parties, and arrested **Islamist** leaders. As a result the FIS has since conducted a reign of terror, which has destabilized the political process and cost many thousands of lives.

**ISLAMIC SCIENCE.** *See* EDUCATION.

**ISLAMIC WORLD.** *See* ORGANIZATION OF THE ISLAMIC CONFERENCE.

**ISLAMIST MOVEMENT.** The movement, also called "political" Islam, was born in large measure as a reaction to the process of Westernization in the Islamic world and the growth of secular, liberal, and Marxist ideologies among Muslim youth. The movement owed much of its organization and ideology to the influence of the **Muslim Brotherhood** of Egypt. Egyptians and foreign Muslims studying at Egyptian institutions spread the message of revolution throughout the Islamic world. They studied the works of Islamic thinkers, such as **Hasan al-Banna** (1906-1949), the "Supreme Guide" of the Ikhwanis; Sayyid **Qutb**, executed in **Cairo** in 1966; and Abu'l A'la **Maududi** (d. 1973), founder of the Pakistani **Jama'at-i Islami** and author of religio-political treatises. They staged demonstrations protesting government policies, Zionism, and the war in Vietnam. They honed their oratorical and martial skills in confrontations with Marxist students on campuses throughout the Islamic world and soon won the majority of offices in student elections.

Many of the Islamist leaders are the product of secular, rather than religious, educational institutions. Many are graduates of technical and medical schools. They share the basic beliefs of the **ulama** but their philosophies are derived through contact with Western ideologies. They see themselves as a vanguard of a revolutionary revivalist movement and teach political sermons to mobilize the masses. They build neighborhood **mosques**, provide soup kitchens for the poor, and aid the families of **martyrs**. They are missionaries who want to make "true" Muslims of the people. Ideologically, they reject the **Traditions** of classical Islam and call for the **ijma'** of the community, not the **ulama**, and the reopening of the "gate of **ijtihad**."

The Islamists are not a monolithic movement, but rather a collection of numerous organizations that want to establish a "true" Islamic state in which sovereignty belongs to God and the **Shari'ah** is the law and constitution. In such a state, they want to enforce all the Islamic punishments, including prohibitions on taking **interest**, playing music, showing television, playing games, and enforcing traditional

**dress** and attendance at **prayers**. They want to turn a Muslim state into an Islamic state.

**ISM.** Personal name. *See* NAMES AND NAMEGIVING.

**ISMAʻIL** (d. 760). Son of the Sixth **Imam, Jaʻfar al-Sadiq**, imam of the **Ismaʻilis**, or Sevener Shiʻites. He was designated by his father to succeed him, but he died before his father. Therefore, Jaʻfar al-Sadiq appointed Musa al-Kazim as imam. This led to schism in the Shiʻite movement and the followers of Ismaʻil proclaimed him the last and Seventh Imam, whereas the Twelvers continued to count six successors. *See* ISMAʻILIS.

**ISMAʻIL, SHAH** (1487-1524). *See* SAFAVID DYNASTY.

**ISMAʻILIS.** A Shiʻite **sect** that recognizes **Ismaʻil**, son of **Jaʻfar al Sadiq**, as the seventh and last **imam**; therefore, they are also called the Seveners (*sabʻiya*). They hold that Ismaʻil will return as the **mahdi** at the end of time, and in addition believe in the exoteric (**zahir**) interpretation of the Koran; also in an esoteric (**batin**) doctrine. The esoteric doctrine consists of two parts: an allegorical interpretation (**taʻwil**) of the Koran and the **Shariʻah**, and truths (haqaʼiq), a system of philosophy and science, coordinated with religion. This doctrine is only known to the initiated who pass through stages of enlightenment according to their intellectual capacity. They try to explain all cosmic and historical developments by the number seven: seven prophets have legislative functions (**Adam, Noah, Abraham, Moses, Jesus**, Muhammad, and Muhammad ibn Ismaʻil). Between each of them there are seven or 12 silent legislators. Regarding the **imam**, some believe him to be merely the lieutenant of the Prophet; others regard him as embodying God's will. The Ismaʻilis are divided into subgroups, such as the **Assassins, Bohras, Druzes, Fatimids, Khojas, Nusairis, Qarmatians**, and others.

**ISNAD (SANAD).** The chain of trustworthy persons, beginning with an eyewitness, who report a saying or action of the Prophet. *See* HADITH.

**ISRAFIL (ASRAFIL).** One of the four archangels, who trumpets the beginning of the **Day of Judgment**. *See also* ANGELS.

**ISTANBUL.** Capital of the **Ottoman empire** since its capture in 1453 by Muhammad the Conqueror (1451-1481). The city, named Constantinople after its founder Emperor Constantine in 330, is strategically important as it is located at the divide of two continents and at an important crossroads of trade. It was the seat of the **Ottoman sultan/caliph** until 1923.

**ISTIHSAN.** "Seeking the good" is a principle in the **Hanafite** school of jurisprudence, which permits the judge to make a decision on the basis of equity and justice.

**ISTISLAH.** Employed especially in the **Malikite** school of jurisprudence, which permits the judge to make a decision on the basis of what is good for the general welfare of the community.

**ITHNA 'ASHARIYYAH.** *See* TWELVER SHI'ITES.

**'IZRA'IL.** Angel of Death. Not mentioned by name, the Koran says: "Say: 'The Angel of Death put in charge of you, will (duly) take your souls: Then shall you be brought back to your Lord'" (32:11). *See also* ANGELS.

-J-

**JABARTI, ABD AL RAHMAN AL-** (1753-1825). Egyptian historian and biographer who wrote a modern history of Egypt, covering the period of French occupation (1798-1803) and its aftermath, which is one of the primary sources for the period. He rejected French materialism and unbelief, but he was impressed by French civic honesty and diligence, which he contrasted with the shortcomings of Egyptian society. He was a pioneer whose ideas found acceptance among **Muslim modernists**.

**JABRITES (JABRIYYAH).** A school of the **Umayyad** period that denied man's free will and asserted that man in all of his actions is subject to the compulsion (*jabr*) of God's sovereignty. Most important of the Jabrites is Jahm ibn Safwan (d.746), who held that salvation was predetermined. Orthodox Islam accepts a measure of free will with the **Ash'arite** concept of "acquisition" **(kasb)**. Popular

Islam tends to a fatalistic acceptance of man's fate (**kismet**). *See also* QADARIYYAH, for a school which accepts man's free will.

**JA'FAR AL-BARMAKI** (d. 803). Member of the **Barmakid** family of **viziers**, tutor of Caliph **al-Ma'mun** (813-833), and adviser of **Harun al-Rashid**.

**JA'FAR AL-SADIQ** (699?-765). Sixth Shi'ite **Imam** and founder of the Ja'farite school of jurisprudence of **Twelver Shi'ism**. He lived in Medina where two of his students, **Malik ibn Anas** and **Abu Hanifa**, became founders of Sunni **schools of law**. Ja'far al-Sadiq appointed his son **Isma'il** as the Seventh Imam, but subsequently he chose another son, Musa al-Kazim. The supporters of Isma'il, the **Isma'ilis**, consider Isma'il the seventh and last imam (except for the **Khojas** who recognize the **Agha Khan**), whereas the Twelvers continued to count their imams from Musa al-Kazim. *See also* SHI'ISM.

**JAHANNAM.** *See* HELL.

**JAHILIYYAH.** *See* IGNORANCE, THE AGE OF.

**JAHIZ, AMR IBN BAHR AL-** (776 -868). Member of the **Mu'tazilite** school who formed his own sub-**sect** supporting the doctrine of free will, named after him *al-Jahiziyyah*. Al-Jahiz, the "Goggle Eyed," was born and educated in **Basra**, and spent several years at the caliphal court in **Baghdad** and Samarra. Called a freethinker, Jahiz was a prolific writer with more than 200 publications to his name, of which about 30 (or 75?) are still extant. His most important work is the seven-volume *kitab al-hayawan* (Book of animals), which presents much scientific information. He published in a variety of fields, including theology, philosophy, linguistics, history, literature, ethics, astronomy, geography, botany, zoology, mineralogy, and music. His *kitab al bayan wa al-tabyin* (Book of eloquence and exposition) is a treatise on rhetoric, which is used as a text even today.

**JALAL AL-DIN RUMI, MAULAWI (JALALUDDIN RUMI, 1207-1273).** Held to be the greatest of all **Sufi** poets, called Shaykh al-Akbar, the "Greatest Master" (or mawlana) by his supporters. Born in Balkh, in present-day Afghanistan, he moved with his father to Konya in Turkey, called Rum at the time; hence his name Rumi. He received a traditional **education** and at age 15 he experienced his mystical "unveiling." He studied at the **Nizamiyyah** in **Baghdad** and traveled widely in the Islamic world. His masterpiece, the *Masnawi*, written in Persian, is a six-volume work of spiritual teachings. He is the founder of the **Mevlevi** order, also known as the "Whirling Dervishes." Jalal al-Din is buried in Konya.

**JAMA'AT-I ISLAMI.** Name of a Pakistani political organization founded by Maulana Abu'l-'Ala **Maududi** (1903-1979) in 1941 that advocates the establishment of an Islamic state patterned after the early Islamic community. It is **pan-Islamic** in nature and looks at the Muslim community as one nation (**ummah**) and rejects nationalism as contrary to Islam. The party opposes capitalism, socialism, forbids the taking of **interest**, **gambling**, prostitution, consumption of **alcohol**, speculation, and hoarding, and demands the promotion of social welfare. Banned in 1953 for its involvement in the Punjab riots against the **Ahmadiyyah** movement, the party gained new prominence when President Zia ul-Haq proclaimed Pakistan an Islamic state in the late 1970s. It has not been very successful in winning votes because of ethnic and sectarian differences in Pakistan and resistance from secular and feudal forces. The party has supported like-minded groups in Afghanistan and elsewhere.

**JAMI, NUR AL-DIN ABD AL-RAHMAN** (1414-1492). The last great poet of classical Persian, a scholar and mystic who was born in Jam and educated in Herat and Samarkand. He settled in Herat where he enjoyed the support of Ali Shir Nawa'i, **vizier** at the court of Sultan Bayqara. His works deal chiefly with moral philosophy and mysticism.

**JANABA.** A state of major impurity that requires the purification of **ghusl**, greater **ablution**. Such impurity is caused by orgasm, copulation, menstruation, and other bodily discharges.

**JANNAH.** "Garden." *See* HEAVEN.

**JARIR, IBN 'ATIYAH** (c. 650-729). A native of the Banu Tamim of Iraq, known as the greatest satirist of the **Umayyad** period and court poet of Ibn Yusuf **al-Hajjaj**, the governor of Iraq. A Bedouin poet and rival of Hammam ibn Ghalib al-**Farazdaq** and Ghiyath al-Taghlibi al-**Akhtal**, his fame was so great "that to be worsted by him was reckoned a greater distinction than to vanquish anyone else" (Nicholson, 245). In addition to his satires, several elegies, and panegyrics in honor of the Caliphs **'Abd al-Malik** and **'Umar** II have been preserved. **Ibn Khallikan** said: "of the four kinds of verses— boasting, laudatory, satirical, and amatory—al-Jarir excelled in all" (I, 295).

**JERUSALEM (AL-QUDS).** A holy city to **Jews, Christians,** and **Muslims** and site of the oldest Muslim archeological treasures, the **Dome of the Rock** and **Al-Aqsa Mosque,** built by Caliph **'Abd al-Malik** in the seventh century. It is the site of Muhammad's **Nocturnal Journey** to heaven in 619. Caliph **'Umar ibn al-Khatab** accepted the surrender of the city in 638, and the inhabitants were given protection and allowed to live autonomously under their own laws and religion in exchange for payment of a poll tax (**jizyah**). In 1099 the Crusaders captured the city and founded the Kingdom of Jerusalem, but in 1187 **Salah al-Din** (Saladin) recaptured the city. The Crusaders gained it again from 1229-1244, but then it remained in **Mamluk** and **Ottoman** hands, until it became part of the British mandate of Palestine in 1920. After the United Nations decided to partition Palestine and the resulting war of 1948, the old part of the city remained in Arab hands until Israel occupied it in 1967 and still holds Jerusalem today.

**JESUS ('ISA).** Recognized in Islam as a **prophet** (19:30, 34), **messenger** (4:171), messiah, and the only creature, besides **Adam,** who has no father (3:52, 59). He is an apostle, but not God (5: 72). He will bear witness on Resurrection Day (4:157). The Koran says: "Such (was) Jesus the son of **Mary:** (it is) a statement of truth, about which they (vainly) dispute (19:34); and "O **People of the Book!** Commit no excesses in your religion: nor say of Allah aught but the truth. Christ Jesus the son of Mary was (no more than) a messenger of Allah, and His word which He bestowed on Mary and a spirit proceeding from Him: so believe in Allah and His Messengers. Say not 'Three:' desist: it will be better for you: for Allah is one God: Glory be to Him: (far exalted is He) above having a son . . ." (4:171). Muslims believe that Jesus was not crucified: "That they said (in boast), 'We killed Christ Jesus the son of Mary, The Messenger of Allah;' But they killed him not nor crucified him. Only a likeness of that was shown to them . . . . . Nay, Allah raised him up unto Himself, and Allah is Exalted in power Wise" (4:157-158). Jesus is believed to have had the power to raise the dead, heal the sick, and breath life into clay birds.

**JEWS.** *See* JUDAISM.

**JIBRIL (JABRA'IL).** The Archangel Gabriel. *See* ANGELS.

**JIHAD.** "Striving." An "effort in the way of God," was originally an obligation to wage war against the unbelievers until they accepted Islam or submitted to Islamic rule. A Muslim who dies in jihad is a **martyr** (*shahid*) and directly enters paradise. Monotheists with a sacred book, like **Christians** and **Jews**, are not forced to convert and enjoy the status of protected subjects. In battle, an enemy is given three choices: accept Islam and enjoy rights of equality with Muslims; submit and become a tribute paying subject with religious freedom and protection of one's property; fight and leave the judgment to God, in which case a defeated enemy becomes part of the **booty**.

These options were historically offered in the siege of a fortified city to encourage the enemy to surrender. In large conquests, as for example in India, Muslim rulers accepted even polytheistic "idol worshippers" as **Peoples of the Book** and therefore not subject to annihilation. **Muslim modernists** quote a Koranic passage: "Fight in the Way of God against those who fight against you, but do not commit aggression . . ." (2:190), maintaining that the obligation of jihad was binding only for the early Islamic period and that jihad also means inwardly waging war against the carnal soul—a kind of moral imperative. The latter is called "The Great Effort" (*jihad akbar*) and is more important as it strives to achieve man's personal perfection; jihad within the **umma** addresses wrongs within the community of Muslims. The third type of jihad is the "martial jihad" which is called "The Small Effort." A number of radical Islamist groups, as for example Jama'at al-Jihad, also known as Al-Jihad, of Egypt and **Osama bin Laden**'s organization, al-Qa'idah, operating from Afghanistan, have proclaimed jihad, the latter to force the expulsion of foreign troops from the territory of Saudi Arabia.

**JILANI, 'ABDUL QADIR AL-** (1077-1166). Theologian, preacher, mystic, and founder of the **Sufi** order that bears his name. Born in Jilan in Persia, he lived in **Baghdad** where his tomb is the object of much veneration. Introduced to Sufism late in life, he became one of the first Sufi **saints** and won great fame for his collection of exhortations called the *Futuh al-Ghayb* (Revelations of the unseen). He called for **jihad** against the self to conquer worldliness and submit to God's will. The **Qadiriyyah** is the first and largest of Sufi fraternities with devotees throughout the Islamic world. 'Abdul Qadir is said to have had 49 sons.

**JINN.** *See* GENIE.

**JIZYAH.** Poll tax levied formerly on non-Muslim monotheists who were possessors of a scripture, the **Peoples of the Book** (*ahl al-kitab*, such as **Christians** and **Jews**). Only adult males of sound mind and body and financial means were to be so taxed. **Women**, children, the aged, beggars, monks, and **slaves** were exempted. In exchange, they enjoyed freedom of life, liberty, and property and were not drafted into the military. In modern days, this discriminatory tax is no longer levied.

**JUBBA'I, ABU ALI MUHAMMAD AL-** (861-915). A celebrated scholastic theologian. He was one of the leading **Mu'tazilites** and an antagonist of his former student, Abu 'l-Hasan **al-Ash'ari**. Juba'i's numerous works were frequently cited but are no longer extant. His son, Abu Hashim 'Abd al-Salam continued his father's work and tried to reconcile his doctrines with orthodox teachings. Jubba'i was born in Jubba, near **Basra**, and he died in **Baghdad**.

**JUDAISM.** Jews are mentioned in the Koran and **Traditions**, called Yahudi (pl. Yahud) and Banu Israel, the Tribe of Israel. They are a **People of the Book**, monotheists with a **scripture**, whose validity was to be corrected with the message of the **Prophet** Muhammad. Virtually all major characters of the Old Testament are mentioned in the Koran and the Traditions. Abraham is recognized as the ancestor of the Arabs and Jews, **Moses** (Musa) is the Law-Giver of the Jews. The Koran appeals to the Jews, saying "O Children of Israel! Call to mind the (special) favour which I bestowed upon you, and that I preferred you to all others" (2:47). It appeals to the Jews to accept Muhammad's message, saying: "It was We who revealed the Torah (to Moses), therein was guidance and light" (5:44), and "We sent Jesus the son of **Mary**, confirming the Torah that had come before him: We sent him the Gospel, therein was guidance and light" (5:46). But the books were corrupted with time and Allah "sent the Scripture in truth [the Koran], confirming the scripture that came before it, and guarding it in safety: so judge between them what Allah hath revealed." When the Jews did not accept Muhammad's invitation to accept the new **revelation**, the Koran warned Muslims not to make them their friends (5:78, 80).

However, Jews lived throughout the centuries in the Islamic world and some 200,000 fled from Granada after the Christian conquest in 1492 and settled in the major cities of the Islamic world. They have continued to speak Latino, their Spanish dialect, to this day. It was only with the establishment of Israel that most Jews left to live in the new State of Israel.

**JUDGE.** "Qadhi." A person of good reputation who is versed in Islamic jurisprudence and acts as a judge in civil and criminal matters. As an institution, it dates from the time of **'Umar II** (r.717-720) who appointed the first judges for Egypt and Syria; subsequently, governors appointed judges in the provinces. Since the late ninth century judges were organized in a hierarchical manner with a chief judge (*qadhi al-qudhat*) at the **'Abbasid** capital. **Islamic law** is God-given and cases are decided by precedent according to a particular school of jurisprudence. A judge could seek the advice of a professional jurist (**mufti**), the litigants appeared personally in court, and written or circumstantial evidence was not admitted. Judges were primarily confined to the cities, and non-Muslims were left under the jurisdiction of their own ecclesiastical courts. Qadhis also acted as guardians of orphans, lunatics, and minors, and administered the pious foundations (**waqf**).

In modern times, states have increasingly secularized the courts, leaving only matters of personal status under the jurisdiction of the **Shari'ah**. Special police courts (*mazalim*) existed since classical times. Military courts and courts set up according to Western models eventually evolved. But recent revivalist movements want to return legal jurisdiction to the traditional system.

**JUM'A.** The day of "general assembly." *See* FRIDAY.

**JUWAYNI, 'ABD AL-MALIK AL-** (1028-1085). **Imam** of the Holy Places (*Imam al-Haramayn*), a **Shafi'ite** jurist and **Ash'arite** theologian who taught in **Baghdad**, Mecca, Medina, and Nishapur where his activities were sponsored by the **Seljuq vizier** Hasan ibn 'Ali **Nizam al-Mulk**. Al-Juwayni was a teacher of al-**Ghazali** and al-

**Ansari**. As a Persian, he held the view that the **caliphate** need not be held by a member of the **Quraysh**. Historians tell us that at his death some 400 of his students broke their pens and refused to study for an entire year.

**JUWAYNI, ALA AL-DIN ATA MALIK Al-** (1226-1283). Born in Juwayn, Khorasan, he received a traditional **education** and traveled widely, visiting the **Mongol** Great Khan in Karakorum. One of the great Persian historians, he accompanied the Mongol founder of the Ilkhanid dynasty, **Hulagu Khan**, on his invasion of Persia. He was governor of **Baghdad** for 24 years and is the author of the *Tarikh-i Jahan Kusha*, translated into English by J. A. Boyle under the title *The History of the World Conqueror*. It is an important source also on the state of the Khwarizm Shahs and the **Isma'ilis** at **Alamut**. He is buried in Tabriz.

**JUWAYRIYYAH BINT AL-HARITH.** Wife of the Prophet. Captured by Muslim forces, she asked to be ransomed, but Muhammad married her and released one hundred of her relatives. He provided a **dowry** of 400 **dirhams**. 'A'ishah was to have said of her: "No woman was ever a greater blessing to her people than this Juwayriyyah."

## -K-

**KA'BAH.** "Cube." A cube-like building, the most holy shrine of Islam, located in the center of the Grand **Mosque** in the holy city of Mecca. The building is about 12 meters long, 10 meters wide, and 15 meters high, made of grey stone with a small entrance on the northern side. On the eastern corner the **Black Stone** is attached at the height of 1.5 meters. Muslims believe that the Ka'bah was erected by **Adam** and rebuilt by **Abraham** after the Flood; a small shrine marks the place where Abraham was said to have stood. The building is covered with a black (during **pilgrimage**, white), gold-embroidered brocade curtain (*kiswa*), which is changed every year. It is cut up into pieces and sold to pilgrims. The Ka'bah is the prayer direction (**qiblah**) toward which Muslims all over the world bow. The surrounding area is sacred territory, forbidden to non-Muslims and in which no animals are to be killed. The Koran says: "And remember Abraham said: 'My Lord, make this a city of peace, and feed its people with fruits, such of them as believe in Allah and the **Last Day**.'" The Ka'bah was repeatedly destroyed and rebuilt and the Black Stone was carried off by **Qarmatian** invaders in 930. The Grand Mosque, surrounding the Ka'bah was enlarged and renovated in the 1950s to accommodate up to two million pilgrims to perform the ritual circumambulation of the shrine.

**KADHI (KAZI).** *See* JUDGE.

**KAFIR.** "Coverer." One who hides, or covers up the truth. An unbeliever, polytheist, and idol worshiper who is condemned to eternal hellfire. Heretics and apostates from Islam were at times killed. **Christians** and **Jews,** as well as other monotheists and peoples of a revealed **scripture,** are not kafirs. They are protected subjects who, on payment of a poll tax, enjoy freedom of religion and property, although in popular terminology they are often included in the term of kafirs. *See also* RIDDAH.

**KAFUR, ABU AL-MISK** (d. 969). "Father of the Muski Camphor." Abyssinian eunuch who became virtual ruler of Egypt and Syria in the second half of the **Ikhshidid dynasty** (935-969). He was tutor of Muhammad al-Ikhshid's sons, Unjur and 'Ali, and after the latter's death in 966, he took the reins of government and held the state together until his death in 969. Kafur was said to have been repellingly ugly (described as a negro of deep black color with a smooth shining skin), a man who loved the society of virtuous men and treated them with marked honor. He was praised as a great sponsor of the arts and sciences.

**KAHIN.** Pre-Islamic soothsayer, usually the guardian of a sanctuary. He was said to have supernatural powers and was consulted in personal matters or to settle disputes. In his pronouncements the Kahin would speak in **rhymed prose,** called **saj.** Some of his opponents called the Prophet Muhammad a kahin. The Koran says the Message is: "Not the word of a poet . . . nor is it the word of a sooth-sayer . . . "(69:41-42).

**KALAM.** The scholastic theology of Islam (from *kalam,* speech, or the Word of God). During the **Umayyad** period no true orthodoxy prevailed in the Islamic world.The **'Abbasid** period marks the creation of a systematic theology. Schools appeared in which new ideas were broached, but most of them again disappeared. Gradually four Sunni theological schools emerged in Medina, **Damascus**, **Basra**, and Kufah. In each of these towns pious men gathered, usually in **mosques**, to discuss religious questions. They debated such questions as sin and the sinner, free will and **predestination**, reason versus **revelation**, etc.

The **Kharijites** (or those who went out) were the first Islamic sect. Originally partisans of 'Ali, they broke with him for his submission to arbitration at **Adhruh** in his controversy with **Mu'awiya**, proclaiming that judgment belongs to God alone (*la hukma illa li-llah*). A radical subgroup, the **Azraqites** (named after their leader Nafi' ibn al-Azraq), proclaimed 'Ali a sinner and therefore an unbeliever (**kafir**) who had to be destroyed. They held that any pious Muslim is qualified for the position of **caliph**, even an Abbysinian **slave**. A quietist group, the **Murji'ites** held, in reaction to the Kharijites, that a sinner is still a Muslim and judgment of a sinner should be left (*irja'*) to the judgment of God. Sins are offset by faith and a believer will not be condemned to eternal hellfire. In political terms, the Murji'ites would give tacit support even to a sinful ruler, and they acquiesced in **Umayyad** rule.

An important dogma in Islam is God's omnipotence—from this would follow that nothing happens without God's will—leaving the believer to accept a helpless **fatalism**. One group, the **Qadarites** (from *qadar*, power), postulated that God is just and therefore leaves man to decide between good and evil. They were influenced by the rationalist **Mu'tazilite** (seceders, from *'itazala*) school, which stood for free will and human responsibility. **Wasil ibn 'Ata** withdrew from a discussion between Murji'ites and Kharijites in which the former declared the sinner a believer while the latter held that he had become an unbeliever. The Mu'tazilites became important under the rule of Caliph **Ma'mun**, who enforced their view that the Koran was created, rather than eternal. One group, the **Jabrites**, proclaimed man's compulsion (*jabr*) and denied man's free will, saying that man is necessarily constrained by the force of God's eternal and immutable decree.

Orthodox Sunni belief took shape lastly under the influence of **al-Ash'ari** (873-935). Al-Ash'ari was originally a Mu'tazilite who broke for various reasons with his circle and used rational methods to espouse a rigid **fundamentalist** view. He favored a literal interpretation of the Koran and was impressed with God's omnipotence—as the creator of good and evil. He held that nothing can infringe on the power of God and denied the existence of all causality. If day follows night, it is only because God in his mercy permits repetition. There is no continuity; God creates the world anew every moment. Although he accepted predestination, he adopted the concept of "acquisition" (**kasb**), which would make man responsible for his deeds. The **Ash'arite** school became the foundation of orthodox scholasticism. It was left to **al-Ghazali** to provide a synthesis of philosophy, theology, and mysticism. For Shi'ite Kalam, *see* SHI'ISM.

**KARAMAT.** God's manifestation of His Grace; supernatural powers to perform miracles which God has bestowed upon **saints**. In popular belief they are miracles performed by saints.

**KARBALA.** A town in present-day Iraq where **Imam Husayn** was martyred in 680. It is a holy city for Shi'ites and a place of **pilgrimage**. Husayn's body is buried there (his head is buried in the Husayn Mosque in **Cairo**).

**KARUBIYUN.** Archangels, namely **Jibril** (Gabriel), **Mika'il**, and **'Izra-'il**. *See* ANGELS.

**KASB.** "Acquisition," the doctrine introduced by **al-Ash'ari** that permits humans a measure of free will. According to the doctrine, God wills both good and evil, that is, God produces the act, but it is "acquired" by the individual to win salvation. In this way, al-Ash'ari was able to reconcile the contradiction seemingly posed between God's omnipotence and man's free will.

**KAYSANIYYAH.** A Shi'ite **sect**, probably named after Kaysan Abu 'Amr, the cruel chief of police of Caliph 'Ali at **Kufah**. Kaysan joined the revolutionary movement headed by **al-Mukhtar**, which supported the **caliphate** of **Muhammad ibn al-Hanafiyah**, the Caliph Ali's son by a Bedouin woman. It was one of the first **sects** in Islam, supported primarily by the newly converted who aimed at avenging the assassination of al-**Husayn** at **Karbala** in 680. After the death of al-Mukhtar, the sect splintered into small groups, which eventually disappeared or merged with the **'Abbasid** revolt.

**KEMALISM.** Policy of secular reforms in the Turkish Republic, named after Mustafa Kemal Atatürk (1881-1938). The policy can be summarized under six principles that became part of the Turkish constitution, encompassing nationalism, secularism, revolutionism, republicanism, populism, and statism. Atatürk and his reformers abolished the **sultanate** in 1922 and the **caliphate** in 1924 and established the Turkish republic. They tried to instill in the people pride as the descendants of "the world's greatest conquering race," rooted in Anatolia from time immemorial. Although the reformers claimed not to be hostile to religion, they abolished **polygamy**, outlawed all religious orders, and adopted the international time and calendar in 1925. Religious laws and courts were abolished and Western civil, penal, and commercial laws adopted. In 1928 Latin numerals and the Latin alphabet were adopted, and the use of the **Arabic** script forbidden. Arabic and Persian vocabulary were replaced with Turkish words and the metric system adopted. In 1934 **women** got the right to vote and, a year later, all citizens had to adopt family names. Finally, Sunday was adopted as the day of rest.

Atatürk was elected President for life, and although many of these reforms were repugnant to devout **believers**, he was able to implement them. The Turkish people saw him as having saved the country from dismemberment after the First World War and therefore accepted his reforms. Since the 1960s there has been a gradual erosion of Kemalism: **madrasahs** were reopened and the great cathedral **mosques** of **Istanbul** again became houses of worship. The movement of Islamic revivalism in the Islamic world has spread also to Turkey: women can be seen in "Islamic dress," something previously forbidden, and an **Islamist** prime minister was elected but subsequently forced to resign through military intervention in 1997.

**KHADIJAH** (d. 619). First wife of the Prophet Muhammad. She was a wealthy lady, about 15 years his senior, who conducted her deceased husband's business and employed Muhammad for some time before she married him. Muhammad gave her 20 she-camels as a **dowry**. She bore Muhammad seven children of whom only the girls survived. They were **Zaynab**, who married Abu al-'As; **Ruqayyah**, who married the third **caliph**, 'Uthman; **Fatimah**, who married the fourth caliph, 'Ali; and **Umm Kulhthum**. Khadijah encouraged Muhammad in his mission and became his first convert. Muhammad did not take another wife as long as Khadijah was alive.

**KHALID IBN AL-WALID** (d. 641). Early Islamic general of the Makhzum clan of **Quraysh** who contributed greatly to the early conquests. He fought Muhammad at the **Battle of Uhud** (625) but converted to Islam in 629. After the death of Muhammad, Khalid defeated a number of false prophets, including **Musaylimah** in 633. He conquered Hira in Iraq, and, together with **'Amr ibn al-'As**, he defeated a Byzantine army at **Ajnadayn** in 634. Temporarily dismissed, he led a contingent in the battle of **Yarmuk** (636). For his services he was given the title *sayf al-Islam* (Sword of Islam). He was rewarded for his service with the governorship of Syria and is buried in the city of Homs.

**KHALIFA.** *See* CALIPH.

**KHALIL IBN AHMAD, AL** (718-791). Arab philologist and compiler of the first **Arabic** dictionary, the *kitab al-'ayn* (Book of the letter 'ayn). It was arranged in alphabetical order according to pronunciation, beginning with the letter 'ayn. A book of his on prosody is lost. Al-Khalil was born in Oman and moved to **Basra**, where he lived in very modest circumstances. Abu 'l Faraj **al-Isfahani** said: "It must be observed that Islamism never produced a more active spirit than al-Khalil for the discovery of sciences which were unknown, even in their first principles, to the learned among the Arabs" (**Ibn Khallikan**, I, 494). Khalil died of an accident when, engrossed in thought, he walked into a pillar when entering a **mosque**.

**KHAMENE'I, AYATOLLAH SAYYIOD ALI HUSAYNI** (b. 1939). Elected as spiritual leader of Iran, after the death of Ayatollah **Khomeyni** in 1989. He was born in **Mashhad** and educated in **Qom**, where he was a student of Khomeyni. Arrested several times during the period of the monarchy, he became a member of Khomeyni's Revolutionary Council and commander of the Revolutionary Guard. He became president of Iran in 1981 and was reelected in 1985 until he succeeded Ayatollah Khomeyni in 1989. Khamene'i is said to be relatively moderate, but he has never enjoyed the power or charisma of his predecessor. *See also* ISLAMIC REPUBLIC OF IRAN.

**KHAN, SIR SAYYID AHMAD** (1817-1898). **Muslim modernist** who demanded reforms and the adoption of Western technology and education. After receiving a traditional **education**, he found work as a writer at the East India Company's court of justice in Delhi in 1841.

He advocated coexistence between Muslims and the British, feeling that Muslim interests would be better protected than under Hindu rule. Among his many publications was a commentary on the Bible and the Koran, pointing out the common source of the **scriptures**. In 1875 Sir Sayyid founded the All-India Muhammadan Anglo-Oriental College at **Aligarh**, which was eventually transformed into Aligarh University. He sought to reconcile faith and reason and favored the adoption of Western concepts, such as science, technology, justice, and freedom. He is credited with being one of the initiators of India's Islamic renaissance and a promoter of the idea of creating a Muslim state, which was implemented long after his death with the creation of Pakistan.

**KHANAQAH (KHANQAH). Sufi** lodge, or monastery, where the devotees live under the direction of a Sufi master. It is often connected with a **mosque** or **madrasah**, and it is most commonly found in Iraq and Iran. The lodges are also called *tekke* and in North Africa *zawiyah* ("corner").

**KHANDAQ.** *See* TRENCH, BATTLE OF THE.

**KHARAJ.** Land tax, adopted from the Byzantines. It was originally levied on non-Muslim subjects, together with the poll tax (**jizyah**). When farmers converted to Islam and Muslim conquerors also acquired land in the early eighth century, the kharaj was levied on all landowners. Originally, the income of the kharaj, often paid in kind, served to defray the cost of the military and administration. Muslims also had to pay the poor tax (**zakat**). Shi'ites dispute the legitimacy of kharaj, because it was introduced by the Sunni **caliph 'Umar ibn al-Khattab**.

**KHARIJITES (KHAWARIJ).** Originally followers of Caliph **'Ali** who deserted him when he agreed to arbitration in the caliphal dispute with **Mu'awiyah** at **Adhruh**. They went out (*yakhraju*) from 'Ali's camp (hence their name) at **Kufah** and settled at Harura. They turned against 'Ali and became a source of rebellions during the **Umayyad** and early **'Abbasid** periods. The Kharijites (pl. *khawarij*, self designation "the People of Paradise") found their supporters primarily among the reciters (*qurra'*) of the Koran, the newly converted, as well as among Arab nomadic tribes that did not benefit from the early conquests. 'Ali defeated the Kharijites decisively at **Nahrawan** in 658, but he was assassinated by a Kharijite in 661.

The Kharijites claimed the right to chose a **caliph** and depose him if he had become a sinner. They recognized **Abu Bakr**, **'Umar**, the first six years of the **'Uthman caliphate**, and the period of 'Ali until the battle of **Siffin** (657). They held that the caliphate is elective and that any pious Muslim is entitled to the caliphate, even if he were an Abyssinian slave. Contrary to other **sects**, they held that a Muslim who had committed a grave **sin** has become an unbeliever (**kafir**). The most radical of the Kharijite **sect** (the **Azraqi**) held that such a sinner is an apostate and has to be killed together with his wives and children. Because of their radicalism, most of them were eventually wiped out. A reaction to their radical views appeared with the rise of the **Murji'ites**, who deferred judgment of sinners to God. A more tolerant group, the **Ibadites**, named after their leader Abdullah ibn Ibad, disassociated itself from the radicals in the second half of the eighth century. They are close to mainstream Sunni Islam and have survived until this day in Oman and in East and North Africa.

**KHATAM.** Meaning "seal," and referring to Muhammad as *Khatam al-nabiyun* (Seal of the Prophets) the last, or final, prophet until the **Day of Judgment**.

**KHATAMI, SAYYID MUHAMMAD** (1943-  ). Elected president of the **Islamic Republic of Iran** in May 1997 with 69 percent of the votes. Largely opposed by the conservatives, his election has been interpreted as the popular desire for a more liberal policy. Khatami was born in Yazd and educated at home and in theology at **Qom**. Subsequently, he earned a doctorate at Tehran University and spent several years as head of the Islamic Center of Iran in Hamburg, Germany. He became a member of parliament in 1980 and minister of education in 1982. After 1969, he served as member of the Supreme Council of the Cultural Revolution. As president of the Islamic Republic of Iran he supported freedom of the press and tried to protect liberals from conservative attacks.

**KHATIB.** A religious functionary who delivers the **Friday** sermon (**khutbah**) in a major **mosque**. Originally, the **khatibs** were tribal spokesmen and intellectual leaders. After the advent of Islam, the **caliph** and his governors in the provinces performed the functions of the khatib, but, eventually, a preacher was assigned to every major mosque. Since it was customary to invoke the name of the caliph (or ruling **sultan**) in the sermon, the khutbah gained an important political aspect. Rebellions started when a challenger had his own name mentioned in the sermon.

**KHAWARIJ.** *See* KHARIJITES.

**KHAZRAJ.** A south Arabian tribe that settled in Medina, who together with the **Aws**, became the Helpers (or **Ansar**) of the first Muslim community. Engaged in internecine warfare with the Aws and members of the three Jewish tribes in Medina, they accepted Muhammad as an arbiter and head of the first Judeo-Arab community. After the Muslim conquest of Mecca in 630, the Ansar were second in rank among converts, after the **Muhajirun**, those early converts who followed Muhammad from Mecca to Medina. *See also* AQABAH, PLEDGE OF.

**KHILAFAT MOVEMENT** (1919-1924). A religio-political movement, headed by the brothers Muhammad Ali and Shaukat Ali, which rose in 1919 in India in response to the defeat of the **Ottoman empire** in the First World War. Although under British control, Indian Muslims continued to recognize the Ottoman **sultan/caliph** as the legitimate head of the Sunni Muslim community. The danger of division of the Ottoman empire and the possibility of occupation of the Holy Places by non-Muslims convinced many that they could no longer live in the **dar al-harb** (Abode of War) under British control. King Amanullah of Afghanistan, who had just secured his country's independence from Great Britain, invited the emigrants (**muhajirun**) to come to his country. Some 18,000 followed his invitation, but most were poor and unskilled people who could not contribute to the development of Afghanistan. When the Turkish government abolished the **caliphate** in 1924 and the Afghan ruler began his secular policies of reform, the Khilafat Movement gradually lost support. Many of the muhajirun returned to India to join the Pakistan movement or moved on to the Soviet Union and Turkey.

**KHIRQA.** A Sufi's woolen robe, bestowed on a disciple by his master.

**KHITAN.** *See* CIRCUMCISION.

**KHOJAS.** A community of Hindus of the Lohana caste that was converted by **Isma'ili** missionaries in the 14th century and adopted the **Nizari** branch of the Isma'ili **sect**. Most recognize the **Agha Khan** as their spiritual leader. They have their own **scriptures** and consider their **imams** god-incarnate. There are, however, Sunni and **Twelver Shi'ite** Khojas who follow their own respective rites.

**KHOMEYNI, AYATOLLAH RUHOLLAH AL-MUSAVI AL-** (c. 1900-1989). Born in Khomeyn, a town about 270 kilometers south of Tehran, Khomeyni received a traditional **madrasa education**. At the age of 27, he taught at Isfahan and later at **Qom**, lecturing on Islamic philosophy, law, mysticism, and ethics. He was quickly involved in political activism, opposing the governments of Reza Khan and his son Muhammad Reza and the growing secularization in Iran. His book, *kashf al-asrar* (Unveiling the secrets) published in 1942, condemned the shah's tyranny, and he made himself the leader of a movement of political protest, which led to his brief imprisonment in 1963. Exiled to Turkey in 1964, Khomeyni went to **Najaf** in Iraq a year later, where he taught for the next 14 years. In his lectures, published under the title, *Guardianship of the Islamic Jurists*, he advocated the establishment of an Islamic state under the leadership of the supreme jurisconsult (*vilayat-i faqih*). Khomeyni next moved to France, but his speeches were reproduced on cassettes and broadcasts from **mosques** throughout the country and made him the major spokesman of the Iranian Revolution. In February 1979 Khomeyni returned to Iran to implement his political ideas. The function of government, he felt, is to enforce the **Shari'ah**, combat oppression, corruption, heresies, and "errors legislated by false parliaments." A reign of terror, the occupation of the American embassy in Tehran, and his proclamation of the export of the revolution led to the increasing isolation of Iran. An indecisive war with Iraq broke out in 1982 that was costly in human and financial resources, and it weakened the state. Khomeyni's **fatwa** of 1989, calling for the assassination of Salman Rushdie for writing *The Satanic Verses*, has left an issue that has contributed to preventing the normalization of relations with the West. Khomeyni's revolution stimulated revivalist movements elsewhere in the Islamic world that oppose Westernization and demand establishment of a purist Islamic state based on the model of the state under the Prophet Muhammad.

**KHUMS.** A fifth (*khums*) of the booty (**ghanima**) of the early Islamic wars that was reserved for the institutional use of the government. In Shi'ism it was the religious tithe collected by the **ulama**, which gave them a measure of independence.

**KHUTBAH.** **Friday** sermon delivered at noon at a congregational **mosque** (*jam´ah masjid*) and during **pilgrimage** and at the time of special festivities. It has political significance because the **khatib** (preacher) traditionally invokes the name of the recognized ruler. Under colonial rule, the khutbah was often read in the name of the "Ruler of the Age," the **Ottoman caliph**, or even in the name of the French president in Algeria. The Khutbah was initially read by the Prophet, later the **Rightly Guided Caliphs**, and under the **Umayyads** by provincial governors. Only in the **'Abbasid** period were khatibs appointed.

**KHWARIZMI, MUHAMMAD IBN MUSA AL-** (ca. 800-846). Mathematician, geographer, and astronomer from Khwarizm, the present Khiva in Uzbekistan, Khwarizmi was the first to compose works on arithmetic and algebra. His *hisab al-jabr wa'l muqabalah* (Calculation of integration and equation) was translated into Latin in the 12th century to become the principal text at European universities. The word "algebra" is derived from the title of his book. He was a pioneer in pointing out the importance of "arabic" numerals and zero instead of the roman numerals used at the time. As court astronomer to the Caliph **al-Ma'mun** at **Baghdad**, al-Khwarizmi compiled the oldest astronomical tables, which were important as they laid the groundwork for the beginning of European astronomy. The mathematical term "algorithm" is derived from his name.

**KINDI, YA'QUB IBN ISHAQ AL-** (801-873). The first important Muslim philosopher who connected Greek philosophical doctrines with the rationalist school of the **Mu'tazilites**. Al-Kindi was born in **Kufah** and became a calligrapher at the caliphal court at **Baghdad**. An adviser at the court of the Caliph al-Mu'tasim (r. 833-842) and a tutor of princes at **Samarra**, al-Kindi faced hostilities from courtiers. He believed in the theory of creation out of nothing (*creatio ex nihilo*) and called for the allegorical interpretation (**ta'wil**) of the Koran. Of some 270 publications on medical topics, alchemy, and mathematics, about 40 are extant. He held the title "Philosopher of the Arabs."

**KISMET.** In popular Islam, the fatalistic acceptance of what God has preordained as one's lot. The **Ash'arite** school of Sunni Islam accepts the idea of acquisition (**kasb**), which permits humans free will to win salvation while at the same time maintaining that God produces all acts. *See also* FATALISM.

**KISWAH.** "Robe." The black, gold embroidered, brocade that covers the **Ka'bah**, except for the area of the **Black Stone**. It is changed each year and cut up and sold or given to pilgrims. To furnish the Kiswah each year was the privilege of the **caliphs**, later the **Mamluk** and **Ottoman sultans**. At present, the Kiswah is woven in Egypt and carried to Mecca in a special procession. After the **Wahhabi** conquest of the **Hijaz** in the early 19th century, the Kiswah procession was prohibited but was resumed after a hiatus of 10 years.

**KITAB.** "The Book." Muslim designation for the Koran, but also for the scriptures (Bible) of the **Christians** and **Jews** who are **Peoples of the Book** (*ahl al-kitab*).

**KIZILBASH.** "Red Heads." Members of seven Turkoman tribes who formed a military and governmental elite under Shah Isma'il (r. 1499-1524), whom they regarded as a **saint** and king. They derived their name from the fact that they wore twelve red stripes on their turbans, each for one of the **Twelver** Shi'ite **Imams**. The Kizilbash were believed to be invincible until they were defeated by the **Ottoman** Sultan Selim at the Battle of Chaldiran in 1514. They remained a force until the 18th century, when they accompanied Nadir Shah Afshar (r. 1736-1747) on his invasions of India and manned fortified bases of occupation in Iran, Afghanistan, and India.

**KORAN (QUR'AN).** The Koran is the sacred book of Islam, containing God's direct revelations through the medium of the Prophet Muhammad. According to dogma it is a miracle, divine in origin, and the uncreated word of God. **Revelation** began in 610 during the holy month of **Ramadhan** when the Angel **Gabriel** called to Muhammad: "Recite! (or Read) in the name of thy Lord." A **hadith** transmitted by **'A'isha** quotes the Prophet telling the story of his first revelation as follows:

> The angel caught me (forcibly) and pressed me so hard that I could not bear it anymore. He then released me and again asked me to read

and I replied "I do not know how to read." At the third time the angel said: "Read in the name of your Lord, who created, created man from a clot. Read! And your Lord is most generous." Then Allah's apostle returned with the inspiration and with his heart beating severely. Then he went to **Khadijah** bint Khuwailid and said, "Cover me! Cover me!" They covered him till his fear was over and after that he told her everything that had happened and said, "I fear that something may happen to me." Khadijah replied, "Never! By Allah, Allah will never disgrace you. You keep good relations with your kith and kin, help the poor and the destitute, serve your guests generously and assist the deserving calamity-afflicted ones." (Bukhari, I,1, Muhsin)

The revelations were collected into one volume. The Koran is divided into 114 chapters (**surahs**), 6,236 verses (**ayahs**), 77,934 words (*harf* pl. *huruf*), and 323,621 letters. The surahs are arranged roughly according to length, beginning with the longest. An exception is the *Fatiha*, or "Opener," which is a short one. The Koran is possibly the most widely read book ever written. Besides serving for worship, it is the textbook from which generations of Muslims have learned to read **Arabic**. Orthodox Muslims believe that the Koran is inimitable (2:23-24) and no authorized translation exists (although the **Ottoman ulama** recognized theTurkish translation as authoritative). The word Qur'an means recitation (or reading) and the book is clearly meant for recitation. The language of the Koran is the written language from which modern standard Arabic is derived.

European Orientalists have attempted to establish a chronology, according to which the Meccan surahs are usually shorter and reflect the period of struggle with the **Quraysh**. Muhammad is the one who warns of the impending **Day of Judgment**, whereas in the Medina period he is a statesman and head of the Islamic community. Passages of the Koran were at first memorized, but already under Caliph **Abu Bakr** (632-634) collection began, and in the period of **Uthman** (644-656) a definitive version was compiled. (Some European scholars [Wansbrough] maintain that the Koran was generated at a much later date.) A science of **exegesis** eventually evolved, which examines hadiths and grammatical and lexicographical factors; Shi'ites permit an allegorical interpretation (**ta'wil**). Schools were established early in Islam where pupils would memorize passages of the Koran; a person who has memorized the Koran holds the honorific title of **Hafiz**. Together with the **Sunnah**, the deeds and pronouncements of Muhammad, the Koran is the basis of **Islamic law (Shari'ah)**.

**KUFAH.** One of the garrison towns (**amsar**) founded in 638 by **'Umar** I on the west bank of the Euphrates River to keep the conquering Arabs apart from the sedentary population. It became the capital of **'Ali ibn Abi Talib** from 657 to 661. In the early **'Abbasid** period (749-762), it was an important cultural center but lost its importance in the 10th century because of **Shi'ite**, **Kharijite**, and **Qarmatian** revolts and because of the transfer of the capital to **Baghdad**. The "kufic" script of **Arabic** was pioneered at Kufah.

**KUFR, AL-.** "Unbelief."A **kafir** is an infidel, one who denies the existence of God or gives partners to God (a polytheist). Surah 109:1-5, titled Al-Kafirun, says: "Say: O ye that reject Faith! I worship not that which ye worship, Nor will ye worship that which I worship."

**KULAYNI, MUHAMMAD YAQUB AL- (KULINI,** d. 940). Shi'ite scholar at **Baghdad** and author of one of the four canonical Shi'ite collections, the *Kitab al-Kafi*, containing more than 15,000 **hadith.** Unlike the Sunnis, the Shi'ite include their **imams** in the chain (**isnad**) of transmitters of a hadith to guarantee its soundness.

**KUNYAH.** Kunyah is the formal name of a person, indicating the relationship of the namebearer to another person, for example Abu Qasim, the father of Qasim. It may also describe a metaphorical relationship or be a nickname as, for example, Abu 'l-Fadhl, father of merit. It is a surname in addition to the *ism*, personal name, to provide additional information; for example Muhammad Abu al-Qasim (Muhammad the father of Qasim). A surname of honor or nickname is called *laqab* as, for example, Nur al-Din, "The Light of Religion," and the *nisbah*, referring to a place, **sect**, and trade, as for example al-Baghdadi (the one from **Baghdad**). The patronymic, *nasab* list the names of ancestors with the word *ibn* (son), for example, Qasim ibn Muhammad—Qasim the son of Muhammad. *See also* NAMES AND NAMEGIVING.

## -L-

**LABID IBN RABI'A** (ca. 560-661). Arab poet and composer of one of the prizewinning poems in the **Mu'allaqat**. He adopted Islam in 630, together with his tribe, and he lived in **Kufah**. Labid abjured poetry, saying "God has given me the Koran in exchange for it" (Nicholson, 119). He was a true Bedouin, extolling the Arab virtues of hospitality, generosity, and bravery.

**LAHAB, ABU.** *See* ABU LAHAB.

**LAKHMIDS.** A dynasty of the Tanukh tribes in southwest Iraq that ruled a buffer state, blocking Arab nomadic expansion to the northeast. The Tanukh established their capital at al-Hira (near the subsequent town al-**Kufah**) in the latter part of the third century. One of their first kings was **Imru' al-Qays** (r. 288-328), whose epitaph is the oldest proto-**Arabic** inscription yet discovered. Under al-Mundhir III (ca. 505-554) the Lakhmid state was at its height. Some among the Tanukh were Nestorian **Christians** and the first and only Christian king was al-Nu'man III (r. ca. 580-602). From his time the kingdom began to decline and was vanquished in the first Muslim conquests. Three of the seven reputed authors of the "Golden Odes" (**Mu'allaqat**) flourished at the Lakhmid court.

**LAQAB.** A honorific title or nickname, added to the name (*ism*), for example: *Nur al-Din*, the Light of Religion. *See also* NAMES AND NAMEGIVING.

**LAST DAY.** The Koran describes the "Folding Up" preceding the **Day of Judgment**, saying:

> When the sun (with its specious light) is folded up; when the stars fall, losing their lustre; when the mountains vanish (like a mirage); when the she-camels, ten months with young, are left untended; when the wild beasts are herded together (in human habitations); when the oceans boil over with a swell; when the souls are sorted out (being joined like with like); when the female (infant), buried alive, is questioned—for what crime she was killed; when the Scrolls are laid open; when the sky is unveiled; when the blazing Fire is kindled to fierce heat; when the Garden is brought near; (then) shall each soul know what it has put forward. (81:1-14)

According to a **hadith**, the Prophet was asked what are the signs of the hour (last Day), and he replied: "They are the disappearance of (religious) knowledge. The appearance of (religious) ignorance.

The taking of alcoholic drinks. The prevalence of open illegal sexual intercourse.

**LAW.** *See* ISLAMIC LAW.

**LAYLAT AL-QADR.** "The Night of Power or Destiny" is a sacred period that fell on the last 10 days of the month of **Ramadhan** of the year 610. According to tradition, the Koran came down from the lowest **heaven** on the night of the 27th (or 29th?) when the Angel Gabriel first spoke to Muhammad. The fate of a person for the coming year is predestined at that time. The Koran says: "We have indeed revealed this (Message) in the Night of Power: and what will explain to thee what the Night of Power is? The Night or Power is better than a thousand months. Therein came down the angels and the spirit by Allah's permission, on every errand: Peace! . . . This until the rise of Morn!" (97:1-5).

**LI'AN.** "Mutual cursing." An oath taken by the wife and the husband when the latter accuses his wife of **adultery**. He makes three oaths that he is truthful and a third time he invokes the curse of Allah on himself if he has lied. The wife can free herself of guilt by performing the same oath and, as a result, the couple is irrevocably **divorced** (24:6-9).

## -M-

**MA'ARRI, ABU 'L-'ALA AL-** (973-1057). Poet, philosopher, and man of letters. He was born in Syria, about 30 kilometers south of Aleppo and educated in his hometown. Blind as a result of smallpox since early childhood, he was gifted with an extraordinary power of memory. After a short stay in **Baghdad**, he retired to Ma'arra, his hometown, and spent the rest of his life in seclusion. He seemed to deny the resurrection of the dead when he said: "We laugh, but inept is our laughter; We should weep and weep sore, Who are shattered like glass, and thereafter Re-moulded no more!" And he seemed to hold Islam no better than other creeds, saying

> Hanifs are stumbling, Christians all astray,
> Jews wildered, Magians far on error's way

We mortals are composed of two great schools -
Enlightened knaves or else religious fools. (Nicholson, 317, 318)

**MADHHAB.** "Direction." A school or rite of Islamic jurisprudence, the **Hanafi, Hanbali, Shafi'i,** and **Maliki schools of Sunni law**. Divergences between the four orthodox schools are based on different **Traditions** or on different interpretations of the same Tradition. Generally, Sunni Muslim are under the jurisdiction of one of the schools, except some **Muslim modernists** and **Islamists**. Shi'ite schools include the **Zaydis** or Fivers and the **Twelvers** adhere to the **Ja'fari** school of jurisprudence. *See also* ISLAMIC LAW.

**MADRASAH.** "Place of Study." General name for a secondary school that functions as a theological seminary, a law school, and a **mosque** and trains religious functionaries in Islamic sciences and law. Usually attached to a mosque with accommodation for students and teachers, the madrasah provides free **education** and, if necessary, support for needy students. The curriculum generally includes the sayings and actions of the Prophet (**jadith**), jurisprudence (**fiqh**), scholastic theology (**kalam**), and Koranic **exegesis** (**tafsir**), as well as such fields as grammar, logic, lexicography, rhetoric (*balagha*), and literature (*adab*). Some of the most famous madrasahs included **Al-Azhar**, founded as an **Isma'ili** institution at **Cairo**, in the 10th century and the **Nizamiyyah** founded by the **Seljuq sultans** in 1065-1067 in **Baghdad**. They became the models for European universities. In the 19th and early 20th centuries secular courses were added to the curriculum and governments regulated such matters as accreditation and curriculum. In many parts of the Islamic world private madrasahs continue to coexist with state-supported institutions.

**MAHDI, AL-.** The "Guide" who will appear at the end of time to fight against evil, restore justice, and unify the world under Islam before the advent of the **Day of Judgment**. A title, first attributed to Muhammad ibn al-**Hanafiyyah**, a son of 'Ali, and later part of the doctrine of the **Hidden Imam** (*Imam Mahdi*) of the **Twelver Shi'ites**. The **Tradition** that the Mahdi is preceded by a "Shedder of Blood" (*al-Saffah*), a name the founder of the **'Abbasid caliphate** adopted, followed by the name al-Mahdi, a name adopted by his grandson, may very well have had the political purpose of legitimiz ing the revolt against the **Umayyad** caliphate. A number of individuals have laid claim to being the Mahdi, including 'Ubayd-ullah (909-934), founder of the **Fatimid** dynasty, **Ibn Tumart** (1077-1130), the **Almohad caliph**, and Muhammad ibn 'Abdullah, who appeared in the Sudan in 1883 and defeated a British expeditionary force. *See* MAHDI OF THE SUDAN.

**MAHDI OF THE SUDAN.** Title of Muhammad ibn 'Abdullah (1844-1885) who became the head of a theocratic regime in the Sudan when he pronounced himself the "Mahdi." He won a wide following and was able to capture most of the Sudan, including the capital Khartoum. He conducted a **jihad** against the British occupation forces and defeated General Charles Gordon at Khartoum in 1885. At his death in the same year, his disciple 'Abdullahi continued to rule for some 14 years until he was defeated and killed in battle by Lord Kitchener in 1899. The Mahdi was born in 1844 in Dongola on the Red Nile. Claiming descent from the **Caliph** 'Ali, he advocated a reformist Islam with emphasis on the teachings of the Koran. A **Sufi shaykh** and head of the Samaniyyah order, the Mahdi was able to mobilize the masses and it was only due to the superior firepower of the British that the Mahdist revolution was finally suppressed.

**MAHMUD OF GHAZNI.** *See* GHAZNAVID DYNASTY.

**MAHR.** The dowry, in pre-Islamic times a bride price given to the father or oldest male relative. In the Islamic period the *mahr* was given to the bride and a **marriage** was not legal without it. Surah 4:4 says: "And give the **women** (on marriage) their dower as an obligation; but if they, on their own good pleasure, remit any part of it to you, take it and enjoy it with right good cheer." The gift remains the property of the woman if the marriage is dissolved "But if ye decide to take one wife in place of another, even if ye had given the latter a whole treasure for dower, take not the least bit back . . ."(4:20). Customs vary in the Islamic world, from giving a symbolic amount to considerable sums that often pose severe hardships on the groom or his family. Therefore, various governments have attempted (usually with little success) to limit the amount of the dowry. In some countries the mahr has amounted to a bride price, paid to the father of the bride. *See also* DIVORCE.

**MAJAH.** *See* IBN MAJAH, ABU 'ABDULLAH MUHAMMAD.

**MAJLIS.** A tribal council (sitting) in pre-Islamic Arabia in which the male members participated in making decisions of common interest. The council was presided over by the chief (**shaykh**), who was essentially an arbiter, rather than a dictator. Although it was a democratic institution, the votes were not counted, but weighed, and the elders, or more prosperous members, carried greater clout. The members of the clan, or tribe, voluntarily submitted to the decision of the council. The concept was continued into the Islamic period in the obligation of the ruler to seek council (**shurah**). The first four **caliphs** were elected by a majlis of **Companions** of the Prophet. Even at present, majlis is the name of the parliament in a number of Muslim states.

**MAKRUH.** Behavior in law that is reprehensible, but not forbidden (**haram**) and therefore not punishable. *See* FIVE PRINCIPAL ACTS IN ISLAMIC LAW.

**MAKTUB.** "It is written," the fatalistic acceptance that the destiny of every individual is preordained and preserved in a book. The Koran says: " Nothing will happen to us except what Allah has decreed" (9:51). *See also* KISMET.

**MALAK** (pl. **MALA'IKA**). *See* ANGELS.

**MALIK.** Title of ancient Arab kings, later of secular Arab rulers. A notable, landowner, chief; also a personal name.

**MALIK IBN ANAS, ABU 'ABD ALLAH** (ca. 710-795). Arab Islamic scholar of the Hijazi school and nominal head of the Malikite school of Islamic jurisprudence. He taught at Medina and stressed the importance of **hadith**, supplementing the **Traditions** with the practice of the community at Medina. His **school of law** (madhhab) bases its decisions on the consensus ('**ijma'**) and permits opinion (**ra'y**) of the doctors of Islamic law, if there is no clear indication in the sources. His work *al-Muwatta* (The beaten path) was the first attempt to codify Islamic law and is the basis of the **Malikite** school of jurisprudence. It gives a survey of law and justice, ritual and practice of religion based on the consensus of the Medina community. Malik was given 70 lashes because of a legal opinion that did not please the **amir**. Mus'ab al-Zubayri described Malik as "one of the most handsome people in his face and the sweetest of them in

eye, the purest of them in whiteness and the most perfect of them in
height and the most excellent in body" (Bewley, 1989, xxviii).

**MALIKITES.** Sunni **school of law** (madhhab), named after **Malik Ibn
Anas.** It advocates the use of **istislah,** which permits making the
welfare of the community (**umma**) a consideration in a legal decision. Major Malikite scholars include 'Abd al-Salam ibn Sa'id al-
Tanuhi Sahnun (776-854), Abu Bakr Muhammad al-**Baqillani** (d.
1012), 'Abd al-Wahhab 'Ali al-**Baghdadi** (d. 1030), Ahmad
Muhammad al-Ma'afiri (1037), and **'Ali Ibn Hazm** (1063). Members
of this school predominate on the east coast of the Arabian Peninsula,
Upper Egypt, the Maghreb, and Mauretania.

**MAMLUK DYNASTY** (1250-1517). A dynasty of Turkic **slaves**
(*mamluk*—one possessed) that rose from being a slave force of the
**Ayyubid** rulers of Egypt to establish their own kingdom. Initially a
woman, Shajar al-Durr (Tree of Pearls), ruled, followed by Aybak,
whom she married and subsequently killed. The first line were called
the Bahri (or River) Mamluks, who ruled from 1250 to 1390,
followed by the Burji (or Citadel) Mamluks from 1382 until the
**Ottoman** conquest of Egypt in 1517. The former were largely
Qipchaq Turks from southern Russia, the latter Circassians from the
Caucasus. To be a member of the ruling class, one had to be
purchased as a slave. Some, like **Sultan** Qala'un, called himself Al-
Alfi (the Thousander), to indicate the amount for which he was
originally purchased. Sultan Qutuz defeated the **Mongols** at **'Ayn
Jalut** in 1260, and Nasir defeated them at Marj Soffar in 1303, thus
stemming the Mongol advance into Syria. The Mamluks supported
Sunni orthodoxy and expelled the Crusaders from Syria. They
controlled the spice trade with India and East Asia until the circum-
navigation of Africa by the Portuguese. Eventually they were
weakened and were easily defeated by the Ottomans. Mamluk, or
slave rulers, existed also in India (1210-1290) and elsewhere.

**MA'MUN, ABU AL-'ABBAS 'ABD ALLAH AL-** (786-833). **'Abbas-
sid caliph** who succeeded his father **Harun al-Rashid** in 813. He
was governor of the eastern provinces at Merv, from which base he
sent an army against his half-brother **al-Amin,** and he eventually
established himself on the caliphal throne in **Baghdad.** To heal the
schism in Islam, al-Ma'mun appointed the Shi'ite **imam,** 'Ali ibn
Musa **al-Ridha,** as his successor in 817. But 'Ali died a year later

and is buried in **Mashhad**. Al-Ma'mun waged successful wars against Byzantium, but he faced numerous revolts. His general, **Tahir ibn al-Husayn**, established the **Tahirid dynasty** (821-873) in Khurasan. Al-Ma'mun supported the **Mu'tazilite** doctrine of the createdness of the Koran and started an inquisition (**mihna**) to force its acceptance. He supported science and art and in 830 founded the famous **House of Wisdom** (*bayt al-hikmah*), where works of Greek learning were translated into **Arabic**.

**MANDEANS.** Originally a heretical **sect** of **Judaism** whose members probably migrated in the first century from Palestine, southeastern Iraq, and Khuzistan in Iran. Persecuted under the Sassanians, the Mandeans became protected subjects (**dhimmis**), being considered scriptuaries (**Peoples of the Book**). Their language is part of the east Aramaic group and is still the cultural language of the Mandeans today. The Koran seems to call them Sabians.

**MANDUB.** "Recommended." A religious duty that is recommended but not essential and fulfillment of which is rewarded. It may be neglected without punishment. Terms synonymous with mandub are **Sunnah**, *mustahabb*, and *masnun. See also* FIVE PRINCIPAL ACTS IN ISLAMIC LAW.

**MANICHAEISM.** A gnostic religion named after its **messenger** Mani (216-277) that emerged in Mesopotamia and quickly spread to North Africa and East Asia. It was to replace all religions before the end of the world. Mani proclaimed the dualism of lightness and darkness, and body and spirit. The scriptures of Manichaeism are the Seven Books of Mani. Mani was imprisoned and died in jail.

**MANSUR, ABU JA'FAR 'ABD ALLAH IBN MUHAMMAD** (714-775). Second '**Abbasid caliph** who consolidated the new dynasty by eliminating all potential rivals to his power. He defeated his uncle 'Abd Allah in 754 and had him assassinated. He summoned his general **Abu Muslim**, who helped him to attain power and had him treacherously killed. He suppressed numerous revolts. In 762 he ordered the building of **Baghdad**, initially called "The House of Peace" (*dar al-salam*), which subsequently, served as the new capital of the empire. During his time Persian influence began to grow, and the **Barmakids**, a family of **viziers**, began their service until their destruction under **Harun al-Rashid** in the early ninth century.

Mansur was given the nickname "Father of the Penny" (or Penny Pincher, *Abu Dawaniq*) because of his parsimoniousness.

**MAQRIZI, TAQI AL-DIN AL-** (1364-1441). Historian and geographer who served as a judge in **Cairo** and subsequently taught theology at **Damascus**. He wrote, among other works, a history of the **Ayyubids** and the **Mamluks** (*al-suluk li-ma 'rifati duwali al-muluk*) and a description of Egypt, called *al-mawa'iz* (The districts). He collected much information that would have been otherwise lost and was characterized as "generally painstaking and accurate, and always resorting to contemporary evidence if it is available" (Nicholson, 453).

**MARABOUT.** Inhabitants of a religio-military outpost in the desert (**Ribat**) who started a **jihad** that led to the establishment of the **Almoravid** dynasty in North Africa. Marabout is also the designation of a **saint** or his descendants who are called upon to dispense blessings (**barakah**), and whose tombs are places of **pilgrimage**.

**MA'RIB.** In ancient times the largest city in southern Yemen and the capital of a Sabean state which lasted from the 10th century BCE to the sixth century CE. It was a rich area, benefitting from the trade in incense and agriculture, made possible by a network of irrigation. When the Ma'rib dam burst in 575, the area quickly declined. The Koran says: "But they (Saba) turned away (from Allah), and We sent against them the flood (released) from the dams, and We converted their two gardens (rows) into 'gardens' producing bitter fruit" (34:16).

    The *Sirah* gives the story how one 'Amr ibn Amr escaped the catastrophe:

> 'Amr saw a rat burrowing in the dam at Marib where they used to hold back the water and then direct it where it was most needed. He perceived that the dam could not last and he determined to leave the Yaman. He proposed to deceive his people in this wise. He ordered his youngest son to get up and hit him in retaliation for his rough treatment; and when he did so 'Amr said publicly that he would not go on living in a land where the youngest son could slap his fathers face. (*Sira*, Gullaume, 693)

He left and God "sent a torrent against the dam and destroyed it," making the country uninhabitable.

**MA'RIFAH.** In **Sufism**, experiential knowledge that, through illumination (kashf), leads to union with God. This knowledge is reached in stages: the devotee (**murid**) passes on the path (**tariqa**) from the stage of common humanity to the stage of purity, then the stage of power, and finally the stage of absorption in God.

**MARJA' AL-TAQLID.** A "source for emulation," the title of a top **mujtahid** of the **Usuli** school of Shi'ism. Shi'ites must find religious truth either by imitation (**taqlid**) or by seeking guidance from a living mujtahid (a religious personage who, through learning, is capable of making independent judgments). A Marja' al-Taqlid has a following and has to have published a book expounding his views. The highest of the mujtahids holds the position of **Ayatollah** al-Uzma. Ayatollah **Khomeyni** held this position.

**MARJ RAHIT.** Place in Syria where a tribal federation led by the Banu Kalb, allied with the forces of the **Umayyad caliph** Marwan, defeated the followers of the anti-caliph **'Abdallah ibn al-Zubayr** in 684. This battle served as an important event in consolidating the power of the Umayyad dynasty.

**MARONITES.** A **Christian sect**, named after its patron saint Maron (d. 410), which is found largely in Lebanon. They were originally Monophysites who were persecuted by the Byzantine church and, therefore, accepted union with Rome in 1495. They were autonomous under the **Mamluk** and **Ottoman empires** and came under French protection in 1516. The Maronite community became increasingly Frenchified and enjoyed French protection after a bloody civil war with the **Druze** community in 1860. After the First World War, the French became the mandatory power of Syria, and they established the State of Lebanon, in which **Christians** held a small majority. After Lebanon's independence in 1944, the office of the president of the republic was reserved for a Maronite, but the changing demographics in Lebanon—in which the Shi'ites became the largest community—led to a bloody civil war (1975-1985), which was stopped only by Syrian intervention. The Taif Accord of October 22, 1994, transferred power from the Maronite presidency to a cabinet in which Muslims and Christians were equally represented.

**MARRIAGE.** "Nikah." Marriage according to Muslim law is a civil contract rather than a religious sacrament. Its legality depends on consent of the parties, expressed in the "declaration and acceptance" (*i jab-o-qabul*). Two male witnesses are required (two **women** equal the testimony of one man), and the amount of a **dowry** has to be determined. A Muslim man can legally marry four women, which **Muslim modernists** want to restrict because of the obligation that a man has to treat all his wives equally.

Shi'ites are permitted temporary marriage (**mut'ah**), which has been explained as a necessity in olden times when a merchant had to travel long distances and be separated from home for months or even years. It is forbidden to marry a blood relation. The Koran says: "Prohibited to you are: Your mothers, daughters, sisters; father's sisters, mother's sisters; brother's daughters, sister's daughters; foster mothers, foster sisters; your wives' mothers; your step-daughters under your guardianship, and two sisters in wedlock at one and the same time" (4:23).

**MARTYR.** "Shahid." Originally a person who is killed in a holy war (**jihad**) against unbelievers or in performing a religious duty. The martyr is freed of all **sin** and goes directly to **paradise** to sit in the nearness of God. The Koran says: "Think not of those who are slain in Allah's way as dead. Nay, they live, finding their sustenance from their Lord" (3:169). A **hadith** quotes the Prophet, saying: "There are seven kinds of martyr other than those killed in the way of Allah. Someone who is killed by the plague is a martyr, someone who drowns is a martyr, someone who dies of pleurisy is a martyr, someone who dies of a disease of the belly is a martyr, someone who dies by fire is a martyr, someone who dies under a falling building is a martyr and a woman who dies in childbirth is a martyr" (Muwatta, 16.12.36). *See also* SHAHID.

**MARY, MOTHER OF JESUS.** Mentioned in the Koran and especially respected in Islam, Mary (Maryam) is the head of the **women** in **paradise**. Muslims believe in her virgin birth of **Jesus**, but they reject the appellation "Mother of God." The Koran says: "And (remember) her who guarded her chastity: We breathed into her from our spirit, and We made her and her son a sign for all peoples" (21:91).

**MARY THE COPT (MARIAT AL-QIPTIYAH).** Christian concubine of the Prophet Muhammad who was the gift of the Christian governor of Egypt in 629. She bore him a son, Ibrahim, who died in infancy.

**MASHHAD (MESHED).** Tomb of a **saint**, a place of martyrdom, which emanates from the spiritual power of the saint and is visited by pilgrims. Also the name of a city in eastern Iran where the eighth **Imam 'Ali ibn Musa al-Ridha** (Reza) is buried. It is the most important shrine of the **Twelver Shi'ites** in Iran after **Karbala**, where Imam **Husayn** was martyred in 680, and **Najaf**, where Imam 'Ali was buried. In 1911 Russian troops, trying to restore Muhammad Ali (1907-1909) to the Qajar throne, bombarded the city and damaged the golden dome of the shrine.

**MASJID.** "Place of prostration." *See* MOSQUE.

**MASLAHA.** In **Islamic law (Shari'ah)** the legal principle that permits or prohibits some act if it serves a useful purpose in advancing the public welfare. It would permit a ruler to levy special taxes in an emergency, or allow such innovations as blood transfusions. Of the four orthodox **schools of law**, only the **Shafi'ite** school accepts this principle with some reservations. Maslaha permits overriding reasoning by analogy (**qiyas**) when a decision is considered harmful or undesirable. The **Hanafite** and **Malikite** schools use the term **istihsan**, an equitable preference to find a just solution, and the **Hanbalis** use the term **istislah**, seeking the best solution for the general interest. *See also* ISTIHSAN.

**MASNAWI.** *See* JALAL AL-DIN RUMI.

**MASTS, BATTLE OF THE.** A sea battle off the Anatolian coast between the new Arab and the Byzantine fleets in 655 that resulted in a great victory for the Arabs.

**MAS'UDI, ALI IBN HUSAYN** (ca. 895-956). Arab historian and geographer from **Baghdad**. A **Muta'zilite**, Mas'udi was called the "Herodotus and Pliny" of the Arabs. He traveled widely from Black Africa to China and settled in Fustat (**Cairo**) where he compiled his 30 volume encyclopedic history. Part of the work was published under the title *muruj al-dhahab* (Meadows of gold). The work begins with the Creation and ends with the reign of **Caliph** Muti' (946-974). In another work, entitled *kitab al-tanbih wa al-ishraf* (Book of admonition and recension), he summarizes his philosophy of history.

About his voyages, he said: "My journey resembles that of the sun, and to me the poet's verse is applicable." He wrote further:

We turn our steps toward each different clime,
Now to the Farthest East, then West once more;
Even as the sun, which stays not his advance
O'er tracts remote that no man durst explore. (Nicholson, 352.)

**MATN.** Text of a **hadith.** *See* HADITH.

**MATURIDI, ABU MANSUR AL-** (d. 944). A theologian from Samarkand who founded his own orthodox school, the *maturidiyah*, in dispute with the **Mu'tazilites.** He accepted man's free will and assurance of salvation; in legal matters he followed **Hanafite** law. He led an ascetic life and was believed to have performed miracles. Maturidi died in Samarkand where his school is still dominant.

**MAUDUDI, SAYYID ABU 'L-A'LA** (1903-1979). Founder of the **Jama'at-i Islami** in India (1941) and one of the ideological fathers of the **Islamist movement.** Born in Aurangabad, India, he was educated in Islamic studies at a **madrasah** and later at the Dar al-Ulum of Heyderabad. His formal **education** was ended at age 16 when his father died, and Maududi started a career in journalism. He founded his own journal entitled *tarjoman al-Koran* (The translator of the Koran) in 1935 and became a prolific writer, opposing Westernization as well as the creation of Pakistan. After partition of India in 1947, he settled in Pakistan and promoted his ideas of an Islamic state, which led to the drafting of a constitution that was, however, never implemented. His conditions necessary for the establishment of an Islamic state included: Affirmation of the sovereignty of Allah; acceptance by the government that it would exercise its powers within the boundaries laid down by Allah; approval that all existing laws that were contrary to the **Shari'ah** would be repealed; and agreement that all laws are to be in accordance with the teachings of Islam. His ideas left a considerable impact on the political life of Pakistan, and the Jama'at-i Islami continued to agitate as a vanguard of Islamist causes. General Zia-ul-Haq staged a military coup against an elected government in 1977, seeking to make Pakistan an Islamic state. Many, but not all, of Maududi's ideas were finally realized. The war against the communist regime in Afghanistan contributed to the growth of an international **Islamist** movement, which has since become a destabilizing factor in a number of Muslim countries.

**MAWALI.** *See* MAWLA.

**MAWARDI, ABU AL-HASAN AL-** (974-1058). Jurist and moralist, famous for his *kitab al-ahkam al-sultaniyyah* (Book of the principles of government), which is a valuable source on the organization of civil administration in the **caliphate**. It was the earliest and most important treatise of Islamic government at a time when the **Abbasid** caliphate was under Shi'ite **Buyid** control. Al-Mawardi defined the functions of the **caliph** as follows: Safeguarding Islam from innovation, providing justice, protecting the borders of Islam, executing the penalties of the **Shari'ah**, garrisoning the borders, compelling unbelievers to convert or submit and pay the poll tax (**jizyah**), levying taxes according to the Koran, regulating the expenditures of the state, appointing the right people to offices, and supervising the administration.

Jurists, philosophers, and Islamic thinkers like al-Mawardi, **Ibn Taymiyyah**, al-**Baqillani**, and **Ibn Khaldun**, have greatly influenced Islamic political theory to the present. Educated in **Baghdad** and **Basra**, al-Mawardi served as a judge in a number of towns before he settled in Baghdad as a juridical expert at the court of the caliph. Writing at a time of Buyid hegemony, he wanted to strengthen the power of the orthodox caliph. Al-Mawardi also wrote handbooks for judges and for guidance in the worldly and religious life, *adab al-dunya wa al-din* (Instructions for this world and the next) as well as a number of treatises on morals and ethics. It was, however, only when al-Mawardi (the name means "seller of rose-water") lay on his deathbed that he consented to have his works published.

**MAWDUDI.** *See* MAUDUDI.

**MAWLA (MAWALI).** Freed **slaves** and early converts to Islam who were, according to Arab custom, attached as clients (*mawali*) to a tribe. They were not fully accepted as equals and were initially taxed like **Peoples of the Book.** The Berbers in North Africa were kept in this inferior position, as were non-Arab converts in the eastern part of the empire. This led to resentment and eventual revolt against the **Umayyads**.

**MAWLAWIYYA (MEVLEVI).** A **Sufi** order founded by **Jalal al-Din Rumi** (1207-1273), known in Europe as the "Whirling Dervishes" because of their ritual dances. Their name derives its origin from *mawlana*, "Our Master," the title given to Rumi. The order predominated in Anatolia (called Rum by the Turks) and was centered in the old **Seljuq** city of Konya, but it also spread to other parts of the Islamic world. It rivaled the influence of the **Bektashi** order, but, because of its ritual dancing and music, the order faced persecution at times.

**MAWLID AL-NABI (MAULID AN-NABI).** Birthday of the Prophet on the 12th of *Rabi ʿal Awwal* of the Muslim **calendar**, which began to be celebrated in the 12th century. Muslims hold special meetings and recite poems, describing the excellence and achievements of the Prophet Muhammad.

**MAYMUNA BINT AL-HARITH** (d. 683). A wife of Muhammad who was **divorced** from her first husband and widowed by the second, when she married the Prophet in 629. She was a "comely widow" 26 years old at the time. Muhammad gave her a **dowry** of 400 **dirhams**. Maymuna was the aunt of the famous general **Khalid ibn al-Walid**; she bore no children and died at about age 80.

**MAZAR.** A tomb, or shrine of a **saint** or **imam**, and a place of **pilgrimage**.

**MAZAR-I SHARIF.** A city with a population of about 70,000 and the capital of Balkh province in northern Afghanistan. According to local belief, the town is built around "The Noble Tomb" of **Caliph ʿAli** (r. 656-661) whose body was brought to this place in the early 15th century. This conflicts with the claim that Ali was buried in **Najaf**, now a holy city to Shiʿites.

**MECCA (MAKKA).** Holy city of Islam with a population of about one million, located about 60 kilometers from Jiddah. In the seventh century the **Quraysh** tribe, to which the Prophet Muhammad belonged, made it its commercial center on the trade routes north to Syria. It was a place of **pilgrimage**, even before the advent of Islam. Muhammad had his first **revelations** there in 610, but he was opposed by the pagan Quraysh and emigrated to Medina (Yathrib) in 622. In 630 the Muslims were able to capture the city and make it their capital and establish the **Kaʿbah** as the most holy shrine of Islam. It has been a place of Muslim pilgrimage ever since. In 930 the **Qarmatians** plundered the city and carried the **Black Stone** away with them until it was returned to the Ka'bah in 951. Mecca lost some of its importance when the Islamic capital was successively moved to **Kufah, Damascus**, and **Baghdad** and was administered by **sharifs** (descendants of the Prophet). In the First World War, Husayn, the sharif of Mecca, revolted against the **Ottoman sultan** and became king of the Hijaz, until the city was conquered by King Abd al Aziz (**Ibn Sa'ud**), who founded the Kingdom of Saudi Arabia. Mecca is sacred territory and off limits to non-Muslims.

**MEDINA (AL-MADINA)**. A city of some 800,000 inhabitants, located in a fertile oasis north of Mecca. The city, called Yathrib in pre-Islamic days and "City of the Prophet" (*Madinat al-Nabiy*) thereafter, sheltered the first Islamic community. When Muhammad came to Medina in 622, the town was inhabited by three **Jewish** and two Arab tribes. He became the head of this community and from this base captured Mecca and unified Arabia under Islam. The tombs of Muhammad and his daughter **Fatimah**, as well as a number of **Companions**, are located in Medina. It was the Islamic capital from 622 until the death of the Prophet in 632. Although it lost some of its former importance, Medina remained a cultural center and, together with Mecca, sacred territory. According to a **hadith**, the Prophet said: "There are **angels** at the entries of Madina, and neither plague nor the Dajjal will enter it" (Muwatta, 45.4.16) After the **Ottoman** conquest of Egypt in 1517, the entire **Hijaz** came under Ottoman administration until the end of the empire as a result of the First World War.

**MEDINA, CHARTER OF.** The Charter regulated the coexistence of the early community and can be seen as the prototype of an Islamic constitution. When Muhammad moved to Medina he gathered with him some of the early converts, his Meccan emigrants (**muhajirun**), who together with the Helpers (**ansar**), were the first **believers** (**mu'min**). The Ansar were members of the Arab tribes, **Aws** and **Khazraj**, who considered Muhammad their Prophet and leader, but there were also three **Jewish** tribes, the **Qaynuqah, Nadir**, and **Qurayzah**, for whom Muhammad was a statesman and commander-in-chief.

The Charter of Medina constitutes the precedent for coexistence of Muslims and non-Muslims to this day. The preamble of the document states: "From the Apostle of God, for those of the **Quraysh** and the inhabitants of Medina who accept Islam and adopt the Faith; and for those who are subservient to them in war and alliance." It had political, civil, and religious sections, stating that Muslims and Jews constitute one political entity with Medina as their sanctuary. God is the sovereign and Muhammad the head, and both should make war or peace together. Each community was responsible for blood money (**diyah**) of their own and everyone had the right to retaliation in self-defense. The Muslims are brothers and constitute one unit against the entire world; if a Jew becomes a Muslim, he will be treated as an equal, and both Jews and Muslims are to offer reciprocal respect and tolerance for the two religions. It set the precedence for the status of **Christians** and Jews as protected subjects (**dhimmis**), who were permitted to live in peace and practice their own religions. Since Islamic law applies only to Muslims, dhimmis were subject to their own religious traditions.

The **millet system** of the **Ottoman empire** continued the autonomy of its subjects until the end of the 19th century, and traces of the system can still be found in Lebanon.

**MESSENGER.** The belief in a Messenger of God is one of the basic dogmas of Islam. The Koran says: "The messenger believeth in what hath been revealed to him from his Lord, as do the men of faith, each one (of them) believeth in Allah, His **angels**, His books, and His messengers" (2:285). According to Tradition (**Sunnah**) the Prophet is believed to have said that there were 124,000 prophets and 315 apostles or messengers. But there are only 25 mentioned in the Koran, and six of them are honored with special epithets: **Adam**, God's chosen one; **Noah**, God's preacher; **Abraham**, God's friend; **Moses**, speaker with God; **Jesus**, God's spirit; and Muhammad, God's Messenger. Muhammad is the last, the "seal of the prophets." He is a witness, a bearer of good tidings, and a warner of impending doom. His message is the culmination of all previous messages. **Prophets** are to guide mankind on the right path to the good life in this world and for salvation in the world to come.

**MEVLEVIS (MAULAWIYYA).** Mystical order named after its founder Mawlana (Master) **Jalal al-Din Rumi**, who are known in the West as "Whirling Dervishes" because of their ecstatic **dances**, which form part of the spiritual exercises. The order flourished in Anatolia, the present-day Turkey, and was forbidden, as were all **Sufi** lodges, by the secular government of Mustapha Kemal Atatürk in 1928. Like the **Bektashi** order and others, it went underground and reappeared when government restrictions were relaxed after the Second World War. *See* JALAL AL-DIN RUMI.

**MIHNA.** "Trial." An inquisition, set up during the ʿ**Abbasid** period (827-848) to force the acceptance of the **Muʿtazilite** dogma of the **"createdness of the Koran."** **Al-Ma'mun** issued a proclamation in 827, declaring that the Koran was created and demanded that all his officials accept his edict. He set up a tribunal. One of its most prominent victims was **Ahmad Ibn Hanbal**, founder of the Hanbali school of jurisprudence, who refused to accept the decree. He was beaten but set free because of his popularity. Eventually, **Caliph** Mutawakkil (833-849) restored the old dogma, namely, that the Koran was not created, which is the orthodox view today.

**MIHRAB.** A niche in the wall of a **mosque** indicating the direction (**qibla**) of the **Kaʿbah** in Mecca, which Muslims all over the world must face during **prayer.** The mihrab is often richly ornamented, adorned with tiles with floral design or Koranic inscriptions. The oldest preserved Mihrab is said to be in the **Umayyad** Mosque in **Damascus** (720).

**MIKA'IL (MIKAL).** One of the Archangels. *See* ANGELS.

**MILLET (MILLAT).** A religio-political community and a system of administrative division in the **Ottoman empire** (1326-1924). Subjects were autonomous under their respective confessional leaders, who had civil and criminal jurisdiction over their flock. The leaders, usually the patriarchs, bishops, or chief rabbis, were responsible for taxation and maintenance of law and order in their communities. Eventually European powers became protectors of various millets: the Russians favored the Orthodox, the French the Catholics, the British the Protestants and certain Shiʿites, etc. The system ended with the defeat of the Ottoman empire in the First World War, but traces of confessional autonomy still remain in Lebanon and other countries in the Middle East where matters of family law are still reserved for the jurisdiction of sectarian communities. The terms millet and milli also mean nation and national, respectively.

**MINA.** A station on the second day of **pilgrimage (hajj)** to Mecca. Pilgrims sacrifice an animal, then throw seven pebbles each at "satan's three pillars" while proclaiming "Allah is most Great." The pilgrims spend the night at Mina and then proceed to Mecca.

**MINARET.** A round, square, or octangular tower of a **mosque** from which the **muezzin** (mu'adhdhin) calls to **prayer**. It either stands separately or is part of the building and has an interior stairway that leads to a balcony for the muezzin. The minaret is ornamented with brickwork or tiles with floral designs or inscriptions in **Arabic**. Some of the **Ottoman** cathedral mosques have as many as four or six minarets.

**MINBAR (MIMBAR).** The raised pulpit in a **mosque** from which the preacher ( **khatib**) delivers his Friday sermon (**khutbah**). Originally it was the chair of the ruler or judge, located on the right side of the prayer niche (**mihrab**). The minbar was first introduced by the 'Abbasid caliphs in the eighth century. It is a wooden structure with several steps, often richly ornamented.

**MI'RAJ.** *See* NOCTURNAL JOURNEY.

**MISKAWAYH, AHMAD IBN MUHAMMAD** (932-1030). A native of Ray, Iran, he acted as secretary and librarian of the **Buyid** ruler in Ray and **Baghdad**. His writings included the fields of philosophy, medicine, and alchemy as well as a history of the world until the year 980 (*kitab al-tajarib al-umam wa ta'aqub al-himam*). It was translated by D. S. Margoliouth with the title *The Eclipse of the Abbasid Caliphate*.

**MONGOL INVASION.** The Mongol invaders of the Islamic world caused terror and wreaked destruction from which it took centuries to recover. According to some sources, the **'Abbasid caliph** sought the help of Chingiz Khan against the neighboring state of the Khwarizm Shahs, and for a short time **Baghdad** was safe. But after the death of Chingiz in 1241, his grandson **Hulagu** moved west. He defeated the **Isma'ili** Assassins in 1256 and in 1258 captured Baghdad and established the Ilkhanid dynasty, which ruled much of the Middle East from 1256 to 1353. The Mongols were eventually stopped by the **Mamluks** of Egypt under Baybars in the battle of **Ayn Jalut** in 1260. Most members of the 'Abbasid family were killed, but an uncle of al-Musta'sim (1242-1258) escaped and continued the 'Abbasid line in **Mamluk** Egypt until the conquest of **Cairo** by the **Ottomans** in 1517.

**MONTAZERI, HUSAYN 'ALI** (1921-). Chairman of the Assembly of Experts of the Iranian revolutionary government and nominated as a successor to Ayatollah **Khomeyni**. He was born in Najafabad, Iran, and educated in Isfahan and **Qom**, where he was a student of Khomeyni. In the 1960s he taught at Qom and became involved in anti-government agitation. Jailed in 1975-1978, he was appointed **Khatib** of Qom by Khomeyni and given a seat on the Islamic Revolutionary Council in 1979. In 1989 he fell out of favor with Khomeyni and is no longer considered in line for succession. *See also* ISLAMIC REPUBLIC OF IRAN.

**MOSES (MUSA).** One of the great prophets recognized in Islam and the one most mentioned in the Koran. His title is "Speaker with God" (*Kalim Allah*). He is a lawgiver and nation-builder who delivered the Israelites from oppression. According to the Koran "(Allah) said: 'O Moses! I have chosen thee above (other) men, by the messages I (have given thee) and the words I (have spoken to thee); take then the **(revelation)** which I give thee, and be of those who give thanks'"(7:-144). Moses performed miracles: "And remember Moses prayed for water for his people; We said: 'Strike the rock with thy staff.' Then gushed forth therefrom twelve springs . . ." (2:60).

**MOSQUE (MASJID).** A place where one prostrates oneself (*sajadah*) five times a day in **prayer**. The mosque has been a center for social as well as political life. It has been a court of law, a center of **education**, and a place where social services are provided to the poor. Major mosques were centers of refuge where the authorities would not arrest an individual. This practice continues the tradition of the Prophet Muhammad who took care of religious as well as political affairs in his home or a yard outside. Eventually cathedral mosques were built where a preacher, **khatib**, delivers the **Friday** sermon **(khutbah)**.

Each mosque has a prayer niche (**mihrab**), which indicates the prayer direction (**qiblah**), and a pulpit (**minbar**) for the preacher. A fountain in the yard provides water for **ablutions**, necessary before prayer. A **madrasah**, Islamic secondary school, is usually part of the Friday mosque, with accommodation for pupils. Major mosques are provided with a **minaret** from which the call to prayer (**adhan**) is broadcast. The mosque and its services are supported by pious foundations (**waqf** pl. *auqaf*), but in modern times the state has increasingly taken control of funding, certification of diplomas, and other matters. Although Friday prayers are to be performed preferably in a cathedral mosque, Muslims may pray at home, in their offices, prayer rooms, and areas set out for prayer. After ablution, prayers, including bowings, kneelings, etc., are performed on a rug. People enter the mosque without shoes or with slippers over their shoes. **Women** do not usually attend mosques, or they are provided a special area for praying.

One Muslim scholar defined the role of the mosque as follows: A base for establishing closer ties to God; a place for scientific and theological sessions; a court for resolving people's differences; a base for military training; a place for concluding contracts and political treaties; a weekly meeting place for rulers to deliver their address to the people; a place for bringing up current political issues; a place for marriage; a place for refugees and helpless people; a gathering place for Muslim combatants before going to battle; and a sanctuary for Muslims as a political means to exert pressure on their tyrannical rulers (Anonymous, *Echo of Islam*. "The Role of the Masjid" Vol. 1, No. 7, October 1981 and No. 8, November 1981).

**MU'ADH IBN JABAL.** A **Companion** of the Prophet of the Khazraj tribe, who, according to tradition, was the first to use opinion (**ra'y**) as a judge. He was sent to be judge in Yemen and, before he departed, the Prophet asked him on what grounds he would judge. He said "According to the scriptures of God." "And if thou findest nought therein?" "According to the **Tradition** of the **Messenger** of God." "And if thou findest nought therein?" "Then I shall interpret with my reason" (Fyzee, 17-18). The Prophet approved his use of independent judgment.

**MU'ALLAQAT.** The oldest collection of pre-Islamic poetry called "the suspended ones" because they were believed to be suspended at the **Ka'bah** as prize-winning examples (some scholars say it refers to a necklace). The *Seven Odes*, collected by Hammad al-Rawiyah (d. ca. 772), are samples of poetry from **Imr al-Qais** (d. ca. 540), Tarafa ibn al-'Abd (d. 564), Zuhair Ibn Abi Sulma (d. ca. 627), **Labid** (d. 661), **'Amr Ibn Kulthum** (d. ca. 600), **Antara** (d. 615), and al-Harith ibn Hilliza (d. ca. 570). They extol the Bedouin virtues of honor, courage, generosity, and loyalty, as well as vengeance and romance.

The *Seven Odes* (there may have been nine and only five are accepted by all) and other collections, like the *Mufadhdhaliyat* of 120 odes, are invaluable sources for pre-Islamic Bedouin life, and the poetry is still appreciated today. *See also* MUFADHDHAL, AL-DABBI AL.

**MU'AWIYAH** (ca. 605-680). First **Umayyad caliph** who disputed the election of 'Ali ibn Abi Talib and, after the arbitration of **Adhruh**, proclaimed himself caliph in 659. After Ali's death in 661, his claim was no longer challenged and he established his capital in **Damascus**, where he had earlier served as governor. He continued the Arab conquests in North Africa and Central Asia and built the first Islamic navy. He stressed capacity as the primary qualification for the office of **caliphate** and started the dynastic principle by appointing his son **Yazid** his successor. When reproached about this, he asserted that Yazid was the most suitable and offered to cancel his appointment if the community could decide on someone more worthy than his son. Mu'awiyah eliminated **Hasan,** son of 'Ali, as a contender by providing a handsome pension for his retirement. Another son, al-**Husayn** refused to acknowledge Mu'awiyah's son and moved from Medina to Iraq, where he and his small following were massacred at **Karbala** in 680.

Mu'awiyah was the first Islamic ruler who set up an office of registry, appointed judges (**qadhis**) to major cities, issued the first coins—patterned after Byzantine and Persian samples—and began a postal service; he reorganized the army, which included Christian mercenaries, into an excellent fighting force and proved himself to be a competent administrator. He cherished **Arabic** poetry and one of the Umayyad's most favored poets was **Akhtal,** a Christian. Later historians characterize Umayyad rule as constituting an Arab kingdom rather than a caliphate. Some felt that the caliphate had come to an end and the institution of worldly dominion had begun.

**MUBAH.** An action that is neutral, neither recommended nor disapproved and that may be left undone without fear of divine punishment. *See* FIVE PRINCIPAL ACTS IN ISLAMIC LAW.

**MUBARRAD, ABU AL-'ABBAS AL-** (826-898). Arab philologist and one of the major representatives of the Basran school of grammarians. Mubarrad was born in **Basra** and came to the caliphal court at **Baghdad** where he remained until his death. His major work *kitab* *al-kamil fi al-adab* (Perfect in literature) has been called the classical *adab* work par excellence. It includes examples of pious sayings, proverbs, poems, and grammatical and lexicographical commentaries. Al- Mubarrad and Abu l'-'Abbas Tha'lab, his rival at **Kufah**, were praised by a contemporary as follows:

> Turn to Mubarrad or to Tha'lab, thou
> That seek'st with learning to improve the mind!
> Be not a fool, like mangy camel shunned:
> All human knowledge thou with them wilt find.
> The science of the whole world, East and West,
> In these two single doctors is combined. (Nicholson, 344)

**MUEZZIN (MU'ADHDHIN).** Islamic functionary who delivers the call for **prayer** from either a **minaret** or the door of a **mosque**. He calls for five prayers: a few minutes after sunset; at night, when the sky is quite dark; at daybreak; a few minutes after noon; in mid-afternoon. Two additional, but not obligatory, prayers are announced after midnight and an hour before dawn. The first muezzin in Islam is said to have been **Bilal** (d. 640s), an Abyssinian slave who converted to Islam.

**MUFADHDHAL, AL-DABBI AL-.** Arab philologist (d. ca. 786) of **Kufah** who was an authority on pre-Islamic poetry. Imprisoned for involvement in a revolt against the **Caliph al-Mansur**, he was pardoned and became tutor to the caliph's son al-Mahdi (775-785). He compiled an anthology of 128 odes (*qasidah*) for his pupil, which is named after him, the *Mufadhdhaliyat*, and he wrote a number of treatises on prosody and proverbs. The *Mufadhdhaliyat* was translated into English by Lady Ann Blunt and put into English verse by Wilfrid S. Blunt (*The Mufadhdhaliat*, London, 1903).

**MUFTI.** A canon lawyer of reputation who gives a formal legal opinion (**fatwa**) in answer to a question submitted to him by either a judge or a private individual. During the **Ottoman empire**, which controlled much of the Sunni Islamic world from the 14th to the 20th centuries, the Grand Mufti was given the title of **Shaykh al-Islam**. He appointed all the muftis in the empire and had the authority to declare legislation by the **sultan/caliph** in conformity with **Islamic law**. After the disintegration of the empire, Muslim countries appointed a Grand Mufti or a council of **ulama**, which issues fatwas on legal issues. In the **Twelver Shi'ite** tradition the **mujtahid**, who was also at times called Shaykh al-Islam, performed a similar role.

**MUHAJIRUN.** "Exiles," or "Emigrants." Designation for the early converts who followed Muhammad from Mecca to Medina or joined him there until the capture of Mecca. Since they were the earliest Muslim converts, they enjoyed a special status in the Muslim community and received a preferential share of the **booty**. Next to them in status were the **Ansar** (Helpers), Medinan converts who rivaled the influence of the Muhajirun until they all merged and came to be called the **Companions** (*ashab*) of the Prophet. Modern Islamist groups summon Muslims to make the migration (**hijrah**) to their camp, that is to say, convert to their concept of Islam.

The Koran says "Those who believe, and emigrate and strive with might and main in Allah's cause, with their goods and their persons, have the highest rank in the sight of Allah: They are the people who will achieve (salvation)" (9:20).

**MUHAMMAD 'ABDUH.** *See* 'ABDUH, MUHAMMAD.

**MUHAMMAD 'ALI** (1769-1848). Viceroy of Egypt and founder of a dynasty that lasted until 1953. Muhammad 'Ali, perhaps of Albanian origin, came to Egypt with an **Ottoman** army, which expelled the French invaders from Egypt in 1801. He headed an Albanian contingent that enabled him to eliminate all rivals to his power to become the unchallenged ruler of Egypt from 1805 to 1848. Benefitting from the example of French administration, he initiated modern reforms in the military, administration, and economy of his state. Ably assisted by his son, Ibrahim, he annexed large areas of the Sudan, eliminated the threat of the unruly Bedouins, destroyed the power of the **Mamluks**, and served the Ottoman **sultan** by defeating the **Wahhabi** uprising in Arabia. Eventually, he even challenged the power of the Ottoman sultan, invading Syria and defeating the Ottoman forces in 1832 and 1839. It was only because of European intervention that he was compelled to withdraw his forces from Syria.

During the reign of his son, Sa'id (1854-1863) the Suez Canal project was started. It was finished under Isma'il (1863-1879). The enormous cost of the construction resulted in the country's bankruptcy and the British invasion of Egypt in 1882. Thereafter,

Egyptian kings had to heed British "advice" in the conduct of their domestic affairs.

Faruq inherited the throne in 1936 when he was still a minor and was subject to the guidance of his regents until July 1937. In 1942 the British ambassador and the commander-in-chief of the British forces in Egypt, accompanied by armored units, forced Faruq to appoint an enemy of his as prime minister. This "humiliation of Faruq" was seen by some as the cause of his subsequent life as a "voluptuary" and habitué of nightclubs to the neglect of the affairs of state. He was overthrown by a revolt of military officers some of whom still control Egyptian affairs today.

The line of Muhammad Ali included the following members:

Muhammad 'Ali (1805-1848)         Husayn Kamil (Sultan) (1914-
Abbas I (1848-1854)                       1917)
Sa'id (1854-1863)                          Ahmad Fu'ad (King) (1917-
Isma'il (1863-1879)                        1936)
Tawfiq (1879-1892)                        Faruq (1936-1952)
Abbas II Hilmi (1892-1914)             Fu'ad (1952-1953)


**MUHAMMAD, MESSENGER OF GOD** (ca. 570-632). He was born in Mecca in the **"Year of the Elephant,"** the son of Abdallah, of the **Hashimite clan** of the **Quraysh**, and Amina of the Zuhra clan. His father died four months before his birth and his mother about six years later. He was nursed by **Halimah**, a Bedouin **woman**, and his grandfather 'Abd al-Mutalib and later his uncle **Abu Talib** acted as his guardians. In about 586 he entered the services of **Khadijah**, a widow some 15 years his senior, whom he married in 595. Khadijah bore him two sons and four daughters, but all except the last born, **Fatimah**, died early. He made several trips to Syria, and in 610, when he was 40 years old, he confessed to Khadijah that he was hearing voices speaking to him. One Monday in the month of **Ramadhan** of the year 610 he had his first **revelation**. Muhammad soon gained a small number of converts. After Khadijah, his cousin and son-in-law 'Ali was one of the first male converts, followed by **Abu Bakr**. Most of the early converts were young men who did not enjoy powerful protectors.

At the time, Mecca was in a stage of transition from a pastoral, nomadic economy to a mercantile one, but the traditional Bedouin values continued. Muhammad's new religion was to substitute the bonds of religion for the bonds of blood. The Meccan **Quraysh**, who were the predominant power, were opposed to Muhammad's message. The new religion constituted a revolution that threatened their economic position and their way of life. Pagan shrines, which brought income from **pilgrimage**, were to be replaced, and the illustrious ancestors of the Quraysh, having been born before Muhammad's message, were to be condemned to eternal hell-fire. Quraysh hostility forced many early converts, who did not have powerful protectors, to emigrate to Abyssinia. When Muhammad's uncle and protector died in 619, **Abu Lahab** became the chief of the **Hashimite** clan and promptly withdrew his protection from Muhammad.

Following an invitation from some tribesmen in Yathrib (Medina), Muhammad fled with a small retinue of Emigrants (**muhajirun**) and established himself as leader of the early community. This flight (**hijrah**) in 622 marked the beginning of the Islamic **calendar**. In addition to the Muhajiruns and the early converts of Medina, the **Ansar** (Helpers), there were also three major Jewish tribes who formed an alliance against the Meccan Quraysh. There was no room for two powers in the **Hijaz** and it was inevitable that Medina and Mecca would have to fight for predominance. Three battles at **Badr** (624), **Uhud** (625), and a defensive battle of the **Trench** (627), convinced the Meccans that they could not prevail, and they made peace in the Treaty of **Hudaybiyah** (628). Two years later, the Muslim forces took Mecca, and by the time of Muhammad's death in 632 most of the Arabian Peninsula was united under Islam.

Muhammad continued to have revelations until his death; they were eventually collected and embodied in the sacred book, the Koran. His model behavior and the actions of the early community served as the basis of the **Sunnah** (Traditions), which, together with the Koran, serve as the two major pillars of Islamic law.

'Ali, Muhammad's son-in-law, described the Prophet as follows:

[He was] neither very tall nor excessively short, but was a man of medium size, he had neither very curly nor flowing hair but a mixture of two, he was not obese, he did not have a very round face, but it was so to some extent, he was reddish-white, he had black eyes and long eyelashes, he had protruding joints and shoulder-blades, he was not hairy but had some hair on his chest, the palms of his hands and feet were calloused, when he walked he raised his feet as though he were walking on a slope, when he turned [for example to someone] he turned completely . . . (Miskat, quoted by Denny, p. 80)

**MUHAMMAD 'UMAR, MULLA** (OMAR, ca. 1960-   ). Supreme leader of the **Taliban** movement and ruler of a major part of Afghanistan. The 40-year-old **mulla** made his reputation as a warrior (**mujahid**) against the Russians and communist government in the 1980s. He is an expert marksman and is reputed to have destroyed several Russian tanks. He was wounded several times and lost one eye. In 1994 he led his force of **mosque** students in a spectacular campaign, which led to the capture of the capital, Kabul, and the conquest of most of Afghanistan. Although he did not finish his Islamic **education**, a **shurah** of about a thousand members of the **'ulama** recognized him as the "Commander of the Faithful" (*amir al mu'minin*).

Muhammad Umar established himself in Kandahar, where the Pashtuns (his ethnic group) predominate, and until his defeat in December 2001 he directed the affairs of state from there. He decreed Islamic **dress**, long beards for men, closed schools for girls, and he relegated **women**—who had been active in the professions—to their homes. Koranic penalties, such as mutilation for theft and stoning for adultery, were introduced, and music of all types was forbidden. The theocratic government of Afghanistan saw itself as part of an Islamic revivalist movement that aims to abolish all traces of Westernization in the Islamic world and endeavors to promote the establishment of a "true" Islamic state. *See also* ISLAMISM.

**MUHARRAM.** "That which is forbidden" or "that which is sacred." The first month of the lunar Islamic **calendar** and a sacred month to Sunnis and Shi'ites. Sunnis celebrate the new year and fast on the 10th of Muharram, and Shi'ites commemorate the martyrdom of **Imam Husayn**, the son of 'Ali, at **Karbala** in 680. The day, called **Ashurah**, climaxes 10 days of mourning for the **Twelver Shi'ites**, in which they conduct processions in communal lamentation with self-flagellations and passion plays, called **ta'ziyahs**, that reenact the events at Karbala. At a time of heightened passions, religious observances often turned into revolts, as during the Islamic Revolution of 1979, when they contributed to the downfall of the Shah of Iran.

**MUHTASIB.** "Censor." A market inspector and overseer of public morals, fulfilling the community's obligation to command the good and forbid the evil (*al-amr bi al-ma ʾrufwa-al-nahy ʿan al-munkar*). He was to discourage sinful behavior, encourage attendance at **prayers**, check measures and weights in the bazaars, and ascertain that foodstuffs were not adulterated. He was usually a jurist (**faqih**), appointed by a **judge** (qadhi), and paid from the public treasury. He was empowered to administer whippings for minor offenses. Since the mid-19th century the urban police has taken over this function in most parts of the Islamic world. The function has been reintroduced in the **Islamic Republic of Iran** and the Islamic Emirate of Afghanistan, where revolutionary guards or **Taliban** activists patrol the streets of major towns to enforce public religious edicts. *See also* HISBAH and MUTATAWI'AH.

**MUJADDID.** "Reformer" or "Renewer." According to **Tradition**, at the turn of each century, a reformer would appear in Islam. Various individuals have claimed this mission, including one **Sufi shaykh** Ahmad Sirhindi (1564-1624). He was called the Renewer of the Second Millennium (*Mujaddid Alf-i Thani*) and his descendants carry the name Mujaddidi and continue to be public personalities. Another person who claimed this title was Mirza Ghulam Ahmad, founder of the **Ahmadi sect** in British India.

**MUJAHID** (pl. **MUJAHIDUN, MUJAHIDIN**). A fighter in a holy war (**jihad**). A fallen mujahid is a **martyr** who is assured **paradise**. In wars of liberation against the French in North Africa and the Soviet occupation in Afghanistan popular forces proclaimed their guerrilla war a jihad and themselves mujahidin. *See* MUJAHIDIN-I KHALQ.

**MUJAHIDIN-I ISLAM.** Religio-political movement founded by Ayatollah Abu 'l-Qasim Kashani in 1945 in Iran. It called for the elimination of secular laws and the establishment of an Islamic state with enforcement of the **Shari'ah**. It also demanded the adoption of a clerical council (as provided for in the Iranian Constitution of 1906) to pass on the compatibility of all legislation with Islamic law. Kashani was banished to Lebanon in 1949 and his movement was superceded by other similar groups.

**MUJAHIDIN-I KHALQ.** Religio-political movement founded in 1965 by Sa'id Muhsin and Muhammad Hanif Nezhad that demanded the establishment of a classless society by combating imperialism, capitalism, dictatorship, and conservative clericalism in Iran. The movement turned increasingly Marxist, which led to a split in its ranks in 1975, but both factions engaged in armed attacks against Muhammad Reza Shah's government. In December 1978 the only surviving member of the original central committee, Mas'ud Rajavi, was freed. The Mujahidin were one of the forces supporting the Iranian Revolution, but they refused to be disarmed and, therefore, turned against the regime of **Ayatollah Khomeyni**. In June 1981 they were responsible for planting a bomb that killed 74 leading members of the revolutionary government. In protracted fighting some 1,200 religious and political leaders were said to have been killed and some 10,000 mujahidin massacred. Rajavi fled to Paris and eventually into exile in Iraq. He formed the National Liberation Army during the Iran-Iraq war, but his forces were badly mauled. After the conclusion of peace between Iran and Iraq, the mujahidin resumed sporadic attacks, but they were decimated to the extent that their activities were reduced to isolated bomb attacks. After 1995 the movement has tried to moderate its policies. *See also* ISLAMIC REPUBLIC OF IRAN.

**MUJTAHID.** "One who strives." One versed in canon law; in Sunni Islam it is the title of the founders of the four orthodox schools of jurisprudence. Shi'ism mujtahids are jurists of the **Usuli** school who, by virtue of their **education**, are entitled to make an independent effort **(ijtihad)** to arrive at a decision regarding Islamic law and **theology**. The mujtahid formulates new rules based on reason **(aql)** and the Koran and Traditions **(Sunnah)**, including those of the **imams**. They differ from Sunni **muftis**, who can give only opinions **(fatwas)**, in the fact that their decisions are authoritative, because the mujtahids are the deputies of the **Hidden Imam**. The founders of the Sunni schools of jurisprudence decided in the 10th century to discontinue the use of ijtihad and called on the **believers** to emulate, or imitate **(taqlid)**, the existing body of law.

**MUKHTAR, AL-** (ca. 622-687). A native of Ta'if and leader of a revolt against **Umayyad** rule in **Kufah** in the name of 'Ali's son, **Muhammad ibn al-Hanafiyyah**. He claimed to avenge the martyrdom of al-**Husayn** at **Karbala** and to establish an egalitarian Islamic state. He captured Kufah in 686 and defeated the Syrian army. He was the first to proclaim himself the Redeemer **(mahdi)** and gained wide support among the Persian and Arab converts whom the Umayyads treated as second-class citizens. Mukhtar tried to emancipate the **mawalis** and was reproached by a leading Arab, who said: "You have taken away our clients who are the **booty** which God bestowed upon us together with this country. We emancipated them, hoping to receive the Divine recompense and reward, but you would not rest until you made them sharers in our booty" (Tabari, quoted by Nicholson). Eventually Mukhtar was defeated in battle and killed at Harura by **Mus'ab ibn al-Zubayr**, brother of **Abdallah Ibn al-Zubayr**, who had himself proclaimed **caliph** in Mecca. Some scholars maintain that Mukhtar's movement contributed to transforming Shi'ism from a political movement to a religious **sect**.

**MULLA.** In Iran and Afghanistan, a preacher and spiritual adviser as well as a teacher in elementary **mosque** schools. A mulla (from *mawla*, master—or *mala'*, meaning to fill, one full of learning) also performs such religious functions as recitation of the **adhan** (call to **prayer**) in the ear of the newborn, and he presides at **marriage** and **burial** ceremonies. He is paid for his services by donations from his parish and often needs to supplement his income by pursuing a trade or agricultural work. Mullas vary in educational background from the barely literate to those with **madrasah education**.

**MU'MINUN.** *See* BELIEVERS.

**MUNAFIQUN.** *See* HYPOCRITES.

**MUNKAR AND NAKIR.** "The Unknown" and the "Repudiating." Two **angels** who interrogate the dead in their graves regarding their opinion about Muhammad and punish the unbelievers severely. If they say: "he is the Apostle of God," they are left unharmed until the **Day of Judgment**. The Koran says: "But how (will it be) when the angels take their souls at death, and smite their faces and their backs?"(47:27). They are described as black angels with blue eyes.

**MUNTAZAR, MUHAMMAD AL-.** The Twelfth **Imam** who disappeared in 878 and is believed to have commenced a period of occultation to return at the end of time as the **Mahdi**. *See also* HIDDEN IMAM and SHI'ISM.

**MUQADDIMAH.** The first volume, Prolegomena, of the monumental history by **Ibn Khaldun**, the *Kitab al-'Ibar* (Book of examples), in which he argues that history is subject to universal laws. He presented a theory of cyclical change of humanity, first from barbarism and primitive nomadism to rural and urban culture then to state and empire, and the growth of luxury, and finally to eventual decline only to become prey to a new wave of barbarians. Ibn Khaldun established a critical methodology for the study of history. He stated:

> The rule for distinguishing what is true from what is false in history is based on its possibility or impossibility: that is to say, we must examine human society (civilization) and discriminate between the characteristics which are essential and inherent in its nature and those which are accidental and need not be taken into account, recognizing further those which cannot possibly belong to it. If we do this we have a rule for separating historical truth from error by means of a demonstrative method that admits of no doubt . . . . It is a genuine touchstone whereby historians may verify whatever they relate. (R. A. Nicholson, 438)

**MUQAFFA, IBN AL-** (720-750). The one with the "withered hand." A Zoroastrian Persian, born in Fars, who adopted Islam and served as secretary to the **'Abbasid Caliphs** al-Saffah and al-**Mansur**. He introduced Persian themes into **Arabic** literature and translated from Persian into Arabic the famous collection of fables Kalilah wa Dimnah, *Khwoda-i-namah* (The book of kings), and a number of other works. He produced an abridgement of Aristotle's works on logic and wrote in a pure style of Arabic; his writings stimulated the development of Arabic prose. His hand was crippled from torture because he was suspected of embezzlement and he was burned at the stake, allegedly for imitating the style of the Koran and translating a book "which corrupted the faith of Muslims." According to another version, he was suspected of intriguing with Caliph Mansur's uncle 'Abdallah ibn 'Ali.

**MUQANNA, HASHIM IBN HAKIM AL-** (d. 785/6). "The Veiled Prophet of Khurasan" who claimed to be an incarnation of God and started a revolt against the **'Abbasid caliph**. He ruled for 14 years but was eventually defeated and committed suicide so as not to fall into the hands of his enemies. He was veiled to conceal his dazzling (or ugly) face and was said to have worn a mask of gold. **Ibn Khallikan** describes him as "low in stature, ill made, blind in an eye, and a stutterer; he never let his face be seen, but always veiled it with a mask of gold, and it was from this circumstance that he received his name" (II, 205). He made his followers believe that he could make the moon rise by placing quicksilver into a well.

**MURABITUN.** Fighters who garrisoned desert outposts (**ribat**) for the defense of the borders of the Islamic world. One force of Berber murabitun succeeded in founding an empire in North Africa and Spain. *See also* ALMORAVIDS.

**MURID.** A "novice," or devotee, of a spiritual master (**murshid**) of a **Sufi** order.

**MURJI'ITES.** "Postponers." The Murji'ites derive their name from the **Arabic** *arja'a*, meaning to defer. It is an early Islamic school that disagreed with the **Kharijites** on the question of **sin** and refused to declare one who had committed a grave sin an **apostate** (murtadd), subject to being killed. They held that judgment should be postponed to God's merciful decision. They were quiescent, accepting the **Umayyad caliphate** for the sake of unity and the well-being of the state, holding that it is better to obey even a sinful ruler than to revolt. The Murji'ites were moderates also in accepting the equality of the newly converted non-Arabs, who were treated as second-class citizens by the Umayyads. They emphasized faith over works. They introduced a quietism that continued to a certain extent even after the demise of the **Murji'ite sect** in the **Hanifite** school of jurisprudence. Murji'ites see justification for their view in the Koranic passage that says: "Others held in suspense (are deferred) for the command of Allah, whether He will punish them, or turn in mercy (relent) to them" (9:106).

**MURSHID.** A spiritual master and guide of a **Sufi** order.

**MURUWWA.** "Manliness." Arab virtue, as exemplified in pre-Islamic nomad poetry. Courage, loyalty, generosity, and hospitality characterized the virtuous man. Examples of this abound in the **Mu'allaqat,** where courage did not require one fighting a superior force, but fighting to the death for one's womenfolk. Loyalty meant devotion to one's tribe or clan, the Arab counterpart of "our country, right or wrong." Or the story of Samuel, the Jew, who sacrificed the life of his son, rather than surrender some coats of armor that were entrusted to him. **Hatim al-Ta'i'** slaughtered three camels to enter-tain three wayfarers who only asked for some milk. Not to protect someone who was in need of help would bring dishonor on the person, his clan, or his tribe. Vengeance must be exacted and it is shameful to take **blood money** for injury. Muruwwa is still a living virtue in tribal societies and is practiced as Pashtunwali by the frontier Afghans and under other names elsewhere.

**MUSA IBN NUSAYR** (640-715). Muslim general who finished the conquest of North Africa and subjugated large areas of Spain. The son of a Christian prisoner, he was appointed governor of Ifriqiyah (698), the present-day Libya and Tunis, from where he started his campaigns. He was "prudent, generous, and brave, and no army put under his command had ever suffered defeat." His lieutenant, the Berber, Ziyad ibn **Tariq**, crossed into Spain and defeated the Visigothic King Roderic before Musa followed with a large army. Musa returned to **Damascus** with fabulous **booty** he had amassed in Spain, but he fell eventually into disfavor and died in poverty.

**MUS'AB IBN AL-ZUBAYR** (647-691). Brother of the anti-**Caliph Abdallah ibn al-Zubayr** and his governor in Iraq. He fought the **Kharijites** and defeated the uprising of al-**Mukhtar** in 687. He was defeated and killed in 691 by the army of the **Umayyad caliph 'Abd al-Malik**.

**MUSA AL-KAZIM** (745-799). Son of **Ja'far al-Sadiq** and the seventh **imam** of the **Twelver Shi'ites**. His brother, **Isma'il**, is recognized as the seventh and last imam of the **Isma'ilis**. Musa was born in Medina and lived there until he was called to **Baghdad**. He was repeatedly imprisoned under the **'Abbasid Caliphs** al-Mahdi and **Harun al-Rashid**. He was given the surname al-'Abd al-Salih (the holy servant) "because of his piety and his efforts to please God." Musa al-Kazim died in prison, probably of poisoning, and his tomb in al-Kazimayn, Baghdad, has become an important place of **pilgrimage** for Twelver (or Imami), Shi'ites. *See also* SHI'ISM.

**MUSAYLIMAH (MASLAMA).** A contemporary of the Prophet Muhammad who claimed prophethood in imitation of Muhammad, for which he was given the name of contempt, "Little Muslim." He was of the Banu Hanifa of Yamama and had a considerable following among his tribe. After the death of Muhammad, the **Caliph Abu Bakr** ordered his general **Khalid ibn al-Walid** against Maslama, who was defeated in a bloody battle at Aqraba in 633. Khalid's army killed some seven thousand of Maslama's followers and suffered the loss of about seven hundred **Companions**. Musaylimah was the most powerful of a number of false prophets who appeared at the time of

Muhammad. The *Sira* (Guillaume, 649), citing letters of correspon-
dence between Musaylima and the Prophet in which the former
wanted to divide Arabia between them, states:

> From Musaylima [he would not have used this term] the apostle of
> God to Muhammad the apostle of God. Peace be upon you. I have
> been made partner with you in authority. To us belongs half the
> land and to **Quraysh** half, but Quraysh are hostile people.

Muhammad said to the messengers: "By God, were it not that
heralds are not to be killed I would behead the pair of you!" Then he
wrote:

> From Muhammad the apostle of God to Musaylima the liar. Peace
> be upon him who follows the guidance. The earth is God's. He lets
> whom He will of His creatures inherit it and the result is to the
> pious.

**MUSLIM.** An adherent of Islam who submits, *aslama*, to Allah's
commands. Muslims reject the term Muhammadan because Muhammad was a man and not a **prophet** with claims to divinity.

**MUSLIM, ABU.** *See* ABU MUSLIM.

**MUSLIM BROTHERHOOD (AL-IKHWAN AL-MUSLIMIN).**
Religio-political organization, founded in Egypt in 1928 by **Hasan
al-Banna**. It is the first **Islamic** revivalist movement in modern times
that spread throughout the Islamic world and inspired subsequent
Islamist groups in Egypt and elsewhere.

**MUSLIM IBN AL-HAJJAJ** (820-875). Islamic scholar from Nishapur
who compiled one of the six canonical **hadith** collections. It is
similar to **al-Bukhari**'s *Sahih* and carries the same title. He traveled
widely collecting **hadith** from all over the Islamic world and died in
his native Nishapur. Muslim claimed that he collected his Sahih from
three hundred thousand **Traditions**. During one of his sessions,
Muhammad ibn Yahya challenged Muslim, saying: "Whoever holds
the pronunciation (of the Koran) to be created, I forbid that person to
attend my lessons;" thereupon Muslim "passed his cloak (*rida*) over
his turban, and, standing up in the midst of the assembly, left the
room" (Khallikan, III349). He held that the Koran is not created, but
that the pronunciation (its utterance) is created.

**MUSLIM MODERNISTS.** *See* SALAFIYYAH.

**MUSLIMS, BLACK.** *See* NATION OF ISLAM.

**MUSTADH'AFUN (MOSTAZAFUN).** A name given to the class of "downtrodden, meek, and poor" in the **Islamic Republic of Iran** to show the regime's sympathy for those who had suffered hardships during the Pahlavi regime. Ayatollah **Khomeyni** claimed that the revolution was made by them and should therefore serve their interests. He referred to a passage in the Koran that states: "And We wished to be gracious to those who were being depressed (*istudha ifun*) in the land, to make them leaders (in faith) and make them heirs" (28:5). Khomeyni renamed the well-endowed Pahlavi Foundation of the Shah the Mustadh'afun Foundation and gave it the task of providing social services for the poor. The war with Iraq and its effect on the economy have made the promise of a better life for the poor an aim rather than an accomplished fact.

**MUT'AH.** "Enjoyment." Temporary **marriage** for a specified time in exchange for a commensurate payment. It can be as short as one day or be valid for years, and children of such marriage are considered legitimate. The partners do not have a right of **inheritance**. It existed in pre-Islamic times, but it is said to have been prohibited by **Caliph 'Umar** (632-634). Only in **Twelver Shi'ism** is the mut'ah marriage still practiced. It has been explained as a necessity in olden times when merchants were away from home for many months or years and therefore deprived of the companionship of their wives. Shi'ites base it on the Koran (4:24), but there are certain conditions: A proper marriage (nikah) must be performed; the woman must be Muslim or of the **People of the Book** (such as **Christians** or **Jews**); she must be chaste; some **dowry** must be specified or the contract is void; there must be a fixed period; and if there is a child, it must belong to the husband (*Baillie's Digest*, from Hughes).

**MUTAKALLIM.** Theologian.

**MUTANABBI, ABU AL-TAYYIB AHMAD** (915-965). Considered one of the greatest Arab poets, al-Mutanabbi was the son of a water carrier, born in **Kufah** and educated in his hometown and **Damascus.** He is said to have been a propagandist for the **Qarmatians,** called al-

Mutannabi (pretender to prophesy) by the Bedouins, for which blasphemy he was imprisoned for two years. After his release he went from one princely court to another, producing panegyrics for Sayf al-Dawla at Aleppo and **Kafur**, the black ruler of Egypt. Nicholson (310) gives one of his erotic preludes:

> She uncovered: pallor veiled her at farewell:
> No veil 'twas, yet her cheeks it cast in shade.
> So seemed they, while tears trickled over them,
> Gold with a double row of pearls inlaid.
> She loosed three sable tresses of her hair,
> And thus of night four nights at once she made;
> But when she lifted to the moon in heaven
> Her face, two moons together I surveyed.

While traveling near **Baghdad**, he was attacked by bandits and fled, but his slave shamed Mutanabbi, author of the verse: "The horse, and the night, and the desert know me (well); the sword also, and the lance, and paper and the pen." Therefore Mutanabbi turned back and fought until he was slain (Khallikan, I, 106).

**MUTATAWI'AH.** Individuals who enforce attendance at prayers and supervise popular morality, similar to the position of the **muhtasib**. In modern times the urban police has taken over this function, except in Saudi Arabia and a few traditional states. In the newly established Islamic states of Iran and Afghanistan, the governments have reintroduced this institution.

**MU'TAZILITES.** Called the "rationalist" theological school, influenced by Greek philosophy, which sees no contradiction between reason and belief. It was founded by **Wasil ibn Ata** in **Basra** in a dispute about whether committing a grave **sin** makes a Muslim an unbeliever. The **Kharijites** maintained that a sinner has become an **apostate** (*murtadd*) and should be killed. The **Murji'ites** (Postponers) on the other hand held that a grave sinner remains a Muslim and that his fate is to be left to God's merciful decision. In the circle of Hasan al-**Basri** (d.728) one person raised this question and Wasil Ibn 'Ata' (d.748) answered that such a sinner is in an intermediate position and he left. Hasan al-Basri said "he has separated himself from us" (*i ïazala*), which gave the new school its name.

The Mu'tazilites held five fundamental principals: affirmation of God's unity (*tawhid*), which denied anthropomorphic divine attributes and the uncreatedness of the Koran; affirmation of man's free will and God's justice; affirmation of promise and threat (*al-wa 'd wa'l-wa 'id*), **paradise** or eternal punishment in **hell**; acceptance of an intermediate state between belief and unbelief, the sinner is neither an infidel nor a believer; the duty of the believer to command the right and forbid the sinful (*al-amr bi'l-ma 'ruf wa-'l-nahy 'an al-munkar*).

The Mu'tazilites enjoyed the support of the **Caliph** al-**Ma'mun** (r. 813-833) who enforced the dogma in an inquisition (**mihnah**), but al-Mutawakkil (847-861) abandoned the doctrine of the **createdness of the Koran**. Orthodox dogma has since accepted that the Koran was not created. The Mu'tazilites call themselves the "People of Justice and God's Unity" (*ahl al- 'adl wa 'l-tawhid*).

**MUTUAL CURSING.** *See* LI'AN.

**MUWAHHID.** "Unitarian." Believer in *tawhid*, divine unity. *See* ALMOHADS and WAHHABIS.

**MYSTICISM.** *See* SUFISM.

## -N-

**NABI.** A **prophet** (pl. *nabiyun* or *anbiya*), "one to whom God has spoken." All **rasuls** (**messengers**) are nabis, but all nabis are not rasuls. A rasul brings a book, a nabi does not.

**NADAWI, ABU AL-HASAN AL-** (1914- ). Indian **Islamist** philosopher and one of the most important theorists of the revivalist movement. He traveled widely in the Islamic world and met many of the founders of the Islamist movement, including **Sayyid Qutb** and Abu A'la **al-Maududi**. He became a member of the **Jama'at-i Islami** in 1941, but he resigned from it in 1978. His book *What the World Lost by Muslims' Deterioration* has been of considerable influence in the Islamic world.

**NADHIR.** "Warner." Muhammad's task was to transmit God's message to the people. He was only a man, not an infallible authority (although Shi'ites would grant him and the **imams** this special quality). He was a "Warner," calling on people to accept his message and prepare for the **Day of Judgment**. The Koran says: "Verily We have sent thee in truth as a bearer of glad tidings and a warner: But of thee no question shall be asked of the companions of the Blazing Fire" (2:119). Other **prophets** also were warners, especially **Noah**, who warned people of the impending flood.

**NADIM, ABU AL-FARAJ AL-** (936-995). A native of **Baghdad**, also called al-Warraq (Stationer), a librarian and bookdealer who gained fame for his *Fihirist* (Catalogue), which listed virtually all publications of the first four centuries of Islam. The book was annotated with information about the authors and included Egyptian papyri, Chinese paper, and leather scrolls. He was a tolerant person, a Shi'ite with **Mu'tazilite** sympathies.

**NADIR, BANU. Jewish** tribe resident in Yathrib (Medina); they cultivated the growing of palms and acted as money lenders and traders in weapons and jewelry. The tribe had come from Palestine to Medina in the first century and became clients of the Banu **Aws**. After the establishment of the Muslim community, they coexisted with Muhammad's government, but they were accused of conspiring with the **Quraysh** and were expelled after the Battle of **Uhud** in 625.

**NAFS.** The "soul," an intellectual substance, incorporeal and immortal. Upon death, the soul leaves the body and the pure soul returns to the intellectual substance created by God. The Koran says: "(To the righteous soul will be said:) 'O (thou) soul, in complete rest and satisfaction! Come back thou to the Lord, well pleased (thyself), and well-pleasing unto Him!... Yea, enter thou My heaven'" (89:27-30).

**NAHRAWAN, BATTLE OF** (659). Battle at a village and canal of the same name near **Baghdad** in which the **Caliph** 'Ali decisively defeated the **Kharijites** commanded by 'Abdullah ibn Wahb al-Rashidi. A survivor of the battle killed 'Ali in 661 in revenge. The Kharijites continued to be a force of rebellion long into the '**Abbasid** period.

**NAJAF.** A town in Iraq where the **Caliph** 'Ali is believed to be buried. The Caliph **Harun al-Rashid** built the tomb of 'Ali there in 791, making it an important Shi'ite place of **pilgrimage**. Afghans believe that Ali's body was brought to Afghanistan and buried at a site that is the present town of Mazar-i Sharif (The Noble Tomb). Al-Najaf is also an important center of Shi'ite **education** where Ayatollah **Khomeyni** taught during his exile in Iraq. The city has been a center of opposition to the Sunni government of Sadam Husayn.

**NAKIR.** See MUNKAR AND NAKIR.

**NAMES AND NAMEGIVING.** Names in **Arabic** generally consist of five elements: First, the personal name, *ism*, as for example, Muhammad, 'Ali, or Husayn—or two names, like Muhammad Ali or Ghulam Siddiq. 'Abd Allah (also spelled Abdullah) is a construct, meaning the Servant of Allah. Second is the formal name, **kunyah**, which denotes a personal relationship, for example, Abu Muhammad, the Father of Muhammad, or Umm Ahmad, the mother of Ahmad. Third, the patronymic, *nasab*, indicates the family origin, the name being preceded by *ibn*, the son of, or *bint*, the daughter of, as for example, **Ibn Khaldun** or Bint Khadijah. Fourth, the group name, **nisbah**, indicates origin or residence, tribe, occupation; for example, al-Harawi, the Herati, or al-Misri, the Egyptian. Fifth, the honorific can be a nickname or title, as for example, al-'Abbas al-Saffah, 'Abbas the "Shedder of Blood," or Muhammad al-Haddad, Muhammad the Smith. The most common name in the Islamic world is Muhammad. Shi'ites prefer the names of their **imams**—'Ali, **Hasan**, **Husayn**. Upon **conversion** a person usually adopts a Muslim name.

**NAQSHBANDIS (NAQSHBANDIYYAH).** A **Sufi** order originating in Central Asia that takes its name from its founder Muhammad Baha al-Din Naqshband (1317-1389). It is most commonly found in Muslim Asia and areas formerly under **Ottoman** control. It advocates strict adherence to the **Shari'ah**, shunning music and **dance**, and unlike other orders prefers silent **dhikrs**. The order was greatly invigorated as a result of the activities of the reformer Shaykh Ahmad Sirhindi (1564-1624), called the "Renewer of the Second Millennium" (Mujaddid Alf-i Thani).

**NASA'I, AHMAD AL-** (830-915). Compiler of the *Sunan* (**Traditions**), one of the six canonic collection of **hadith**. He traveled in Egypt and Syria and seemed to be a supporter of the party of 'Ali (*shi'atu 'ali*). **Ibn Khallikan** quotes a witness in **Damascus**, saying: "This doctor was an advocate for the rights of the **caliph** 'Ali; so the people began to strike him on the sides, nor did they discontinue till they thrust him out of the **mosque**. He was then borne to Ramla where he expired" (I, 58). He was buried in Mecca.

**NASKH.** *See* ABROGATION.

**NATION OF ISLAM.** Originally a black religio-nationalist movement, founded in the 1930s by W. Fard (or Farrad). After his mysterious disappearance in 1934, his deputy, who adopted the name Elijah Muhammad, founded in 1936 the Temple of Islam in Chicago and established his national headquarters there. Elijah Muhammad claimed prophethood and evolved an Islamic body of doctrines as well as a basis for economic self-sufficiency. During his 41-year period of leadership he established more than 100 temples and numerous small businesses. He forbade the use of **alcohol** and drugs and the consumption of pork. Malcolm X, a deputy of Muhammad, left the Nation of Islam in March 1964 and converted to orthodox Islam, founding his own organization. A gradual trend to Islamic orthodoxy began, which accelerated after the death of the founder in February 1975, when his son **Imam** Warith Deen Muhammad assumed the position of Supreme Minister. He adopted the name "American Muslim Mission" for his organization, but he eventually disbanded it to accept union with Sunni Islam. Muhammad Ali, the boxing champion, was a celebrated convert. Louis Farrakhan continued the "Nation of Islam" on a more black-nationalist line, but there seems to have been a rapprochement between the groups.

**NAWAWI, YAHYA IBN SHARAF AL-** (1233-1277). **Shafi'ite** jurist and **hadith** scholar who flourished in **Damascus**. He is the author of *minhaj al-talibin* (Search of the investigators), which, with its commentaries, is a text of Shafi'ite jurispridence. His *Forty Hadith* and *Gardens of the Pious* are among his most important works. Nawawi was born in Nawa, south of Damascus, and he died there.

**NIDHAM AL-MULK.** *See* NIZAM AL-MULK, HASAN IBN 'ALI.

**NIGHT OF POWER.** *See* LAYLAT AL-QADR.

**NIHAVAND, BATTLE OF** (640). Al-Nu'man ibn Muqarrin defeated a Sassanian army under Firuzan, which led to the collapse of the Sassanid dynasty. Both generals died in the battle and Yastdijird III fled in 651, but he was killed by a miller with whom he had sought refuge. It was the last great battle of the Persians and three years later the Muslim Arabs reached the Oxus (Amu Dariyah) River and the Indian border.

**NIKAH.** *See* MARRIAGE.

**NISBAH.** "Noun of relationship." Part of the name of a person, indicating a group, origin, tribe, or occupation, for example, Jamal al-Din al-Afghani—Jamal, the Afghan. *See* NAMES AND NAMEGIVING.

**NIYYAH.** "Intention." A formula expressed before **prayer** or commencement of a **pilgrimage** to validate a ritual act. The formula vows: "I intend to offer to God only, with a sincere heart, this morning (or, as the case may be) and with my face toward Mecca, two (or more) **rak'ah** prayers **fardh**" (**Sunnah**, nafl, etc.).

**NIZAM AL-MULK, HASAN IBN ALI** (1018-1092). Grand **vizier** of the Great **Seljuq** rulers Alp Arslan and Malik Shah (1063-1092). He contributed to the centralization of government and developed the system of military feudalism (*iqta*). He founded orthodox theological schools (**Nizamiyyah**) in **Baghdad, Damascus**, and other major cities to counter Shi'ite propaganda. He appointed **al-Juwayni** and **al-Ghazali** to teach in the Nizamiyyah. **Hasan al-Sabah** studied there, before he founded his order of the **Assassins**. Nizam al-Mulk (his title, meaning "Order of the Realm") was the author of a book on governance, entitled *Siyasat-Nama*. It provided instruction on statecraft but also contained attacks on Shi'ites and, especially, **Isma'ilis**. He was assassinated by an Isma'ili follower of **Hasan al-Sabah**.

Nizam al-Mulk was born in Nawkan, near Tus in Iran. He had memorized the Koran at age 11, and he continued with **Shafi'ite** teachers at Nishapur. He became secretary to the **Ghaznawid** ruler before he started his 20 years at the Seljuq court. Legend has it that when Nizam al-Mulk traveled near **Nihavand**, the site of a battle at the time of **Caliph 'Umar**, he said: "Happy is the man who is with them (the **martyrs**)." When a boy from Dailam in the dress of a **Sufi** called out to him and when the vizier reached out his hand, the boy stabbed him in the heart with a dagger (Khallikan, I, 414-415).

**NIZAMIYYAH, AL-MADRASA AL-.** The first real academy of Islam in **Baghdad**, built under the **Seljuq vizier Nizam al-Mulk** in 1065-

1067 and therefore named after him. It represented the **Shafi'ite** school of Sunni Islam and offered the complete curriculum of the Islamic sciences. It promoted **Ash'arite** orthodoxy and counted among its scholars and students the most brilliant minds. **Al-Ghazali** lectured there for four years, and the school survived the catastrophe of the **Mongol invasion** in 1258 to become the model for similar institutions elsewhere.

**NIZARIS (NIZARIYYAH).** A branch of **Isma'ilis** who gave allegiance to Nizar, son of the **Fatimid Caliph** Mustansir (d. 1094) and his descendants. Headed at one time by the Shaykh of **Alamut, Hasan al-Sabbah**, the order lasted for 150 years until the **Mongol** conquest of Alamut. The **Agha Khan** claims descent from this **sect**.

**NOAH (NUH).** In the Koran Noah is a warning **prophet** who was saved from the flood: "They rejected him (Noah), but We delivered him, and those with him in the ark, and We made them inherit (the earth), while We drowned in the flood those who rejected our signs. They see what was the end of those who were warned (but heeded not)" (10:73). He is said to have lived to be 950 years old (29:14). *See also* NADHIR.

**NOBLES.** *See* SHARIF.

**NOCTURNAL JOURNEY (MI'RAJ).** Journey of Muhammad from Mecca to **Jerusalem** and, in the company of the Angel **Gabriel,** to the Seventh Heaven. He was riding a white animal, called **Buraq**, which was the size of a mule with a woman's head and a peacock's tail and two wings. Muhammad is said to have brought from **heaven** the instructions for the five ritual **prayers**. The Koran says: "Glory to (Allah) who did take his servant for a journey by night from the sacred **Mosque** whose precincts We did bless—in order that We might show him some of Our Signs" (17:1). A number of **hadith**, narrated by Abu Dhar, **Malik ibn Anas**, and **Ibn Hazm**, describe the Mi'raj as follows: Gabriel descended, opened my chest and washed it with the water of **Zamzam** spring. He brought a golden tray full of wisdom and faith and poured it into my chest, and then closed it. He took hold of my hand and ascended to the sky . . . ." Muhammad saw **Adam, Moses, Jesus,** and **Abraham** in heaven and God prescribed 50 prayers, which He finally reduced to five. After entering several heavens, Muhammad was admitted to paradise "where there were strings of pearls and its soil was of musk" (Bukhari, VII, 345). This is how the daily five prayers were prescribed.

**NU'MAN, ABI ABDULLAH AL-** (d. 974). Arab jurist who served at the **Fatimid** court in Egypt as judge and as **Isma'ili** propagandist. He is credited as the founder of Isma'ili jurisprudence. He was described as a man of great talent, learning, and accomplishments; a prolific author, and an upright judge. He created the juridical and legal system of the Fatimid state and seemed to work toward reconciliation with Sunnism. Of 44 works attributed to him, 18 are still extant.

**NUR MUHAMMADI.** The Light, or blessing **(barakah)**, which inspired the Prophet Muhammad and became inherent in his descendants according to Shi'ite Islam. From this derives the dogma of the infallibility of the Twelve **Imams**. The Nur Muhammadi is also an important **Sufi** concept.

**NUSAYRIS.** *See* 'ALAWIS.

**NUWAS, ABU** (753-813/15). *See* ABU NUWAS.

-O-

**OATH.** "Yamin." The Koran enjoins **believers** to be responsible for an oath and, if one breaks an oath, one must make atonement: "And make not Allah's (name) an excuse in your oaths against doing good, or acting rightly, or making peace between persons; for Allah is one who heareth and knoweth all things" (2:224) and "Allah will not call you to account for what is void in your oaths, but He will call you to account for your deliberate oaths: for expiation feed ten indigent persons on a scale for the average for the food of your families; or clothe them; or give a slave his freedom. If that is beyond your means, fast for three days . . . ." (5:89).

**OCCULTATION.** "Ghaybah." *See* CONCEALMENT and SHI'ISM.

**OMAR.** *See* 'UMAR.

**ORGANIZATION OF THE ISLAMIC CONFERENCE (OIC).** The Organization of the Islamic Conference was established in Jidda,

Saudi Arabia, in 1971 to promote Islamic solidarity and foster political, economic, social, and cultural cooperation among Muslim states. The organization comprises 45 member countries, including some with only a minority Muslim population, as for example, the African countries of Sierra Leone, Uganda, and Cameroon, with Muslim populations of 30 percent, 16 percent, and 22 percent, respectively. In addition to accomplishing the above tasks, the OIC sees its mission as one of fighting racial discrimination, eradicating colonialism, supporting international peace and security, safeguarding the Holy Places, and assisting the Palestinians in regaining their rights and liberating their land. It is a pan-Islamic organization that wants to unite the Islamic community (**ummah**), which is not just territorial but also includes all Muslims wherever they may be. The foundation of the organization was shocked into action as a result of the arson attack on the **Al-Aqsa mosque** in **Jerusalem** by an Australian Zionist in August 1969. The OIC organizes conferences on matters of common interest and supports publications on religious and political subjects. Affiliated institutions include the Islamic Development Bank, the Al-Quds (Jerusalem) fund, the Islamic Commission of the International Crescent (equivalent of the Red Cross), and others. In spite of political and sectarian differences, the organization includes representatives from primarily Shi'ite Iran, as well as predominately Sunni Saudi Arabia.

**ORTHODOXY.** The major **sect** in Islam, "The People of the **Tradition** and the Community" (*ahl al-sunnah wa'l-jama'a*), are called Sunnites. They comprise about 80 percent of Muslims and claim to represent orthodoxy in distinction to the Shi'ites and other, smaller, groups. *See* SUNNIS.

**OSAMA BIN LADIN.** *See* USAMA BIN LADIN.

**OSMAN.** *See* 'UTHMAN.

**OTTOMAN EMPIRE (OSMANLI,** 1342-1922). Named after Osman ('Uthman) the first of a Turkish dynasty, which lasted until the end of the First World War and comprised at the height of its power an area from the borders of Iran westward across North Africa, south to Yemen, and north to the gates of Vienna. The empire emerged from a small principality in northwestern Anatolia and in less than a century included much of the Balkans and Anatolia. A setback, 223 when **Timur-i Lang** (Tamerlane) defeated the Ottoman **Sultan** Bayezit in the Battle of Ankara in 1404, proved to be only temporary and, in 1453, Mehmet the Conqueror reunited the empire and captured the city of Constantinople. Renamed **Istanbul**, the city remained the capital of the Eurasian empire. The empire achieved its greatness under **Sulayman the Magnificent**, so called in the West, and known as "The Lawgiver" (al-Qanuni) to his people.

The spectacular military success of the Ottoman empire was due largely to its institutions and skill in military technology. It had an infantry army, drafted primarily from Christian subjects in the Balkans, equipped with firearms at a time when its neighbors were still fighting a cavalry war. Ottoman rulers were able to stay in power by surrounding themselves with a bureaucracy and officers corps of their **slaves**, who held the highest offices in the state. The government was based on a system of military feudalism and tax farming, which worked well so long as the checks and balances were maintained. Members of the subject class were organized into autonomous nationalities (**millets**), which provided tranquility and left Muslims, **Christians**, and **Jews**, subject to the jurisdiction of their traditional courts.

The Ottomans had a powerful navy, which, for a time, made them the masters of most of the Mediterranean, but a gradual decline set in when Ottoman expansion had reached its maximum extent. After an unsuccessful siege of Vienna in 1529, Hungary was annexed, but when the Ottomans again laid siege to Vienna in 1683, Hungary was lost and Ottoman weakness was clear to the world. Russia and Austria gained territory in the Balkans and the Ottomans lost control of the seas. Decline was gradual but, by the 19th century, only the distrust and rivalry of European powers prevented the empire from being dismembered. The Young Turk revolution of 1908 ended the power of the **sultan/caliph**, and Ottoman participation in the First World War on the side of the Central Powers led to the end of the empire and the emergence of the Republic of Turkey in 1923.

## -P-

**PAN-ISLAMISM.** The concept of political unification of the Islamic world to gain strength for defense against European imperialism. The idea was propounded by Sayyid Jamal al-Din **Afghani** and his disciple **Muhammad Abdu** in the late 19th century. They advocated reforming the Islamic world by selectively borrowing Western technology and administration. In exile in Paris, both collaborated in a journal called *al-'Urwat al-Wuthqa* (The firmest bond) and a magazine entitled *al-Manar* (The minaret). Afghani was a revolutionary. He enjoyed the support of **Sultan Abd al-Hamid** (1876-1908), whose claim to the **caliphate** would have made him the head of a pan-Islamic empire. Unity was not to be attained; rather, nationalism and, for a time socialism, became the ideologies of the 20th century, and only with the foundation of the **Organization of the Islamic Conference** in 1969 have new attempts been made at creation of a pan-Islamic organization.

**PARADISE.** *See* HEAVEN.

**PARTY OF ALLAH.** *See* HIZBULLAH.

**PASDARAN.** Revolutionary Guards, organized like a regular army in support of the Iranian Revolution. They organized *komitehs* to fight counterrevolutionary forces throughout Iran. The Guardians provided a check on the power of the regular army, operating under the ministry of defense. During the Iran-Iraq war, they are said to have numbered up to 400,000. *See also* ISLAMIC REPUBLIC OF IRAN.

**PASSION PLAYS.** *See* HUSAYN IBN 'ALI and HUSAYNIYYAH.

**PENSIONS.** For pensions paid to the early Muslim communities, *see* 'UMAR IBN AL-KHATTAB.

**PEOPLES OF THE BOOK.** Peoples of the Book (*ahl al-kitab* also called *dhimmis*) are adherents of monotheistic religions with a revealed scripture such as **Christians** and **Jews**. As the Islamic empire grew, Zoroastrians in Iran, Buddhists in Transoxania, and Hindus in India were included in this category. They were invited to believe in Muhammad and the Koran (3:110) because the Christian and Jewish scriptures promised the prophesy of Muhammad. The Peoples of the Book were protected subjects—"peoples of the covenant" (*ahl al-dhimma*)—and under the jurisdiction of their own laws. They had to pay a special poll tax (**jizyah**) but were usually exempt from military service. In the **Ottoman empire** (1281-1924) they were organized according to **sects** or nationalities (**millets**) under their respective bishops, patriarchs, and rabbis, who had civil and criminal jurisdiction over their communities. They often held high financial, clerical, and professional positions in the empire. The treatment of dhimmis varied with time and place: generally well treated, discriminating restrictions were, however, at times imposed on them, especially under the **caliphs 'Umar II** (717-20), **Harun al-Rashid** (786-809), **Mutawakkil** (847-61), and the **Fatimid** Caliph **al-Hakim** (996-1021). Since the 19th century and with the emergence of nation-states in the Middle East, most countries have given equal citizenship to non-Muslims and the poll tax obligation has been abolished.

**PILGRIMAGE.** Pilgrimage (**hajj**) to the **Ka'bah** in Mecca once in a lifetime is an obligation for Muslims who are in good health and have the means to afford the cost. A pilgrim cannot borrow the cost and must have paid the alms tax (**zakat**) on the money he pays for the trip. It is the "right' of God upon men (3:97). According to tradition, it is a practice dating from **Abraham**, which was subsequently corrupted and restored to its proper function by the Prophet Muhammad.

There are two types of pilgrimage: the *hajj* and the *umrah*, the greater and lesser pilgrimage. The pilgrim begins the hajj in a state of consecration (**ihram**) in which one keeps away from things forbidden, performs **ablutions** and puts on ihram clothing, consisting of two unsewn linen sheets. The hajj is performed in the last month of the lunar calendar, the Dhu 'l-Hijjah, and takes several days to complete. The pilgrim performs the circumambulation, walks seven times around the **Ka'bah**, approaches the **Black Stone** and touches it, if possible, and proceeds to the **Station of Abraham** and performs a **prayer**. After performing the rites in the Grand **Mosque**, the pilgrims perform the rite of *sa'y*, walking or running between the hills of Safa and Marva. Then they set out for the plain of **'Arafat**, stopping on the way at **Mina** and upon return at Muzdalifah, where they spend the night. An animal is slaughtered as a sacrifice (this may be substituted by **fasting** for three days).

A person who has performed the pilgrimage obtains the honorific title "Hajji," "Pilgrim;" and one who dies during the process has become a **martyr** and wins immediate entrance to **paradise**. In recent years an increasing number of individuals has performed the hajj and the presence of more than two million pilgrims has led to major accidents. Fires, crowds out of control, and political demonstrations have led to fatalities, and it is becoming increasingly difficult to channel the flow of pilgrims smoothly.

Shi'ites visit, in addition to Mecca and Medina, the **Atabat**, the shrine cities of Iraq where six of the twelve Shi'ite **imams** are buried, and **Mashhad** and **Qom**, which contain numerous shrines.

**PILGRIMAGE, FAREWELL.** In 632, in the final days of Muhammad's life, he set out on a **pilgrimage** to Mecca, accompanied by some 90,000 persons. On the first day of his pilgrimage he preached to the pilgrims, and the following day he set out for **Mina**, then he halted in the valley of **Arafat** and delivered his farewell address. In it he supported the sanctity of life and property, opposed usury, prohibited bloodshed, forbade changes in the **calendar**, appealed for the rights of wives, proclaimed the equality and brotherhood of all Muslims, and called for kind treatment of **slaves**. The Prophet then had a **revelation** that states: "This day have I perfected your religion for you, completed My favor upon you, and have chosen for you Islam as your religion" (5:3).

**PILLARS OF ISLAM. See** FIVE PILLARS OF ISLAM.

**PIOUS FOUNDATION.** *See* WAQF.

**PIR.** The Persian word for a spiritual guide of a mystical **(Sufi)** order who initiates the novice **(murid)** in the Sufi practices. The **Arabic** equivalents for the term pir are **murshid** or **shaykh**.

**PLUNDER.** *See* GHANIMA.

**POLL TAX.** *See* JIZYAH.

**POLYGAMY.** Permitted in Islam, the Koran limited previously unlimited polygamy to a maximum of four wives. The Koran says: "Marry **women** of your choice, two, three, or four; but if ye fear that ye shall not be able to deal justly (with them), then only one, or that which your hand possesses [a slave]" (4:3).

Muslim modernists reason that it is impossible to treat several women equally, and therefore discourage polygamy. They hold that during the time of the early conquests men had to marry the wives of **martyrs**. Women had to be integrated into the clan and, when a man died, a brother or close relative had to marry the widow. But in modern society those conditions no longer exist. *See also* MARRIAGE.

**POLYTHEISM.** Polytheism (**shirk**) is a **sin** that cannot be forgiven. *See* KAFIR and IDOLATRY.

**PRAYER.** The Koran says God alone listens to prayer (3:38) and the best way to pray is with humility and in seclusion (7:55). There are several types of prayer, the ritual prayer, *salat*, which Sunnis perform five times a day, and the **du'a'**, or personal prayer for special occasions.

The time for the ritual prayer is announced by the **muezzin** from a **minaret**, balcony, or from the door of a **mosque**. The five prayers are performed a few minutes after sunset, at night when the sky is quite dark, at daybreak, a few minutes after noon, and in mid-afternoon. A person goes to the nearest mosque, prayer room, or performs his prayers at home, or at work. A carpet, or mat, is usually spread out on which the person prays, facing Mecca, the prayer direction (**qiblah**). In mosques people line up in rows and follow the prayer leader (**imam**) to perform their bowings (rak'ah) in unison. **Women** pray at home, or in a mosque in a special area behind the men. Before prayer a person performs the ritual washing (**ghusl** or **wudhu**), recites his intention (**niyah**) to offer his prayer to God. **Friday** prayer should be performed in a major mosque where the preacher (**khatib**) gives his sermon (**khutbah**). According to a **hadith**, **'Umar ibn al-Khattab** used to say: "Do not intend to do your prayer at either sunrise or sunset, for the horns of Shaytan rise with the rising of the sun and set with its setting" (Muwatta, 15.949). *See also* FIVE PILLARS OF ISLAM.

**PRAYER DIRECTION.** *See* QIBLAH.

**PRAYER NICHE.** *See* MIHRAB.

**PREDESTINATION.** "Qadar." On the question of free will and predestination the Koran says: "All bounties are in the hands of Allah: He granteth them to whom he pleaseth"(3:73); and "O Allah! Lord of Power (and Rule) Thou givest power to whom Thou pleasest, and Thou strippest off power from whom Thou pleasest: Thou endowest with honor whom Thou pleasest and Thou bringest low whom Thou pleasest: in Thy hand is all good. Verily, over all things Thou hast power" (3:26). These and similar passages in the Koran are taken by some schools, such as the **Jabrites** (from *jabr*, compulsion), to deny free will. The **Ash'arites** maintained that God wills "what is preserved on the table," seemingly denying man's free will, but they accept the idea of acquisition (**kasb**), which holds that God produces the act, but it is acquired by His creatures. There exists a measure of fatalism in popular Islam, manifest in such expressions as "it is written" (*maktub*), "it is decided" (*maqdur*), or "it is my lot (*kismat*)," that is, the "**Kismet**," that is known in the West. *See also* FATALISM.

**PRESERVED TABLET.** "Al-Lauh al-Mahfudh." The belief that human actions were recorded before **creation** upon a "preserved tablet" in **heaven** has led some schools to deny the capacity of free will. The Koran says: "Of all things have We taken account. In a clear Book (of evidence)" (36:12). *See also* PREDESTINATION.

**PRIDE.** The Koran considers pride a **sin**. It was out of pride that **Iblis** (a fallen angel) refused to bow before **Adam** (2:34, 7:13, 38:74-76). The causes of pride are affluence, a sense of superiority, and whims and desires.

**PRIESTS.** There is no priesthood in Sunni Islam, and all Muslims have equal rights and duties. There is no ordination of its functionaries, no teaching office that issues decrees of dogma, and no ritual that cannot be performed by any believer. Legislative power belongs to God and the head of state is to follow the God-given law (**Shari'a**). The '**Alim** (pl. **ulama** ) is a learned man, qualified to interpret the law, acting in the name of the community (**ummah**).

The **Usuli** school of **Twelver Shi'ism** has permitted the creation of a hierarchy of clergy to act as intermediaries between the **Hidden Imam** and the **believers**. This led to the principle of "governance of the jurist" (**vilayat-i faqih**), which has led to the establishment of theocratic rule in the **Islamic Republic of Iran**.

**PROFESSION OF FAITH.** *See* SHAHADA.

**PROPHETS.** A prophet is a bringer of good tidings and a **warner**. The Koran says: "To every people (was sent) a **Messenger**: when their

Messenger comes (before them), the matter will be judged between them with justice, and they will not be wronged."(10:47).

**PULPIT.** *See* MINBAR.

**PUNISHMENTS.** There are three types of punishments in **Islamic law**: **Hadd** punishments are defined in the Koran or Traditions (**Sunnah**) and include **adultery, fornication,** false accusation of adultery, **apostasy,** drinking **alcoholic** beverages, theft, and highway robbery. **Qisas,** retaliation, is exacted for blood shed but is optional for the aggrieved. And **Ta'zib** results from the judge's discretional decision.

**PURDAH.** A woman's garment, also called *burqah* or *chatri,* that covers the entire body and is worn primarily in South Asia and Afghanistan. *See also* CHADOR and VEIL.

**PURIFICATION.** In preparation for **prayer** a person must observe ritual purity (*tahara*) and **wudhu',** minor ablution, is obligatory. It requires one to: wash the hands, wash the face and beard, wash the arms up to the elbows, rub the scalp, and wash the feet up to the ankles. Major ablution, **ghusl,** is obligatory on **Fridays** and on the **'Id al Fitr** and **'Id al-Adha** and after sexual intercourse, menstruation, and childbirth. It consists, in addition to *wudhu',* in washing the head by pouring water over it, washing the body—beginning with the right side—and washing the crevices of the body. If there is no water available, sand can be used for a symbolic purification. *See also* ABLUTION.

-Q-

**QADARIYYAH.** An early Islamic school of theology that upheld the Divine Decree (*al-Qadar*), God's omnipotence, but nevertheless accepted the idea of free will against the proponents of **predestination.** Qadar (power) seemed to denote the power of God to determine human actions, and the power of man to determine his own actions (Allah will leave to stray those who do wrong: Allah doeth what He willeth, 14:27-32). Their opponents held that men act under compulsion (**jabr**), hence they were called the **Jabrites.** The contradiction has been resolved for orthodox Islam by **al-Asha'ri**'s postulation of **kasb**. *See also* ASH'ARITES.

**QADHI (KAZI).** *See* JUDGE.

**QADIANIS.** *See* AHMADIS.

**QADIRIYYAH.** A **Sufi** order named after Shaykh Abdul Qadir al-**Jilani** (1088-1166), an ascetic preacher, acclaimed one of the most popular **saints** in the Islamic world (*qutb al-qutb*—saint of saints). His tomb in **Baghdad** is a place of **pilgrimage**, maintained by the Naqib, custodian of the shrine, who is the descendant and hereditary head of the Qadiriyyah Sufi fraternity. From Iraq they spread in numerous branches across Asia and Africa.

**QADISIYAH, BATTLE OF** (637). A place near the present city of **Najaf** where **Sa'd ibn abi Waqqas** met the Persian general Rustam in a decisive battle in which the Muslims captured Iraq. They sacked the capital Ctesiphon (Mada'in) and gained an enormous amount of **booty**. Like Yarmuk, this battle became a turning point in the history of Muslim conquests in the east.

**QANUN (KANUN).** Civil law in the **Ottoman empire**, issued by the **sultan** and collected into codes of law, the *Kanun-Name*. The name comes from the Greek, in which it designates religious (canon) law. A qanun had to be accompanied by a **fatwa**, indicating that it is not in conflict with any provision in **Islamic law (Shari'ah)**. Qanuns were easily changed to adapt to changing situations and enabled Ottoman rulers to borrow from their Persian and Byzantine neighbors and later from the West. In most countries of the Islamic world a dual system of God's law and King's law (or local tradition) has coexisted to this day.

**QARI'.** "Reciter." A person who is versed in the science of reading the Koran correctly. A number of individuals have won fame as reciters of the Koran and have been in great demand for their skills.

**QARMATIANS (CARMATIANS).** A religio-political movement of **Isma'ilis**, named after Hamdan Qarmat who led a revolt against the **'Abbasid Caliphate** and created a state in 894. The **Qarmatians** were located primarily in **Kufah** and Bahrain, the coastal areas of eastern Arabia, and southern Iraq. The state was organized on the basis of egalitarian, communist system with shared property. The people elected their **imam** and an advisory council and organized workers and artisans into guilds. The **sect** was messianic and revolutionary. Successors of Qarmat sacked Kufah, occupied Oman, and in 929 sacked Mecca and carried off the **Black Stone**, returning it only some 20 years later. Parts of the Qarmatian state survived until the end of the 11th century. Nasir-i Khusraw, the poet and world traveler, says of the Qarmatian state

> It is ruled by the six sons of Abu Sa'id in common; in their palace there is a dais on which sit a council and from which they promulgate their orders and degrees after they have come to an agreement. They are assisted by six **viziers** who sit behind them on another platform. All matters are decided by them in consultation . . . . These princes possess 30,000 negro slaves . . . who are employed in agriculture and gardening. The people have to pay neither taxes nor tithes. To anyone who becomes poor or gets into debt, advances are made from public funds until his affairs are in good state again. Only the capital has to be paid back, no **interests** are claimed . . . . (quoted by Ronart, pp. 433-34.)

**QASIDAH.** An ode, composed for the purpose of gaining "a rich reward in return for praise and flattery," it consists of about 25 verses to more than a hundred. It follows a rigid pattern and depicts Bedouin life, then proceeds to the erotic prelude (*nasib*), which is followed by a eulogy or invective (*hija'*) for reward or to hurl invective at a person. Nicholson calls it "an illustrative criticism of Pre-Islamic life and thought" (78-79).

**QAYNUQAH.** One of three Jewish tribes in Medina who were merchants and jewelers and attained a measure of wealth. They were allied with the Muslim community until the Battle of **Badr** (624), when they were accused of collaborating with the Meccans and expelled from the Arabian Peninsula.

**QIBLAH.** The direction of prayer was toward **Jerusalem** until 623, and afterward it was directed toward the **Ka'bah** in Mecca. In **mosques** all over the world the prayer niche (**mihrab**) indicates the direction of Mecca. Outdoors a stone or landmark indicates the direction. The qiblah has a special sanctity: animal sacrifices are performed with the animal's head pointing in the direction of Mecca, and Muslims are buried with the head facing the qiblah. The change in the prayer direction was announced in the Koran: "We see the turning of thy face (for guidance) to the heavens: now shall We turn thee to a Qibla that shall please thee. Turn then thy face in the direction of the Sacred Mosque: Wherever ye are, turn your face in that direction" (2:144). Another **Surah** presents the change as a test from God: "And we appointed the Qibla to which thou wast used, only to test those who followed the **Messenger** from those who would turn on their heels" (2:143).

**QISAS.** *See* RETALIATION.

**QIYAS.** "Compare." Reasoning by analogy, an extension of personal judgment (**ra'y**) is one of the four pillars of Islamic law. By analogical reasoning, general principles found in the Koran, the **Traditions** (**Sunnah**), and the consensus of the doctors of law (**ijma**) are employed in judging a case. For example, the Koranic prohibition of wine applies to all intoxicating substances, including narcotic drugs, because they have a similar effect, even though they are not mentioned by name in the Koran.

**QIZILBASH.** *See* KIZILBASH.

**QOM.** One of the holy places of **Twelver Shi'ism** Islam in Iran located south of Tehran. Some 400 imamzadeh (descendants of Shi'ite **imams**) are said to be buried there, including Fatima (d. 816), sister of the eighth imam Ali al-**Ridha**. Her shrine is a celebrated sanctuary and an important object of **pilgrimage**, and it is visited prior to visiting the holy places of **Mashhad** and **Karbala**. Iran's largest theological college, the Fayziyyah, was opened there in 1920. Because of the fact that the most holy places of pilgrimage, Najaf and Karbala, are located in present-day Iraq, Qom and Mashhad are the only shrine cities readily available to Iranian pilgrims. Ayatollah **Khomeyni** taught in Qom, and the city became his headquarters after the Iranian revolution. It has continued to be the seat of the highest Shi'ite clergy.

**QUR'AN.** *See* KORAN.

**QURAYSH.** A tribe which ruled over the city-state of Mecca and conducted trade between the Arab Peninsula and Syria. It was divided into the subtribes of **Umayya**, Makhzum, Zuhra, Taim, and

Hashim, among others. The Quraysh ruled Mecca and were the guardians of the **Ka'bah** when it was still a pre-Islamic shrine. The dialect of the Quraysh became the classical standard of **Arabic** because the Koran was revealed in it (but some claim that it was the language of the wider Arab community). The Prophet Muhammad was of the **Hashimite** clan. Initially leaders of the Quraysh opposed Muhammad and his invitation to **conversion,** so that he was forced to flee to Medina. They waged a number of wars against the early Muslim community, but they eventually surrendered when Muhammad entered Mecca in 630. The Quraysh subsequently held leading positions, including the **caliphate,** in the **Umayyad** and **'Abbasid** dynasties, so that it came to be accepted by the Arabs that the caliphate is reserved for members of the Quraysh.

**QURAYZAH.** One of three **Jewish** tribes at Medina who were in a treaty relationship with the Prophet Muhammad. Accused of collaborating with the Meccans in the **Battle of the Trench** in 627, some 600 were killed and the rest expelled from the Arabian Peninsula.

**QUTAYBAH IBN MUSLIM** (669-715). Arab general and governor of Khurasan, who was responsible for **Umayyad** conquests in Central Asia. Various expeditions led him to Bukhara, Samarkand, Khiwa, and as far east as Farghana, establishing nominal Islamic rule. After the death of the **Caliph al-Walid** (715), he refused to recognize his successor and was killed by rebellious soldiers.

**QUTAYBAH, MUHAMMAD IBN MUSLIM AL-DINAWARI IBN-AL-** (828-889). Historian, philologist, and literary critic of Persian origin, living in **Baghdad.** For a short time he acted as judge in Dinawar, before moving to Baghdad. He was a master of every known branch of science and a prolific author. His major works include *kitab al-ma 'arif* (The book of knowledge), a manual of history and genealogies; a *adab al-katib* (Guide for secretaries) on orthography, philology, synonyms, and grammar; and *uyun al-akhbar* (Sources of information), a work in 10 books, each of which covers a different subject. He died quite suddenly, after he uttered a loud cry, and he was buried in Baghdad.

**QUTB.** "Pole." The head of the hierarchy of **Sufi saints**.

**QUTB, SAYYID** (1906-1966). A leading member of the **Muslim Brotherhood** (*Ikhwan*) and one of the "Founding Fathers" of the modern **Islamist** movement. Born in a village near Asyut, he attended a village school and by the age of 10 had memorized the Koran and thus earned the title of **Hafiz**. He then transferred to a teacher's training school and graduated in 1933 with a B.A. degree in **education**. He briefly taught at the Dar al-'Ulum in **Cairo** and then found employment in the ministry of education. Winning a fellowship, he came to the United States where he earned the M.A. degree in education at the University of Northern Colorado's Teachers' College. His experience in the West caused an intellectual transformation— he was shocked by racism, sexual permissiveness, and the pro-Zionist attitude of the American people.

Upon returning to Egypt, Qutb joined the Muslim Brotherhood and became editor of its paper, *al-Ikhwan*. Originally he supported the Free Officers who toppled the monarchy in Egypt in 1952, but then he opposed the Nasser regime when it became clear that the government was not going to Islamize the state. Arrested several times, Qutb was executed on August 29, 1966. In his writings Qutb stated that "true Islam existed only in the time of the Prophet and his **Companions**," and he called for the reestablishment of the state according to the early example. He advocated the use of violence to overthrow the existing Muslim rulers as they had strayed from the Islamic way. He rejected capitalism, communism, nationalism, liberalism, and secularism as ideologies that have failed and demanded the establishment of an Islamic state. He called for the public ownership of "fire, grass, and water," and he demanded the redistribution of wealth not properly acquired. His teachings inspired the formation of such radical Islamic movements as Jama'at **al-Takfir wa al-Hijrah** (Excommunication and Exile), al-**Jihad** (Holy War), and **Jama'at al-Islamiyah** (Islamic Society) in Egypt, as well as others in many parts of the Islamic world.

-R-

**RABB.** One of the 99 beautiful names of Allah (*al-asma' al-husna'*). It means "nourisher, sustained provident being," and "master or lord" and also appears in such compounds as "The Lord of the Worlds" (*rabb al- 'alamin*). Allah is the Lord and the **believers** are his servants, or slaves (**'Abd**). The Koran says: "It is Allah who is my Lord and your Lord; then worship Him. This is a way that is straight" (3:51).

**RABI'AH AL-'ADAWIYYAH** (714(?)-801). Famous female mystic of the tribe of 'Adi who was born in **Basra** and died in **Jerusalem**. She led an ascetic life in the desert near Basra and attracted many disciples to her idea of Divine Love and union with God. Miracles were attributed to her. She wrote **Sufi** poetry, some of which is still extant. Kidnaped in youth and sold into **slavery**, she was manumitted because of her piety. Her grave was a much-visited object of **pilgrimage**. One verse of Rabi'ah quoted by Shaykh Al-Suhrawardi states:

> I reserve my heart for Thy converse, (o Lord!) And leave my body to keep company with those who desire my society. My body is thus the companion of the visitor, but my dearly beloved is the companion of my heart. (Khallikan, I 156.)

**RAHIM.** One of the beautiful names of Allah, generally translated as "compassionate," and found in such phrases as *al-rahman al-rahim* "The Compassionate, The Merciful." It occurs in the **Basmala**, the invocation of all **Surahs** except Surah 9, in which it says: In the Name of the Merciful, the Compassionate" (*bi- 'sm 'llahi 'r-rahmani 'r-rahim*).

**RAHMAN.** *See* RAHIM.

**RAIDS.** *See* GHAZWAH.

**RAJ'AH.** The return, referring to the return of the **Hidden Imam** in **Twelver Shi'ism**. *See also* SHI'ISM.

**RAJM.** Stoning, one of the **Hadd** punishments commanded in the **Traditions**. *See* HADD.

**RAK'AH.** A complete series of bowings (*ruku'*) performed during **prayer**.

**RAMADHAN (RAMAZAN).** The ninth month of the Islamic lunar **calendar,** during which daylight **fasting** is obligatory. Fast (sawm) begins with the sighting of the new moon (*laylat al-ruyah*) until dawn when a white thread can be distinguished from a black one. It ends with the ʿId al Fitr. In addition to not eating any food, it is also prohibited to drink any liquids, including saliva—which can be ejected—or engage in sexual relations. Children, the sick or elderly, travelers, and **women** menstruating, giving birth, or breast feeding are exempted. It is the sacred month in which the Koran was first revealed in the **Night of Power** (*Laylat al-Qadr*), when the Battle of **Badr** was fought, and when the Muslims captured Mecca. The Ramadhan War (Yom Kippur War, October 1973), started by Egyptian President Anwar Sadat to break the impasse in the Arab-Israeli conflict, was indicative of the religio-historical significance of the conflict. The Koran says: "The Night of Power is better than a thousand months. Therein come down the **angels** and the Spirit (**Gabriel**) by Allah's permission." *See also* IʿD AL-ADHA.

**RAMLA.** *See* UMM HABIBAH, BINT ABI SUFYAN.

**RASHIDUN.** *See* RIGHTLY GUIDED CALIPHS.

**RASUL.** "**Messenger.**" Muhammad was the *Rasul Allah*, the Messenger of God. Other **prophets** accorded the title rasul, include **Abraham**, **Noah**, Lot, Ismaʿil, **Moses**, Shuʾaib, Hud, Salih, and **Jesus** (Isa).

**RATIONALISTS.** *See* MUʿTAZILITES.

**RAWDHAH KHANI (RUZEH KHANI).** Ritual mourning, commemorating the martyrdom of **Husayn**, the son of **Caliph** ʿAli, in which Shiʿites reenact the events of 680. On **Ashurah**, the 10th day of **Muharam** (but also at other times), meetings in **mosques** or homes are held for communal mourning and lamentation. Some mourners conduct processions through the streets, flagellating themselves and cutting the skin of their heads or bodies. Shiʿite communities stage passion plays, called **Taʿziyeh**, in public squares, and coffee houses, dramatizing the events of their **imam**'s death.

**RAʾY.** "Informed opinion." Resort to the personal opinion of the jurist (**faqih**) in cases where the Koran and **Sunnah** do not give any clear decision regarding a point of law or theology. It was employed during the first two centuries of Islam as a "third source" of Islamic law. Ra'y is permitted primarily by the **Hanafi school** of Sunni Islam.

**RAYHANA BINT ZAID.** Wife of Muhammad who belonged to the Jewish tribe Nadhir and had married into the Banu Qurayzah of Medina. Taken as a captive, she converted and married the Prophet in the month of Muharram 628. She died before Muhammad during the **Farewell Pilgrimage**. According to some sources, Rayhana decided to remain a concubine, so that she could keep her former religion.

**RAZI, ABU BAKR AL-** (865-925). Persian physician, philosopher, and universal thinker from Rayy in present-day Iran, known in the medieval West as Rhazes. He published works on various diseases and their symptoms which were translated into Latin, Greek, and modern Western languages. His first medical book, dedicated to the Samanid Prince al-Mansur (*kitab al-mansuri*), established him as a medical authority. In more than 100 medical treatises, he described the medical achievements up to his time. As philosopher, he postulated, in addition to God, the world soul, time, space, and matter as eternal principles. As a youth he sang and played the lute, but later he renounced this in saying that: "music proceeding from between mustachoes and a beard had no charms to recommend it" (Khallikan, III, 312). A failed alchemical experiment caused him to be whipped by al-Mansur, which caused him to be blinded.

**RAZI, FAKHR AL-DIN AL-** (1149-1209). Persian philosopher, theologian, and commentator on the Koran, said to have been one of the last encyclopedic writers of Islam. He was an adherent of the **Ash'arite** school, and violent opponent of **Mutazilism**. His most important works are *kitab al-muhassal* (The resume) about philosophical and theological ideas, as well as the commentary on the Koran, entitled *mafatih al-ghayb* (The key to God's secret). **Ibn Khallikan** described Razi as "the pearl of the age, a man without a peer; he surpassed all his contemporaries in scholastic theology, metaphysics, and philosophy" (II,652). He was born in Rayy and died in Herat in present-day Afghanistan.

**RAZZIA.** *See* GHAZWAH.

**RECITER.** *See* QARI'.

**RECOMPENSE.** Mankind will be judged according to actions, good or evil, and will be recompensed by God in this world or in the world to come. The Koran says: "That Day will every soul be requited for what it earned; no injustice will there be that Day, for Allah is swift in taking account" (40:17). Nations rise and fall as recompensed by God: "And thou wilt see every nation bowing the knee: every nation will be called to its record: 'This day shall ye be recompensed for all ye did'" (45:28).

**REFORM OR REVIVAL MOVEMENTS.** *See* SALAFIYYAH.

**REFORMER.** See MUJADDID.

**REMEMBRANCE.** In **Sufism,** *dhikr,* is the remembrance of God. It is the glorification of God by repeating a fixed phrase in a ritual order, accompanied by bodily movements and rhythmic breathing, until a trance or unity with God is achieved. The Koran is also called *dhikr, reminder,* and the **Peoples of the Book** are called *ahl al-dhikr.*

**RENEWER.** *See* MUJADDID.

**REPENTANCE.** Return (*tawbah*) of an individual to God after falling into **sin** or error. Repentance wipes out sins, if it is made in a state of belief and is accompanied by the will to abstain from sin in the future. A nominal believer will not suffer perpetual damnation. The Koran says: "But those who reject faith after they accepted it, and then go on adding to their defiance of faith—never will their repentance be accepted" (3:90).

**RESURRECTION.** *See* DAY OF JUDGMENT.

**RETALIATION.** "Qisas." The principle of "An eye for an eye, a tooth for a tooth," requires retaliation for killing or the shedding of blood. It is the system of pre-Islamic blood revenge in which retaliation could be targeted against any male member of the offender's family, clan, or tribe. In a tribal conflict, peace could be restored when the party with a blood debt made material amends. **Women** could be given in **marriage** or blood money (**diyah**), in the form of cash, camels, or other livestock was paid. In Islam a court has to decide the offense and the aggrieved is permitted to kill a murderer or inflict an injury of equal nature. Blood money must be paid if the relatives of the aggrieved accept it, or they can pardon the culprit.

In most Islamic countries the state has prohibited qisas, but in tribal and traditional societies in the Middle East qisas is still practiced. The British, during their rule in India, codified tribal law to the extent that exact amounts of blood money were stipulated for an injury to the body, the face, the loss of a limb, or the loss of life. The Koran stipulates: "O ye who believe! The law of equality is prescribed to you in cases of murder: The free for the free, the slave for the slave, the woman for the woman. But if any remission is made by the brother of the slain, then grant any reasonable demand, and compensate him with handsome gratitude. This is a concession and a mercy from your Lord. After this whoever exceeds the limits shall be in grave chastisement" (2:178).

**REVELATION.** "Wahy." Guidance for mankind is given in the form of revelation by a **prophet**. Every prophet receives a message from God, which he conveys to his people to guide them on the Right Path. There are three types of revelation: inspiration, revelation "from behind a veil," and the message conveyed to the heart of the prophet by an **angel**. The Koran says: "It is not fitting for a man that Allah should speak to him except by inspiration, or from behind a veil, or by the sending of a **Messenger**" (42:51). Divine revelation is necessary to guide humanity to attain the ultimate truth.

**REVENGE.** *See* RETALIATION.

**REWARD.** God will reward the good by opening **paradise** to them, and good actions will be rewarded at least tenfold. The Koran says: "He that doeth good shall have ten times as much to his credit: he that doeth evil shall only be recompensed according to his evil" (6:160).

**REZA.** *See* RIDHA, 'ALI AL-.

**RHYMED PROSE.** "Saj'." Rhymed prose, one of the oldest forms of **Arabic** literary speech, also used in the **revelations** of Muhammad. It was the speech of the **Kahin**, the soothsayers, dealers in oracles whose form of expression was thought to possess magical powers. From saj' evolved another poetic form, the *rajaz*, which had a somewhat irregular iambic meter that is said to have been adopted from the rhythm of the gait of the camel. Because he used this medium of expression, Muhammad was accused by his enemies of being a Kahin. The Koran says: "This is verily the word of an honored **messenger**, it is not the word of a poet . . . nor is it the word of a soothsayer" (69:40-42).

**RIBA'**. *See* INTEREST.

**RIBAT**. Originally a fortified camp on the edges of the desert for the protection of Muslim communities. They were manned by religious fighters who often followed a purist, revivalist concept of Islam. The **Almoravids** were such a community, which succeeded in founding an empire in North Africa and Spain.

**RIDDAH**. "**Apostasy**" is forbidden in Islam. An apostate has become an infidel (**kafir**); he may lose his property and is considered **divorced** from his wife because a Muslim woman may not be married to a non-Muslim. Some radical **sects**, like the seventh-century **Kharijites**, would even kill an apostate and his family. After the death of Muhammad, some of the Arab tribes considered their alliance with the Prophet terminated and the **caliphate** of **Abu Bakr** (632-634) was devoted to forcing them to renew their loyalty and convert others in what came to be known as the "Riddah Wars." During European colonial occupation, **Islamic laws** of apostasy could not be enforced and missionary activity, though with little success, was permitted. After independence, many Muslim states adopted Western legal institutions and, although apostasy was considered forbidden, they did not enforce punishments.

**RIDHA, 'ALI AL- (REZA,** 765-818). The eighth of the **Twelver Shi'ite imams**. He resided in Medina and was called to **Baghdad** by the **'Abbasid Caliph** al-**Ma'mun** in 817 to be his successor. He gave him his daughter Umm Habib in **marriage** and had coins struck in his name. The 'Abbasid caliph wanted to end the schism in Islam, but al-Ridha died before him, reputedly of poisoning.'Ali al-Ridha's death ended 'Abbasid attempts at unifying the Islamic community. Al-Ridha is buried beside **Harun al-Rashid** and his shrine has become one of the most venerated places of **Twelver Shi'ite pilgrimage**. The city of **Mashhad** has grown around the shrine. A companion chided the poet **Abu Nuwas**, saying: "I never saw a more shameless fellow than you; there is not a sort of wine nor beast of chase but you have made some verses on it; and here is 'Ali Ibn Musa ar-Rida, living in your own time, and yet you have never noticed him." In a poem Abu Nuwas excused himself, saying: I am unable to utter praises suited to the merits of an imam to whose father (the **angel**) Gabriel acted as a servant" (Khallikan, II, 213).

**RIDHA, MUHAMMAD RASHID** (1865-1935). Islamic revivalist and reformer. Born near Tripoli, Syria, he left for Egypt in 1897 and cooperated with Muhammad **Abduh** in publishing the monthly journal *Al-Manar* (The lighthouse) in **Cairo**. The journal demanded reform and the revitalization of Islam and Islamic society. Ridha advocated the reinterpretation of Islam on the basis of the Koran and the **Sunnah** through the exercise of **ijtihad** (informed reasoning in deciding matters of doctrine in **Islamic law**). Like his mentors **Afghani** and Abdu, he wanted the Islamic community to progress by acquiring the positive aspects of European civilization. He opposed nationalism and secularism and demanded the restoration of the **caliphate**. But he wanted the Islamic world to gain strength to stem the tide of European colonialism and to fight tyranny and stagnation at home. He published a number of works, including *The Caliphate of the Supreme Imamate* as well as a biography of Muhammad Abduh and a commentary on the Koran. His teachings inspired both moderates and conservatives.

**RIFA'I, AHMAD IBN ALI AL-** (1106?-1183). Islamic mystic and founder of a religious fraternity, named after him the Rifa'iyyah. He was a native of Iraq and educated in **Basra**, and he attracted a large following with his teachings. He was an ascetic and inspiring teacher whose students believed that he could perform miracles. The order is centered primarily in Egypt, Syria, and Turkey; it stresses poverty, abstinence, and self-mortification. Because of their ecstatic dances, the Rifa'iyyah are know as the "Whirling Dervishes" in the West.

**RIGHTLY GUIDED CALIPHS (RASHIDUN).** The first four caliphs in Sunni Islam are called the Rightly Guided successors to the Prophet (*al-khulafa al-rashidun*). **Abu Bakr** (r. 632-634), **'Umar ibn al-Khattab** (r. 634-644), **'Uthman ibn 'Affan** (r. 644-656), and **'Ali ibn Abi Talib** (r. 656-661) were contemporaries and closest to Muhammad and succeeded him after his death in the leadership of the Islamic community. Abu Bakr was elected by a council of **Companions** and contributed to the consolidation of the Islamic state in the **Riddah** wars. During 'Umar's **caliphate** the Islamic domains extended into Persia and North Africa; he adopted the title **caliph** and "Prince of **Believers**" (*amir al-mu'minin*) and created some of the first institutions of the Islamic state. His assassination brought

'Uthman to the caliphate. He is said to have collected the text of the Koran as it exists today, but his rule was generally described as consisting of six good and six bad years. Nepotism increased and the Umayyads succeeded to leading positions in the empire. 'Uthman's assassination resulted in civil war and the gradual beginnings of schism, which eventually divided the Islamic world into the orthodox Sunnis and the Shi'ites who denied the legitimacy of the first three caliphs and considered 'Ali the rightful successor to Muhammad. 'Ali's tenure was challenged by **Mu'awiyah**, a second cousin of 'Uthman, and neither force of arms nor arbitration had resolved the dispute when 'Ali was assassinated in 661. This ended the period of the patriarchal caliphs and ushered in the **Umayyad caliphate** (661-750), which many considered an Arab kingdom rather than a true Islamic theocracy.

**RIGHT PATH, THE.** Muslims are enjoined to follow the Right Path (*al-sirat al-mustaqim*), which leads directly to God and salvation (11:56).

**RITUAL PRAYER.** *See* PRAYER.

**ROSARY.** The Muslim rosary (*subhah* or *misbahah*) has 33 beads, divided into three sections, sometimes adding up to 99 or more beads. A person recites or thinks of the 99 beautiful names of God as he walks in public or sits in a coffee house. Probably originating in India, use of the rosary came into the Islamic world and was generally used after the 15th century. It is accepted by most schools, except for the **Hanbalis**, and even non-Muslims in the Mediterranean regions carry the rosary to busy their fingers.

**ROWZEH.** Persian name for **fasting** (*sawm*).

**RUH.** "Spirit or life." Allah gave life to **Adam** when he blew his *ruh* into him. "The faithful spirit" (*ruh al-amin*) and "the Holy Spirit' (*ruh al-quds*) seem to refer to the angel **Gabriel** who was the means of communication in bringing the message of Allah to Muhammad. Ruh Allah, the Spirit of God, is the title of **Jesus** in the Koran.

**RUKU' (RAK'AH).** *See* PRAYER.

**RUM.** "Rome," a term referring to the Eastern Roman (Byzantine) empire. After the conquest of Asia Minor by the **Seljuq** Turks, they were referred to as the Rum Seljuqs. During **Ottoman** times (13th to 20th centuries) their European possessions came to be called Rumelia, as compared to Anatolia, but Persians and Arabs continued to call Turks Rumis (those from Rome).

**RUMI.** *See* JALAL AL-DIN RUMI.

**RUQAYYAH.** Daughter of Muhammad by **Khadijah**. Ruqayyah married the son of **Abu Lahab**, an enemy of the Prophet, but she was **divorced** before consummation of the **marriage**. She accepted Islam at the same time as her mother and then married **'Uthman** ibn 'Affan and went into Abyssinian exile with him. She died at the time of the Battle of **Badr** (624).

**RUZEH KHANI.** *See* RAWDHAH KHANI.

-S-

**SABBAH, HASAN AL-.** *See* HASAN AL-SABBAH.

**SACRED MONTHS, THE.** From the time of **Abraham** four months (Dhu 'l-Qa'dah, Dhu 'l-Hijjah, **Muharram**, and Rajab) were sacred months. During the first three it was forbidden to wage war, loot, or plunder, and general peace prevailed. Fairs were held in certain places where Bedouin poets competed for prizes and honors. The **Mu'allaqat** was one of these collections of pre-Islamic poetry. The 10th of Rajab was celebrated in Islam as the day when **Noah** entered the ark. The Koran says: "It is no crime in you if ye seek of the bounty of your Lord (during **pilgrimage**)" (2:198), which has been interpreted to mean that commerce can continue even during the month of pilgrimage.

**SACRIFICE.** Islam took over the custom of ritual sacrifice from pre-Islamic times. It is in commemoration of the Prophet **Abraham**'s sacrifice, but **Muslim modernists** now see it as an act of social welfare and charity. On the 10th of Dhu 'l-Hijjah pilgrims are required to make an animal sacrifice at **Mina**, usually of camels, cows, sheep, and goats. Those who cannot afford the cost may substitute a number of **fast** days. The pilgrims may eat some of the flesh and donate the rest to the poor. Formerly, the meat was buried because it could not be kept, but nowadays much of it is transported to feed poor people in countries of great need. An animal sacrifice is optional in celebration of the **'Id al-Adha,** which marks the end of the month of **pilgrimage,** or the birth of a child, or in expiation of a **sin.** The Koran says: "The sacrificial camels We have made for you as among the signs from Allah: in them is (much) good for you: then pronounce the name of Allah over them as they line up (for sacrifice); when they are down on their sides (after slaughter), eat ye thereof, and feed such as (beg not but) live in contentment" (22:36).

**SADAQA.** Voluntary **almsgiving** to the needy. It can be given pubicly or secretly and is one of the principal forms of making atonement. In addition there is also the mandatory charity, **zakat.** If one has nothing to give, to refrain from evil is also considered a sadaqa.

**SA'D IBN ABI WAQQAS.** *See* WAQQAS, SA'D IBN ABI.

**SADR, MUSA AL-** (1928-1978?). An Iranian born Shi'ite cleric who became a dominant factor in Lebanese politics. Educated in **Qom** and at Tehran University, and subsequently in **Najaf,** Iraq, he came to Lebanon in 1959, where he became a religious leader in Tyre. He established a vocational institute in the vicinity of Tyre and wrote the covenant of the "Movement of the Deprived" (*al-mahrumin*) in 1974. He founded the Lebanese Resistance Detachments (AMAL). In August 1978 he visited Libya with two companions and disappeared. He is believed by his followers to have been killed by the Libyan leader Mu'ammar al-Qadhdhafi. **Amal** and **Hizbullah** are offshoots of the newly politicized Shi'ite movement in eastern and southern Lebanon.

**SAFAVID DYNASTY** (1501-1732). A dynasty named after Shaykh Safi al-Din (d. 1334), a **Sufi saint,** who established the Safavid order in Ardabil in northwestern Iran. A descendant of the **shaykh,** Shah Isma'il, founded the dynasty in 1501, unified the country, and established **Twelver Shi'ism** as the religion of the new state. He created a personal force, the **Kizilbash** (Red Heads), and a tribal force, the Shah Sevan (Friends of the Shah) as praetorian guards. His tribes venerated **Isma'il** and thought him invincible. It was only when the **Ottomans** defeated the Shah in the battle of Chalidran in 1514 that the ruler lost some of his charisma. But the Safavids retained some of the quasi-divine status. An Afghan army finally defeated the Safavids in the battle of Gulnabad in 1722.

**SAFFARID DYNASTY.** *See* YAQUB IBN LAYTH, AL-SAFFAR.

**SAFIYYAH BINT HUAYY.** The 17-year-old widow of Kinanah, chief of the Jews of Khaybar, married Muhammad. She was captured in the Battle of Khaybar in 629 and enslaved, but she converted to Islam and was set free. She died long after the Prophet in 674 and left a third of her estate to her Jewish nephew.

**SAINTS.** "Awliyah, Friends of God." In popular Islam there exists a cult of saints who are the source of a special blessing (**barakah**). They were often the founders of **Sufi** orders and their tombs are objects of **pilgrimage**. Devotees fasten pieces of cloth from a garment to the enclosure or a tree nearby of a saint's tomb to find recovery from an affliction, or they may wear the cloth as a talisman. Some saints are believed to perform miracles (**karamat**) and dispense **amulets**, and are patrons of communities or tribes. The terms for saints are **pir** (spiritual master), **wali** (friend), *murabit* (the North African *marabout*), *shafi* (intercessor), and **shaykh** (leader). They are believed to have the power of **intercession**, and the ability to give advice, and bestow blessings. A person becomes a saint by acclamation and is often associated with a shrine. They receive offerings of money from their devotees. Although saint cults are frowned upon by orthodoxy, they are an expression of popular Islam, which could not be suppressed. **Twelver Shi'ism** accepts only a lesser type of sainthood, the imam-zadeh shrines, and the Sunni **Wahhabis** of Saudi Arabia and the **Hanbali school of law** reject the cult of saints as sinful innovations.

**SAJ'.** Rhymed Prose. The oldest form of poetic speech in Arabia and the style used in the Koran.

**SAJDAH.** Prostration, as during prayer. A person stands, then lowers himself to the ground, and touches the ground with both hands and the forehead. *See* PRAYER.

**SALADIN.** *See* SALAH AL-DIN.

**SALAF.** "Ancestor." The virtuous forefathers, and a person who draws on the Koran and the **Sunnah** as the only valid sources of Islam. The Salaf included the Prophet's **Companions** and the early generations of Islam, ending with Ahmad **Ibn Hanbal** in the ninth century, although a number of later Islamic scholars are included. *See* SALA-FIYYAH.

**SALAFIYYAH.** A reform movement in Islam that tried to respond to stagnation and weakness in the Islamic world and advocated a return to the basics of Islam on the basis of the Koran, the **Sunnah,** and the practices of the Pious Fathers **(Salaf).** It included such scholars as **Ibn Hanbal, Ibn Taymiyyah** and, in the 19th century, **'Abd al-Wahhab,** whose ideas influenced later reformers. Most importantly, they influenced an Egyptian reform and revival movement at the turn of the century inspired by Jamal al-Din **Afghani** (18 39-1897) and **Muhammad Abduh** (1849-1905). Impressed by the threat of European colonialism, they demanded a reinterpretation of Islam in the light of modernity and rejected the blind adherence to legal decisions of the past *(taqlid).* They felt that **revelation** and reason were fully compatible and favored **education** in the sciences and adoption of those technologies of the West that would strengthen the Islamic world. A conservative trend, promoted by **Rashid Ridha,** inspired an **Islamist** movement that demanded the establishment of an Islamic state in which the **Shari'iah** is the supreme law and all manifestations of Western culture are eliminated. Inspired by the Iranian revolution and the writings of Ayatollah **Khomeyni** (ca. 1900-1989), **Hasan al-Banna** (1906-1949), and **Abu 'l-A'la Maududi,** radical Islamic parties emerged that used Islam as a political doctrine of action. The **Taliban** of Afghanistan, the **Jihad** of Egypt, and the **Islamic Salvation Front** of Algeria seek to create a new Islamic society.

**SALAH AL-DIN, YUSUF IBN AYYUB (SALADIN)** (1138-1193). Military and diplomatic genius who founded the **Ayyubid** dynasty of Egypt. He replaced the **Fatimid** kingdom and restored orthodoxy to Egypt. He conducted a **jihad** against the Crusaders and in the battle of Hittin (1187) recaptured **Jerusalem**. He was respected as a tolerant ruler and became a hero in the Islamic world. He was born in Takrit, Iraq, the son a Kurdish officer in the service of Nur al-Din, and he was educated in the **Shafi'ite** tradition. At the age of about 30 he joined forces with a Syrian army and gained control of Egypt. After the death of his suzerain Nur al-Din in 1174, he proclaimed himself independent under nominal **'Abbasid** suzerainty with the title of **sultan**. His mausoleum is located in **Damascus**.

**SALAMAH BINT ABI UMAYYAH (UMM SALAMAH, d.681).** A widow of Abu Salamah with children who became the wife of

Muhammad, after she had rejected a proposal by **Abu Bakr** and **'Umar I**. She confessed to Muhammad that she was jealous, but he replied that "Allah will remove her jealousy." Her **dowry** is said to have consisted of a bed stuffed with palm leaves, a bowl, a dish, and a hand mill. She died at age 59, surviving most of Muhammad's wives.

**SALAT.** *See* PRAYER.

**SALMAN THE PERSIAN (AL-FARISI). Companion** of the Prophet and first Persian convert to Islam who is credited with having suggested the construction of a trench (*khandaq*) that protected the Muslim community in Medina from a Meccan attack in the battle of the **Trench** (627). Salman was a **Christian slave** who purchased his freedom and converted to Islam. He is also said to be one of the founders of **Sufism** and is considered by some Shi'ite **sects** a divinely inspired individual. His tomb is located in Mada'in.The Shi'ite **Alawis** put Salman on a par with Muhammad and 'Ali.

**SALVATION.** "Naja." **Believers** are promised "gardens with rivers flowing beneath, their eternal home [in paradise]" (5:119). A good Muslim will find salvation, a bad one will suffer in purgatory until his sins are atoned. An unbeliever will suffer the pains of eternal hellfire.

**SAMA'.** A **Sufi** practice, *sama*, "listening" is used in musical gatherings together with dhikr, **"remembrance,"** to achieve ecstacy or union with God.

**SAMANID DYNASTY** (819-1005). A dynasty, named after its eponymic ancestor Saman, that reached its greatest extent under Nasr II ibn Ahmad (913-943) and included eastern Iran, Tranoxania, and present-day Afghanistan. Virtually independent of the **'Abbasid caliphs**, the Samanids defeated the **Saffarids** and captured 'Amr **ibn Layth** (d. 901). They established their capital at Bukhara, which was one of the great centers of Islamic civilization. Under the Samanids, there was a great revival of Persian culture. They patronized Persian language and literature, which asumed its modern form during this period. The first Persian poet of the Islamic period Rudaki (d. 940) and the great physicians and philosophers **Ibn Sina** (Avicenna) and Abu Bakr **al-Razi** flourished at the Samanid court. Eventually the Samanids succumbed to the **Ghaznawids** and Qarakhanids.

**SAMARRA.** Capital of the 'Abbasid caliphate founded by al-Mu'tasim (r. 833-842) in 836, when his Turkish bodyguard became a menace to **Baghdad.** The name is a corruption of "pleased is he who sees it" (*surra man ra 'a*). The city flourished in 847-861 under the Caliph al-Mutawakkil but after 688 it began its decline, and in the 10th century it was deserted. Remnants of the 'Abbasid architecture can still be seen, and the tombs of the **imams** 'Ali al-Hadi (d. 868) and Hasan al-Askari (d. 874) make it an important place of **pilgrimage** for **Twelver Shi'ites.**

**SAMUEL, IBN ADIYA AL- (SAMAW'AL).** Sixth-century **Jewish** poet who lived in a castle called al-Ablaq north of Medina. His name has become proverbial as the epitome of unlimited loyalty when he sacrificed his son rather than surrender armor entrusted to him. The Bedouin poet **Imru' al-Qays** was pursued by men of the king of al-Hira and entrusted five suits of armor to Samaw'al, before moving on. When the pursuers got to the gates of the castle, they demanded the armor—they had managed to capture his son while out on a hunting trip—and threatened to kill him. Samaw'al sacrificed his son rather than betray a trust. Hence, the Arab saying: "more loyal than Samaw'al."

**SANAD.** *See* ISNAD.

**SANCTUARY OF PEACE, THE.** The city of Mecca is called the "sanctuary of peace" in the Koran (28:57, 29:67). The Koran says that **Abraham** prayed to God that the city of Mecca be designated a city of peace, because of the location of the **Ka'bah** in it (2:126).

**SANUSIYYAH.** A **Sufi** fraternity in North Africa founded by Muhammad Ibn Abi al-Sanusi in 1833. The order won many followers in Libya, Egypt, and the Saharan desert region, where it established peace and security and introduced a puritanical practice of Islam. Under Sayyid Muhammad al-Mahdi ((1859-1902) and Ahmad al-Sharif al-Sanusi (1905-1925) they fought the **Ottoman,** French, and subsequently Italian governments, and in 1951 their leader, Idris, became king of Libya. In 1969 the monarchy was overthrown in a military revolt under Colonel Mu'ammar al-Qadhdhafi.

**SATAN.** *See* IBLIS.

**SA'UD, IBN.** *See* IBN SA'UD.

**SAWDAH BINT ZAM'AH.** Wife of Muhammad. She and her first husband adopted Islam in Mecca and went into Abyssinian exile. When her husband died, she was the first woman after **Khadijah** whom Muhammad married. The **marriage** was in the month of **Ramadhan** in 620 and she received 400 **dirhams** as **dowry**. Described as a charitable woman, large and heavy, as she grew older, she deferred to **'A'ishah** to please Muhammad. She died in Medina in 676.

**SAWM.** *See* FASTING.

**SA'Y.** "Walking or running." One of the rituals of **pilgrimage** after circumambulation of the **Ka'bah**, *sa'y* consists of jogging between the hills al-Safa and al-Marwah within the area of the Grand **Mosque**. At each stop the pilgrim says certain **prayers**. The practice goes back to a tradition, according to which **Hagar**, concubine of **Abraham** and mother of his son Isma'il, was running between the hills in search of water for her son.

**SAYYID.** "Lord, Master." Title of a tribal chief in pre-Islamic times, it came to be a title of honor for the descendants of the Prophet through **al-Husayn**, son of **Fatimah** and **'Ali ibn Abi Talib**. Especially honored in **Shi'ism**, but also in **Sufism**, sayyids attained a measure of political influence. In some countries sayyids live in their own communities and do not intermarry with the local population. Although not an aristocracy, sayyids enjoyed a number of privileges, including at times 'dispensation from physical punishment. In most Arab countries the term now is equivalent to "Mister."

**SAYYID AHMAD.** *See* BARELVI, SAYYID AHMAD.

**SCHOOLS OF LAW.** "Madhhab," meaning direction. By the middle of the ninth century, four Sunni schools became established and gained general acceptance in the orthodox Islamic community. These schools, named after their teachers, evolved out of the legal practices in various areas of the Islamic world. They are:

The Malikite School was named after **Malik ibn Anas** who died in Medina in 795. Malik placed great importance on **Sunnah**, but he supplemented the Traditions with the practices of the community of Medina. He employed **ijma'**, consensus of the doctors of law, and permitted consideration of the welfare of the community (**istislah** and istihsan) and informed opinion (ra'y). At present the Malikite School is found primarily in North Africa and parts of Central and West Africa.

The Hanifite School, named after **Abu Hanifa** (d. 767) who taught at **Kufah**, Iraq, is considered the most liberal in the use of legal techniques. It gives preponderance to the use of informed opinion, **ra'y**, and also permits the use of preferential judgment (istihsan) and reasoning by analogy (**qiyas**). The school is the largest of the four and is found primarily in Iraq, Syria, Turkey, Central Asia, and India.

The Shafi'ite School, named after Idris al-**Shafi'i**, a member of the **Quraysh** who died in Egypt in 820. Shafi'i rejected the use of *ra'y* and *istihsan*, but permitted *ijma'*, consensus of the community (rather than the scholars), and makes this, in addition to the Koran and the Sunnah of the Prophet, the basis for argument by reason of analogy (**qiyas**). The Shafi'ite School is prevalent in northern Egypt, the **Hijaz**, southern Arabia, East Africa, and South East Asia.

The Hanbali School, named after Ahmad **Ibn Hanbal**, an Arab who died at **Baghdad** in 855, wants to confine the sources of Islamic law solely to the Koran and the Sunnah. The school permits the use of reasoning by analogy (qiyas) only when the Koran, ijma', and even a weak **hadith** are not available. Everything else is sinful innovation (**bid'ah**). Hanbal favored a literalist interpretation of the Koran and Sunnah and rejected informed reasoning. This school is dominant in Saudi Arabia.

All four schools are considered orthodox, and individuals are under the jurisdiction of their particular school (**madhhab**). Because of interference by **caliphs** in matters of dogma, such as the question of the **createdness of the Koran**, the jurists decided in the 10th century that the "Gate of **Ijtihad**" was closed, and **believers** were henceforth bound to imitate or emulate the law (**taqlid**). The jurist **Ibn Taymiyyah** (d. 1328) and the founder of "Wahhabism," '**Abd al Wahhab** (d. 1792), became major exponents of this school.

According to Muslim jurists the fundamental human condition is liberty. But since it is in human nature to be weak, covetous, and ungrateful, it is in the interest of the individual and society that limits be set on human freedom of action. These limits, **hadd**, constitute the law. They were ordained for the soul of man to define his relationship to God. The principle of liberty of mankind limits man only in cases about which revealed information exists, or in which a need for limi-tations was felt. The majority of human actions do not come under the scope of law. The criteria for good and evil were therefore more than just two. There are five general classes of acts: Actions obligatory on believers (**fardh**), as for example, the **Pillars of Islam**, **prayers**, etc; Actions desirable or recommended, but not obligatory (**mandub**), like the manumission of slaves; Actions that are indifferent (**mubah**); Actions that are objectionable but not forbidden (**makruh**), like the eating of certain types of fish; Actions which are forbidden (**haram**), like the drinking of wine.

The **Kharijites, Twelver, Fiver** Shi'ites, and the other **sects** differ from the orthodox interpretation. The Fivers are closest to the Sunnis, and the Twelvers recognize the Koran and the Sunnah of the Prophet as well as of the **imams**, whom they consider infallible. In the absence of the **Hidden Imam**, qualified scholars (**mujtahid**) continue the practice of ijtihad. See also ISLAMIC LAW and SHI'ISM.

**SCRIPTURES.** "Kitab." With the Koran Muslims gained a scripture like that of the **Christians** and **Jews**. The Prophet announced that to him was revealed the Koran in the **Arabic** language, so that the Arabs too would have a scripture which they could understand: "We have sent it down as an Arabic Qur'an, in order that ye may learn wisdom"(12:2). The Book provides verbal guidance and the **prophets** provide practical instructions. The Book is preserved on a tablet which is called the "Mother of the Book" (13:39, *umm al-kitab*). The Koran says that **Moses** received the Torah (tawrat), David the Psalms (*zabur*), and **Jesus** the Gospel (injil) and Muhammad the Koran - each successive book confirms the preceding ones, but the Koran is the last, free of any accretions or falsifications. *See also* KORAN.

**SEAL OF THE PROPHETS, THE.** Muhammad is called the "Seal of the Prophets," meaning that he is the final **prophet** and that the institution of prophesy after him is ended.

**SECEDERS.** *See* KHARIJITES.

**SECTS.** According to a **hadith**, Muhammad has said that there will be 73 sects in Islam, but only one will be saved. Some theologians deny that there are any sects in Islam because all agree on the essentials. In addition to the majority of Muslims, the Sunnis, there are a number of sects and movements which disagree on specific details; they comprise: the **Kharijites**, and the **Shi'ites** ( in cluding the **Twelvers, Zaidites, Isma'ilis, Qarmatians, Assassins, Bohras**, and **Khojas**) and those derived from them (the **Druzes, Nusairis**,

Bahai'is, and **Ahmadis**). There are also other small groups. The Twelvers (or **imamis**) are the largest of the Shi'ite sects.

**SELJUQ DYNASTY** (1038-1194). A dynasty named after its eponymic ancestor, Seljuq, who established **sultanates** in Iraq, Persia, and Anatolia (Asia Minor). The Great Seljuqs (1038-1194) controlled Persia, Iraq and Syria, and the **Rum** Seljuqs (1077-1307) established a state in Anatolia. The Seljuqs helped to restore Sunni orthodoxy to their domains after the rule of the Shi'ite **Buyids** at **Baghdad** and the **Fatimids** in Syria. The Great Seljuqs attained the height of their power under their **sultan** Tughril Beg and his immediate successors, Alp Arslan (1063-1072) and Malik Shah (1072-1092). They defeated the Byzantines in the battle of Manzikert (1071), which opened Anatolia to the Turks and established an empire in which learning and the arts flourished. In addition to reestablishing orthodoxy, the great **vizier Nizam al-Mulk** (1018-1092) contributed to the consolidation of **Ash'arite** dogma. The Rum Seljuqs continued to rule after the breakup of the Great Seljuq sultanate and until the **Mongol** conquest.

**SERMON.** *See* KHUTBAH.

**SEVENERS.** *See* ISMA'ILIS.

**SEVEN ODES.** *See* MU'ALLAQAT.

**SHADHILI, ABU 'L-HASAN 'ALI AL-** (1196-1258). Islamic mystic born in Tunisia who established himself in Egypt where his devotees founded the Shadhiliya **Sufi** fraternity. The order has many adherents in North Africa, Syria, Palestine, Iraq, and portions of southern Arabia. Shadhili died in the Egyptian desert on his way to the Holy Cities and his tomb is a much venerated shrine.

**SHAFI'I, MUHAMMAD IBN IDRIS AL-** (767-820). Eponymous founder of the Shafi'ite school. He was born in Khurasan (Gaza?) and traveled widely in the Arab world and is buried in **Cairo**. He was the first to formulate the classical theory of the bases of **Islamic law**, the Koran, the Traditions (**Sunnah**), reasoning by analogy (**qiyas**) and consensus (**ijma'**), and restricted the use of informed opinion (**ra'y**). Famous members of his school include **al-Ah'shari** (d. 935), **al-Mawardi** (d. 1058), **al-Ghazali** (d. 1111), and **al-Nawawi** (d. 1277). Al-Shafi'i spent his childhood in Mecca, and at the age of seven was able to recite the Koran by heart. He continued his **education** in Medina as a pupil of **Malik ibn Anas,** founder of the **Malikite** school, and reached the rank of **mufti** at the age of 15. Finally, he settled in al-Fustat (**Cairo**), where he won a large following. Today, Shafi'ites are found predominantly in Syria, the southern part of the Arabian Peninsula, East Africa, and Southeast Asia. *See also* SCHOOLS OF LAW.

**SHAFI'ITES.** *See* SCHOOLS OF LAW and SHAFI'I, MUHAMMAD IBN IDRIS AL-.

**SHAHADA.** "Testimony." The profession of faith that contains the formula "There is no god but Allah and Muhammad is the **Messenger** of Allah." It is the first of the **Five Pillars of Islam.** This formula (*kalima*) is part of the ritual prayer and an expression of piety. It makes a person a Muslim if he testifies before two witnesses to it. There are six conditions, which are: It must be recited aloud; it must be perfectly understood; it must be believed in the heart; it must be professed until death; it must be recited correctly; it must be professed and declared without hesitation. *See also* ISLAM.

**SHAHID.** "Witness." *See* MARTYR.

**SHAHRASTANI, ABU 'L-FATH MUHAMMAD IBN 'ABD AL-KARIM** (1076-1153). Muslim theologian from Shahrastan in Khurasan who specialized in the history of religion. He studied in **Baghdad** but returned to his hometown to spend the rest of his life there. A member of the **Ash'arite** school, he examined in his *kitab al-milal wa 'l-nihal* (Book of religions and sects) various Islamic and non-Islamic religions, **sects,** and philosophical currents. His work has been translated into German by T. Haarbrücker (Halle, 1850-1851). It was said of Shahrastani: "He knew by heart a great quantity of traditional information, his conversation was most agreeable, and he used to address pious exhortations to his auditors" (Khallikan, II, 675).

**SHAJAR AL-DURR** (d. 1257). "Tree of Pearls." Former **slave** and wife of the **Ayyubid** ruler Malik al-Salih (1240-1249), who adopted the title "**Sultana** of Egypt" after the death of her husband. As a sign of her authority, she had coins struck in her name. Subsequently, she married 'Izz al-Din Aybak, the commander of her Turkish body guard, and surrendered her title to Aybak. When Aybak took a second wife, she had him assassinated and was finally killed herself. This ended the unprecedented rule of a woman in the Islamic world.

**SHA'RANI, ABD AL-WAHHAB AL-** (1493-1565). **Shafi'ite** Islamic scholar and original thinker who tried to find a synthesis of **Sufism** and the **Shari'ah**. He studied and resided in **Cairo** where he practiced the trade of a weaver. He was a tolerant person who pleaded for social justice and the equality of all and is said to have objected to the institution of **polygamy**. Nicholson (464) said of him he "could beat the scholastic theologians with their own weapons. Indeed, he regarded theology as the first step towards Sufism, and endeavored to show that in reality they are different aspects of the same science." He was a member of the Shadhiliyyah Sufi fraternity. See SHADHILI, ABU 'L-HASAN 'ALI AL-.

**SHARI'AH.** "The path to the water hole." *See* ISLAMIC LAW.

**SHARI'ATI, 'ALI** (1933-1977). Iranian social and religious critic who provided the radical interpretation of Islam for the revolution. Born in Mazin, a village near **Mashhad**, and educated in Islamic studies in Mashhad, he worked as a teacher and in the 1950s became a political activist, supporting the Mussadeq government. Arrested for a short time, he traveled to Paris and earned a doctorate in sociology from the Sorbonne in 1964. He was one of the founders of the National Front and edited its paper *Iran Azad* (Free Iran). Upon his return to Iran, he was arrested. Jailed several times, he left Iran for London, where he died under mysterious circumstances. He was a modernist Shi'ite reformer who criticized the **ulama** for "believing without thinking." He was attacked by the conservative 'ulama as an agent of **Wahhabism**, communism, and **Christianity**. He emphasized independent reasoning and the principle of permanent revolution. He became famous as a fighter for progress and against the rule of the Iranian monarch and is credited by Iranians as the "Father of the Iranian Revolution" of 1979. He is buried in **Damascus**.

**SHARIATMADARI, MUHAMMAD KAZIM** (1903-1986). Senior religious leader in Iran and celebrated authority in his native Azerbaijan. Born in Tabriz of an Azari (Turkish) family, he was educated in **Najaf** and **Qom**. He was active as a religious teacher, before again moving to Qom where he was elevated to the rank of **Ayatollah** in 1961. Although imprisoned for a short time, he remained loyal to the Pahlavi regime. After the ouster of the Shah in

1979, he joined the religio-political leadership. He differed with Ayatollah **Khomeyni** and the conservatives by demanding implementation of the Iranian constitution of 1906 and noninterference by the clerics in government affairs. Shariatmadari's son-in-law was accused of plotting a coup in April 1982 and of having been in contact with members of the American CIA. Shariatmadari died in 1986 of natural causes.

**SHARIF.** "Noble." In pre-Islamic times the title of a Bedouin tribal chief. Subsequently a male descendant of the Prophet through **Fatimah** and her son **Hasan**. The descendants of **Husayn** carry the title of **Sayyid**. Sharifs (pl. *shurafa*) can be recognized by their green turbans. Since the 13th century, the position of the Grand Sharif of Mecca was hereditary in the **Hashimite** clan. Sharif Husayn was appointed as governor by the **Ottoman** ruler but he led the Arab Revolt in the First World War against the Ottoman government.

**SHAYKH (SHEIKH).** "Old Man." In pre-Islamic times the title of a Bedouin chief who had to earn dignity through actions of bravery, generosity, and the ability to lead his tribe successfully in battle. In Islam, it was the designation for the heads of **Sufi** orders and leading Islamic scholars.

**SHAYKH AL-ISLAM.** Honorary title for Islamic scholars since the ninth century, and in the **Ottoman empire** the title of the Grand Mufti of **Istanbul**. He issued legal decisions (**fatwas**) testifying that the **sultan**'s laws were not in conflict with the **Shari'ah** and appointed the **muftis** of the major Ottoman cities. The title was abolished in Turkey in 1924. In Iran it was the title of a local paramount official.

**SHAYKHIS (SHAYKHIYYAH).** An Iranian Shi'ite movement founded by Ahmad al-**Ahsa'i** (1753-1826) that had syncretist features and therefore aroused the hostility of the **ulama**. He claimed to be the "Bab" (Gate) to the **Hidden Imam**. One of his successors, Sayyid Ali Muhammad, founded the **Babi sect**, an offspring of which is the Bahai religion. *See also* BAB.

**SHAYTAN.** *See* DEVIL and IBLIS.

**SHEKH.** *See* SHAYKH.

**SHI'AH.** "Party." The supporters of 'Ali Ibn Abi Talib to succeed the Prophet Muhammad in leadership of the Islamic community were called the "Party of Ali" (*shi 'at 'ali*). The party eventually developed into a **sect** combining many trends. It counted its own **imams** until the sect consolidated into those who supported the legitimacy of the Fifth Imam, the Seventh Imam, and the Twelfth Imam, which became subsects within Shi'ism. *See also* SHI'ISM.

**SHI'ISM.** The **sect** of the partisans of 'Ali developed a doctrinal basis only gradually. The party began as an Arab political movement that was strongly supported by non-Arab converts and eventually developed into a **sect**. The fundamental doctrine of Shi'ism is the exclusive right to the **caliphate** by members of 'Ali's family (**ahl al-bayt**), declaring the first three Sunni **caliphs** usurpers. Like the Sunnis, the Shi'ites accept the exoteric, literal, interpretation of the Koran but also believe in an inner, esoteric, interpretation of a body of secret knowledge. This secret knowledge was believed to have been transmitted by Muhammad to 'Ali and his descendants. The **imam** (Shi'ite term for the leader) has therefore also a spiritual function that exceeds that of the Sunni caliph. The imam became the only authoritative source of doctrine, which led to the eventual doctrine of the infallibility of the imam. The Divine Light, which came to the imams from **Adam** and a succession of prophets through Muhammad, gave them a special **barakah** (blessing) and special authority. Some Shi'ites claim that the Angel **Gabriel** had brought the message wrongly to Muhammad instead of to 'Ali. The trends of legitimism and esoterism merged with others and consolidated into three major sects.

They are: the **Zaydis**, the **Isma'ilis**, and the Imamis (or Twelvers). The Zaydis, are followers of Zayd, a grandson of **Husayn**. They are also called the **Fivers** because Zayd was the fifth of the imams. Those who did not accept Zayd continued to count imams until the seventh, Isma'il, and are called Seveners, or Isma'ilis. Isma'il was appointed by his father and later repudiated, but his followers rejected the repudiation. The Seveners eventually split into three major groups (also called **Batiniyyah** because they believe in an inner, *batin*, interpretation of the Koran and the teachings of Islam): the **Fatimids** of Egypt, the **Qarmatians** of **Basra** and Bahrain, and the **Assassins** of **Hasan al-Sabah**.

Finally there are the **Twelvers** (also called Ja'fariyyah after the sixth imam **Ja'far al-Sadiq**), who recognized **Musa al-Kazim** as the seventh imam and continued to count 12 imams to Muhammad al-

Muntazar, who is believed not to have died when he disappeared as a child but went into occultation as the **Hidden Imam**. They are the largest of all Shi'ite sects.

The Shi'ite concept of the state assigns the imam the functions of interpreting and applying the Koranic laws. The imam is infallible and sinless and is inspired by the Prophet or God. In the absence of the imam the **ulama** is collectively responsible for the guidance of the community. The hierarchy of Islamic scholars culminating in the **Ayatollah** al-'Uzma permitted the establishment of the theocratic regime in Iran founded by Ayatollah **Khomeyni**.

The Shi'ite imams include the following:

1. 'Ali ibn Abi Talib (d. 661)
2. Hasan (d. 669)
3. Husayn (d. 680)
4. Ali Zayn al-Abidin (d. 712)
5. Zayd (d. 760) Imam of the Zaydis
5. Muhammad al-Baqir (d. 731)
6. Ja'far al-Sadiq (d. 765)
7. Isma'il (d. 760)
7. Musa al-Kazim (d. 799)
8. 'Ali al-Ridha (d. 818)
9. Muhammad al-Jawad (d. 835)
10. 'Ali al-Hadi (d. 868)
11. Al-Hasan al-'Askari (d. 874)
12. Muhammad al-Muntazar (878) Last imam of the "Twelvers."

The eponymic ancestor of the **Safavid dynasty** was Shaykh Safi al-Din who established the Safaviyyah Sufi order at Ardabil in northwestern Iran. Shah Isma'il, the first of the Safavid rulers, imposed Shi'ism on most of Iran and began a theocracy that lasted until 1732. *See also* ASSASSINS; FATIMIDS; HIDDEN IMAM; TWELVER SHI'ITES; USULI; and VILAYAT-I FAQIH.

**SHI'ITE.** *See* SHI'ISM.

**SHIRK.** "Polytheism." It is a **sin** that cannot be forgiven. Islam espouses a strict monotheism that rejects "giving partners to God." The Koran says: "Allah forgiveth not (the sin of) joining other gods with Him; but he forgiveth whom He pleaseth other sins than this; one who joins other gods with Allah, hath strayed far, far away (from the right)" (4:116); and "Wonderful Originator of the heavens and the earth: How can He have a son when He hath no consort?"(6:101).

**SHURAH.** "Council, Advice." Islamic rulers are enjoined to seek the advice of a council of experts; the Prophet, himself, did so and the Koran says: "consult them in affairs (of moment), then, when thou hast taken a decision, put thy trust in Allah, for Allah loves those who put their trust (in Him)"(3:159). It was started under **Caliph 'Umar** (634-644), who set up a council of six of the oldest and most respected **Companions** of the Prophet. The concept of shurah has been interpreted by **Muslim modernists** as a legitimization of parliamentary democracy. The term shurah is synonymous with **majlis** (tribal council), which is the term used in Iran for parliament.

**SHU'UBIYYAH.** A political and literary movement among the **mawali** during the ninth and 11th centuries that attacked the claimed superiority of the Arab Muslims over those of other races. It was especially connected with the Persian intelligentsia who engaged in a literary feud contrasting their ancient culture with the **Age of Ignorance** of the Arabs.

**SIBAWAYH, ABU BISHR AL-** (d. 796). Arab philologist and grammarian of Persian descent. For a long time, his *al-kitab fi al-nahw* (Book) was the most authoritative work on **Arabic** grammar. Al-**Jahiz** said of it: "Never was the like of such a book written on grammar, and the books of other men have drawn their substance from it." Sibawayh studied at **Basra** and became an outstanding member of the Basra school of grammarians. He abstracted grammatical rules from the Koran and **Traditions**, and from classical poetry and proverbs. His work left a lasting influence on Arabic linguistics.

**SIFAH (SIFAT).** "Attributes." God has seven attributes, as distinct from His Essence, including: life—his existence has neither beginning nor end; knowledge—God is omniscient; power— God is almighty; will —God can do what He wants; hearing—Allah hears all without an ear; sight—Allah sees all things; and speech—Allah speaks to His servants like he spoke with **Moses**. This has encouraged the acceptance of a literalism and anthropomorphism in Islam. Some scholars also include God's 99 beautiful **names** as additional attributes.

**SIFFIN.** A town on the right bank of the Euphrates that became famous for the battle fought between **'Ali** and **Mu'awiyah** in July 657. After three days of fighting, Ali's forces seemed to gain the upper hand when Mu'awiyah appealed for arbitration of the dispute, culminating in the arbitration at **Adhruh**. The battle of Siffin and subsequent

arbitration resulted in the creation of a new force of former support-
ers of 'Ali, the **Kharijites**, who now turned against him. The **Caliph**
Ali was subsequently assassinated by a Kharijite and the schism in
Islam began.

**SIJISTANI, SULAYMAN ABU DAWUD AL-** (817-888). Native of
**Basra** and compiler of one of the six canonical collections of Sunni
**hadith**. His work, the *kitab al-sunnan* (Book of traditions) contains
a collection of some 4,000 hadith, said to have been collected from
a pool of some 500,000. He used a measure of personal opinion
(**ra'y**) in authenticating his choices. Abu Dawud said a man requires
only four things for his religious conduct: Deeds are to be judged by
the intentions; proof of a man's sincerity in Islamism is his abstaining
from what concerns him not; the believer is not truly a believer until
he desireth for his brother that which he desireth for himself; and the
lawful is clear and the unlawful is clear, but between them are things
that are doubtful (Khallikan I, 590).

**SILSILAH.** "Chain." In **Sufism**, a spiritual lineage to the Prophet
through a succession of Sufi **shaykhs**, or for Shi'ites to **Imam** 'Ali.

**SINF.** "Guild." According to some authorities, the Muslim organization
of crafts into guilds was started by the **Qarmatians**, which action
then influenced the foundation of craft guilds in the rest of the
Islamic world and medieval Europe.

**SIN(NER).** Sin is primarily disobedience to the law of God. There are
two types of sin: major and minor. Disbelief and giving partners to
God are great sins that cannot be forgiven and deserve eternal
hellfire. The next category of great sins are murder, **adultery**, and
homosexuality. Next come theft, robbing of orphans, and receiving
**interest**. A final category includes drinking wine, false accusation of
unchastity, the practice of magic, and fleeing from the battlefield. A
minor sin, committed intentionally, can become a major sin. Some
theologians hold that a Muslim sinner will remain in hell for all
eternity (**Kharijites**), but the orthodox view is that God will pardon
all sins or the Prophet will intercede for the sinner. A **martyr** who
dies for his faith is free of sin and goes directly to **heaven**. For
Sunnis, only Muhammad is believed to be sinless while the Shi'ites
hold that their **imams** are impeccable.

**SIQILLI, JAWHAR AL-** (d. 992). "The Sicilian." **Fatimid** general who conquered Fez in 960, al-Fustat in 969, and the **Hijaz** in 976. He ruled as governor of Egypt and founded **Cairo** where he remained until ousted by the **Caliph** al-Mu'izz (952-975). He was a Christian slave, probably from Sicily, hence his name. Siqilli was presented to the Caliph **al-Mansur** (946-952) and inherited by the Caliph al-Mu'izz. The latter set him free and made him his personal secretary, then minister, and finally commander-in-chief of the army. His repeated attempts at conquering Syria failed and he retired.

**SIRHINDI, AHMAD AL-FARUQI AL-** (1564-1624). A **Sufi** reformer claiming descent from the **Caliph 'Umar** I, called the Renewer of the Second Millennium (*Mujaddid Alf-i Thani*). He was born and received his early **education** in Sirhind, Punjab, India. At age 28 he joined the **Naqshbandi** Sufi fraternity in Delhi. A collection of his letters details his teachings and activities. Some of his descendants carry the family name **Mujaddidi** and are active in Naqshbandi and political affairs.

**SLAVERY.** Slavery existed in pre-Islamic times, as elsewhere, and was mainly the result of war. Islam did not abolish it. Unlike the New World, where slaves were employed in a plantation economy to cultivate sugar, cotton, and tobacco, slaves in the Islamic world were largely employed as domestic servants and soldiers. As domestics, they became part of the family, and as soldiers they became the protectors of their masters, the **caliphs** and **sultans**. Eventually the slave forces made themselves independent and as sultans became the rulers of many parts of the Islamic world. They founded the **Mamluk** (slave) Sultanates in Egypt and Syria (1250-1517), and slave dynasties in India, and supported the **Ottoman** sultans, who were themselves the sons of slave **women**. The egalitarian **Kharijites** proclaimed that anyone qualified for the position of caliph, even an Abyssinian slave. Islam encouraged the manumission of slaves and **Abu Bakr**, the first caliph, is said to have spent his wealth on purchasing and freeing slaves.

Slavery in Islam was a condition from which recovery was possible. A contract (*kitaba*) enabled a slave to acquire his freedom in exchange for a future, or installment, payment. If a slave woman bore a child to a Muslim man, she could no longer be sold and was free when her master died. (Muwatta, 38.5.6). The **Zakat**, the poor tax, is also to be used to purchase the freedom of slaves (9:60). Once freed, a slave generally enjoyed all civil rights as a Muslim citizen.

Slavery was officially abolished in the 19th and 20th centuries and in 1962 also in Saudi Arabia.

**SOUL.** *See* NAFS.

**STATION OF ABRAHAM.** "Maqam Ibrahim." A shrine near the **Ka'bah** where a stone with the footprint of Abraham is said to be kept. According to tradition, Abraham stood at this stone when he laid the foundations of the Ka'bah and left his footprint on the stone. The Koran says: "The Station of Abraham; whoever enters it attains security; **pilgrimage** thereto is a duty men owe to Allah" (3:97).

**SUBHAH.** *See* ROSARY.

**SUCCESSION TO MUHAMMAD.** Schisms appeared in Islam over the question of succession to the Prophet to head the Islamic community. Muslims divided into three major groups: the Sunnis, Shi'ites, and **Kharijites.** The Sunnis held that the successor (khalifa—caliph) should be elected and, especially the Arabs, felt he must be of the **Quraysh** tribe; the Shi'ites hold that he should be of the family of the Prophet and three major subsects recognize either the Fifth (**Zayd**), the Seventh (**Isma'il**) or the Twelfth (al-Muntazar) as their **imam**. The egalitarian Kharijites would elect any pious man, "even an Abyssinian slave."

**SUFI(ISM).** "Tasawwuf." A member (*mutasawwif*) of one of the Sufi orders, a devotee of a mystical "path" (*tariqa*) or discipline that consists of graded esoteric teachings leading through a series of initiations to the status of an adept. The objective of the "path" is to achieve direct experiential knowledge (**ma'rifah**), which through illumination (**kashf**) leads to communion with God (*fana' fi llah*); it is achieved through personal devotion and a mastery of the techniques taught by the **shaykh**. The name comes probably from the **Arabic** "suf" meaning wool, the coarse, wool garment worn by the early mystics. Sufism was systematically developed after the ninth century; al-Qushairy (d. 1072) was first to suggest stages of approach to the experience of God. The great Muslim philosopher **al-Ghazali** (d. 1111) succeeded in reconciling Sufism with orthodox Islam.

Sufi orders originated among the urban artisan classes that organized into brotherhoods, following a particular spiritual leader or saint (**pir**, shaykh, or **murshid**). Sufi lodges (**khanaqah**, tekke, zawiyya, ribat) were founded at the residence or tomb of a venerated *pir* and supported with contributions from the disciples (**murid**). Members meet regularly in homes or public places to perform remembrance (**dhikr**), pronounce ecstatic recitations of the names of Allah, or read passages of the Koran, accompanied by rhythmical breathing and physical movements; or engage in listening (**sama'**), participation in an ecstatic spiritual recital with music and dance. Of about 200 orders, 70 are still active in the Islamic world. The line of famous mystics goes from the Persian al-**Hallaj**, executed in 922, to the pantheist Sufi Muh-yi al-Din **ibn-'Arabi** (1165-1240), the Egyptian ibn al-Farid (1181-1235), who extolled Divine Love, to the great Persian poets of the thirteenth century Sa'di, Hafiz, and **Rumi**. Famous founder of Sufi fraternities include '**Abd al-Qadir al-Jilani** (1077-1166), the patron saint of the **Qadiriyyah**; Shihab al-Din **al-Suhrawardi**, of the Suhrawardiyyah; Ahmad al-**Rifa'i** (1106?-1182) of the Rifa'iyyah; Muhammad Naqshband (1317-1389) of the **Naqshbaniyyah**; and the eponymic ancestor of the **Safavid dynasty**, Shaykh Safi al-Din, who founded the Safaviyyah Sufi order in Ardabil in northwestern Iran. *See also* RABI'AH AL-'ADAWIY-YAH and HASAN AL-BASRI.

**SUFYAN.** *See* ABU SUFYAN.

**SUHRAWARDI, SHIHAB AL-DIN YAHYA** (1154-1191). Muslim mystic and philosopher who traveled widely in the Middle East. His major work is *hikmat al-ishraq* (Wisdom of illumination) which combined Shi'ite views with speculative philosophy of **Ibn Sina** and **Sufi** theosophy. **Ibn Khallikan** says of him:

> As-Suhrawardi was the first man of his time in the philosophical sciences, all of which he knew perfectly well. In the science of the fundamentals of jurisprudence he stood pre-eminent; he was gifted with great acuteness of mind and the talent of expressing his thoughts with precision. His learning was greater than his judgment (Khallikan, IV, 154).

He was executed as a heretic in Aleppo and came to be known as "Suhrawardi the Martyr."

**SUHRAWARDI, SHIHAB AL-DIN AL-** (1144-1234). Eponymic founder of the Suhrawardi **Sufi** fraternity, which is represented mainly in the Indian subcontinent. He lived at the caliphal court in **Baghdad** where he attracted a large following as Grand Master of the Sufi order. It was described as "not so much an Order as a school of mystic philosophy which has had a great influence on the teaching of many of the African Orders and fosters the growth of **fatalism** amongst them" (Canon Sell, 46.). His major work is the *awarif al-ma 'arif* (Divine gifts of knowledge) which is one of the most celebrated works on Sufism. **Ibn Khallikan** called him "a pious and holy **shaykh**, most assiduous in his spiritual exercises and the practice of devotion." He was born in Suhraward and died at Baghdad.

**SULAYMAN THE MAGNIFICENT** (1494-1566). **Ottoman sultan,** called the "Magnificent" in Europe and "The Lawgiver" (*al-Qanuni*) by the Ottomans. During his reign, the empire reached its high point of power and success. His army captured Belgrade in 1521, Rhodes in 1522, and defeated the Hungarians at Mohacs in 1526 to take direct control of the country in 1541. Vienna was able to withstand a siege in 1529. His navy successfully fought the Portuguese, British, and Dutch fleets in the Indian Ocean and the "Holy League" in the Mediterranean. He concluded a trade agreement with King Francis of France (r. 1515-1547), which granted the French considerable trade privileges. The "Capitulations" granted at a time of Ottoman power were to weaken the state in subsequent centuries and permitted virtually unlimited European economic penetration. After Sulayman, the empire suffered a gradual decline, but it continued to exist until its defeat in the First World War.

**SULTAN.** "Power." Title, indicating de facto power, but eventually an independent king. The title was first assumed by Mahmud of Ghazna (r. 998-1030), but it was struck on coins for the first time by the **Seljuq** Toghrul Bey (d. 1063) at a time when the **caliphate** was in decline. The position of sultanate was legitimized as the "pious sultanate," in which the sultan was to perform all the functions the caliph no longer could. For a time, the fiction of caliphal supremacy was maintained, but eventually sultans became independent kings. The **Ottoman** sultanate was abolished in 1922.

**SUNNAH (SUNNAN).** "Path, Way." The customary way of life of the ancient Arabs. In Islam, the Sunnah comprises the Prophets's example: What he said, what he did, and what he approved or disapproved. In addition to the Koran, the Sunnah provides guidance in personal behavior as well as in matters of **Islamic law (Shari'ah)** where it forms, together with the Koran, reasoning by analogy **(qiyas)** and the consensus of the scholars **(ijma'),** the Four **Pillars of**

**Islamic Law**. Matters not clearly stipulated in the Koran are supplemented from the "model behavior" of the Prophet on the assumption that he led an exemplary life. The Koran says: "Ye have indeed in the **Messenger** of Allah an excellent exemplar"(33:21). **Hadith** is the story of a particular occurrence, and **Sunnah** is the rule of law deduced from it. Eventually, even the examples of the Prophet's **Companions** and their successors were taken as worthy of emulation. Shi'ites also follow the Sunnah of the infallible **imams**.

**SUNNI (SUNNITES)**. The Sunnis are called the "people of custom and community" (*ahl al-sunnah wa 'l-jama'a*) or "orthodox" Muslims, who comprise about 80 percent of the Muslim population. They recognize the first four **caliphs** as rightful successors to the Prophet Muhammad and accept the legitimacy of the **Umayyad** and **'Abbasid caliphates**. They are divided into four **schools of law**: the **Hanafi, Maliki, Shafi'i**, and the **Hanbali** schools, the Hanafi being the largest and the Hanbali school the most restricted in its interpretation of the Koran and the **Sunnah**. Much of what has been described in this work is part of the Sunni tradition.

**SURAH**. A chapter in the Koran. There are 114 chapters arranged roughly according to length, beginning with the longest, except for the **Fatiha**, "Opener," which is a short one. Each surah has a special title and all, except the ninth, begin with the **Basmalah** formula.

**SUYUTI, JALA AL-DIN AL-** (1445-1505). Scholar of Persian origin who flourished in **Cairo**. A prolific writer with some 500 publications (some only short pamphlets) to his name, including a history of Cairo, a history of the **caliphs**, and a commentary on the Koran. His major work is *al-Muzhir* (The flowering) , in which he examines **Arabic** dialects and philology. He favored magical practices in medicine and rejected philosophy and logic. Suyuti knew the Koran by heart when he was eight years old. He traveled widely, but his vanity and arrogance frequently got him into trouble. He said about himself: "When I made the **pilgrimage**, I drank of the water of the well **Zemzem** with various intentions: among others that I should arrive in jurisprudence to the eminence of Shaykh Sirajuddin al-Bulqini, and in **Tradition** to the distinction of the Hafiz Ibn Hajr" and he left no doubt that he surpassed his teachers in erudition (*History of the Caliphs*, viii).

**-T-**

**TABARI, MUHAMMAD IBN JARIR AL-** (839-923). Islamic scholar from Tabaristan, Iran, whose *Annals of Prophets and Kings* (*tarikh al-rusul wa 'l-muluk*) is a history of the world from its creation to the 10th century. It is the first history of the world in **Arabic** and an important source for the early history of the **caliphate**. He also produced a 30-volume commentary (**tafsir**) on the Koran. The Annals have been translated into English, German, and French. Tabari is said to have memorized the Koran at age seven. He traveled widely and studied with famous scholars, including **Ibn Hanbal**, before he settled down in **Baghdad** as teacher of Traditions (**Sunnah**) and jurisprudence (**fiqh**). Tabari refused to accept an appointment as judge to dedicate all his time to his research. **Ibn Khallikan** praised him as

> a jurisconsult of the **sect** of **al-Shafi'i**,...a high and sure authority as a doctor, veracious, learned, versed in dogmas and secondary points of the law, exact in his researches on the principles of Jurisprudence, conscientious, virtuous, and holy in his conduct.

But he was not impressed by his poetry, saying that Tabari "composed poetry as good as might be expected from a jurisconsult" (II, 597). Tabari died at Baghdad in 923.

**TABI'UN.** "Successors." A class of people who had been in personal contact with **Companions** of the Prophet. They were important transmitters of **Traditions**, as were the *Tabi'un al-Tabi'in*, the next generation of "successors of the successors."

**TAFSIR.** "Explanation." Commentary on the Koran, a branch of Islamic theological science. *See also* EXEGESIS and TA'WIL.

**TAGHRI BIRDI, ABU AL-MAHASIN AL-** (1411-1469). Egyptian historian who wrote a history of Egypt from the Muslim conquest to his time, entitled *al-nujum al-zahirah fi muluk misr wa 'l-qahirah* (The brilliant stars regarding the kings of Egypt and Cairo). It is an important source on the history of the Bahri **Mamluk sultanate** (1250-1390).

**TAHIRID DYNASTY** (822-873). First quasi-independent state, named after Tahir ibn Husayn (775-822), who helped **al-Ma'mun** win his struggle for the **caliphate** against his brother **al-Amin**. For his help,

Tahir was appointed governor of Khurasan and the Islamic east, and he made Nishapur his capital. Toward the end of his life, Tahir made himself independent, having the **khutbah** read in his name, but his descendants continued to pay tribute to the **caliph** at **Baghdad**. Tahir was the descendant of a Persian slave, who made his fame as a military commander, nicknamed *Dhu al-Yaminayn* (the Ambidextrous), because he could yield a sword effectively with either hand. During their short rule, the Tahirids provided a period of prosperity in Khurasan until they were succeeded by the **Saffarids**.

**TAHTAWI, RIFA'A RAFI' AL-** (1801-1873). Egyptian modernist and reformer, born in Tahta, Upper Egypt, and educated at **Al-Azhar**. He was sent to accompany the first mission of Egyptian students to France and took advantage of the opportunity to study the French language, literature, and political philosophy. He was impressed by what he saw: the orderly life of the people, their social morality and seeming love of work, their intellectual curiosity and patriotism, and their democratic spirit. Upon his return he worked as a translator, and in 1836 he founded the School of Translation. In his writings, he advocated educational reforms, modern development, and parliamentary democracy. He wanted **education** for the people as well as the rulers and called for reform of the ornate and obfuscating style of **Arabic**. He was forced into exile for a number of years (1851-1854), but upon his return he resumed his cultural mission.

**TAKBIR.** The *takbir* consists in saying God is Most Great (*Allahu Akbar*). It is part of the canonic prayers and a pious exclamation.

**TAKFIR.** "Excommunication." *See* EXCOMMUNICATION.

**TAKFIR WA AL-HIJRAH, JAMA'AT AL-.** "Excommunication and Exile." The name given to a radical **Islamist** group in Egypt led by Shukri Ahmad Mustafa (b. 1942) who was executed in 1978. He taught that only members of his movement, founded in 1972, were true Muslims and that **Islamic law**, as compiled by the jurists of the traditional schools, was man-made and therefore to be rejected. He denied the legitimacy of Muslim rulers and wanted to establish an Islamic state ruled by a pious **amir**. The group was involved in the "bread riots" in 1977, attacking night clubs and bars in **Cairo**. They kidnaped Shaykh Muhammad Husayn al-Dhahabi of **Al-Azhar** University and killed him. The government reacted with mass arrests and tried some 465 members in military courts, executing five members, including Shukri. *See also* EXCOMMUNICATION.

**TALAQ.** "Repudiation, **Divorce**." Originally it meant "unshackling" an animal, but the term came to mean the repudiation of a wife by a man. To divorce his wife, a man has to say "I divorce thee" three times in succession in front of witnesses. In many Muslim countries this traditional process is no longer practiced and in some, such as Tur-key, Western procedures have been adopted.

**TALHAH IBN 'UBAYDULLAH** (596-656). Member of the **Quraysh** and **Companion** of the Prophet, he became a candidate for the **caliphate** and fought in succession for all of the first four **caliphs**. He was finally killed in the **Battle of the Camel** in 656 and was buried in **Basra**.

**TALIBAN.** A neo-fundamentalist movement recruited from students (*talib*, pl. *tullab*) of **mosque** schools and **madrasahs**, who were organized into a military force and captured most of Afghanistan. The movement was headed by Maulawi **Muhammad 'Umar** (Omar), who was proclaimed Commander of the **Believers** (*amir al-mu'minin*) and set up a theocratic government with himself as the head. After the capture of Kabul, the capital of Afghanistan, the movement decreed that **women** be restricted to the home, men wear long **beards,** and discard Western dress. The Taliban brought peace to the 85 percent of the country during their four year rule. But they closed girls schools and prohibited women, who had been active in the professions, the bureaucracy, business, etc., to continue their chosen careers. The Taliban started to enforce Islamic punishments, including the cutting off a hand or a foot for theft, and stoning for **adultery**. In the countryside their policies caused little change. But in Kabul, a modern city with a population of a million and a half, this change had a profound impact. The Taliban government was recognized only by Pakistan, the United Arab Emirates, and Saudi Arabia. Western recognition was not forthcoming in view of the discrimination against women, and the fact that Afghanistan had become a major producer of opium and its derivatives. Their collaboration with **Osama bin Ladin** and the attack on the New York World Trade Center led to American retaliation and the destruction of the Taliban regime.

**TAMERLANE.** *See* TIMUR-I LANG.

**TAQIYYAH.** *See* CONCEALMENT.

**TAQLID.** "Imitation." The obligation in Sunni Islam to imitate, or emulate, the law as frozen by the four orthodox **schools of law** that agreed to close the "gate of **ijtihad**" in the ninth century. Henceforth innovation (**bid'ah**) was forbidden. Various modernist and radical movements reject taqlid. Shi'ites accept the taqlid of their **mujtahids**.

**TARIQ, ZIYAD IBN** (670-720). Berber commander of a force under **Musa Ibn Nusayr** (640-715) that crossed from Ceuta into Spain in 711. Out on a mission of reconnaissance, he found little resistance and opened Spain to Muslim conquest, defeating the Visigothic King Roderic at the battle of Wadi Bakka. Tariq encouraged his troops, saying: "My men! Whither can you fly? [flee] The sea is behind you and the enemy before you; nothing can save you but the help of God, your bravery and your steadiness. Be it known to you that you are here as badly off as orphans at a miser's table. The foe is coming against you with his troops, his arms and all his forces; you have nothing to rely on but your swords, no food to eat except what you may snatch from the hands of the enemy" (Khalikan, III, 477). Gibraltar got its name from him, "Mountain of Tariq" (*Jabal al-Tariq*).

**TARIQA.** "Path." *See* SUFISM.

**TASAWWUF.** *See* SUFISM.

**TAWBAH.** "Repentance." First station of the **Sufi** path. *See* REPENTANCE.

**TAWHID (TAUHID).** The doctrine of the unity of God, a strict monotheism; to give partners to God is an unforgivable sin. The Koran says: "Say: He is Allah, the One; Allah, the Eternal, the Absolute; he begetteth not, nor is He begotten; and there is none like unto Him" (112:1-4).

**TA'WIL.** "Interpretation." The science of interpreting the Koran and its complement, commentary (**tafsir**), began by 'Abdallah ibn al-'Abbas in the late seventh century. Ta'wil is an allegorical interpretation practiced mainly by Shi'ites, especially **Isma'ilis** and mystics, whereas tafsir focuses on the exoteric, literal meaning of the Koran.

Some Islamic scholars claim that everything, including the modern sciences, can be found in the Koran; they base this on a verse in the Koran that says: "Nothing have We omitted from the Book"(6:38).

**TAXATION.** There are three types of taxes in Islam: the poor tax (**zakat**), the poll tax (**jizyah**), and the land tax (**kharaj**). A kind of tithe (**'ushr**) eventually also became a land tax. Zakat is a transfer payment to help the poor and amounts in some countries to from 2.5 to 10 percent of liquid assets, or 5 to 10 percent on agricultural products. It is a wealth, rather than an income, tax. The jizyah, or poll tax, was levied on non-Muslim men, who did not pay the zakat and did not serve in the armed forces. **Women,** children, the elderly, beggars, monks, and **slaves** were exempt. The kharaj was originally levied on non-Muslims but since the eighth century also on Muslims. It was paid largely in kind. In many parts of the Islamic world, a military feudalist system was set up in which land taxes were levied by officers or government officials to compensate them for their administrative or military duties, or by local notables contracted as tax farmers in exchange for a percentage of the income from land. In most countries the jizyah has been abolished and the Islamic taxes replaced by an income tax, with the zakat levied independently by the **ulama**. In oil-rich countries, such as Saudi Arabia, the government levies only the zakat. Shi'ites reject the legitimacy of kharaj and 'ushr because they were introduced by **'Umar ibn al-Khattab** and are not mentioned in the Koran, but they accept a **khums.** They also consider zakat a charity rather than a religious tax. *See* KHUMS.

**TAYAMMUM.** Symbolic purification by sand or stone where there is no water to perform the ritual **ablutions** of **wudhu** and **ghusl.** If water is available but barely enough for drinking, or because of illness of a person or fear of contracting a disease, Tayammum is permissible.

The practice goes back to a **hadith,** which relates that the Prophet "struck his hand on earth once, then he shook off its dust and wiped with it the back of the (right) hand with the left or the back of the left with the (right) hand, then wiped his face with both hands." (Bukhari, 7:8)

**TAYMIYYAH.** *See* IBN TAYMIYYAH, AHMAD.

**TA'ZIR.** Discretionary punishments for offenses that are not specified in the Koran or **Traditions**. Ta'zir permits the judge considerable discretion in a wide range of punishments, including admonition, reprimand, threat, boycott, public disclosure, fines, imprisonment, and flogging. It is usually imposed for less serious offenses and differs from the **hadd** offenses for which punishment is prescribed in the Koran or Traditions. In exceptional cases the death penalty has been allowed as a ta'zir punishment.

**TA'ZIYEH.** "Consolation." Shi'ite passion plays in remembrance of the martyrdom of Imam **Husayn** at **Karbala** in 680. They are performed on the 10th of **Muharram** in public places. The Ta'ziyah is perhaps the earliest serious drama developed in the Islamic world. *See also* 'ASHURA.

**TEKKE.** Turkish term for **Sufi** retreat. *See* KHANAQAH.

**TENTH OF MUHARRAM.** *See* 'ASHURA' and MUHARRAM.

**TESTIMONY OF FAITH.** *See* SHAHADAH.

**THEOLOGY.** *See* KALAM.

**TIJANIYYAH. Sufi** order founded in the 19th century by Ahmad ibn Muhammad al-Tijani (1737-1815) in Fez, present-day Morocco. It gained considerable support in North Africa at the expense of the **Qadiriyyah** Sufi order. It was criticized for its political activities, especially its cooperation with the French. The members of the order believe that their chain of blessing led directly to Tijani from the Prophet Muhammad.

**TIMUR-I LANG (TAMERLANE,** 1336-1405). The "Lame Timur" was a military genius and the last of the great nomadic conquerors. He was born of humble origin in Kesh, a town near Samarkand in present-day Uzbekistan. He claimed descent from the family of Chingiz Khan, but his real link to the family was his **marriage** to a **Mongol** noble woman. He carried a number of titles, but only in 1388 did he call himself **sultan**. He was called the Lame Timur because he was disabled on the right hand and foot. An infirmity he suffered in war, or according to some sources, while stealing sheep. In 1941 Soviet scholars opened his tomb and found a skeleton, which they identified as his. Timur claimed to wage **jihad,** but in fact he fought primarily against Muslim states. His wars did not follow a general strategy of conquest. He moved from the Volga to the

Ganges in India and from Mongolia to Syria. He defeated his opponents wherever he went, but he could not establish permanent rule over these areas. He was the most destructive of nomadic invaders, using terror as a tactical weapon. Timur sacked and destroyed Delhi, **Damascus, Baghdad,** Isfahan, Herat, and many other Islamic cities. He weakened the power of the Golden Horde in Russia, defeated the **Ottomans** at the battle of Ankara in 1404 and weakened the power of Muslim rulers in China and India. Timur built towers of skulls of the people he slaughtered and, while he destroyed many centers of Islamic civilization, he created his own cultural center in Samarkand. He seemed to be content with **booty**. Only in India did the house of Timur continue with the establishment of the Moghul dynasty in 1524.

**TIRMIDHI, ABU JA'FAR (TIRMIZI,** 816-907). A **Shafi'ite** jurist "the ablest of them all in that age, the most devout and the most abstemious." When asked to comment on the Prophet's saying that "God descended to the heaven of the world" (i.e., the lowest of seven heavens) and that "what could be more exalting than the lowest heaven?" Tirmidhi replied: "The descent is intelligible; the manner how is unknown; the belief therein is obligatory, and the asking about it is a blamable innovation" (Khallikan, II, 601).

**TIRMIDHI, MUHAMMAD IBN 'ISA AL- (TIRMIZI,** 825-892). Islamic **hadith** scholar who compiled the *Jami 'al-Tirmidhi* (Collection of Tirmidhi), one of the six canonical collections of **Traditions** in which he examined the differences between the **schools of law**. He was born and died in the village of Bugh near Tirmidh, Transcaspia. He was a pupil of **al-Bukhari** and, although blind, he was one of the great Traditionists.

**TIRMIZI.** *See* TIRMIDHI.

**TOMBS.** Monuments and **tombs** of saints and rulers exist in most parts of the Islamic world; they are forbidden by the **Hanbali School of law**. During their conquests in Arabia the **Wahhabis** destroyed gravestones and monuments but spared the tomb of the Prophet. They also sacked the holy places of the Shi'ites at **Najaf** and **Karbala** in 1802.

**TRADITIONS.** *See* HADITH and SUNNAH.

**TRENCH, BATTLE OF THE.** "Khandaq." The battle between the forces of the Muslim community in Medina and the Meccans in 627. A Meccan army of some 10,000 men faced a Muslim force of about 3,000 and the Muslims were saved when, at the suggestion of a Persian convert, **Salman**, they built a defensive trench. After two weeks of desultory long-distance fighting a heavy storm blew away some of the Meccans' tents and disunity started, forcing the Meccans to lift the siege. This was the last encounter with the Meccans and only 10 people were killed on both sides. The event caused a boost in the morale of the Muslim community and a loss of prestige for the Meccans. The last of the Jewish tribes of Medina, the Banu **Qurayza**, was annihilated, having been accused of collaboration with the Meccans.

**TULUNID DYNASTY** (868-905). A dynasty founded by a deputy of the **'Abbasid caliphate** in Egypt, named Ahmad ibn Tulun (868-884), a Turkish slave from Bukhara. He had distinguished himself as a military commander, fighting the Byzantines, and became the **caliph**'s bodyguard. Once appointed deputy governor in Egypt, he remained in de facto control. His state's wealth was based on its agriculture and a flourishing textile industry. Ibn-Tulun established his capital at al-Qata'i (now **Cairo**), where he built the famed Tulunid **mosque**. When the 'Abbasid caliph tried to dislodge him, Ibn Tulun had the **Khutbah** read in his name as a sign of his independence. When Ahmad died in 884, he was succeeded by his son Khumrawayh (884-895), who was able to add Syria to his possessions. Having been unable to oust him, the Caliph al-Mu'tadid (892-902) gave Khumrawayh his daughter in **marriage**. The latter displayed such prodigality on the occasion of his marriage that the state was seriously weakened and was finally recaptured by the forces of Caliph al-Muktafi in 905. The Tulunid example of the sudden rise of a **slave** to political power and the tendency of governors to make themselves independent was to become a common event in the Islamic world.

**TURABI, HASAN** (1932-    ). Sudanese lawyer and politician who became head of the Sudanese Muslim Brotherhood in 1964. Born in Kassla, eastern Sudan, he studied law at the universities of Khartoum, London, and the Sorbonne and obtained a Ph.D. degree in law from the Sorbonne in 1964. Upon his return to Sudan, he formed the Front for Islamic Constitution and acted as its secretary-general until

1969. Jailed for a few years from 1969, he joined the Numeiri government and was appointed attorney general (1977-1983). He demanded the introduction of **Islamic law** in 1983. Imprisoned for a short time in 1985 and 1989, and after the overthrow of the Jaafar Numeiri regime in 1985, Turabi founded the National Islamic Front, which came in third in the national elections. After the military coup of General Omar al-Bashir in June 1989, the new military government implemented many of Turabi's ideas. He has inspired **Islamist** revivalists in other Muslim countries and has been accused of assisting the group that attempted to assassinate Egyptian President Husni Mubarak in June 1995. His most important publication is *taj-did al-fikr al-islami* (The renewal of Islamic thought).

**TURBAN.** A headdress consisting of a long piece of fabric, usually wound around a skullcap. It has existed since pre-Islamic times. The color, size, and shape of a turban usually indicated the ethnic, sectarian, or tribal identity of a person. Rulers would bestow turbans as an honor for distinguished service. In the 19th century the Kufiyyah of the Arabs came into use and the fez was worn by administrative and military officals. In some parts of the Middle East, fur caps came to be used. As a sign of Islamist revival, government officials in Afghanistan were ordered to wear a turban, rather than the previous choices of headgear.

**TUSI, MUHAMMAD IBN AL-HASAN AL-** (995-1067). Shi'ite theologian and compiler of one of the four canonical works on **Traditions** of the Prophet. His works include also the 20-volume *Fihrist* (Catalogue), which comprised all treatises on Shi'ite subjects published to his time. He was born in Tus, Iran, but he spent most of his life in **Baghdad**. He finally left for **Najaf**, a center of Shi'ite learning, to escape from Sunni persecution.

**TUSI, NASIR AL-DIN AL-** (1201-1274). Shi'ite scholar, philosopher, astronomer, and mathematician born in Tus, Persia. He was probably an **Isma'ili**, who collaborated with the **Mongols** and entered the services of **Hulagu** Khan, founder of the Ilkhanid dynasty (1256-1353). Tusi made original contributions to the fields of mathematics and astronomy. Hulagu built an observatory and library for him at Maragha where he compiled his astronomical tables (*al-zij al-il-khani*) showing the planetary movements. Another of his many publications was a treatise on Shi'ite dogmatics.

**TWELVER SHI'ITES.** Also called Imamis, or Ja'faris, and in **Arabic** *Ithna 'Ashariyyah*; they recognize the twelfth as the last **imam** in descent from 'Ali, the cousin and son-in-law of the Prophet Muhammad. *See also* SHI'ISM.

## -U-

**'UBAYDAH, IBN AL-JARRAH ABU** (d. 639). **Companion** of the Prophet and important commander from Mecca. He participated in many battles and saved Muhammad's life when the Prophet was wounded in the Battle of **Uhud** in 625. He participated in the election of the first **Caliph Abu Bakr** (r. 632-634) and was appointed commander-in-chief in Syria and governor of **Damascus** by the Caliph **'Umar I** (r. 634-644). His tomb in Damascus is a much venerated shrine.

**'UBAYDAH, MA'MAR IBN AL-MUTHANNA ABU** (728-825). Arab philologist and historian who represented the **Basra** school of grammarians and was a proponent of the anti-Arab *Shu'ubiyyah* movement. Because of his extraordinary learning, he was summoned to the court of **Caliph Harun al-Rashid** (786-809), where he is said to have earned the animosity of many courtiers. Abu 'Ubaydah is said to have been of Judeo-Persian origin and is credited with some hundred publications, only a few of which are extant. Al-Jahiz said of him: "There was never on earth a **Kharijite** or an orthodox believer more learned in all the sciences than he." But **Ibn Khallikan** quotes Ibn Qutaybah in saying:

> The unusual expressions (of the **Arabic** language), the history of the (ancient) Arabs and their conflicts, were his dominant study; yet, with all his learning, he was not always able to recite a verse without mangling it; even in reading the Koran, with the book before his eyes, he made mistakes (Khallikan, III, 388-389).

**UBAYDULLAH IBN ZIYAD** (648-686). Son of **Ziyad ibn Abihi**, appointed by the **Umayyad caliph** governor of Khurasan and subsequently of Iraq. He successfully fought **Kharijite** and Shi'ite revolts. His army under Sa'd ibn abi **Waqqas** was responsible for the massacre of **Husayn** and his forces at **Karbala** in 680.

**UHUD, BATTLE OF.** On March 21, 625, a year after the defeat at the Battle of **Badr**, the Meccans again manned an expedition against the Muslim community in Medina. This time they collected a force of some 3,000 men headed by **Abu Sufyan** with 3,000 camels and 200 horses. They engaged Muhammad's force of some 700 men and defeated the Muslims. **Khalid ibn al-Walid**, then fighting on the side of the Meccans, was one of the decisive officers. Muhammad blamed the defeat of his men on their lack of devotion and called it God's trial of the sincerity of the faith of the Muslims. Although suffering great losses, and the Prophet himself wounded, the Muslim community was able to recover from this defeat. Muhammad accused the **Jewish** tribe, Banu **Nadir**, of collaborating with the enemy and expelled them from the **Hijaz**.

**'UKAZ.** A town in the **Hijaz** near Mecca that was the most important fair ground of pre-Islamic Arabia. It was a place of **pilgrimage** and a cultural center where Bedouin poets would compete for prizes. The *Seven Odes* (**Mu'allaqat**) were suspended there and at the **Ka'bah** as prize-winning samples of Bedouin poetry. Annual fairs and periods of peace during three months made it possible for tribesmen to congregate. During this time, Meccan caravans could travel unmolested.

**'ULAMA'.** A collective term for the doctors of Islamic sciences. An 'alim (pl. 'ulama') is "one who possesses the quality of 'ilm, knowledge, or learning, of the Islamic traditions and the resultant canon law and theology." An 'alim is the product of a religious institution of higher **education (madrasah)**. He is educated to be a religious functionary, as, for example, a judge (**kadhi**) who gives legal decisions in accordance with the **Shari'ah**, a preacher (**khatib**) who reads the **Friday** sermon, a jurist (**faqih**) or a canon lawyer (**mufti**) who gives a formal opinion (**fatwa**) as to the legality of a case. Often described as the Islamic "clergy," the 'ulama' is not tightly organized. It requires no ordination or hierarchy of authority, although in the **Ottoman empire** the **Shaykh al-Islam** was the grand **mufti** of **Istanbul** and appointed all muftis in the major cities. After independence, chief muftis were established in major cities, but the decision of one mufti is not necessarily binding on others. Only in **Twelver** Shi'ism has there been a development toward a centralized church with the victory of the **Usuli** branch of jurisprudence. *See* SHI'ISM.

'UMAR IBN 'ABD AL-AZIZ (OMAR, II 682-720). The eighth **Umayyad caliph** (r. 717-720) who solved the second-class status of the newly converted (**mawali**), giving them equality with Arab Muslims in matters of **taxation** and pensions if they had fought in the early conquests. He gave **Peoples of the Book**, the protected subjects (**dhimmis**), freedom of religion but limited their religious performances to the privacy of their homes. Crosses could not be worn in public and bells could not be sounded; they had to pay a poll tax (**jizyah**), but they did not have to serve in the military.

'Umar discontinued the practice of cursing **'Ali** at **Friday prayers**. The system introduced at this time was the model for subsequent Muslim states and extended throughout the **Ottoman empire** (1281-1924) where the **millets** (ethnic-sectarian) groups enjoyed cultural and juridical autonomy. With the emergence of nation-states, the poll tax and other limitations began to disappear. Although Abbasid historians did not give the Umayyads a good press, they did respect Umar II as a pious and just caliph.

'UMAR, 'ABD AL-RAHMAN. *See* 'ABD AL-RAHMAN 'UMAR.

'UMAR IBN AL-KHATTAB (OMAR I, 585-644). One of the early **Companions** of the Prophet who converted to Islam in 617 and became the second **caliph** in 634 after the death of **Abu Bakr**. He was a close adviser to the Prophet and gave him his daughter, **Hafsah**, in **marriage**. After the Prophet's death, he offered his allegiance to Abu Bakr and thus facilitated the election of the first Sunni caliph. 'Umar took the title "Prince of **Believers**" (*amir al-mu'minin*) and during his short period as caliph, the Muslim armies conquered Syria and Palestine (640), Egypt (639-642), Tripolitania (643), and defeated the Persians at **Nihavand** (642). Umar made administrative reforms; he established a system of pensions, the **Diwan**, which allocated funds to the Prophet's wives and to Muslims, ranked according to their dates of conversion. He ordered a cadastral survey for taxation of the newly conquered lands and founded the garrison towns of **Basra**, **Kufah**, and Fustat. He was assassinated in 644 by a slave who was a partisan of 'Ali.

'UMAR, MULLA MUHAMMAD. *See* MUHAMMAD 'UMAR, MULLA.

**UMAYYA, BANU.** A branch of the **Quraysh** to which **Caliph 'Uthman** and **Mu'awiyah** belonged. Mu'awiyah, founder of the **Umayyad** dynasty (661-750), challenged Caliph **'Ali** to demand vengeance for the murder of his clansman, 'Uthman, and eventually succeeded to the caliphate.

**UMAYYAD CALIPHATE** (661-750). The Umayyads gained power after **Mu'awiyah** successfuly challenged the succession of **'Ali**. He demanded that the murder of **'Usman** be avenged and implied that 'Ali was implicated in the deed. Mu'awwiyah's first measure was to establish the Islamic capital at **Damascus**, where he had been governor and had the protection of his army. Mu'awiyah had himself proclaimed **caliph** in 660 and, after the assassination of 'Ali in 661 by a member of the **Kharijite sect**, there was no challenge to his claim. He gave **Hasan**, son of the Caliph 'Ali, a handsome pension to renounce his claim, strengthened his army, and built the first Muslim navy. He paid the pensions of the soldiers and rendered justice according to the example of his predecessors. He issued coins fashioned after the Byzantine and Persian examples and appointed governors for the provinces. Mu'awiyah expanded the domains of the Islamic world from Central Asia across North Africa.

He broke precedence by appointing his son **Yazid** (r. 680-683) as his successor. **Husayn**, son of the Caliph 'Ali, challenged the authority of Yazid and moved from his retirement in Medina to **Kufah** to follow an invitation of his supporters. He encountered an Umayyad army of some 4,000 man and his group was wiped out almost to a man. The martyrdom of Husayn at **Karbala** sealed the schism in Islam. Yaszid's army defeated another challenger, 'Abdallah **ibn Zubayr**, near Medina in 683. **'Abd al-Malik** (r. 685-705), the fifth of the Umayyad rulers, began to reorganize the empire along **Arabic**-Islamic lines. His general, **al-Hajjaj**, pacified Iraq and suppressed a number of revolts. 'Abd al-Malik Arabized the administration of the empire, minted the first Islamic coins, and started construction of the great **Dome of the Rock** in **Jerusalem**. His was the greatest period of Umayyad power. **'Umar II** (r. 717-720) continued the reforms, but he also ended **Christian** participation in government and the army. He was later called the "Renovator of Islam."

But **'Abbasid** historians, perhaps to justify the 'Abbasid revolt, called the Umayyads Arab kings, rather than caliphs, who established secular rule, based on dynastic succession. Historians have attributed the fall of the Umayyads to lack of an Islamic ideology, revival of Arab tribalism, and government of the Arabs for the Arabs. Only three caliphs, Mu'awiya, Abdul Malik, and Umar II, were great rulers. The Umayyads, like subsequent Islamic rulers, did not have a clear rule of succession, and their governors and the generals who brought them great victories were eliminated as soon as they had accomplished their tasks. The pietist opposition, the **Kharijites**, the Shi'ites, and Iranian revivalism under the cover of international Islam all contributed to the 'Abbasid revolt, which ended the 'Umayyad empire in 750. Umayyad caliphs included the following:

| | |
|---|---|
| 660 Mu'awiyah ibn Abi Sufyan | 717 'Umar ibn 'Abd al-Aziz |
| 680 Yazid | 720 Yazid II |
| 683 Mu'awiyah II | 724 Hisham |
| 684 Marwan ibn al-Hakam | 743 al-Walid |
| 685 'Abd al Malik | 744 Yazid III |
| 705 al-Walid | 744 Ibrahim |
| 715 Sulayman | 744-50 Marwan II. |

**UMMAH** A term for the Medina community that included Muslims and **Jews**, but was subsequently the term for the Islamic community, the Islamic "nation." It is not a territorial designation and includes Muslims wherever they may be. Arabs also use the term for the Arab nation.

**UMM HABIBAH BINT ABI SUFYAN.** Wife of Muhammad (also called Ramla) who was married to him in 629 when she was in Abyssinian exile. She was the daughter of **Abu Sufyan**, chief of the **Quraysh** and half sister of **Mu'awiyah**, the first **Umayyad caliph**. She was 35 years old at **marriage** and the Negus is said to have provided a **dowry** of 400 **dinars**. She died in about 646.

**UMM AL-KITAB.** A term used in the Koran, meaning "Mother of the Book." It refers to the **Preserved Tablet** in **Heaven** as well as to verses in the Koran. The Koran says: "Allah doth blot out or confirm what He pleaseth: with Him is the Mother of the Book"(13:39).

**UMM KULTHUM.** Daughter of the Prophet Muhammad from **Khadijah** who was to be married to her cousin 'Utaybah, son of **Abu Lahab**. Muhammad did not permit the **marriage**, because Abu

Lahab was one of his worst enemies. She eventually married the future **Caliph 'Uthman** after the death of his wife **Ruqayyah**, another daughter of Muhammad. Umm Kulthum remained with 'Uthman until her death in 631. She had no children.

**UMM AL-MU'MININ.** "Mother of the **Believers**," a title given to **'A'isha**, the wife of Muhammad.

**UMM AL-QURRA.** "Mother of Cities," a title given to Mecca in the Koran (6:92). The Koran says: "Thus We have sent by inspiration to thee an **Arabic** Qor'an: that thou mayest warn The Mother of Cities and all around her" (42:7).

**UMM SALAMAH.** Wife of Muhammad. *See* SALAMA BINT ABI UMAYYAH.

**'UMRAH.** The lesser **pilgrimage** that can be performed at any time of the year, unlike the **Hajj** which can be performed only during the month of pilgrimage (*Dhu 'l-Hijjah*). The Umrah consists of two ceremonies, the circumambulation (*tawaf*) of the **Ka'bah** and the *sa y*, walking and running seven times between the hills of al-Safa and al Marwa. Unlike the Hajj, the Umrah is not obligatory.

**UNBELIEVER.** *See* KAFIR.

**'UQBAH IBN NAFI'** (622-683). Arab general and governor of Ifriqiyyah (Tunis, 662-674) and the Maghrib (Northwest Africa) in 682. He founded the city of al-Qayrawan (Kerouan) in 670. With the support of Berber contingents, he fought Byzantine forces and advanced as far as Tangier (682), but he was eventually forced to retreat. Separated from his troops with only a small force, 'Uqbah was killed. The village called Sidi 'Uqbah grew at the place of his tomb.

**'URF.** Local customs or laws, as distinguished from sacred law (**Shari'ah**). In the Islamic world a dualism has remained: the "King's law" and "God's law." Rulers could legislate and thus adapt the legal system to the changes of times, but these laws ('urf, **qanun**, *siyasa*) were not to be in conflict with the sacred law. They had to be accompanied by a legal decision (**fatwa**), testifying to this fact (although this was at times ignored). The Shari'ah is God's will; 'urf and qanun can be changed at the will of a ruler or government.

'**URWA AL-WUTHQA, AL-**. *The Firmest Bond* was the title of a weekly magazine published in Paris in 1884 by **Jamal al-Din Afghani** and **Muhammad Abduh**. It advocated revivalist, **pan-Islamist** activism to save the Islamic world from Western imperialism and has had a considerable influence on revivalist movements to this day. The title comes from a verse in the Koran (2:256 and 31:22).

**USAMA BIN LADIN** (OSAMA, 1953- ). Son of a Saudi family engaged in the construction business and a leading member of the radical **Islamist** movement. He graduated from Abdul Aziz University in Jeddah in 1979 and joined other "**Afghanis**" in the war against the communist regime in Afghanistan. He was stripped of his Saudi citizenship because of his anti-government agitation and found protection in Sudan. The American government accused him of instigating a number of terrorist attacks, including the bombing of the American embassies in Kenya and Tanzania. He proclaimed a **jihad** against the United States to force it to withdraw its forces from the territory of Saudi Arabia. Usama secretly left Sudan and found protection in Afghanistan, where he commanded a force of some 4,000 Arab fighters, called al-Qaida. American retaliation, the bombing of a chemical factory in Sudan, and the fortified camp of Usama, did not succeed in achieving his arrest. As a result the **Taliban** regime of Afghanistan was outlawed by the United Nations and the country placed under a boycott. The attack of the New York World Trade Center resulted in American intervention and the destruction of the al-Qaida network.

**USAYBI'AH, IBN ABI** (1230-1270). A native of **Damascus** who studied medicine, specialized in ophthalmology, and became head of the major hospital in **Cairo**. He won fame for his *'uyun al-anba' fi tabaqat al-atibbah* (Sources of information on the classes of physicians) which includes the biographies of some 600 **Arabic** and Greek physicians.

'**USHR**. "Tenth." A tithe levied by the state for public expenses that eventually became a land tax. Shi'ites dispute the legitimacy of the 'ushr because it was not mentioned in the Koran and was introduced by '**Umar II**.

'**USMAN**. *See* UTHMAN.

**USUL.** "Root." Usul al-fiqh, the sources of jurisprudence. *See* USULI SCHOOL.

**USULI SCHOOL (USULIYAH).** One of two schools of jurisprudence in **Twelver** Shi'ism, the Usulis are the "followers of principles" and the **akhbaris** (akhbariyah) the "followers of tradition." First expounded by Aqa Muhammad Baqir Bihbihani (1706-1790), the Usuli branch gained dominance in Iran in the 19th century and led to the centralization of the religious establishment as the representatives of the **Hidden Imam**. Whereas the Akhbari theologians based their legal argumentation on the Shi'ite **Traditions**, the Usulis used deductive reasoning based on the premises in the Koran and Traditions. This permitted the learned doctors (**mujtahids**) to claim a position of intellectual and moral leadership in the community. Eventually a hierarchy of mujtahids developed that culminated in a circle of the most prominent, requiring every believer to follow a living source for emulation (**marja' al-taqlid**). With the founding of the **Islamic Republic of Iran** in 1979, Ayatollah **Khomeyni** claimed supreme political powers with the establishment of the government of the highest jurist (**vilayat-i faqih**), whose **fatwa** is binding on the **believers**.

**'UTHMAN, IBN 'AFFAN** (r. 644-656). **Companion** of the Prophet, who married in succession **Ruqayyah** and **Umm Kulthum**, daughters of Muhammad by **Khadijah** (*see* WIVES OF THE PROPHET). He spent some time with refugees in Abyssinia. He was the third of the Sunni **caliphs**, whose tenure marked the beginning of division in Arab unity. 'Uthman was a member of the **Umayyad** clan of the **Quraysh** and was elected as a compromise candidate because he was a weak, old man. Opposition began over the division of revenues, which forced 'Uthman to reduce pensions. Muslim historians say that 'Uthman was a good ruler during his first six years. When he lost the Prophet's seal, six years of corruption and nepotism ensued. The partisans of '**Ali** (*shi 'at 'ali*) disputed the legitimacy of the first three caliphs. Malcontents in the provinces and the pious opposition resented the supremacy of the Umayyads, most of whom were enemies of the Prophet and only recent converts. 'Uthman proclaimed the Arabian peninsula sacred territory, forbidden to non-Muslims. He conceived of the Arabs as a ruling elite and tried to prevent them from assimilation in the newly conquered lands by keeping them stationed in **garrison towns**. During his reign, the final version of the Koran is said to have been compiled to prevent the development of regional differences. Discontent increased with **Zubayr ibn al-Awwam** and **Talha ibn 'Ubaydullah**, two important companions of the Prophet among the opposition. A band of insurgents, headed by Muhammad ibn Abi Bakr, moved against Medina and assassinated 'Uthman in 656.

-V-

**VEIL.** In the pre-Islamic Middle East the veil was a status symbol, worn only by aristocratic ladies and subsequently by urban **women**; it became obligatory for Muslim women only in the ninth century. **Christian** and **Jewish** women also wore the veil, whereas Muslim peasant and nomad women only wore a kerchief as the veil would have interfered with agricultural labor and the mobility of the nomads. Increasing urbanization led to a variety of veils from full body covers to those that revealed parts of the face. Modernization and the growth of Western influence in parts of the Islamic world have led to a demand for making the veil optional. **Muslim modernists** pointed out that there is no clear indication in the Koran which makes the veil obligatory. Traditionists point to the example of the Prophet, who ordered a partition, **hijab**, put up in his room, separating the women from the daily conduct of affairs of state. They point to a passage in the Koran, which says: "O Prophet! Tell thy wives and daughters, and the believing women, that they should cast their outer garments over their persons (when out of doors): That is most convenient, that they should be known (as such) and not molested" (33:59). And "Say to the believing women that they should lower their gaze and guard their modesty; that they should not display their beauty and ornaments except what (ordinarily) appear thereof; that they should draw their veils over their bosoms and not display their beauty except to their husbands, their fathers, their husbands' fathers, their sons, their husbands' sons, their brothers or their brothers' sons. Or their sisters' sons, or their women, or the slaves whom their right hands possess, or male attendants free of sexual desires [eunuchs], or small children who have no carnal knowledge of women" (24:31). The reference to women's breasts seems to forbid the pre-Islamic practice of Arab women baring their breasts to incite their men to bravery in battle. There is widespread disagreement on the obligation of seclusion and the wearing of the veil. Young women in many parts of the Middle East, and even Europe, have adopted "Islamic dress," consisting of a kerchief that covers the hair, but leaves the face free. *See also* HIJAB.

**VERSE.** *See* AYAH.

**VILAYAT-I FAQIH.** A term used by Ayatollah **Khomeyni** in 1969 in a lecture in **Najaf,** which translates as the "guardianship of the Islamic jurist." It was implemented in 1979 when Khomeyni became the highest secular and religious authority in the **Islamic Republic of Iran.** The basis for Khomeyni's claim to temporal leadership is the **usuli** school of **Twelver** Shi'ism, which became dominant in the 19th century and gave exclusive right to interpret Islamic law to the **mujtahids.** In his book on Islamic government (a compilation of lectures at **Najaf**), Khomeyni claimed for the highest jurist (**faqih**) the right to govern and the obligation of the people to obey him. Khamene'i, his successor, however, no longer is endowed with a special charisma but he continues the line of spiritual leadership in Iran.

**VIZIER (WAZIR).** "One who carries a load." Title first given to ministers in the **'Abbasid** period and subsequently in other Islamic states. The grand vizier is a prime minister, ranking second only to the **sultan.** Some families held the vizierate for several generations; as for example, the **Barmakids** under the 'Abbasids or the Chandarlis under the **Ottomans.** The Koran commanded the Prophet to "consult the intelligent and the learned" among his **Companions,** and it has **Moses** ask of God to "give me a vizier from my family . . . add to my strength through him, and make him share my task"(20:29-32). In al-**Ghazali**'s *Counsel for Kings,* the king is to observe three principles in his treatment of the vizier: not to punish him in haste when vexed with him, not to covet his wealth when he grows rich, and not to refuse him a (necessary) request when he makes one (Ghazali, 107).

## -W-

**WAFA', ABU AL-** (BUZJANI, 940-997). Mathematician and astronomer from Buzjan, Khurasan, who came to **Baghdad** at age 19 and remained there until his death. He made his major contribution in the development of spherical trigonometry and geometrical constructions. His commentaries on Euclid, Diophanus, and **al-Khwarizmi**, as well as his astronomical tables, are lost. A moon crater was named in his honor.

**WAHB IBN MUNABBIH** (ca. 728). Arab chronicler of the **Umayyad** period and author of the *kitab al-maghazi* (Book of wars) describing the early wars and conquests of the Arabs. A native of Yemen, Wahb was a great transmitter of narrations and legends and "possessed information concerning the origin of things, the formation of the world, the history of the prophets and of (ancient) kings" (Khallikan, III, 671).

**WAHHAB, MUHAMMAD IBN 'ABD AL-** (1703-1792). *See* 'ABD AL-WAHHAB, MUHAMMAD IBN.

**WAHHABIS (AL-WAHHABIYYAH).** A puritanical Islamic revivalist movement in the Arabian Peninsula that calls itself Unitarians (*muwahhidun*), founded by Muhammad Ibn 'Abd al-Wahhab (1703-1792). 'Abd al-Wahhab allied himself with the tribal chief Muhammad ibn Sa'ud and conquered large areas of the Arabian Peninsula, including the Holy Cities of Mecca and Medina. They were defeated by Ibrahim, son of **Muhammad Ali**, the viceroy of Egypt, in 1818. During their raids, they destroyed some of the most holy shrines, including the tomb of **Husayn**, the son of 'Ali. About 100 years later, **Ibn Sa'ud** ('Abd al-'Aziz ibn 'Abd al Rahman al-Sa'ud) was able to conquer much of the Arabian Peninsula and establish the Kingdom of Saudi Arabia.

Unitarianism (for the unity of God, **tawhid**) was established as the dominant school of Islamic jurisprudence in Saudi Arabia. It espouses a puritanical fundamentalism and opposes developments during the classical period of Islam as innovations (**bid'ah**). Wahhabism rejects **Sufism, intercession, saint** cults, and considers the Koran and the early **Traditions** of the Prophet the only bases of **Islamic law**. Wahhabis enforce attendance at prayers and maintain a religious police to promote virtue and forbid vice. In recent years their practices have been somewhat mitigated and great cathedral **mosques** were constructed in Mecca and Medina and elsewhere. The **Taleban** rulers, although of the liberal **Hanifite** school, seem to have adopted the fundamentalist policies of Wahhabism in Afghanistan.

**WAITING PERIOD, THE.** "Iddah." The time a widow or **divorced** woman must wait before she can marry again. For widows the time is four months and 10 days, for divorced **women** it is three months. A child born during the waiting period is counted the offspring of the divorced or diseased man. For a pregnant woman the period extends to the birth of the child. The husband is responsible for the support of the woman during the waiting period; he can also take her back and continue the marriage.

**WAJIB.** "Obligatory" or "Necessary." Like **fardh** an essential duty, the fulfillment of which will be rewarded and neglect of which will be punished. *See* FIVE PRINCIPAL ACTS IN ISLAM.

**WALI.** A "friend" or "patron", one who is "near" to God. Also the title of a governor of a province (*wilayat*). Shi'ites call 'Ali the "Wali Allah," meaning "the Friend of God' and the "Vicegerent of God," thus the rightful successor to Muhammad's leadership of the Muslim community. *Wali* also means guardian of a minor, benefactor, helper, or a Muslim **saint** (pl. *awliya*).

**WALI ALLAH, SHAH** (1703-1762). One of the most important Muslim intellectuals of 18th century India. Shah Wali Allah studied with his father and at age 15 he became a disciple of the **Naqshbandiyyah Sufi** order. He taught in Delhi and in 1731 left on a **pilgrimage** to Mecca and Medina where he studied **hadith, fiqh,** and **Sufism.** On his return to Delhi, he published in **Arabic** and Persian. He attributed the decline of the Islamic world to the discontinuance of the spirit of **ijtihad** and the dominance of the dogma of imitation or emulation of the law (**taqlid**), as it was established by the four orthodox **schools of law**. He called for an intellectual revolution as a precondition to political change in India. He tried to create a united front for the purpose of establishing an Islamic state. His followers subsequently advocated a zealous puritanism, resembling the teachings of **Wahhabism**.

**WALID, IBN 'ABDUL MALIK AL-** (668-715). Sixth **Umayyad caliph** during whose reign (705-715) the conquest of Spain began in 711 and the eastern part of the empire expanded to the Indus River. Walid was a great builder, who started the construction of the **Al-Aqsa mosque** and rebuilt the mosque of the Prophet in Medina. He continued the Arabization policy of his father and built the Umayyad mosque on the site of the Church of St. John in **Damascus**. The booty from territorial conquests permitted a period of unprecedented prosperity.

**WALID.** *See* KHALID IBN AL-WALID.

**WAQF.** "Detention." Pious foundation (pl. *awqaf,* also called *habs*), real estate, or property given to God in perpetuity in support of religious and charitable institutions. It provided for the construction of **mosques,** schools, hospitals, bridges, and the support of **education,** soup kitchens, and other social services. It was usually administered by a member of the **ulama.**

A **Hanifite** definition of waqf is

> the tying-up of the substance of a thing under the rule of the property of Almighty God, so that the proprietary right of the waqif [donor] becomes extinguished and is transferred to Almighty God for any purpose by which its profits may be applied to the benefit of His creatures. (Asaf A. A. Fyzee, p. 269)

There are certain conditions for establishing a waqf: the property must be real estate or a durable object; the property must be given in perpetuity; the doner must be of sound mind and legally fit; the purpose must be an act of charity; and the beneficiary must be alive. Eventually private awqaf were established to protect property from confiscation. Such provisions reserved for the donor and his descendants the use of a part of the property. It is said that in the later **Ottoman** period as much as a third of all lands comprised waqf property. Like church property in some Western countries, waqf property was exempt from **taxation** and could not be easily confiscated by the state. Nevertheless, governments took over control of awqaf when they had the power to defy popular resentment. In Turkey three-fourths of arable lands consisted of waqf land; these lands were "nationalized" in 1925, and a minister (not a member of the ulama) took over their administration. In 1830 the French government took over the waqf (there called *habous*) in Algiers, where at the end of the 19th century almost one-half of arable land was dedicated to God (Fyzee, p. 266-267). It has been recognized that waqf property quickly deteriorated, as there was very little incentive for maintenance. Furthermore, the loss of taxation was a compelling reason for governments to take over the property.

**WAQIDI, MUHAMMD IBN 'UMAR AL-** (747-823). Arab historian from Medina, invited by the **Caliph Harun al-Rashid** (r. 786-809) to **Baghdad**, where he won fame for his *Kitab al-Maghazi* (Book of Muhammad's campaigns). It served as an important source for biographies of the Prophet. His study of transmitters of **hadith** was important in evaluating the soundness of chains of transmitters.

**WAQQAS, SA'D IBN ABI** (603-675). Arab general, said to have been the seventh convert to Islam. He defeated the Sassanian forces at the Battle of **Qadisiyah** (637) and was appointed governor of **Kufah**. He retired from politics after the assassination of the **Caliph 'Uthman** in 656.

**WAR.** War between Muslims is forbidden, unless it is in defense against aggression. The Koran says: "If two parties among the **believers** fall into a fight, make ye peace between them: but if one of them transgresses beyond bounds against the other, then fight ye (all) against the one that transgresses until it complies with the command of Allah; but if it complies, then make peace between them with justice, and be fair: for Allah loves those who are fair (and just)" (49:9). This means that an aggressor should be fought but reconciliation must be attempted. The only legal war is **jihad**. *See* DAR AL-HARB.

**WARNER.** *See* NADHIR.

**WASI.** "Inheritor." The title Shi'ites give to **'Ali**, son-in-law and cousin of the Prophet, whom they consider the rightful successor to lead the Islamic community.

**WASIL IBN 'ATA'** (d. 748). Theologian and founder of the **Mu'tazilite** school in **Basra**. Some claim that he was the first exponent of the five Mu'tazilite principles. A native of Medina, he came to **Baghdad** and became a student of **Hasan of Basra** (d. 728). One day the question was raised whether a person who has committed a grave **sin**

was a believer or not. According to one version, the **Murji'ites** held that the question should be postponed to the merciful decision of God, and the **Kharijites** declared a sinner a **kafir** destined for hell. Wasil held that the person was in between belief and unbelief and then he withdrew and formed his own circle. Hasan said that "he separated from us" (*i 'tazala 'anna*) and his followers came to be called the Mu'tazilites. Wasil had a long neck, for which he was ridiculed by his enemies, and he had a speech impediment that prevented him from pronouncing the letter "r;" therefore, he substituted words without the letter "r" in his speeches.

**WAZIER.** *See* VIZIER.

**WHITE STREAK, THE.** The time when a believer can eat during **Ramadhan** "until the white thread of dawn appear to you distinct from its black thread" (2:187).

**WINE.** *See* ALCOHOL.

**WITNESS.** *See* SHAHID.

**WIVES OF THE PROPHET.** As long as he was married to **Khadijah**, Muhammad did not take any other wives. He married **'A'isha**, and **Hafsah** (a widow), the daughters of the subsequent **caliphs Abu Bakr** and **Umar**; then he took a number of widows, including **Umm Habibah**, the daughter of his erstwhile enemy **Abu Sufyan**, and **Sawdah**, **Zaynab** bint Khuzaymah, Umm **Salama**, and **Safiyyah**. One wife, **Zaynab** bint Jahsh, was **divorced**, and one, **Juwayriyyah**, was a political **marriage**, as was his taking a **Jewish** and a **Christian** concubine, **Rayhana** and **Mary the Copt**. The Tabaqat also lists **Maymuna**, and a number of **women** who proposed to Muhammad or whom he married and divorced. The wives who outlived Muhammad received a yearly pension of 10,000 **dirhams**. A'ishah was his favorite wife, who outlived him by 46 years and was subsequently called the "Mother of the **Believers**." The descendants of Khadijah's daughter **Fatimah** and her husband **'Ali** ibn Abi Talib are the **Shi'ite imams**.

**WOMEN.** In the tribal society of pre-Islamic Arabia women were part of the estate of her husband, father, or close male relative. The birth of a girl was considered a misfortune and it was common to have female infants buried alive. The Koran refers to it, saying: "When news is brought to one of them of (the birth of ) a female (child), his face darkens, and he is filled with inward grief! With shame does he hide himself from his people, because of the bad news he has had. Shall he retain it on (sufferance and) contempt, or bury it in the dust? Ah, what an evil (choice) they decide on" (16:58,59). Islam brought change: It gave women a right to **inheritance**, limited the number of wives to four—although as a result of slavery— there was no limit to the number of concubines. Women have a soul, like men, but the functions of the two differ: The woman is respected as a mother and the man is responsible for her support. The Koran says: "Men are the protectors and maintainers of women, because Allah has given the one more (strength) than the other, and because they support them from their means" (4:34).

But even since the early period of Islam, women played important roles in society. **Khadijah**, the wife of Muhammad, conducted business with Syria in which Muhammad was employed for a time. **Fatimah**, the wife of the Prophet, is the example of the virtuous woman, and **'A'isha** is the transmitter of a great number of **hadith**. She participated in the **Battle of the Camel** in 656 during the civil war against 'Ali. Shajar al-Durr (Tree of Pearls) was sultan of Egypt in the beginning of the **Mamluk** sultanate. **Rabi'ah al-'Adawiyyah** is a much revered female mystic.

In **Islamic law** the man possesses the right to punish a disloyal wife. **Adultery** requires four witnesses or a confession of the culprits to be punished, and an accusation of adultery by a husband can be voided, if the woman swears to her innocense (*see* LI'AN). It takes the testimony of two women for that of one man in a **Shari'ah** court, but punishments and fines are half those for a man. A woman does not have to fight in war and does not share in the **booty**, and she is not to be killed in war.

The position of Muslim women continues to be influenced by **Tradition** today. The number of women in public life is still limited even in more Westernized states. Traditional occupations include the medical fields, education, business, and menial labor in the textile trades and agriculture. Although in urban areas a greater number of women attend public schools, illiteracy is much greater among women than men. As a result of the emergence of independent states in many parts of the Islamic world, women gained leading positions in social and political life, including the position of prime minister in several states of South Asia. Many discriminatory practices against women were outlawed. Women protest that, although limitations in public life were valid for a tribal society during the early period of Islam, present times call for a reinterpretation of old traditions. The recent resurgence of **Islamist** movements in many parts of the Islamic world has led to a demand to limit the spheres of female activity. An extreme example of this is the policy of the **Taliban** in Afghanistan, who, after their conquest of Kabul in 1994, closed schools for girls and restricted women to their homes. It caused innumerable hardships because many women were the sole support of their families. Even the most radical Islamist groups do not call for such measures.

**WORSHIP.** Laws concerning worship (**'ibadat**) refer to obedience and submissiveness to God and include such duties as ritual **prayers**, **fasting, almsgiving**, and the **pilgrimage.** *See* FAITH.

**WUDHU.** The lesser **Ablution**.

**WUQUF.** "Station, Halt." The standing position during **prayer**. The obligation of "standing before the Lord" in the plain of Arafat on the ninth day of **pilgrimage**. The various schools differ as to the time a pilgrim has to be there, but pilgrimage would be invalid without the *wuquf.*

## -Y-

**YAQUB IBN LAYTH AL-SAFFAR** (867-879). Yaqub, the coppersmith (*saffar*), was the founder of a kingdom that came to be named after him, the Saffarid dynasty (867-1495). He began as a bandit, in which profession he showed great courage and generosity, and he may have been a **Kharijite**, before he turned orthodox. Appointed as commander of the army of Sistan, he captured Herat, Kerman, and raided into Fars. The **'Abbasid caliph** recognized his power and appointed him governor of Balkh and Tokharistan. From there, he expanded his realm further east to Kabul, Afghanistan, and then turned to the west to conquer Nishapur from the Tahirids. Encouraged by his conquests, he demanded the province of Fars, but the Caliph Mu'tamid (r. 870-892) sent an army against him and scored a decisive victory. Yaqub was succeeded by Amr (r. 879-901) but another defeat ended the

Saffarid's control of Persian territory, although the Saffarids continued to control parts of Sistan for several centuries.

**YAQUBI, IBN WADIH AL-** (d. 897). Arab historian and geographer who won fame for his *tarikh ibn wadih* (World history), which starts with the creation and continues to his time. His *kitab al-buldan* (Book of countries) provides statistical and topographic data on the Islamic world from Iran westward across North Africa. A **Twelver** Shi'ite and the son of a freed **slave**, he spent his childhood in **Baghdad** and subsequently lived in Armenia and Khurasan before moving to Egypt.

**YAQUT AL-HAMAWI** (1179-1229). Arab writer of Greek origin who came to **Baghdad** as a **slave** and was manumitted there. He was a prolific writer, but only three of his works are extant: *mu 'ajam al-buldan* (Geographical dictionary), *mu 'ajam al-udaba '*(Dictionary of men of letters) , and *mushtarik* (Gazetteer). He traveled widely and eventually settled in Aleppo.

**YARMUK, BATTLE OF AL-**. A tributary of the Jordan River where in 636 a Muslim force under the command of **Khalid ibn al-Walid** defeated a Byzantine army. Khalid's army of about 25,000 faced a superior Byzantine army of some 50,000 men, headed by Theodorus, brother of the Byzantine ruler Heraclius. Most of the Byzantine forces were killed, including Theodorus. This meant the loss of Syria (except for **Jerusalem**) by the Greeks.

**YATHRIB.** The pre-Islamic name of Medina. *See* MEDINA.

**YAWM AL-QIYAMAH.** "Resurrection." *See* DAY OF JUDGMENT.

**YAZID IBN MU'AWIYAH** (r. 680-683). The second **Umayyad caliph**, appointed by his father, **Mu'awiyah**, as his successor, thus establishing the precedent of dynastic succession. The pious opposition in Medina and the followers of '**Ali** ibn Abi Talib in Iraq contested the appointment. The **Kufans** invited **Husayn**, the son of 'Ali, from Medina but were unable to protect him from the army of Yazid and on the 10th of **Muharram** 680, Husayn and his small group of followers were massacred. Yazid's forces defeated the opposition of Medina in the Harra. Once consolidated in power, Yazid sponsored the arts and introduced feasts with music and wine to his court.

**YAZIDIS.** Followers of a Kurdish enthno-sectarian community that probably derives its name from **Yazid**, the son of **Mu'awiyah**. Its modern creed was shaped by the **Sufi Shaykh** Adi ibn Musafir (d. 1160?) of Lalish near Mosul, Iraq. The **scriptures** of the Yazidis are the *Book of Revelation* and the *Black Book.* Their religion is said to have Sabaean, Muslim, Christian, and Zoroastrian elements and, because of the secrecy of their belief, they have been called devil worshipers and have been exposed to long periods of persecution. The tomb of Shaykh Adi is located near Mosul and is the location of an annual **pilgrimage**.

**YEAR, ISLAMIC.** *See* CALENDAR.

**YUSUF IBN TASHFIN** (d. 1106). **Almoravid** ruler (1061-1106) who founded Marrakesh in 1062 and eventually controlled virtually all of Muslim Spain after he defeated King Alfonso VI of Léon and Castile in 1086.

## -Z-

**ZAB.** Two tributaries of the Tigris. The Greater Zab with its source near the Iraqi-Iranian border was the site of a battle in January 750 between the last **Umayyad Caliph** Marwan II and **'Abbasid** forces. The Umayyads were decisively defeated and replaced by the 'Abbasid **caliphate**.

**ZABUR.** "Psalms." Book given to David, mentioned in the Koran. It is one of a series of books, including the Torah, the Gospel, and the final **revelation**, the Koran. The Koran says: "Say: We believe in Allah, and in what has been revealed to us and what was revealed to **Abraham**, Isma'il, Isaac, Jacob, and the Tribes, and in (the Books) given to **Moses**, **Jesus**, and the Prophets from their Lord; we make no distinction between one or another among them, and to Allah do we bow our will (in Islam)" (4:163).

**ZAHIR.** The literal meaning, especially of the Koran, the opposite of the esoteric (*batin*). *See* BATINITES and ZAHIRITES.

**ZAHIRITES (ZAHIRIYYAH).** A school of jurisprudence, founded by Dawud al-Isfahani (d. 884), which demands an exoteric, **zahir**, interpretation of the Koran and the **Sunnah**. The Zahirites were "literalists," rejecting acceptance of authority (**taqlid**), the use of opinion (*ra'y*) by the jurist, and reasoning by analogy (**qiyas**), in interpreting the law. The Zahirites were established as an orthodox school in Iraq and then spread to other parts of the Islamic world. **Ibn Hazm** (d. 1064) was one of the school's most important proponents in Spain. It was also the school of jurisprudence of the **Almohad** ruler Yaqub al-Mansur (1184-1199), but it never found acceptance as a fifth orthodox **school of law**.

**ZAKAT.** A tax incumbent on all Muslims. The Koran says: "Alms are for the poor and the needy, and those employed to administer the (funds); for those whose hearts have been reconciled (converted to truth); for those in bondage and in debt; in the cause of Allah; and for the wayfarer; thus it is ordained by Allah" (9:60). It is one of the obligations subsumed under the code of rituals called the **Five Pillars of Islam** and can be given in cash or in kind. Now largely voluntary, as much as 2.5 to 10 percent was customary.

According to the *Muwatta* of **Imam Malik ibn Anas**, zakat is paid on three things: the produce of cultivated land, gold and silver, and livestock. But there is no zakat obligation on less than five camels, on less than five awaq (two hundred **dirhams** of pure silver), or on less than five awaq of dates (1,500 double-handled scoops) (17.1.1-3.). Shi'ites look at zakat as charity rather than as a religious tax. *See also* SADAQA.

**ZAMAKHSHARI, MAHMUD AL** (1075-1144). Theologian and philologist of Persian origin, who was born at Zamakhshar and died at Korkanj in Transcaspia. **Ibn Khallikan** calls him: "The great master (**imam**) in the sciences of Koranic interpretation, the **Traditions**, grammar, philology, and rhetoric, was incontrovertibly the first imam of the age in which he lived." He was a **Mu'tazilite**, supporting the **createdness of the Koran** and, in spite of his origin, an opponent of the anti-Arab **shu'ubiyyah** movement. His Koran commentary *al-kashshaf* (The revealer) was original and his **Arabic** grammar (*al-mufassal*) is still used as a reference work today. Zamakhshari lost a foot as a result of an accident and he carried a certificate with him to show that this was not the result of amputation for committing a crime.

**ZAMZAM.** "Abundant Water." A sacred well at the southeast corner of the **Ka'bah**, which the Angel **Gabriel** conjured to save **Hagar** and her son Isma'il from dying of thirst. Muslims drink from it during **pilgrimage** and treasure the water for its presumed healing qualities.

**ZANJ.** Arab name for the black inhabitants of the east African coast (Zanzibar) who were transported as **slaves** to work in the swampland of southern Iraq. As many as 5,000 slaves worked in the area, and they finally rose in rebellion, led by 'Ali Muhammad al-Zanji, and under the banner of the **Qarmatian sect**. They captured **Basra** and cut off the trade route to the Gulf. The Zanj were defeated and their capital, al-Mukhtara (The Chosen), was taken in 883, but their uprising speeded the **'Abbasid** decline. Black slaves were usually employed as domestics or soldiers; the employment of large numbers of slaves in mines or plantations was an exception.

**ZAWIYAH.** "Corner." A place of worship or **Sufi** lodge. *See* KHANA-QAH.

**ZAYD IBN 'ALI** (698-740). A grandson of **Husayn** and **imam** of the **Zaydiyyah** (or **Fiver**) Shi'ites. He fought the **Umayyads** but was defeated and killed in 740. *See* ZAYDIS.

**ZAYD IBN HARITH.** A **slave** given to Muhammad by his wife **Khadijah** and later adopted as a son by Muhammad. Zayd **divorced** his wife **Zaynab** when the Prophet wanted to marry her. A **revelation** permitted the **marriage**, which would have been prohibited because adoption made Zayd a blood relative. He was the second male convert to Islam after 'Ali.

**ZAYD IBN THABIT** (d. 666). Secretary of the Prophet and in charge of distributing the **booty** after the **Battle of Yarmuk** (636). In the wars of **apostasy** a large number of reciters of the Koran were killed and it was considered necessary to compile a definitive version from fragments, palm leaves, bones, and "the hearts of men." He was charged by **Caliph Abu Bakr** with the collection of texts of the Koran, a task he is believed to have later completed during the caliphate of **'Uthman**. When Ibn 'Abbas held the stirrup of Zayd, the latter exclaimed: "How, you, who are the uncle of the blessed Prophet, hold my stirrup?" Ibn Abbas replied: "Yes it is thus we do with the learned." Caliphs **'Umar I** and 'Uthman considered him "without an equal as a judge, as a jurisconsult, a calculator in the division of **inheritance**, and a reader of the Koran" (Khallikan, I, 372). Zayd is buried in **Damascus**.

**ZAYDIS. (ZAYDIYYAH).** The followers of **Zayd ibn 'Ali** (d. 740), the fifth Shi'ite **imam**. They are closest to Sunni Islam and recognize the Koran and the **Sunnah** as the bases of their theology. They require that the imam be a descendant of either **Hasan** or **Husayn** and have de facto power as well as special doctrinal knowledge and political ability. Also an important qualification was that the imam excell in piety and valor, possess personal grace, and be free from physical defects. The Zaydis founded a state in Yemen in 897 and for a time they also existed in Iran. Their theology is a mixture of **mu'tazilite** and **murji'ite** doctrines and they accept **Abu Bakr**, **'Umar I**, and part of **'Uthman**'s tenure as legitimate. Zaydis do not practice **taqiyah** and **mut'ah marriage** and are opposed to **Sufism**. On the question of **sin** and the sinner, they believe the sinner is an unbeliever, but they do not demand that he be killed. They now constitute the majority of the population in southwestern Yemen. From the 10th century until 1962, their imam was also the head of state.

**ZAYNAB BINT JAHSH.** Wife of the Prophet who was married to his adopted son, **Zayd ibn Haritha**. When Muhammad came to visit Zayd, he refused to enter the house when he learned that Zayd was not at home. Sensing that Muhammad was interested in her, Zayd **divorced** Zaynab and she became the Prophet's wife. A **revelation** said: "When Zayd no longer had any need of her, We married her to you" (33:37). She received a **dowry** of 400 **dirhams**.

**ZAYNAB BINT KHADIJAH.** Oldest daughter of Muhammad and **Khadijah**. She married Abu 'l-'As ibn al-Rabi' before the advent of Islam and had two children, 'Ali and Umama. 'Ali died young and Umama grew up and married 'Ali ibn Abi Talib after **Fatima**'s death. Zaynab became Muslim and emigrated with her father to Medina. Her husband refused to convert; he was captured by the Medinans, and Zaynab won his release when she sent her necklace as ransom. When Abu 'l-'As converted, Muhammad gave Zaynab back to him. She died in about 630, before the death of the Prophet.

**ZAYNAB BINT KHUZAYMAH.** Wife of Muhammad, called "Mother of the Poor" because she spent much of her wealth on charity.

Muhammad married her in the month of **Ramadhan** in 625 and gave her a **dowry** of 400 **dirhams**. She was **divorced** by her first and widowed by her second husband. Zaynab died at age 30 after only eight months of **marriage**.

**ZAYN AL-'ABIDIN** (658-712?). Son of **Husayn** ibn 'Ali and Sulafa, the daughter of Yazdegird III, the last Sassanian ruler. He is the fourth of the Shi'ite **imams** and all the imams were his descendants. He was called Ibn al-Khiaratain (the son of two preferred ones) because a **hadith** quotes the Prophet as saying: "Of all the human race, Almighty God has preferred two (families); the tribe of Kuraish amongst the Arabs, and the Persians amongst the foreign nations." He had a reputation as a pious man and noted traditionist and jurist.

**ZIKR.** See DHIKR.

**ZINAH.** See ADULTERY.

**ZIONISM.** Jewish religo-nationalist movement founded in the late 19th century through the initiative of Theodor Herzl (1860-1904), a Paris correspondent of the *Neue Freie Presse* of Vienna. In his book, *Der Judenstaat*, Herzl asked the European governments to grant the Jewish people an area where a Jewish homeland could be established. He suggested Argentina, Palestine, or some other possible area, but the First Zionist Congress in Basel, Switzerland (1897), demanded, the establishment of a homeland in Palestine. The Zionist movement grew and a Jewish National Fund was created, which specialized in land acquisitions in Palestine.

Attempts at winning the **Ottoman sultan Abd al-Hamid**'s approval for the settlement of Jews in Palestine in exchange for financing the Ottoman debt were unsuccessful. But during the First World War, the British foreign secretary Arthur Balfour, trying to win the support of world Jewry, wrote a letter to Lord L. W. Rothschild in which he stated that his government favored "the establishment in Palestine of a national home for the Jewish people," with the proviso that "nothing shall be done which may prejudice the civil and religious rights of existing non-Jewish communities" (*Encyclopedia of Zionism and Israel*, 103).

The defeat of the **Ottoman empire** and the establishment of a British mandate for Palestine facilitated further Jewish immigration. The Arab population became increasingly hostile, fearing that unlimited Jewish immigration would lead to a loss of their political power. The result led to armed clashes between the communities, which turned into war after the United Nations decreed to divide Palestine into Jewish and Arab states, with Jerusalem under a UN Trusteeship. Rather than helping to implement the Partition Plan, the British terminated the mandate in May 1948 and thus did not prevent the outbreak of war between the communities. Thus the Zionist objective was achieved.

**ZIYAD IBN ABIHI** (ca. 626-675). Proclaimed a half brother by **Caliph Mu'awiyah** to tie him to the **Umayyad** regime, even though his name, the "Son of His Father" (*ibn abihi*) indicates that there was some doubt as to his descent (**Abu Sufyan** was rumored to be his father). He became governor of **Kufah**, later also **Basra** and the eastern provinces, where he distinguished himself in fighting **'Alid** and **Kharijite** forces and thus contributed to the consolidation of the **Umayyad caliphate**. He ruthlessly restored order in Iraq and Iran and maintained an elaborate spy system. Ziyad also wanted control of the Hijaz and wrote to the caliph: "Commander of the faithful! My left hand holds Iraq in submission unto you, and my right hand is unoccupied and waits to be employed in your service; appoint me therefore governor of **Hijaz**" (Khallikan, 621). This was not granted, but Iraq prospered under his reign.

**ZIYAD, TARIQ IBN.** *See* TARIQ IBN ZIYAD.

**ZIYARAH.** "Visitation." A visit to the graves of individuals for the purpose of praying for the dead. Also, **pilgrimage** to a shrine that can be undertaken at any time.

**ZUBAYR, IBN AL-AWWAM** (d. 627). A cousin of the Prophet and the fifth convert to Islam who fell in the **Battle of the Camel** fighting against 'Ali. His wife, Asma', was the daughter of the **Caliph Abu Bakr,** and his son, Abdallah **ibn al-Zubayr,** fought the **Umayyads** as counter-caliph in Mecca.

# BIBLIOGRAPHY

The sources listed in the following sections are a representative selection of books and articles in the field of Islamic studies. They are organized in four parts: I. Reference, II. History, III. Islam, and IV. Islamic Politics and Society.

Part I includes bibliographies, essential even at a time when one can access the Library of Congress catalog from a home computer. Most important are J. D. Pearson's *Index Islamicus,* which covers virtually all articles published on any aspect of Islamic studies in most European languages from 1905 to the present. The *Guide to Islam* (1983), by David Ede, is still indispensable. It lists a wide range of reference materials and historical works from pre-Islamic to modern times, as well as publications on religious thought, law, art, and other topics, with ample annotations. Specialized bibliographies include works on political Islam by Yvonne Haddad and John L. Esposito's *The Islamic Revival since 1988: A Critical Survey and Bibliography* and Yvonne Haddad, John O. Voll, and John L. Esposito's *The Contemporary Islamic Revival: A Critical Survey and Bibliography.* Ahmad S. Moussalli lists an excellent bibliography in his *Historical Dictionary of Islamic Fundamentalist Movements in the Arab World, Iran, and Turkey.*

Indispensable for the serious student of Islamic history for the period between CE 600 and 1500 is R. Stephen Humphreys's *Islamic History: A Framework for Inquiry,* which combines a bibliographic study with an inquiry into method, surveying the principal reference tools available to historians of Islam. It is the most recent study of its type.

The most important reference works for the advanced student are the *Encyclopaedia of Islam,* a second edition (*EI2*) of which was begun in 1954 and is still not completed (a CD-ROM edition exists up to the letter "S"), and the *Shorter Encyclopaedia of Islam,* which appeared in 1953 (reprinted in 1961) under the editorship of H. A. R. Gibb and J. H. Kramers. These works are complemented by the *Encyclopaedia Iranica* to include greater coverage on Shi'ism and the eastern part of the Islamic world. It includes more contemporary materials, but the transliteration system may pose problems for the beginner. Furthermore, it is also still far from completion and cross listings of Persian terms in English are therefore not always available. A beginning student will therefore prefer to consult Cyril Glassé's *Concise Encyclopedia of Islam* and Stephan and Nandy Ronart's *Concise Encyclopaedia of Arabic Civilization*.

For reliable chronologies the reader may refer to C. E. Bosworth's *The New Islamic Dynasties: A Chronological and Genealogical Manual*, and Robert Mantran's *Great Dates in Islamic History*.

Part II lists works on the history of individual countries, including the Arab world, Iran, the Ottoman empire, and Turkey, and a limited amount of books and articles on Central Asia, an area that has been defined as the "Central Islamic Lands." One section includes general histories as well as the pioneering work of M. G. S. Hodgson, entitled *The Venture of Islam: Conscience and History in a World Civilization*.

Part III contains books and articles on various aspects of Islamic studies, including sections on the Prophet Muhammad, Koran, mysticism, and modernism.

Part IV covers politics and society, with special emphasis on political Islam. Samples of the writings of the major ideologues of political Islam, as for example Sayyid Abu'l A'la al-Maududi's *First Principles of the Islamic State*, Sayyid Qutb's *Milestones*, Hasan al-Banna's *Collections* and Ayatollah Khomeyni's *Islam and Revolution* have been presented in translations. An important work on political Islam is Ahmad S. Moussalli's *Historical Dictionary of Islamic Fundamentalist Movements in the Arab World, Iran, and Turkey*.

It must be stressed, however, that the following selection is necessarily only a representative sample of the considerable volume of material produced in the field of Islamic studies.

## CONTENTS

I. Reference

II. History

III. Islam

IV. Islamic Politics and Society

# I. Reference

## Bibliographies

Amin, S. H. *Islamic Law in the Contemporary World: Introduction, Glossary and Bibliography.* Glasgow: Royston House, 1985.

Creswell, K. A. C. *A Bibliography of the Architecture, Arts and Crafts of Islam to 1960.* Cairo: American University at Cairo Press, 1961.

Ede, David. *Guide to Islam.* Boston, MA: G. K. Hall, 1983.

Geddes, Charles L. *Guide to Reference Books for Islamic Studies.* Denver, CO: American Institute of Islamic Studies, 1985.

Haddad, Yvonne, and John L. Esposito. *The Islamic Revival since 1988: A Critical Survey and Bibliography.* Westport, CT: Greenwood Press, 1998.

Haddad, Yvonne, John O. Voll, and John L. Esposito. *The Contemporary Islamic Revival: A Critical Survey and Bibliography*. Westport, CT: Greenwood Press, 1991.

Humphreys, R. Stephen. *Islamic History: A Framework for Inquiry*. Princeton, NJ: Princeton University Press, 1991.

Meghdessian, Samira R. *The Status of the Arab Woman: A Select Bibliography*. New York: Greenwood Press, 1980.

Shimoni, Yaacov. *Biographical Dictionary of the Middle East*. New York: Facts On File, 1991.

Zwaini, Laila al-, and Rudolph Peters. *A Bibliography of Islamic Law, 1980-1993*. Leiden: E. J. Brill, 1994.

## Encyclopedias and Handbooks

Adamec, Ludwig W. *Historical Dictionary of Afghanistan*. 2d. rev. ed. Lanham, MD: Scarecrow Press, 1997.

Bidwell, Robin. *The Dictionary of Modern Arab History*. New York: Kegan Paul International, 1997.

Bosworth, Clifford Edmund. *The New Islamic Dynasties: A Chronological and Genealogical Manual*. Edinburgh: Edinburgh University Press, 1996.

Freeman-Grenville, G. S. P. *The Muslim and Christian Calendars, Being Tables for the Conversion of Muslim and Christian Dates from the Hijra to the Year A.D. 2000*. London: Oxford University Press, 1963.

Gibb, Hamilton A. R., and J. H. Kramer. *Shorter Encyclopedia of Islam*. London: Luzac and Co, 1961.

Glassé, Cyril. *The Concise Encyclopedia of Islam*. San Francisco: Harper and Row, 1989.

Hazard, H. W. *Atlas of Islamic History*. 3d ed. Princeton, NJ: Princeton University Press, 1954.

Hiro, Dilip. *Dictionary of the Middle East*. Houndmills, Basingstoke: Macmillan, 1996.

Houtsma, M. T. et al., eds. *Encyclopedia of Islam: A Dictionary of the Geography, Ethnography, and Biography of Muhammadan Peoples, Prepared by a Number of Leading Orientalists*. 4 vols. Leiden: E. J. Brill, 1913-1936; Supplement, 1938.

Moussalli, Ahmad S. *Historical Dictionary of Islamic Fundamentalist Movements in the Arab World, Iran, and Turkey*. Lanham, MD: Scarecrow Press, 1999.

Pearson, J. D. *Index Islamicus, 1906-1955: A Catalogue of Articles on Islamic Subjects in Periodicals and Other Collective Publications.* Cambridge: W. Heffer, 1958. Supplements continuing.

Reich, Bernard, ed. *Political Leaders of the Contemporary Middle East and North Africa: A Biographical Dictionary.* New York: Greenwood Press, 1991.

Ronart, Stephan, and Nandy Ronart. *Concise Encyclopaedia of Arabic Civilization.* Vol. 1. *The Arab East.* New York: Praeger, 1960.

Simon, Reeva S. et al. *Encyclopedia of the Modern Middle East.* New York: Macmillan Reference USA, 1996.

Ziring, Lawrence. *The Middle East: A Political Dictionary.* Santa Barbara, CA: ABC-CLIO, 1992.

## Biographies

Abbott, Nabia. *Aishah, the Beloved of Mohammed.* Chicago: University of Chicago Press, 1942.

Fischel, Walter J. *Ibn Khaldun in Egypt: His Public Functions and His Historical Research: A Study in Islamic Historiography.* Berkeley: University of California Press, 1967.

Haq, Mahmmudul. *Muhammad. Abduh: A Study of a Modern Thinker of Egypt.* Aligarh, India: Institute of Islamic Studies, Aligarh Muslim University, 1978.

Haykal, Muhammad Husayn. *The Life of Muhammad.* Translated from the 8th edition by Ismail Ragi A. Faruqi. London: Shorouk International, 1983.

Keddie, Nikki R. *Sayyid Jamal ad-Din "al-Afghani": A Political Biography.* Berkeley: University of California Press, 1972.

Kinross, Lord. *Atatürk: A Biography of Mustafa Kemal, Father of Modern Turkey.* New York: Morrow, 1965.

Monroe, Elizabeth. *Philby of Arabia.* London: Faber and Faber, 1973.

Philby, H. St. John. *Harun al-Rashid.* New York: Appleton-Century, 1934.

X, Malcolm. *The Autobiography of Malcolm X* (1965). New York: Ballantine Books, 1992.

# II. History

## General

Cleveland, William L. *A History of the Modern Middle East*. Boulder, CO: Westview Press, 1994.

Fisher, Sydney Nettleton, and William Ochsenwald. *The Middle East: A History*. New York: McGraw-Hill, 1990.

Goldschmidt, Arthur Jr. *A Concise History of the Middle East*. 4th ed. Boulder, CO: Westview Press, 1991.

Hitti, Philip. *The Near East in History: A 5000 Year Story*. Princeton, NJ: Princeton University Press, 1961.

Hodgson, G. S. Marshall. *The Century of Islam: Conscience and History in a World Civilization*. 3 vols. Chicago: University of Chicago Press, 1974.

Lapidus, Ira. *A History of Islamic Societies*. Cambridge: Cambridge University Press, 1988.

Mansfield, Peter. *A History of the Middle East*. New York: Penguin Books, 1991.

## Arab World

Burkhardt, John L. *Travels in Arabia* (1829). London: F. Cass, 1968.

Fernea, Elizabeth. *A View of the Nile*. New York: Doubleday, 1970.

———. *Guests of the Sheikh*. New York: Doubleday, 1965.

Hitti, Philip K. *History of the Arabs from the Earliest Times to the Present*. 8th ed. New York: St. Martin's, 1964.

Hourani, Albert. *Arabic Thought in the Liberal Age, 1789-1939*. London: Oxford University Press, 1962.

Lewis, Bernard. *The Arabs in History*. 4th ed. London: Hutchinson's, 1966.

Monroe, Elizabeth. *Philby of Arabia*. London: Faber and Faber, 1973.

Morony, Michael. *Iraq after the Muslim Conquest*. Princeton, NJ: Princeton University Press, 1984.

Muir, Sir William. *The Caliphate, Its Rise, Decline and Fall, from Original Sources* Beirut: Khayats, 1963. Orig. Publ. in 1915.

Watt, W. Montgomery. *Muhammad at Mecca*. Oxford: Clarendon, 1953.

———. *Muhammad, Prophet and Statesman*. London: Oxford University Press, 1961.

# Iran

Arberry, J. J., ed. *The Legacy of Persia.* Oxford: Clarendon, 1968.

Bakhash, Shaul. *The Reign of the Ayatollahs: Iran and the Islamic Revolution.* New York: Basic Books, 1986.

Binder, Leonard. *Iran: Political Development in a Changing Society.* Berkeley: University of California Press, 1962.

Browne, Edward G. *A Literary History of Persia.* 4 vols. Cambridge: Cambridge University Press, 1951-1953. Orig. publ. in 1928.

Frye, Richard N., ed. *The Cambridge History of Iran.* Vol. 4. *From the Arab Invasion to the Saljuqs.* Cambridge: Cambridge University Press, 1975.

Hiro, Dilip. *Iran under the Ayatollahs.* London: Routledge and Kegan Paul, 1985.

Keddie, Nikki R. *Religion and Rebellion in Iran: The Iranian Tobacco Protest of 1891-1892.* New York: Humanities Press, 1966.

Savory, Roger. *Iran under the Safavids.* Cambridge: Cambridge University Press, 1980.

# Ottoman Empire and Turkey

Armstrong, Harold C. *Grey Wolf, Mustafa Kemal: An Intimate Study of a Dictator.* London: Barker, 1932.

Atil, Esin. *The Age of Sultan Suleyman the Magnificent.* New York: Harry N. Abrams, 1987.

Berkes, Niyazi. *The Development of Secularism in Turkey.* Montreal: McGill University Press, 1964.

Davis, Fanny. *The Ottoman Lady: A Social History from 1718 to 1918.* New York: Greenwood, 1986.

Gerber, Haim. "Social and Economic Position of Women in an Ottoman City, Bursa, 1600-1700." *International Journal of Middle East Studies* 12 (1980): 231-44.

Gibbons, Herbert A. *The Foundation of the Ottoman Empire.* Oxford: Clarendon Press, 1916.

Heyd, Uriel. *The Foundations of Turkish Nationalism.* London: Harwell Press, 1950.

Inalcik, Halil. *The Ottoman Empire: Conquest, Organization and Economy.* London: Variorum, 1978.

Itzkowitz, Norman. *Ottoman Empire and Islamic Tradition.* New York: Knopf, 1973.

Karpat, Kemal H. *The Ottoman State and Its Place in World History.* Leiden: E. J. Brill, 1974.

Kinross, Lord (Patrick Balfour). *Ataturk: A Biography of Mustafa Kemal, Father of Modern Turkey*. New York: Morrow, 1965.

Landau, Jacob M., ed. *Ataturk and the Modernization of Turkey*. Boulder, CO: Westview Press, 1984.

Merriman, R. B. *Suleiman the Magnificent, 1520-1566*. Cambridge, MA: Harvard University Press, 1944.

Moorehead, Alan. *Gallipoli*. New York: Harper, 1956.

Shaw, Stanford J. *History of the Ottoman Empire and Modern Turkey*. 2 vols. Cambridge: Cambridge University Press, 1976.

**South Asia and Central Asia**

Adamec, Ludwig W. *Historical Dictionary of Afghanistan*. Lanham, MD: Scarecrow Press, 1997.

————. *Afghanistan's Foreign Affairs to the Mid-Twentieth Century: Relations with the USSR, Germany, and Britain*. Tucson: University of Arizona Press, 1974.

Ahmad, Aziz. *An Intellectual History of Islam in India*. Edinburgh: Edinburgh University Press, 1969.

Dupree, Louis. *Afghanistan*. Princeton, NJ: Princeton University Press, 1973.

Gregorian, Vartan. *The Emergence of Modern Afghanistan*. Stanford, CA: Stanford University Press, 1969.

Mujeeb, M. *Islamic Influence on Indian Society*. Delhi: Meenakshi Prakashan, 1972.

Schimmel, Annemarie. *Islam in the Indian Subcontinent*. Leiden: E. J. Brill, 1980.

Smith, Vincent. *The Oxford History of India*. Pt. 2, *India in the Muhammadan Period*. Oxford: Clarendon, 1920.

# III. Islam

**General**

Adams, Charles J. "The Islamic Religious Tradition." In *Religion and Man*. Edited by W. Richard Comstock. New York: Harper and Row, 1971, 553-617.

Arberry, A. J. *Aspects of Islamic Civilization as Depicted in the Original Texts*. London: Allen and Unwin, 1964.

Endress, Gerard. *An Introduction to Islam*, Trans. Carole Hillenbrand. New York: Columbia University Press, 1988.

Gibb, H. A. R. *Mohammedanism.* 2d ed. London: Oxford University Press, 1962. Reprinted with revisions, 1970.

Haddad, Yvonne Yazeck. *Contemporary Islam and the Challenge of History.* Albany: State University of New York Press, 1982.

Hodgson, Marshall G. S. *The Venture of Islam.* Chicago: University of Chicago Press, 1974.

Jeffery, Arthur, ed. *Islam: Muhammad and His Religion.* New York: Liberal Arts, 1958.

Lane, Edward William. *An Account of the Manners and Customs of the Modern Egyptians.* London: J. M. Dent, 1954.

Lewis, Bernard, ed. and trans. *Islam from the Prophet Muhammad to the Capture of Constantinople.* Vol. 1. *Politics and War.* Vol. 2. *Religion and Society.* New York: Harper and Row, 1974.

Rahman, Fazlur. *Islam.* Garden City, NY: Doubleday, 1968.

## Islamic Studies

Farah, Caesar E. *Islam: Beliefs and Observances.* Woodbury, NY: Barron's Educational Series, 1968.

Gibb, H. A. R. *Studies on the Civilization of Islam.* Edited by S. J. Shaw and W. R. Polk. Boston: Beacon Press, 1962.

Gibb, H. A. R., and Harold Bowen. *Islamic Society and the West.* 2 vols. London: Oxford University Press, 1950.

Grunebaum, G. E. von. *Classical Islam: A History 600-1258.* Translated by Katharine Watson. London: Allen and Unwin, 1970.

Haddad, Yvonne Yazbeck. *Contemporary Islam and the Challenge of History.* Albany: State University of New York Press, 1982.

Lewis Bernard, ed. *Islam and the Arab World: Faith, People, Culture.* New York: Knopf, 1976.

Nasr, Seyyid Hossein. *Islamic Science.* London: Luzac, 1976.

Piscatori, James P. *Islam in a World of Nation-States.* Cambridge: Cambridge University Press, 1986.

Rahman, Fazlur. *Islam and Modernity: Transformation of an Intellectual Tradition.* Chicago: University of Chicago Press, 1982.

Schimmel, Annemarie. *Islam in the Indian Subcontinent.* Leiden: E. J. Brill, 1980.

Smith, Wilfred Cantwell. *Islam in Modern History.* New York: New American Library, 1957.

Watt, W. Montgomery. *The Majesty That Was Islam: The Islamic World 661-1100.* London: Sidgwick and Jackson, 1974.

## Muhammad

Abbott, Nabia. *Aisha, the Beloved of Mohammed.* Chicago: Chicago University Press, 1942.

Andrae, Tor. *Mohammed: The Man and His Faith.* New York: Harper and Row, 1960.

Glubb, John Bagot. *The Life and Times of Muhammad.* London: Hodder and Stoughton, 1970.

Guillaume, A. *The Life of Muhammad: A Translation of Ibn Ishaq's Sirat Rassul Allah.* London: Oxford University Press, 1968.

Haykal, Muhammad Husayn. *The Life of Muhammad.* Translated from the 8th edition by Isma'il Ragi A. Faruqi. London: Shorouk International, 1983.

Rodinson, Maxine. *Mohammed.* Translated by A. Carter. London: A. Lane, Penguin Press, 1971.

Watt, W. Montgomery. *Muhammad at Mecca.* Oxford: Clarendon Press, 1953.

———. *Muhammad at Medina.* Oxford: Clarendon Press, 1953.

———. *Muhammad: Prophet and Statesman.* London: Oxford University Press, 1964.

## Koran

Arberry, A. J., trans. *The Holy Koran: An Introduction with Selections.* London: Allen and Unwin, 1953.

———. *The Koran Interpreted.* 2 vols. London: Allen and Unwin, 1955.

Jeffery, A. *The Qur'an as Scripture.* New York: Russell Moore, 1952.

Pickthall, Muhammad N. *The Glorious Koran: A Bilingual Edition with English Translations, Introduction and Notes.* Albany: State University of New York Press, 1976. Reprint of 1938 edition.

## Mysticism

Arberry, A. J. *An Introduction to the History of Sufism.* London: Longmans, 1942.

Birge, John Kingsly. *The Bektashi Order of Dervishes.* Hartford, CT: Hartford Seminary Press, 1937.

Gilsenan, Michael. *Saint and Sufi in Modern Egypt: An Essay in the Sociology of Religion.* Oxford: Clarendon, 1973.

Keddie, Nikki R., ed. *Scholars, Saints, and Sufis: Muslim Religious Institutions since 1500.* Berkeley: University of California Press, 1972.

Nicholson, R. A. *Studies in Islamic Mysticism.* Cambridge: Cambridge University Press, 1967. Reprint of 1921 edition.

Rice, Cyprian. *The Persian Sufis.* 2d ed. London: Allen and Unwin, 1969.

Schimmel, Annemarie. *Mystical Dimensions of Islam.* Chapel Hill: University of North Carolina Press, 1975.

Trimingham, J. Spencer. *The Sufi Orders in Islam.* Oxford: Oxford University Press, 1971.

## Modernism

Adams, Charles C. *Islam and Modernism in Egypt: A Study of the Modern Reform Movement Inaugurated by Muhammad 'Abduh.* New York: Russell and Russell, 1968.

Ahmad, Aziz. *Islamic Modernism in India and Pakistan, 1857-1964.* London: Oxford University Press, 1967.

Badawi, M. A. Zaki. *The Reformers of Egypt.* London: Croom Helm, 1978.

Chehabi, H. E. *Iranian Politics and Religious Modernism: The Liberation Movement of Iran under the Shah and Khomeini.* Ithaca, NY: Cornell University Press, 1990.

Ikram, S. M. *Modern Muslim India and the Birth of Pakistan.* Lahore: Shaikh Muhd Aswal, 1965.

Keddie, Nikki R. *Sayyid Jamal ad-Din al-Afghani: A Political Biography.* Berkeley: University of California Press, 1972.

Martin, Vanessa. *Islam and Modernism: The Iranian Revolution of 1906.* London: Tauris, 1989.

# IV. Islamic Politics and Society

## Political Islam

Abrahamian, Ervand. *Radical Islam: The Iranian Mojahedin.* London: Tauris, 1989.

Adams, Charles J. "The Ideology of Mawlana Maududi." In *Religions and Politics in South Asia.* Edited by Donald Smith. Princeton, NJ: Princeton University Press, 1966, 371-97.

Affendi, Abdelwahab. *Turabi's Revolution: Islam and Power in Sudan.* London: Grey Seal, 1991.

Ahmad, Akbar S. *Postmodernism and Islam: Predicament and Promise.* New York: Routledge, 1992.

Ahsan, Abdullah. *OIC: The Organization of the Islamic Conference.* Islamization of Knowledge Series. Herndon, VA: International Institute of Islamic Thought, 1988.

Amad, Queyamuddin. *The Wahabi Movement in India.* Calcutta: K. L. Mukhopadhyay, 1966.

Arjomand, Said Amir, ed. *Authority and Political Culture in Shi'ism.* Albany: State University of New York Press, 1988.

———. *From Nationalism to Revolutionary Islam.* London: Macmillan, 1984.

———. *The Shadow of God and the Hidden Imam.* Chicago: University of Chicago Press, 1984.

Ayubi, Nazih N. *Political Islam: Religion and Politics in the Arab World.* London: Routledge, 1991.

Azmeh, Aziz al-. *Islam and Modernity.* London: Verso, 1993.

Banna, Hasan al-. *Five Tracts of Hasan al-Banna (1906-1949).* Translated by Charles Wendell. Berkeley: University of California Press, 1975.

Binder, Leonard. *Islamic Liberalism: A Critique of Development Ideologies.* Chicago: University of Chicago Press, 1988.

———. *Religion and Politics in Pakistan.* Berkeley: University of California Press, 1961.

Burgat, Francois. *The Islamic Movement in North Africa.* Austin: Center for Middle East Studies, University of Texas, 1993.

Butterworth, Charles E. *Political Islam.* The Annals of the American Academy of Political and Social Sciences, 524 (November, 1992).

Dekmejian, Richard H. *Islam in Revolution: Fundamentalism in the Arab World.* Syracuse, NY: Syracuse University Press, 1985.

El-Affendi, Abdelwahab. *Turabi's Revolution: Islam and Power in Sudan.* London: Grey Seal, 1991.

Esposito, John L. *The Iranian Revolution: Its Global Impact.* Gainesville: University of Florida Press, 1990.

———. *Islam and Politics.* 3d ed. Syracuse, NY: Syracuse University Press, 1991.

———. *The Islamic Threat: Myth or Reality?* rev. ed. New York: Oxford University Press, 1995.

Esposito, John L., and John O. Voll. *Islam and Democracy.* New York: Oxford University Press, 1996.

Faruqi, Ziya-ul-Hasan. *The Deoband School and the Demand for Pakistan.* Bombay: Asia Publishing House, 1963.

Hunter, Shireen, ed. *The Politics of Islam Revivalism.* Bloomington: Indiana University Press, 1988.

Husain, Mir Zohair. *Global Islamic Politics.* New York: HarperCollins, 1995.

Keddie, Nikki R. *An Islamic Response to Imperialism: Political and Religious Writings of Sayyid Jamal ad-Din al-Afghani.* Berkeley: University of California Press, 1968.

Kerr, Malcolm. *Islamic Reform: The Political Theories of Muhammad Abduh and Rashid Rida.* Berkeley: University of California Press, 1966.

Khomeini, Ruhollah al-Musavi. *Islam and Revolution: Writings and Declarations of Imam Khomeini.* Translated and edited by Hamid Algar. Berkeley: Mizan Press, 1981.

Kramer, Martin. *Hezbollah's Vision of the West.* Washington, DC: Washington Institute for Near East Policy, 1989.

Marty, Martin E. *The Glory and the Power: The Fundamentalist Challenge to the Modern World.* Boston: no pub., 1992.

Mawdudi, Sayyid Abu'l-A'la. *First Principles of the Islamic State.* Translated and edited by K. Ahmad. Lahore: Islamic Publications, 1960.

Mitchell, Richard P. *The Society of the Muslim Brothers.* London: Oxford University Press, 1969.

Moussalli, Ahmad S. *Historical Dictionary of Islamic Fundamentalist Movements in the Arab World, Iran, and Turkey.* Lanham, MD: Scarecrow Press, 1999.

———. *Islamic Fundamentalism: Myths and Realities.* Ithaca, NY: Ithaca Press, 1998.

———. *Moderate and Radical Fundamentalism: The Quest for Modernity, Legitimacy and the Islamic State.* Gainesville: University Press of Florida, 1999.

Nasr, Seyyed Vali Reza. *Mawdudi and the Making of Islamic Revolution.* New York: Oxford University Press, 1996.

Norton, Augustus Richard. *Amal and the Shi'a: Struggle for the Soul of Lebanon.* Austin: University of Texas Press, 1987.

Roy, Olivier. *Islam and Resistance in Afghanistan.* Cambridge: Cambridge University Press, 1986.

Salem, Elie Adib. *Political Theory and Institutions of the Khawarij.* Baltimore, MD: Johns Hopkins University Press, 1956.

Sayeed, Khalid Bin. "The Jama'at-i-Islami Movement in Pakistan." *Pacific Affairs* 30, no. 1 (March 1957).

Sivan, Emmanuel. *Radical Islam*. New Haven, CT: Yale University Press, 1985.

Turabi, Hasan al-. "The Islamic State." In *Voices of Resurgent Islam*, Edited by John L. Esposito. New York: Oxford University Press, 1983, 241-51.

Vatikiotis, P. J. *The Fatimid Theory of State*. Lahore: Orientalia, 1957.

Warburg, G. R., and U. M. Kupferschmidt, eds. *Islam, Nationalism and Radicalism in Egypt and the Sudan*. New York: Praeger, 1983.

Watt, W. Montgomery. *Islamic Fundamentalism and Modernity*. London: Routledge, 1988.

Wendell, Charles. *Five Tracts of Hasan al-Banna (1906-1949)*. Berkeley: University of California Press, 1975.

## Women

Abaden, Nermin. *Marriage in Islam*. Jerico, NY: Exposition Press, 1972.

Abbott, Nadia. *Aisha: The Beloved of Mohammad*. London: Saqi Books, 1986.

————. *Two Queens of Baghdad*. London: Saqi Books, 1986.

Afkhami, Mahnaz, and Vaziri, Haleh. *Claiming Our Rights: A Manual for Women's Human Rights Education in Muslim Societies*. Bethesda, MD: Sisterhood Is Global Institute, 1996.

Ahmad, Lelia. *Women and Gender in Islam: Historical Roots of a Modern Debate*. New Haven, CT: Yale University Press, 1992.

Amrouch, Fadham. *My Life Story: The Autobiography of a Berber Woman*. New Brunswick, NJ: Rutgers University Press, 1989.

Badran, Margo. *Feminists, Islam and Nation: Gender and the Making of Modern Egypt*. Princeton, NJ: Princeton University Press, 1995.

Hawley, John S., ed. *Fundamentalism and Gender*. New York: Oxford University Press, 1994.

Keddie, N., and B. Baron, eds. *Women in Middle East History: Shifting Boundaries of Sex and Gender*. New Haven, CT: Yale University Press, 1992.

Najjar, Orayb Aref. *Portraits of Palestinian Women*. Salt Lake City: Utah University Press, 1992.

Nashat, Guity, ed. *Women and Revolution in Iran*. Boulder, CO: Westview Press, 1983.

Sharawi, Huda. *Harem Years*. New York: Feminist Press, 1987.

# ABOUT THE AUTHOR

Ludwig W. Adamec (B.A., in political science; M.A., journalism; Ph.D. Islamic and Middle East studies, UCLA) is a professor of Middle Eastern studies at the University of Arizona and was director of its Near Eastern Center for 10 years. Widely known as a leading authority on Afghanistan, he is the author of a number of reference works on Afghanistan and books on Afghan history, foreign policy, and international relations, including *Afghanistan 1900-1923: A Diplomatic History; Afghanistan's Foreign Affairs to the mid-Twentieth Century;* a six-volume *Political Gazetteer of Afghanistan*; the *Historical Dictionary of Afghan Wars, Revolutions, and Insurgencies*; and the *Historical Dictionary of Afghanistan*. His most recent publication is the *Historical Dictionary of Islam*.